THE HUMAN TOLL

Is the Nature of Regulation under the Australian Skills Quality Authority Destructive?

THE HUMAN TOLL:

IS THE NATURE OF REGULATION UNDER THE AUSTRALIAN SKILLS QUALITY AUTHORITY DESTRUCTIVE?

ISBN: 978-0-6452012-0-8

- Get Raelene's FREE compliance tips from her famous #30days30tips:

  http://rto-doctor-academy.thinkific.com/courses/30days30tips
- Join the private Facebook group 'ASQA and the Human Toll':

  ASQA and the Human Toll.
- See the back page of this book for your FREE e Course.

Author: Raelene Bartlett

Title: The Human Toll:

Subtitle: The Destructive Nature of Regulation Under the Australian Skills Quality Authority

Subjects: Education; Adult Education; Australian Skills Quality Authority; ASQA; Compliance; Vocational Education and Training (VET); International Education; CRICOS; Regulation; Compliance; Trauma; Post Traumatic Stress Disorder (PTSD); Anxiety; Vicarious Trauma

Disclaimer

The material in this publication is of the nature of general comment only and does not represent professional advice. It is not intended to provide specific guidance for particular circumstances, and it should not be relied upon as the basis for any decision to take action or not take action on any matter which it covers. Readers should obtain professional advice where appropriate, before making any such decision.

The stories that have been included in this book have been provided by individuals who have experienced negative circumstances under ASQA's regulation. They have contributed their experiences under a Collaboration Agreement where they have declared that all information provided is true and correct.

To the maximum extent permitted by law, the author and publisher disclaim all responsibility and liability to any person, arising directly or indirectly from any person taking action or not taking action based on the information in this publication.

Contents

Acknowledgements

> *History, despite its wrenching pain, cannot be unlived, but if faced with courage, need not be lived again*
>
> **- Maya Angelou.**

I would like to thank those who have contributed to this book, especially those who have bravely shared their stories. For many people, sharing their story was too risky and despite their good intentions, they withdrew their stories at various stages of the book writing and publication process. I have no doubt that sadly, there will be a second edition and they will have another opportunity.

For those who have shared their professional expertise with the intention of helping the VET sector heal, I thank you sincerely for your contribution.

For those people for whom the #enoughisenough campaign was designed to support, we sincerely hope that this book provides you with a level of comfort to help you realise that you are not alone. May we never have to tell stories like this again and that the national VET regulator learns from these experiences.

Raelene Bartlett

RTO Doctor

Preface

> **You must be the change you want to see in the world**
> **- Mahatma Gandhi**

People often ask me, *"Why do you dislike regulators so much?"*

My family and friends who know little about Australia's VET sector say, *'I don't really understand what it is you do or why, but I know you're needed whatever it is you do!'*

I think I can answer both together.

The truth is, I actually don't have anything against regulators! Once upon a time, I too was once a regulator! I guess that's partly why I see things the way that I do. I've seen both sides of the fence; the provider's perception and the regulator's perception. However, I also see something that many others don't - an independent analysis of how things can and should be. I also have very high expectations of our regulatory framework and those responsible for it.

With so many millions of dollars of taxpayer's money being allocated to it each year, quite a number of major reviews into operations and efficiency each identifying how far ASQA has to go before they can be trusted and recognised as a best-practice regulator, I am still shocked each day at the level of incompetence that makes me question whether establishing the national VET regulator has really achieved what it was set out to.

I am one of those people who calls a spade a spade and will often have foot in mouth disease! I tell it like it is, no sugar coating and, as some colleagues would say, often without the diplomacy that one might ordinarily expect. So, consistent with my character, I call things out when they are wrong, corrupt, a conflict of interest, incompetent or just plain stupid...sometimes, the issues are all of those things combined!

You see, having been a regulator once, I truly understand what is required to be a good regulator. I worked as a regulator with the Department of Education Services in Western Australia in International and Higher Education Regulation. During that time, I learned first-hand about the critical nature of my work, how important it was to ensure that procedural fairness was afforded to all clients and always, always act with integrity and be accountable for everything I do. One of the first things I had to do when commencing my employment there was a course in 'Accountable and Ethical Decision-Making in the Public Sector' and so when I hear reports of potentially corrupt, unscrupulous behaviour by ASQA personnel (including those who have now left the public service voluntarily or were walked out, who will ever truly know?) I get really, really angry.

When I see audit reports riddled with errors and incompetence that have led to insane recommendations that are just signed off willy nilly, it makes my blood boil, especially when those insane recommendations are made out of spite, laziness and incompetence.

As my family and friends know, I do come from the school of hard knocks. I didn't grow up with a silver spoon, nor all the bells and whistles of a rich upbringing. I came from a background of a single parent Mother, an alcoholic Father, and a very dysfunctional childhood. Everyone that knows me knows that I've got a soft spot for battlers and social justice. As Martin Luther King once said, 'the time is always right to do what is right'.

I am a Christian and I do believe that I have a responsibility to advocate for and support my brothers and sisters in their time of need, not turn them away and certainly not to exploit them. I've spent my life learning and growing because I believe in the value of education. I would never ask anyone to do anything I am not prepared to do myself. I'm a constant learner and thrive on becoming a better version of myself to enable me to fulfill my purpose and help others. I recognise not everyone has the skills or courage or ability to stand up for themselves or others and so it is a role I have undertaken my whole life, it's one that sits comfortably with me.

Keeping the regulator accountable for their decision-making, positive and/or negative is what I do well. Advocating for justice and the truth to be told is probably what I excel at most.

I endeavour to ensure that the truth gets told because if it's not, the next generations will always be walking on unstable, flaky foundations. I don't want my children and grandchildren to live their lives in a world where everyone is so self-absorbed that they go after whatever they want, whenever they want and no matter what the cost.

This book started out as a bit of a challenge. A challenge by ASQA that my last book was so poorly written and so poorly researched that it didn't deserve the attention it received or the academic result it did prior to publication (a Distinction). I was advised that I had fabricated untruths that couldn't be traced back. I deny these allegations knowing full well I provided copious references and resources to demonstrate how I came to my findings. But that's just like ASQA isn't it? They're in denial, too lazy to look and when they can't immediately see something in front of their eyes, they just deem you not compliant anyway.

I try hard to help clients put their best foot forward at the Tribunal and will continue to serve the VET sector as the face and head of the #enoughisenough campaign. Some of the testimonials from people I work with provide some insight into who I am and the work that I do. Hopefully, this provides you, my reader, with an indication of how I can assist you further:

"Raelene Bartlett is a legend in the education space. Her knowledge of the applicable law, the Standards and her experience in acting for many hundreds of providers is without parallel. Her dedication to her clients and her stubborn adherence to her vision of a broader, fairer, and more open education space for providers sets her apart from other players in the space. She has a passion for her clients and importantly for their students and this guides her every move."

"When you work with Raelene, you understand that you are entering into a different paradigm. There is no 'near enough is good enough'. Perfection is the only option. Her loyal following from her clients and has earned the fearful respect of the regulator. For that reason, Raelene is to be commended for the work that she does and cannot be recommended highly enough."

"We approached Raelene when we got the cancellation notice from ASQA as we wanted someone who could combine the legal mind with compliance knowledge and help us with not only rectification but develop an overarching strategy to fight what was very obviously a wrong and out of proportion decision by ASQA. Raelene was the right choice for us in that she personally took over the project and executed it ensuring that all the responses were meticulously charted out, as well as being apt. She also stuck with us as a client until the very end, ensuring a positive outcome, unlike some in the industry who tend to bail out when things get to the hairy end. The result was overwhelmingly positive."

"Raelene remains one of very few people I have known with a zero-error approach and capacity to do so.

"We remain grateful to her for what she brought to the table for us and gave us not only hope, but led the strategy and execution, freeing us to focus on ensuring that the wolves did not circle the RTO when under stress. Thank you Raelene and the team at RTO Doctor."

"Raelene changed the paradigm of how we deal with regulators. She forces them to play by the rules rather than letting them throw their

weight around unchallenged. As a result, even after multiple attempts to sanction or cancel us they have never been successful. Also, Raelene has worked with our RTO to become as compliant and bullet-proof as possible.

Now regulatory interaction is an occasional annoyance, not an existential threat."

"With our RTO facing a cancellation decision by ASQA at the Tribunal and having already engaged and worked with four different compliance consultants, it was with great fortune we were referred to Raelene Bartlett, Founding Director of RTO Doctor, to assist us with our fight with ASQA. As we worked closely with Raelene, we felt a sense of relief that we had finally found a consultant that didn't claim to know compliance but actually knew compliance!!!"

"The work we undertook with Raelene for our response submissions to ASQA was enlightening and we wondered how and why our previous consultants were not imparting the calibre of knowledge nor delivering to the required standards that needed to be met."

"Raelene's approach to compliance is exceptionally multi-faceted. Not only does she address non-compliances, but Raelene also has incredible foresight to ensure continued compliance which one can only possess through her passion and experience within the VET sector."

"Raelene has been instrumental in winning our case after two years with ASQA and we have no hesitation in recommending her and RTO Doctor. We want to thank Raelene for saving our RTO and look forward to engaging her for all our future compliance/audit needs!"

"I've worked with Raelene over several years and seen first-hand her invaluable assistance in reforming RTOs to prepare for proceedings in the Administrative Appeals Tribunal and helping me to prepare for hearings. Her knowledge, diligence and attention to detail are first-rate, and I would happily recommend her to any RTO."

"Raelene has unparalleled experience in monitoring compliance of RTOs. Upon receipt by an RTO of an unfavourable audit report from ASQA, Raelene knows how to jump right in and identify the issues. ASQA audit reports are not for the faint hearted! They are often lengthy documents, and they are difficult to understand. Raelene's expertise in understanding the finer details of ASQA audit reports means that she knows how to break down each allegation of non-compliance and analyse the evidence relied upon by ASQA in forming an unfavourable conclusion."

"Raelene helps RTOs to understand the basis for a finding of non compliance and then helps RTOs rectify the alleged non compliances. She prepares sophisticated evidence reports to provide to ASQA, and she works collaboratively with solicitors and barristers to give evidence before the Administrative Appeals Tribunal where required."

Want to see more? Visit:

https://rtodoctor.com.au/services/sanction-management/testimonials.

Why this book?

> **History will record that the greatest tragedy of social transition was not the clamour of bad people, but the appalling silence of the good**
>
> **- Martin Luther King.**

There are many people in Australia's VET sector who have a comprehensive understanding of what has been bubbling under the surface for decades. Some people have chosen to exploit those chunks in the armour of the sector, others have either chosen to be silent for fear of rocking the boat, however well-intentioned their silence may be. They may also have chosen to maintain their silence through fear; fear for themselves, for their families, fear of losing their income, fear of retaliation from the national VET regulator for themselves, their employers or their colleagues. Some other people, however, have been waiting for an opportunity to share their story and make sure that this tragic period of history in Australia's VET sector does not go without being recorded.

As will be seen through this book, Australia's VET sector has a long history of change and reform and when people start taking their lives, losing their marriages and homes, becoming homeless and experiencing domestic violence and miscarriages as a result of the manner in which regulation is being implemented, when governments don't listen, this is the price our country pays.

The intention of this book is to stand as a living testimony for those whose stories are being told. It is also to hopefully create change that will hopefully transform and challenge the antagonistic, toxic behaviours and decisions of the regulator and finally make it accountable to some '*body*', somewhere.

> ***We can easily forgive a child who is afraid of the dark; the real tragedy of life is when men are afraid of the light."***
>
> **— Plato**

The #enoughisenough Campaign

> "History protects us from historicism - from a historicism that calls on the past to resolve the questions of the present."
>
> **- Michel Foucault**

It was mid-2016. I found myself locked up in a building upstairs in metropolitan Melbourne with a number of people, including one of ACPET's senior employees, trying to facilitate one of the worst RTO closures I've ever been involved in throughout my entire career. It didn't start out as a closure though, there were many twists and turns before it got to that point. It's typical of the VET sector really. Add a little bit of an ASQA audit, a rogue auditor, students who don't really want to be studying but are forced to by the government or they lose their parenting payment. The young Mums from some of the shadier parts of Melbourne who, despite the risks, bring their babies to what is effectively a riot outside the RTO just so they can get their face on the Channel 7 news and say, *'Look at me! Look at me!'* Surely it sounds like an episode of Kath and Kim? No sadly, not a Kath and Kim episode, but real life in Australia's Vocational Education and Training sector.

Up until this point, as much as I had concerns about Australia's national VET Regulator ASQA, I was always willing to give them the benefit of the doubt and often defended their practice. After all, there are many RTOs whose compliance is just dreadful and they deserve to be caught. This RTO though was not one of those. This is what I would soon realise would become a familiar pattern of destruction of people's lives that I could no longer turn a blind eye to. These were good people who were losing everything because of a rogue ASQA auditor, high on his moment of power and the ability (and narcissistic desire) to destroy others. This was the beginning of the #enoughisenough campaign.

In the next few years, my anger and outrage at what was fast becoming an increasingly prevalent problem of not just narcissistic auditors but also incompetent ones whose findings were the cause of regulatory decisions that just should not have been made. Unfortunately, with the lack of oversight not just of incompetent auditors but also poor policy, a regulator whose performance was less than ideal, the problem proliferated. It was of course also the time of the VET FEE Help saga throughout the country and the media demonisation of RTOs as a result of the findings coming out of ASQA and their audits. The media of course were feeding off the findings of ASQA's strategic review and their audits but what they didn't know at the time was everything that we've uncovered since about ASQA's performance, the quality of research they undertake and the auditors who are intent on destruction.

Of course, it wasn't all ASQA's fault and sometimes, they did actually get it right. What everyone failed to acknowledge at the time however was that poor government policy was never going to end well - but someone had to be the scapegoat and it was never going to the government. That government policy allows certain conduct that was never intended and allowed providers to generate millions of dollars was of course the providers who were just greedy, who exploited students, who were dodgy, unethical and morally corrupt. But what about the people who made the policy? What about those who developed the scheme? Those who monitored the scheme? Those who had a responsibility to the Australian taxpayer to ensure that taxpayer funds were being appropriately spent? You can still hear the consequences of the poor government policy in today's Senate meetings. Recently, on 25 March 2021, we heard Senators asking the Minister whether or not there is suitable and adequate oversight of the new apprenticeships funding so that it doesn't blow out and get exploited like the VET FEE-Help scheme.

Slowly, as time went by, more and more people started sharing their concerns about the regulator, its auditors and what was happening to Australia's VET sector. I was facing more and more of these cases where the destruction to human life, students and the public interest at the hands of the regulators and/or its representatives and I knew something needed to change.

As an ex-regulator, I knew that the way that regulation was taking place in this sector was not conducive to collaborative partnerships, good policy and the public interest. After all, when you have the new regulator come out on their public appearance admitting that it is their intention to close down as many RTOs as possible, you know their intentions are not about their legislated purpose and that something much bigger and much worse is festering. In those days, I would make sure that I ran no more than four of these matters per year as the physical and emotional toll on me personally was too much and, after each one, I would need to take a few days to recover. Now today, I'm lucky if I have less than five or six matters running concurrently such is the regulator's wrath.

The #enoughisenough campaign began formally around mid-2019 as a collective of individuals in the Vocational Education and Training ("VET") industry in Australia who chose to come together to collaborate for the betterment of the VET sector and to advocate for reform of the sector's regulatory framework. It was widely acknowledged that individually, some members had been working on attempts at reform individually for some years and that collectively, we could make a bigger impact. This was strengthened by the fact that we all shared the same goals and visions for Australia's VET sector and similar values. While we all come from a variety of different backgrounds, we considered (and still do) that this was actually one of our biggest strengths in guiding true reform.

All of us, individually and collectively have taken on these roles and actions voluntarily with no benefit (financial or otherwise) in order to advocate on behalf of the sector but also put ourselves at substantial risk in the process. Some of us have risked our businesses, our reputations and our own livelihoods because we believe that future generations have the right to have a viable VET sector that will continue to provide skills well into the future. As the campaign group though has somewhat quietened with few contributors, some of us continued working behind the scenes to ensure that the concept grew and became a trusted, respected leader in advocacy for stakeholders of the VET sector.

In early 2020, the foundations of the International Centre for Education Advocacy (ICEA) began. Based on a social enterprise framework, the overall goal of the ICEA is to ensure natural justice and procedural fairness in decision-making that relates to education providers while ensuring an opportunity to advocate for the rights and responsibilities of education providers is available and accessible. The ICEA is like nothing Australia's VET sector has ever seen before and is still in its infancy but there is hope that together, with the stakeholders of Australia's VET sector, we can become a driving force behind future policy decisions and VET Reform consultations and activities and will also be invited to take a place on ASQA's recently announced Roundtable.

All proceeds from the sale of this book are being donated to the ICEA.

The International Centre for Education Advocacy ("ICEA")

> *"Change will not come if we wait for a smoother person or some other time. We are the change we've been waiting for. We are the change we seek."*
>
> **- Barack Obama**

As per its business plan, the ICEA exists to support education providers in their day to day existence by holding accountable government and other decision-making bodies whose decision-making undermines or threatens the existence and/or operations of those education providers. The ICEA operates as an organisation who pursues the development and implementation of sound educational policies that promote and enhance equality in the provision and regulation of quality education.

Governments, regulators and other policy making bodies make decisions regularly that impact the ability of education providers to provide for and meet their stakeholder needs. Often, those education providers at the coalface of educating tomorrow's leaders for future problems are hampered by policies, legislation and interventions that are largely misunderstood causing a barrier to business and education service provision. The ability of a niche education provider to lobby a government or pursue unjust, adverse decision-making or policy is often beyond their capability, makes them a target and/or, has the ability to so drastically influence future decision-making and regulation of that provider that attempts to be a voice for what is right are silenced and therefore never heard. Often legislative reforms are undertaken that intentionally or not, undermine the ability of education providers to not only succeed in the provision of quality education and training, often in niche markets, but it perpetuates the inherent bias that comes with legislation and policy making that is either insufficiently scrutinised, or not scrutinised at all prior to becoming law.

Currently existing solutions that are similar in nature are also completely different in their makeup, structure and approach to achieving their purpose. Stakeholders of ICEA report that systematically, other similar organisations:

- Have failed to adequately represent them as businesses;
- Failed to represent them in policy and legislative reform opportunities at State and Commonwealth level;
- Do not provide sufficient power or voices around the country to make a real impact on State, Commonwealth or global policy debate and legislative reform;
- Are too self-absorbed as an organisation to truly consider and represent the core values and needs of its stakeholder group;
- Is not truly representative of its members;
- Fails to adequately support its membership in all geographical areas it purports to;
- Do not have sufficient educational background or experience to challenge the status quo and demand better for its members;
- Do not care about the state of health about the education sector more generally and only purports to be accountable to its members;
- Are at no time completely transparent in its dealings with:
    - Government;
    - Its membership;
    - Education providers generally;
    - Regulators; and
    - The legal system.
- The lack of awareness and engagement with industry, education providers and the community means that it does not, and cannot, truly represent their stated interests; and
- Do not, and will not, ever have the capacity to support its members or other education providers in challenging decision-

making through the courts on behalf of its members and the sector.

Attempts at challenging the status quo and establishing new member based bodies to better represent education providers are not new. In fact, over the past few decades, there have been multiple attempts by various bodies at trying to achieve a similar purpose. These include, for example, but are not limited to:

- Some private peak bodies already in place;
- Australian Vocational Education and Training Quality Practitioners and Consultants Association ("AVQPCA");
- Independent Education Providers Association ("IEPA"); and
- Australian Institute of Training and Development Professionals ("AITD").

The solution offered by ICEA is a complex one because it captures all of what each of the above associations do or tries to do and more. It will challenge legislation, bills and policy without ever compromising its values and vision and always in the pursuit of its purpose, has an advisory committee, driven by those who have committed to the #enoughisenough cause and will provide guides and codes of practice on areas that education providers are continually challenged with.

The ICEA will be driven by and have, as its foundation, a model of social enterprise which has at its core, a Community of Practice. The ICEA and its members will be passionate about using their businesses and the ICEA platform for driving social impact, having a space for mutual support, encouragement and celebration. It will also provide a hub for sharing advice, collaborating and supporting each other to provide a business and campaign that is driven by a public, community cause and provides solutions that are founded in, and supported by its social mission. It is designed to work for the public good of education, in the public interest which benefits not just members, but the education sector more broadly. Critically, one of its most important functions will be to, upon approval of the Board, run test cases in the Federal Court of Australia where required, in order to challenge unlawful or simply wrong regulatory decisions that have the potential to impact the sector as a whole. More information regarding ICEA can be obtained by contacting the author directly but one thing is for sure, we are hoping that the ICEA will contribute to the future of Australian VET being radically changed.

ASQA - Why So Much Disdain?

> "The problem is not the problem; the problem is your attitude about the problem."
> **- Captain Jack Sparrow**

Regulatory Ambit

Australia's VET/IE system is significant, complex and an important contributor to Australia's economy. However, Bowman and McKenna[1] report that:

> *Twenty years after the introduction of a national training system, it is still difficult to find a consistent statement about its purpose, objectives and key elements.*

It should come as no surprise then that the regulatory ambition of the VET/IE sector in Australia is just as complex.

The regulation of Australia's VET/IE sectors has historically been a shared responsibility between the Commonwealth, the States and Territories. On 1 July 2011, a national regulator, the ASQA was established under the NVR Act; it shares this responsibility with the Training and Accreditation Council ("TAC") in Western Australia and the Victorian Registration and Qualifications Authority ("VRQA") in Victoria. This is further complicated by the State and Territory governments who provide funding to certain providers and may also, under a Memorandum of Understanding, share regulatory responsibility with the national regulator via delegation.

1 Kay Bowman and Suzy McKenna, *The Development of Australia's National Training System: A Dynamic Tension Between Consistency and Flexibility* (NCVER, 2016) 16 [2].

These delegated arrangements are noted in the schools' sector (primary and secondary schools across Australia and certain public providers, specifically Technical and Further Education ("TAFE") colleges.

Adding further complexity, ASQA also shares its regulatory functions with the Tertiary Education and Quality Standards Agency (TEQSA) for all organisations, public or private, who provide higher qualifications in Australia.

While higher education includes qualifications under the Australian Qualifications Framework (AQF) between AQF Levels 5 and 10, some of these qualifications are also delivered in the VET sector. TEQSA is the ESOS Agency[2] for the purposes of the *Education Services for Overseas Students Act 2000* (Cth.) ("ESOS Act") for ELICOS[3] and Foundation Program[4] providers.

The Council of Australian Government (COAG) Industry Skills Council (CISC) has overall responsibility for industry competitiveness, productivity, labour market pressures, skills development and national training arrangements. The Australian Industry Skills Committee (AISC) was established in May 2015 after the National Skills Standards Council (NSSC), established in July 2011 (which replaced the National Quality Council) was disbanded.

Since Australia has endeavoured to formalise the national framework underpinning the VET sector, it has seen many changes. Those changes appear to occur in a cyclic manner with the fundamental premise to provide a national system that encourages quality and compliance with a set of '*Quality Standards.*'[5]

In that context, '*someone*' needed to monitor compliance with those Standards, and this has inevitably resulted in this shared responsibility

2 *Education Services for Overseas Students Act 2000* (Cth.) s 5.

3 ELICOS - English Language Intensive Courses for Overseas Students.

4 Foundation Programs courses are those courses defined by the legislative instrument *Education Services for Overseas Students 2000 - Foundation Program Standards.*

5 *National Vocational Education and Training Regulator Act 2011* (Cth.) s 231A

between the Commonwealth, States and Territories. On 1 July 2011, the VET/IE landscape changed immeasurably with the introduction of the NVR Act and the VET Quality Framework ("VQF").[6]

COAG's intention for ASQA was to maximise efficiency and facilitate greater consistency of regulation'.[7] The situation is best described in the following diagram:[8]

6 The VQF includes the *Standards for Registered Training Organisations (RTOs) 2015* (Cth.) ("Standards for RTOs"), the *Fit and Proper Persons Requirements 2011* (Cth.) ("FPP Requirements"), the *Financial Viability Risk Assessment Requirements 2011* (Cth.) ("FVRAR"), the *National Vocational Education and Training Regulator (Data Provision Requirements) Instrument 2020* ("DPR") and the Australian Qualifications Framework (2nd Edition) ("AQF").

7 Valerie Braithwaite, *All Eyes on Quality: Review of the National Vocational Education and Training Regulator Act 2011 Report* (January 2018).

8 Bowman and McKenna (n 3).

Figure 1 National frameworks for VET products and providers initiatives since the late 1980s

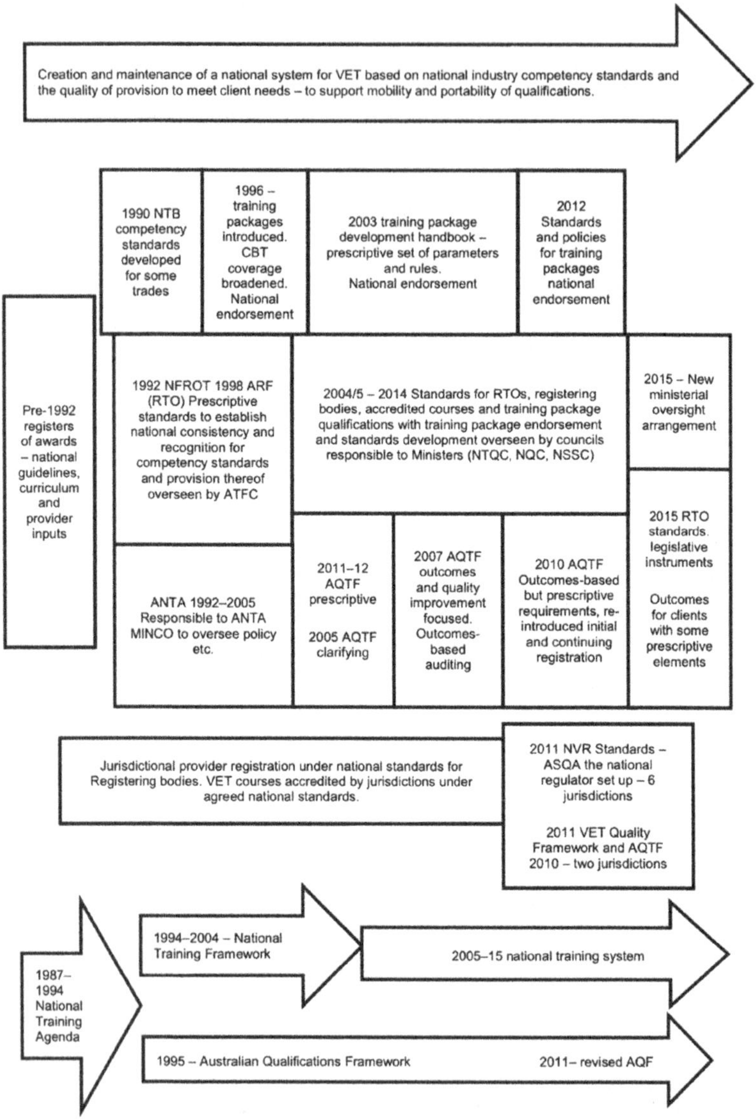

Notes: NTB = National Training Board; NFROT = National Framework for the Recognition of Training; ARF = Australian Recognition Framework; ATFC = Australian Training Framework Committee; MINCO = Ministerial Council; AQTF = Australian Quality Training Framework; ASQA = Australian Skills Quality Authority; NTQ = National Training Council; NQC = National Quality Council; NSSC = National Skills Standards Council.

The development of Australia's national training system

ASQA is responsible for regulating all Registered Training Organisations ("RTOs") nationally.[9]

Braithwaite[10] found:

> As of November 2017, ASQA was responsible for regulating 4,061 RTOs, while Victoria and Western Australia, who have not referred their powers, regulate 242 and 235, respectively.

These numbers are in a constant state of flux due to a range of factors including those considered by this book. This book is focussed on the human toll and experiences of those who have somehow found themselves participating in this poorly managed, monitored and intimidating circus of ASQA and its appeals process which includes the Administrative Appeals Tribunal (AAT), specifically, people who are otherwise known as the victims of ASQA's predatory regulatory practices. TAC and the VRQA operate under very different appeals processes, therefore will not be considered by this book.[11]

ASQA's Role and Operation

In its review of ASQA's operations and processes, PricewaterhouseCoopers ("PwC") found that, '*Given ASQA's position as a national VET regulator, PwC could not identify any directly comparable regulatory organisations against which to assess ASQA*'.[12] While some might argue that TEQSA is a comparable regulator, in terms of numbers of providers regulated

[9] With the exception of two (2) jurisdictions under limited circumstances TAC and VRQA refused to hand over their powers to the Commonwealth and these regulators both operate independently of ASQA.

[10] Braithwaite (n 9) 13 [4].

[11] There are limited circumstances where providers that are registered in either Western Australia or Victoria cannot maintain registration under their respective State regulators. These include where the provider is registered on the Commonwealth Register of Institutions and Courses for Overseas Students (CRICOS), where they are delivering nationally recognised training online or in an ASQA regulated jurisdiction and where they are providing ELICOS.

[12] Pricewaterhouse Coopers, '*ASQA Process Review: Final Report*' (2013) [10].

and the self-accrediting nature of the majority of its providers, TEQSA's regulatory model is quite dissimilar.[13]

ASQA is an independent statutory agency meaning that a delegate exercises powers under the relevant legislation independently although the Minister remains accountable for the decision.[14] It performs a number of roles while operating on an almost full cost-recovery basis. ASQA's independence as a national regulator[15] means that *it is not subject to direction from anyone in relation to the performance of its functions or the exercise of its powers*.

The Chief Commissioner (now the Chief Executive Officer due to legislative changes)[16] of ASQA is delegated power from the Minister[17] to make those decisions to which this book relates, while the NVR Regulator is authorised to delegate their power to a range of people and bodies that make up government authorities,[18] occupational licensing and other bodies[19] and to certain self-regulating RTOs.[20] This provides the foundation for legal decision-making under the NVR Act.

ASQA has four main responsibilities under the NVR Act being:

- Registration of training providers and courses under the NVR Act[21];
- Manage changes to registration and courses;
- Ensuring compliance with the VET Quality Framework (VQF); and
- Accreditation of courses.

---

13 Tertiary Education Standards Agency, '*What Approach to Quality Assurance and Regulation*' (Web Page) <https://www.teqsa.gov.au/what-we-do>.

14 Judith Bannister, Anna Olijnyk and Stephen McDonald, Government *Accountability - Australian Administrative Law*, (Cambridge University Press NS, 2nd Edition, 2018).

15 *National Vocational Education and Training Regulator Act 2011* (Cth.) s 159.

16 Ibid s 155.

17 Ibid s 223.

18 Ibid s 224.

19 Ibid s 225.

20 Ibid s 226.

21 Training providers and courses are registered separately under the NVR Act however a course cannot be registered if the provider is not registered.

ASQA exerts its ESOS Agency responsibilities below[22] concurrent with its responsibilities under the NVR Act where relevant.

Findings are usually determined under the NVR Act first and either eliminated or further assessed against the ESOS Act requirements subsequent to the initial findings including:

- Registration of training providers and courses;[23]
- Manage changes to registration and courses;
- Ensure compliance with the ESOS Act and National Code[24]; and
- Undertake enforcement action against providers who do not comply with the Act or legislative instruments made under the Act.

ASQA's legal representatives often refer to, and rely upon their responsibilities in fulfilling the objectives of the NVR Act as one of the key reasons why a stay decision should not be granted prior to a review decision taking place by the Tribunal.[25] ASQA lawyers appear to have less need recently to reinforce these responsibilities at the outset or in their Statements of Issues, Facts and Contentions as it would appear that it is not uncommon now for Tribunal members to identify ASQA's

[22] It should be noted that a provider cannot be registered under the ESOS Act for VET courses if it is not registered as an RTO first, albeit some applications are reviewed concurrently (*Education Services for Overseas Students Act 2000* (Cth.), s 6E(1)(b).

[23] Training providers and courses are registered separately under the ESOS Act however a course cannot be registered if the provider is not registered.

[24] The *National Code of Practice for Providers of Education and Training to Overseas Students 2018* ("National Code") is a legislative instrument made under s 33 of the ESOS Act.

[25] *VETiS Consulting Services Pty Ltd ('VETiS') v Australian Skills Quality Authority* [2019] AATA 341 (7 March 2019) [5], *Institute of Training Pty Ltd ('Institute of Technical Training') v Australian Skills Quality Authority* [2018] AATA 4127 (5 November 2018) [39], *Technical Education Australia Pty Ltd ('Technical Education Australia') v Australian Skills Quality Authority* [2018] AATA 3047 (23 August 2018) [104 - 105], *Trades College Australia Pty Ltd ('Trades College Australia') v Australian Skills Quality Authority* [2018] AATA 1703 (12 June 2018) [16], *Australian Institute of Technical Training Pty Ltd ('Australian Institute') v Australian Skills Quality Authority* [2018] AATA 1281 (11 May 2018) [53-54], *Sher-E-Punjab Pty Ltd ('Sher-E-Punjab') v Australian Skills Quality Authority* [2018] AATA 46 (15 January 2018) [104-106].

responsibilities without any provocation in its decision-making.[26] It would ordinarily be expected that ASQA lawyers would point toward these responsibilities and spell them out more explicitly when defending their regulatory decisions during stay proceedings. However, it would appear that Tribunal Members have become so acquainted with ASQA's responsibilities (and arguments) that ASQA lawyers no longer refer to this in as much detail as it once used to as a Statement of Facts, Issues and Contentions; these issues will be addressed later in this paper.

In the context of ASQA's regulatory ambitions, s 4A of the NVR Act provides a number of outcomes, which are measured annually in ASQA's report.[27] The very crux of vocational education and training though, producing job ready graduates for, and endorsed by industry, could be seen as a measure or outcome of the success of ASQA's regulatory performance. It would not be uncommon for a student enrolled in a vocational education and training course to have as a measurable outcome that they are '*job ready after training that has been endorsed by industry*'. This is aligned with what Braithwaite describes as '*desirable student outcomes*'.[28]

This student outcome though is a different measure and regulatory ambit to what is provided for in the Objects of the NVR Act at s 4A and yet, under the current student-centred audit model, this should be a key focus. This outcome is something that is completely disregarded by ASQA in its legal decision-making.

---

26 *Business Institute of Australia Pty Ltd ('Business Institute') v Australian Skills Quality Authority* [2019] AATA 669 (16 April 2019) 11 [30], '*Technical Education Australia'* [107], *Metro College of Technology Pty Ltd and Australian Skills Quality Authority* (Unreported) [34], '*Trades College Australia'* [27-28].

27 ASQA's reporting requirements are detailed in s215 of the *National Vocational Education and Training Regulator Act 2011* (Cth.).

28 Valerie Braithwaite, (n 9) [9].

There are many examples of cases that have come before the Tribunal[29] where graduates have been endorsed by industry as being suitable graduates and employer satisfaction is high or, the provider meets additional licencing and/or accreditation requirements, yet this evidence is completely disregarded by ASQA and considered irrelevant.

The relevance of meeting additional licencing requirements and not ASQA's was an issue discussed by Senior Member Puplick in *Pacific Flight Services v Australian Skills Quality Authority*[30] where the Member states that '*the Tribunal does not accept that there are such inconsistencies between ASQA and CASA regulations and requirements that it is legitimate to give priority to one over the other*'.[31]

However, if CASA as the aviation regulator has no concern over the training and assessment practices of the provider and yet ASQA does, the inconsistencies that Senior Member Puplick refers to must exist.

In summary, while COAG's intention for there to be a uniform and consistent framework across all jurisdictions, it is clear that this has still not been achieved and there remains significant tension in the ability of the sector to achieve it. The ambition of Australia's regulatory framework in the VET/IE sector and ASQA's role and operation is to ensure that there is a consistent quality framework that guides its operation; providing monitoring mechanisms and accountability to the public and government. How it goes about achieving this however, and how that performance is measured is something that requires further investigation and discussion.

29 As well as others who were prevented from accessing merits review due to and including some of the reasons outlined in this paper; For example, *Success Fast-Track Pty Ltd v Australian Skills Quality Authority* [2012] AATA 531 (10 August 2012), *Australian Institute of Trades Pty Ltd as trustee for the Institute of Hotel Management Australia v Australian Skills Quality Authority* [2017] AATA 2912 (1 August 2017) and *Pacific Flight Services Pty Ltd v Australian Skills Quality Authority* [2019] AATA 745 (23 April 2019).

30 *Pacific Flight Services v Australian Skills Quality Authority* [2019] AATA 745 (23 April 2019).

31 Ibid at [4].

The Size of the VET/International Sectors in Australia

In its March 2019 statistics, the Commonwealth[32] confirmed:

> Australian international education, as well as being one of Australia's largest export industries and contributing nearly $35 billion to the Australian economy in 2018, is also a significant creator of jobs in Australia.

This is an increase from the Department's figures in 2017 showing that international education contributed $30.8 billion to the Australian economy with 27% of those enrolments in the VET sector. Even with the global COVID-19 pandemic, Australia's Technical and Vocational Education and Training ("TVET") sector remained strong in 2021 at $9.4 billion, with 3.4% market growth in 2021. Its annualised market growth size between 2016-2021 however demonstrates the decrease in size due to the pandemic.[33]

It is important to recognise however that there is often much crossover between the different sectors (Schools, VET, Higher Education and ELICOS) and in many cases, students will often follow an integrated pathway or package. A common example of such a package might be that the student arrives and completes 12 weeks of English language study with an ELICOS provider. They then complete a Certificate III, Certificate IV, Diploma and Advanced Diploma with an RTO then finish their study in Australia with a bachelor's degree at university.

Advice to Parliament about the size of Australia's VET sector outside the international education market in November 2018 included:

> In 2017, an estimated 4.2 million students were enrolled in VET with an Australian training provider, representing almost

---

32 Department of Education and Training (DET) 'Jobs supported by international students studying in Australia' (Research Snapshots, March 2019) <https://internationaleducation.gov.au/research/Research-Snapshots/Documents/RS_Job%20supported%202018.pdf>.

33 IBISWorld 'Technical and Vocational Education and Training in Australia - Market Size 2007-2027 <https://www.ibisworld.com/au/market-size/technical-vocational-education-training/>.

> a quarter of the Australian population aged 15-64 years. In comparison, in the same year, there were 1.5 million higher education students enrolled with an Australian higher education provider, and 3.8 million school students enrolled in Australia...The majority of students (60.2%) were enrolled with a private training provider only, while the next largest group were enrolled with a TAFE institution only (16.1%).[34]

This helps demonstrate why the VET/IE sector is constantly under the spotlight in the media and is often used as a political handball.

The VET/IE system in Australia is a complex web, partly due to non-harmonised jurisdictions in the attempt by COAG[35] referred to earlier to develop uniform, national regulation of the sector while integrating components of the General Skilled Migration ("GSM") program and the ELICOS sector.

Further complicating this regulatory framework is that some of these programs are offered across primary and secondary schools, both government and private schools as well as the TAFE and University sector, including Non-Self-Accrediting Institutions ("NSAIs") operating in the University space.[36]

The regulation of the VET/IE sector is perhaps so complex because it lacks clarity in what it is trying to achieve, as well as the often-interchanging political portfolios that it tends to fall into. Internationally

---

34 Joint Standing Committee on Migration, Parliament of Australia, *Report of the Inquiry into Efficacy of Current Regulation of Australian Migration and Education Agents* (February 2019) <https://www.aph.gov.au/Parliamentary_Business/Committees/Joint/Migration/Migrationagentregulatio/Report>.

35 Council of Australian Governments, '*Council of Australian Governments' Meeting Communiqué*', (February 2009) 5 [2].

36 While technically, Technical and Further Education ("TAFE") institutions are classified as Registered Training Organisations (RTOs), they are often not recognised as such by the public and media. There is evidence (see Bibliography reference to The Hon Simon Birmingham) that they are not regulated in the same manner as '*traditional*' RTOs and receive preferential treatment due to their status as government entities. Under this umbrella of complex regulatory oversight, is further regulation by State and/or Territory funding bodies and delegated powers of regulation to State/Territory regulators for certain education and training providers.

known as Technical Vocational Education and Training ("TVET"), Todd and Dunbar on behalf of UNESCO[37] state:

> TVET cuts across every sector of the economy and relies on effective dialogue and interaction between education and training providers, labour market stakeholders including employers, worker representatives, and other stakeholders. In addition, TVET is expected to contribute towards a wide range of (sometimes contradictory) socioeconomic goals, including full employment, increased productivity and competitiveness, social cohesion, equity and sustainability...Given this context it is no surprise that governments have experienced difficulty in formulating, planning, managing, implementing and evaluating effective TVET and skills development policies, strategies and plans.

The Braithwaite Report[38] identified that 'there is a real need for transparency around ASQA audits to inform the sector on where systemic weaknesses lie'. The issues presented in this paper are only the tip of the iceberg; there are sadly many more that still require investigation. The writer submits that from an ethical standpoint at least, there is an obligation on the Commonwealth, in particular, the Attorney-General and the relevant Ministers, to investigate these matters further. Some of the additional critical concerns that have not been discussed in this paper that require further investigation include for example, but are not limited to:

- Auditors can be deemed by the Regulator to be beyond reproach in their decision-making and findings related to the level of compliance of providers that leads to Notices and sanctions under the Act when contracted by ASQA. Yet, when presenting evidence on behalf of RTO clients in their capacity of private Consultants, ASQA dismisses the validity and reliability of their

37 Robin Todd and Muriel Dunbar, UNESCO, '*Taking A Whole of Government Approach to Skills Development*' (2018) 14 [1.1:2].

38 Valerie Braithwaite, (n 9) 8 [3].

evidence and the Tribunal subsequently considers their opinions differently.

- Is there a conflict of interest where ASQA auditors are also acting as rectification Consultants for RTOs who are deemed allegedly not compliant by ASQA?

- The Honourable Ian Callinan in his recent review of the AAT[39] stated that, 'the acting head of ASQA referred to "*ghost colleges*", little more than addresses operated by people who provided no real training or tuition'. This statement was denied by ASQA[40] publicly however, this is an argument that ASQA lawyers often use and refer to in Tribunal proceedings.[41] This suggests that the view is held by more than those litigating on behalf of the Commonwealth but is representative of a culture of belief within the regulatory body itself.

  - In the context of the issues highlighted in this paper, and those yet to be investigated but recommended for further review, what is the public interest that both ASQA and the AAT are desperately trying to protect in accordance with their legislated objectives?

One of the key findings of previous research that this writer has undertaken[42] is that there needs to be more transparency about the audit process and the legal decisions being made at all points in the legal decision-making process. This would ensure that the foundation upon which external review is being sought is not only sound but legally valid and reliable.

39 Hon Ian Callinan AC, *Review: Section 4 of the Tribunals Amalgamation Act 2015 (Cth.) Report*, (July 2019) [at 6.96].

40 Tim Dodd, 'Regulator Denies Ghost College Claims', *The Australian* (online, 25 July 2019) 5 <https://www.theaustralian.com.au/higher-education/regulator-denies-ghost-college-claims/news-story/38b7c6e9ed9d426743fe37e6374d0499>.

41 *Sher-E-Punjab Pty Ltd v Australian Skills Quality Authority* (n 31), *Australian Institute of Technical Training Pty Ltd v Minister for Education and Training* (n 31) and *Business Institute of Australia Pty Ltd v Australian Skills Quality Authority* (n 32).

42 Raelene Bartlett, '*National Vocational Education and Training Regulator Act 2011 (Cth.): An Investigation Into Merits Review*', 2020.

Unqualified Auditors

The NVR Act provides for the Standards for VET Regulators 2015[43] which have the following purpose:

> To ensure:
>
> - the integrity of nationally recognised training by regulating RTOs and VET accredited courses using a risk-based approach that is consistent, effective, proportional, responsive and transparent;
> - consistency in the VET Regulator's implementation and interpretation of the RTO Standards and Standards for VET Accredited Courses; and
> - the accountability and transparency of the VET Regulator in undertaking its regulatory functions.

The term '*auditor*' is defined under these Standards[44] with Standard 1 providing a reference to the national competency standard for auditors[45] engaged by the national regulator for performing some of its functions as a regulator, including that the '*VET Regulator makes decisions consistent with the principles of natural justice and procedural fairness*'.[46]

ASQA is empowered under various sections[47] of the NVR Act to conduct audits in order to perform some of its functions as the National VET Regulator.[48] ASQA engages various staff and consultants to undertake these regulatory functions, including audits in accordance with ss 182-184 of the Act. While ASQA does use its own staff where possible to conduct its regulatory functions, in the 2017/2018 Annual Report,

43 *Standards for VET Regulators 2015* made under ss 189(1) of the National Vocational Education and Training Regulator Act 2011 (Cth.).
44 Ibid, see the Glossary at Part 1 'auditor'.
45 *Standards for VET Regulators*, Standard 1.9(c), sch 1.
46 Ibid, Standard 1.10.
47 The NVR Act provides for audits under s 17(3) and s 35, in the performance of its duties under various other sections of the Act. Part 5, Divisions 1 and 2 of the Act provide for investigations and searches of premises.
48 NVR Act s 157.

ASQA spent $968,000 on its panel auditors and a further $687,000 on '*Consultants*'.

The same report states that '*The consultancy contracts were for a range of services including internal and external audit and financial management*'.[49]

These costs to the Australian taxpayer were again considered later in this report in the context of '*the public interest*'.

Regulatory audits can be triggered by any range of events in addition to those identified for the purposes or registration and change of scope of registration. They can be triggered for factors including, but not limited to issues such as:

- a provider seeking to add a new delivery location;
- a provider seeking to increase their student capacity;
- ASQA's receipt of complaints;
- general compliance monitoring;
- national strategic reviews; or as previously referred to,
- an investigation.

What follows is a general overview of the audit process under ASQA. While audits are a standard requirement for many institutions, both public and private to maintain standards, in the current ASQA regulatory environment, audits are generally triggered as opposed to being a part of standard operating procedure.

The audit process usually begins with a desktop review of the evidence (*in some cases, the audit may actually end there because a legal decision has already been made to reject or cancel registration for*

[49] Australian Skills Quality Authority, ASQA Annual Report 2017-2018, 106.

example).[50] The audit will usually be conducted by an ASQA panel auditor or an ASQA Regulatory Officer. A finding will generally be made that the level of non-compliance is minor, serious or critical although, in recent months, a new finding is being made of '*concerning compliance*'.

Historically, ASQA would provide RTOs who had been deemed not compliant with 20 working days to rectify any non-compliance identified at audit. ASQA has in recent times suggested that this was a discretionary power that it '*volunteered*' and was not obliged by law to provide. On 1 July 2018, ASQA removed this option for applications for initial registration. Where a legal decision has not been made after completion of the desktop audit, a site visit will be conducted; these are usually performed by the same auditor who undertook the desktop audit.

The auditor will then usually make a recommendation which is communicated to the Manager of Regulatory Operations in the relevant jurisdiction who will then approve the audit report for release. The correspondence can either be in the form of a provision of 20 working days to rectify any non-compliance or, the issue of a Notice.[51] In either case, the provider will typically have 20 working days in which to respond to the audit report (*and if relevant, the Notice*) and they may provide new evidence to be considered at this point. The evidence may or may not be reviewed by the same auditor or regulatory officer.

Upon consideration of the response, ASQA will make a new decision that either the provider is compliant, and no further action is taken, alternatively, they may issue a Notice[52] if one wasn't previously or affirm the previous Notice. If the Notice is affirmed, the provider then

50 *Providers may at this point receive one of a number of 'Notices' from ASQA including, for example, a 'Notice of intention to impose a sanction' or a 'Notice of intention to cancel registration'; Since 1 July 2018, applicants for initial registration as an RTO are issued with a 'Notice' rejecting their application for any non-compliance.*

51 *Ibid.*

52 *Ibid.*

has access to external review[53] provisions under the NVR Act[54] if it is a reviewable decision[55] under that Act.

ASQA summarises this process as follows:

> Responsibility for regulatory decisions by ASQA resides with its Commissioners, with some decisions being made jointly by all three Commissioners, and others by a single Commissioner or senior staff holding a delegation...The streaming of decisions will be based upon an analysis of a range of factors, including:
>
> - how serious the impact of the decision may be on the VET industry and its reputation, and
> - whether ASQA has identified serious concerns about the provider in question.
>
> Decisions which have the most severe impact on a training provider such as cancellation or non-renewal of registration will generally be made jointly by all three Commissioners, while decisions with a lesser impact will usually be made by a single Commissioner or a senior staff member holding delegated authority.
>
> If a decision is made jointly by ASQA's Commissioners, a review of that decision can only be made by an external authority (such as the Administrative Appeals Tribunal). In these cases, the provider cannot apply for an internal ASQA reconsideration of the decision.

Amendments to the Education Services for Overseas Students Act 2000 (Cth.) ("ESOS Act"), which took effect on 1 July 2016,

53 *Providers also have access to internal review mechanisms however they do not form part of this research.*
54 *NVR Act s 203.*
55 *Ibid s 199.*

> enable ASQA to delegate certain CRICOS decisions, which previously had to be made jointly by all three Commissioners.[56]

The ASQA website clearly states that the decision will be made jointly by all three Commissioners, however, the standard correspondence that a provider will receive from ASQA in the '*most severe of circumstances*' reads somewhat differently.

The generic template letter[57] that will usually be issued to a provider in the '*most severe of circumstances*' provides 'In accordance with section 37(2) of the NVR Act, ASQA hereby gives you notice that the Chief Commissioner for the Commissioners *(as opposed to three Commissioners as stated on the ASQA website)* has made a decision to cancel your registration under section 39 with effect from...'.[58]

However, some RTOs receive a very different letter[59] regarding the decision to cancel their registration which is completely at odds with the explanation provided by ASQA and states 'In accordance with section 37(2) of the NVR Act, ASQA hereby gives you notice that it (*as opposed to the three Commissioners or the Chief Commissioner on behalf of the three Commissioners as per the previous point*) has made a decision to cancel your registration under section 39 with effect from 29 April 2019'. All cases referred to were eligible for external review and all correspondence was issued by the same staff member.

56 *Australian Skills Authority, 'Changes to ASQA's Decision-Making Processes', (Web Page)* <https://www.asqa.gov.au/news-publications/media/asqa-announces-further-changes-protect-sectorhttps://www.asqa.gov.au/news-publications/media/asqa-announces-further-changes-protect-sector>.

57 The generic template letter referred to is the standard correspondence received by providers. The example used however is 'Letter from Benn Gramola to Name Withheld, 29 May 2019 [3]'.

58 Australian Skills Quality Authority, 'Notice of Decision to Cancel NVR Act Registration' template (no version number, date); as stated in Raelene Bartlett, '*National Vocational Education and Training Regulator Act 2011 (Cth.): An Investigation Into Merits Review*', 2020.

59 Letter from Benn Gramola to Name Withheld, 29 March 2019 [3], professional correspondence held on client's file - RTO Doctor, at 23 January 2019 [3], professional correspondence held on client's file - RTO Doctor, at 15 January 2019 [2], at 22 November 2018 [2], at 11 April 2018 [3], at 30 August 2017 [3], at 11 August 2017 [2].

Competency Requirements of ASQA Auditors

In November 2020, the writer of this book published an article on LinkedIn that was directly relevant to the competency of ASQA auditors. With over 90 comments on a public forum, it demonstrates just how out of touch the national VET regulator is and how big an issue this is for the sector. Amongst these comments is an update after this information went to the Senate Estimates Committee. For the purposes of transparency, and to highlight the gravity of this issue, comments from the article have been included. The purpose in highlighting this article and the plethora of feedback is this; each of the testimonials provided in this book have suffered as a result of these critical issues. In what other regulatory system does such physical, psychological, emotional and financial harm occur where those responsible for the audit process and therefore findings were under such a cloud of validity and reliability but the destruction occurred anyway? First though, the article.

Competency Requirements for ASQA Auditors: The Standards for VET Regulators 2015, Standards for RTOs 2015 and the ELICOS Standards 2018

The #enoughisenough campaign has as one of its primary goals to consistently seek transparency and accountability from the Australian Skills Quality Authority (ASQA), Australian Parliament and the Ministers responsible for Australia's Vocational Education and Training (VET) and Australia's international education industry.

I am in the midst of preparing a response for a client who is currently at the AAT appealing a cancellation decision and once again, I can't help but turn my mind's eye to the qualifications and experience (as well as vocational/educational competency) of ASQA auditors to audit specific programs.

The Standards for VET Regulators 2015 are a legislative instrument made under subsection 189(1) of the *National Vocational Education and Training Regulator Act 2011*. The Standards for VET Regulators 2015, as per the Preliminary information in Part 1, should be read in conjunction with:

- VET Quality Framework;
- Standards for Registered Training Organisations 2015;
- Standards for Training Packages; and
- Standards for VET Accredited Courses 2021.

The Standards for VET Regulators 2015 provide the minimum qualifications for auditors on behalf of the National VET Regulator at Schedule 1. For the purposes of transparency and clarity, these requirements are:

Schedule 1 – Competency Requirements

AUDITORS

The VET Regulator must ensure that each auditor holds at a minimum the following qualifications or equivalent competencies as determined by the VET Regulator:

- TAE40110 Certificate IV in Training and Assessment (or its successor); and
- BSB51607 Diploma of Quality Auditing (or its successor).

In undertaking the above qualifications, the auditor must complete the following units of competency, or have equivalent competencies as determined by the VET Regulator:

from the Business Services Training Package (or its successor):

- BSBAUD402B Participate in a quality audit (or its successor);
- BSBAUD501B Initiate a quality audit (or its successor);
- BSBAUD503B Lead a quality audit (or its successor); and
- BSBAUD504B Report on a quality audit (or its successor).

from the Training and Education Training Package (or its successor):

- TAEASS502B Design and develop assessment tools (or its successor);
- TAEDES501A Design and develop learning strategies (or its successor); and
- TAEASS503A Lead assessment validation processes (or its successor).

An audit team may comprise a lead auditor and one or more auditors, and include technical advisers when required, who provide specific knowledge or expertise to the audit team. Technical advisers must operate under the direction of an auditor. Any technical adviser involved in an audit is not required to comply with the minimum competency requirements specified for auditors above.

COURSE ACCREDITATION ASSESSORS

The VET Regulator must ensure that each application for a VET accredited course is considered by a course accreditation assessor who holds at a minimum the following qualification or equivalent competencies as determined by the VET Regulator:

- TAE40110 Certificate IV in Training and Assessment (or its successor); and
- BSB51607 Diploma of Quality Auditing (or its successor)

In undertaking the above qualifications, the course accreditation assessor must complete the following units of competency, or have equivalent competencies as determined by the VET Regulator:

- TAEDES402A Use training packages and accredited courses to meet client needs (or its successor); and
- TAEDES504A Research and develop units of competency (or its successor).

The ESOS Act 2000 provides for an ESOS Agency (*in this case, the National VET Regulator ASQA*) at s6C of the ESOS Act.

In relation to the ELICOS Standards 2018, a legislative instrument is established (Education Services for Overseas Students (ESOS Agency—ELICOS and Foundation Programs) Determination 2016 under s 6C(2).

That legislative instrument, at s6 recognises the National VET Regulator as the ESOS Agency for an ELICOS provider who is a registered VET provider. Interestingly, the ELICOS Standards were obviously updated in 2017/2018, prior to the commencement of this legislative instrument which remains in force and sunsets in October 2026.

The Preliminary section of the Standards for VET Regulators 2015 clearly states which legislative instruments they should be read in conjunction with and NOWHERE are, or have, the ELICOS Standards been listed (*ever, not even in the Standards for VET Regulators 2011 where there was no Schedule 1 requirement at all*). Even worse, as can be seen in the screenshot from the Standards for VET Regulators 2015, there is nothing even remotely aligned to the ELICOS Standards 2018 even mentioned in the purpose of the Standards for VET Regulators 2015!

PART 1 – Preliminary

Name of Standards

These Standards are the *Standards for VET Regulators 2015.* These Standards should be read in conjunction with the:

- VET Quality Framework
- Standards for Registered Training Organisations
- Standards for Training Packages
- Standards for VET Accredited Courses

Purpose

The purpose of these Standards is to ensure:

- the integrity of nationally recognised training by regulating RTOs and VET accredited courses using a risk-based approach that is consistent, effective, proportional, responsive and transparent;
- consistency in the VET Regulator's implementation and interpretation of the RTO Standards and Standards for VET Accredited Courses; and
- the accountability and transparency of the VET Regulator in undertaking its regulatory functions.

Context:

The Standards require a risk-based approach to the regulation of RTOs that is informed by assessments of RTO compliance with the Standards for RTOs on an ongoing basis. This risk management approach enables VET Regulators to more actively and regularly apply strategies to reduce the regulatory burden for high-performing RTOs with a history of strong compliance and to increase regulatory action for those RTOs considered as higher risk. This is achieved through regulatory strategies that can include:

- *an active and dynamic risk assessment process that is based on compliance history, performance data, outcomes of complaints against RTOs, and industry and learner intelligence;*
- *varying the type and regularity of audits, based on risk assessments;*
- *recognising and not duplicating the decisions of other relevant regulators; and*
- *delegating regulatory powers to low-risk RTOs, such as the ability to amend their scope of registration.*

Regulation must be sufficient to assure the quality outcomes of the Standards for RTOs and the Standards for VET Accredited Courses, with VET Regulators using the strength of their regulatory tools to deter non-compliance. The regulatory approach should engender self-evaluation and improvement within RTOs in a way that makes regulation valued for what it contributes to RTOs, industry stakeholders and learners.

Here is the issue though:

The Standards for VET Regulators 2015 and the Schedule 1 requirements have absolutely no alignment with the requirements of the ELICOS Standards 2018.

Schedule 1 – Competency Requirements

AUDITORS

The VET Regulator must ensure that each auditor holds at a minimum the following qualifications or equivalent competencies as determined by the VET Regulator:

- TAE40110 Certificate IV in Training and Assessment (or its successor); and
- BSB51607 Diploma of Quality Auditing (or its successor).

In undertaking the above qualifications, the auditor must complete the following units of competency, or have equivalent competencies as determined by the VET Regulator:

from the Business Services Training Package (or its successor):

- BSBAUD402B Participate in a quality audit (or its successor);
- BSBAUD501B Initiate a quality audit (or its successor);
- BSBAUD503B Lead a quality audit (or its successor); and
- BSBAUD504B Report on a quality audit (or its successor).

from the Training and Education Training Package (or its successor):

- TAEASS502B Design and develop assessment tools (or its successor);
- TAEDES501A Design and develop learning strategies (or its successor); and
- TAEASS503A Lead assessment validation processes (or its successor).

An audit team may comprise a lead auditor and one or more auditors, and include technical advisers when required, who provide specific knowledge or expertise to the audit team. Technical advisers must operate under the direction of an auditor. Any technical adviser involved in an audit is not required to comply with the minimum competency requirements specified for auditors above.

COURSE ACCREDITATION ASSESSORS

The VET Regulator must ensure that each application for a VET accredited course is considered by a course accreditation assessor who holds at a minimum the following qualification or equivalent competencies as determined by the VET Regulator:

- TAE40110 Certificate IV in Training and Assessment (or its successor); and
- BSB51607 Diploma of Quality Auditing (or its successor)

In undertaking the above qualifications, the course accreditation assessor must complete the following units of competency, or have equivalent competencies as determined by the VET Regulator:

- TAEDES402A Use training packages and accredited courses to meet client needs (or its successor); and
- TAEDES504A Research and develop units of competency (or its successor).

On 29 January 2019, **Education Issues Australia** reported that:

> *Just last year ASQA enrolled 28 regulatory employees (30%) to acquire mandatory qualifications. Even if they did meet the requirements of ELICOS Standard P6.4 and held the Sch 1 requirements of the Standards for VET Regulators 2015, surely this loophole needs to be closed? Surely the person who is qualified under that Standard should be responsible for writing that section of the audit report where they operate in a team? (e.g. Just because someone is identified as a Lead Auditor, does not mean that they should be writing the entire report, making recommendations based on that audit report etc. where they are not qualified to do so). ASQA told @Louise_ Pratt they had 93 Audit Staff and "on occasion ASQA employs staff that do not hold all of the mandatory qualifications.*

This finding from Education Issues Australia was also supported by the following evidence from the publicly available ASQA Annual Report 2018-2019:

Capability development

ASQA's Performance Development Framework (PDF) underpins capability development. The objectives of the PDF are to:

- clarify and align individual roles and work efforts to the outcomes of ASQA's strategic direction
- build high performance for individuals and teams
- develop employee's skills and capability.

Over 2018-19, ASQA actively invested in developing workforce capability, supporting a range of learning and development opportunities for its employees. These opportunities included:

- enrolment of 28 regulatory employees in the Diploma of Quality Auditing; Certificate IV in Training and Assessment and/or; Diploma of Vocational Education and Training

Source: **Education Issues Twitter Page**, 29 January 2019.

All of this got me thinking...

1. How could an ASQA auditor who likely doesn't meet the Sch 1 requirements of the Standards for VET Regulators 2015 validly and reliably audit any course? This is not the first time I have asked this question and I have never had an adequate response, yet hundreds of regulatory decisions have been made by ASQA on this basis since it was established and commenced operating on 1 July 2011. It should not be forgotten that a large number of ASQA staff then and now, were previously State-based employees/regulators.

2. How could an ASQA auditor who likely doesn't meet the Schedule 1 requirements of the Standards for VET Regulators 2015 validly and reliably audit an ELICOS course?

3. How could an ASQA auditor who has done a quick and nasty auditing course (*remember those same short courses that ASQA sanctions providers for running which don't meet the AQF Volume of Learning?*) as identified above validly and reliably audit an ELICOS course?

4. How does an ASQA auditor who, in most cases, would never even qualify to be an ELICOS teacher (*and certainly don't meet the requirements of ELICOS Standard P6.4*) validly and reliably conduct an audit on an ELICOS course?

5. How does an ASQA auditor, in any of the above scenarios conduct an audit on, report an audit outcome, make a recommendation of any kind (*let alone a sanction*) while not being qualified (*even remotely*) to do so?

Just because a section of the Education Services for Overseas Students ("ESOS") ESOS Act (*for the purposes of the ELICOS Standards 2018 for example*) provides them with the authority to, does not equate to them being qualified. Surely this is an abuse of power and in a court of law, could be considered invalid evidence? This leaves the door open for absurd abuses of power.

This issue is of course closely related to the many discussions and concerns that I have raised over the years that ASQA auditors **MUST** hold the same competency and currency requirements or above as the very providers, trainers and assessors that they are auditing under the Standards for Registered Training Organisations 2015; however, as is highlighted previously, there is **NO** requirement. While legislatively, auditors are required under the Standards for VET Regulators 2015 to hold specific qualifications, as was disclosed by Education Issues Australia above, this is clearly not always the case.

To be very clear about what I am referring to, I firmly believe that all ASQA auditors **MUST**, at a minimum, meet the following requirements in addition to the Schedule 1 requirements of the Standards for VET Regulators 2015:

Minimum Competency Requirements

1. In addition to the requirements specified below, ASQA auditors' duties are performed only by persons who have:

    a) vocational competencies at least to, but preferably higher than, the level being delivered and assessed by the provider being audited;

    b) current industry skills (within the last 12 months) directly relevant to the training and assessment delivered and assessed by the provider being audited;

    c) current registration or licensing by the relevant industry body, agency or authority where one exists, that is directly relevant to the training and assessment delivered and assessed by the provider being audited; and

    d) current knowledge and skills in vocational training and learning that informs their training and assessment.

Where relevant and required, industry experts **must** also be involved in the audit process, including, but not limited to finalising the audit findings and recommendations, working alongside the audit team to complete the audit process.

2. ASQA ensures that all auditors undertake professional development in the fields of:

    - the knowledge and practice of vocational training;
    - learning and assessment including competency-based training and assessment; and
    - contemporary best-practice audit approaches.

3. All ASQA auditors must complete a minimum of six audits supervised by an experienced (no less than 3 years) auditor who meets the requirements of 1 above and holds qualifications equivalent to PSP50416 - Diploma of Government Investigations*.

Individuals working under the supervision of an experienced auditor

4. Where the auditor, in conducting an audit, participates in the audit process and they do not hold the competency and currency requirements outlined, the individual works under the supervision of an experienced auditor and does not determine audit outcomes.

5. ASQA ensures that any individual working under the supervision of an experienced auditor under Clause 4**:

    a) holds the training and assessment credential specified in Item 6 of Schedule 1 of the Standards for Registered Training Organisations 2015;

b) vocational competencies at least to, but preferably higher than, the level being delivered and assessed by the provider being audited;

c) current industry skills (within the last 12 months) directly relevant to the training and assessment delivered and assessed by the provider being audited;

d) current registration or licensing by the relevant industry body, agency or authority where one exists, that is directly relevant to the training and assessment delivered and assessed by the provider being audited; and

e) current knowledge and skills in vocational training and learning that informs their training and assessment.

6. Where ASQA engages an individual under Clause 5, it ensures that audits comply with the Standards for VET Regulators 2015 and Clauses 1-4 above.

7. Without limiting Clauses 4-6, ASQA:

   a) determines and puts in place:

      i) the level of the supervision required; and

      ii) any requirements, conditions or restrictions considered necessary on the individual's involvement in the provision of audits and collection of assessment evidence; and

   b) ensures that auditors providing supervision, monitor and are accountable for all training and audit provision and collection of supervision and audit evidence by the individual under their supervision.

Auditing the delivery of the training and assessment qualifications for trainers and assessors

8. To audit any AQF qualification or skill set from the Training and Education Training Package (or its successor) ASQA must ensure all trainers and assessors auditing the training and assessment hold a qualification at least one level above that the level being delivered which may include (but is not limited to) a Bachelor degree or higher specialising in adult education and/or competency based training***.

9. ASQA must ensure that any person working under supervision for the purposes of Standard 8:

   a) does not determine audit outcomes; and

   b) meets the requirements of Clause 5.

Independent validation of auditor qualifications, experience, registration and licensing

10. ASQA must undertake an independent validation**** of its auditors' qualifications, experience and currency annually in accordance with the above requirements, including its audit system, tools, processes and outcomes in accordance with the requirements contained in the above.

11. The outcomes of this independent validation must be disclosed in ASQA's annual corporate plan under the Public Governance, Performance and Accountability Act 2013.

I also firmly believe that there needs to be accountability and penalties for the National VET regulator ASQA and individual auditors where these requirements are breached. Let me explain...

Currently, there are a range of offences and civil penalties under the NVR Act for RTOs who do not meet similar requirements under the Standards for RTOs 2015. These are listed below:

- s 103 Offence—issuing VET qualification without providing adequate assessment;
- s 104 Civil penalty—issuing VET qualification without providing adequate assessment;
- s 105 Offence—issuing VET statement of attainment without providing adequate assessment;
- s 106 Civil penalty—issuing VET statement of attainment without providing adequate assessment;
- s 107 Offence—issuing VET qualification without ensuring student satisfied requirements;
- s 108 Civil penalty—issuing VET qualification without ensuring student satisfied requirements;
- s 109 Offence—issuing VET statement of attainment without ensuring student satisfied requirements; and
- s 110 Civil penalty—issuing VET statement of attainment without ensuring student satisfied requirements.

I believe that the regulator should also be just as liable for its actions which have the potential to cause just as much impact to the Australian population if they do not perform their functions under the NVR Act. So that the wider Australian community is clear about the legislated functions of the National VET Regulator (ASQA), these are provided below directly from the legislation. These same functions are what ASQA lawyers often refer to when pursuing providers in the AAT based on the findings of auditors to whom the qualifications, experience and currency of this article refer to.

157 Functions of the National VET Regulator

(1) The National VET Regulator has the following functions:

(a) to register an organisation as an NVR registered training organisation;

(b) to accredit courses that may be offered and/or provided by registered training organisations;

(c) to carry out compliance audits of NVR registered training organisations;

(d) to promote, and encourage the continuous improvement of, a registered training organisation's capacity to provide a VET course or part of a VET course;

(e) if requested to do so by the Minister, or on the Regulator's own initiative, to advise and make recommendations to the Minister on matters relating to vocational education and training;

(f) if requested to do so, in writing, by the Education Minister for a State or Territory, or on the Regulator's own initiative, to advise and make recommendations to the Education Minister for the State or Territory on specific matters relating to vocational education and training in the State or Territory;

(g) if requested to do so, in writing, by the Chair of the Ministerial Council, or on the Regulator's own initiative, to advise and make recommendations to the Ministerial Council on general matters relating to vocational education and training in all jurisdictions;

(h) to collect, analyse, interpret and disseminate information about vocational education and training;

(i) to publish performance information, of a kind prescribed by the regulations, relating to NVR registered training organisations;

(j) to conduct training programs relating to the regulation of registered training organisations and/or the accreditation of courses;

(k) to enter into arrangements with occupational licensing bodies, other industry bodies, or both, for the purpose of ensuring compliance by NVR registered training organisations with this Act;

(l) to cooperate with a regulatory authority of another country that has responsibility relating to the quality or regulation of vocational education and training for all, or part, of the country;

(m) to develop relationships with the Regulator's counterparts in other countries;

(n) to develop key performance indicators, to be agreed by the Minister, against which the Regulator's performance can be assessed each financial year;

(o) to develop service standards that the Regulator must meet in performing the Regulator's functions;

(p) any other function relating to vocational education and training that is set out in a legislative instrument made by the Minister;

(q) such other functions as are conferred on the Regulator by or under:

  (i) this Act; or

  (ii) the *Education Services for Overseas Students Act 2000*; or

  (iii) the *Higher Education Support Act 2003*; or

  (iv) the *VET Student Loans Act 2016*; or

  (v) any other law of the Commonwealth;

(r) to do anything incidental to, or conducive to, the performance of any of the above functions.

(2) When preparing advice for the purpose of paragraphs (1)(f) and (g), the National VET Regulator may consult with VET Regulators in non-referring States.

(3) The Minister must not set out a function in a legislative instrument under paragraph (1)(p) unless the Ministerial Council has agreed to the function.

Note 1: For how the Ministerial Council gives agreement, see section 191.

Note 2: Section 42 (disallowance) and Part 4 of Chapter 3 (sunsetting) of the *Legislation Act 2003* do not apply to a legislative instrument that sets out a function (see regulations made for the purposes of paragraphs 44(2)(b) and 54(2)(b) of that Act).

(4) In performing the National VET Regulator's functions, the Regulator must apply the Risk Assessment Framework.

(5) In performing the National VET Regulator's functions, the Regulator must have regard to any reports or information the Regulator receives about matters relating to this Act.

(5A) Without limiting subsection (5), in performing the National VET Regulator's functions, the Regulator must have regard to any advice provided by the Advisory Council (whether or not the advice was given in response to a request by the National VET Regulator or the Minister).

(6) A failure to comply with the requirements of subsection (4), (5) or (5A) in relation to the performance of a function of the National VET Regulator does not affect the validity of the performance of the function.

(7) The National VET Regulator has the power to do all things that are necessary or convenient to be done for or in connection with the performance of the Regulator's functions.

Note: Other functions may be conferred on the National VET Regulator by State law, see Division 2 of Part 8.

Source: National Vocational Education and Training Regulator Act 2011

In my line of work, I have seen multiple examples of deliberate misfeasance by ASQA auditors and advocate strongly for justice to be done where I can individually and as a founder of the #enoughisenough campaign. It is of significant concern that issues such as these continue to go unaddressed despite the multitude of appearances that ASQA has before the Australian Parliament. It is even more concerning that despite multiple approaches about a range of issues, a range of Ministers have not shown any interest in addressing some of these issues. As a representative of the Australian VET and international education community, I have not ceased and will not stop demanding why these matters continue to exist and I will continue to expose them; not just for the betterment of our community but to ensure that we have a solid foundation for skills training in future generations.

People were encouraged to share their comments and opinions which have been copied below:

** The PSP50416 - Diploma of Government Investigations is just a suggestion but it could be others, or the course may not even exist and needs to be accredited. Further, it may be appropriate to look at other regulatory frameworks to see how/what they do. This is just a starting point for discussion and consideration.*

*** In other words, the person being supervised is vocationally qualified and holds a current TAE, however, has not yet* *successfully completed the Schedule 1 requirements of the Standards for VET Regulators 2015. This could be amended to reflect other competencies that may be missing but is a starting point for discussion and consideration.*

**** This could be amended to reflect other competencies that may be missing but is a starting point for discussion and consideration.*

***** This definition should be an independent statutory body who reports directly to the Minister. This is a starting point for discussion and consideration.*

Comments from the LinkedIn article as at the time of publication of this book:

Eva Godwin • 1st 5mo •••
Training Services Manager at WA Local Government Association (WALGA)

Raelene you are a brilliant mind - thanks for sharing your detailed research and thanks for your continued commitment for our industry

Like Reply

Danny Angeth • 1st 1y •••
RTO Quality and Compliance Officer at Chandler RTO

Very true

Like Reply

Marc Miles • 1st 1y •••
Training and Compliance professional

Danielle Jones

Like Reply

Fazluz ZAMAN • 1st 1y •••
Tertiary Academic | Lecturer | VET Trainer | Education Quality and Compliance Administrator | Curriculum Desi...

ASQA publishes RTO name list for non compliance but TEQSA's risk Management works oppositely, allow to hide the uni status

Like · 1 Reply · 1 Reply

Michelle-Anne Kenny • 2nd 1y •••
Vocational Education Professional

I am trying to imagine an auditor holding a dance or musical theatre qualification LOL Maybe we'd never get audited :)

Like · 2 Reply · 1 Reply

<u>From the writer:</u>

Something that I did not write in the article but should have:

> Someone can be a qualified auditor in accordance with Schedule 1 of the Standards for VET regulators 2015 and not meet the requirements to conduct independent validation under the Standards for RTOs 2015. Go figure!
>
> How many ASQA auditors have audited validation clauses and not met the same requirements I wonder?

1.9. The RTO implements a plan for ongoing systematic validation of assessment practices and judgements that includes for each training product on the RTO's scope of registration:

a) when assessment validation will occur;

b) which training products will be the focus of the validation;

c) who will lead and participate in validation activities; and

d) how the outcomes of these activities will be documented and acted upon.

1.10. For the purposes of Clause 1.9, each training product is validated at least once every five years, with at least 50% of products validated within the first three years of each five year cycle, taking into account the relative risks of all of the training products on the RTO's scope of registration, including those risks identified by the VET Regulator.

1.11. For the purposes of Clause 1.9, systematic validation of an RTO's assessment practices and judgements is undertaken by one or more persons who are not directly involved in the particular instance of delivery and assessment of the training product being validated, and who collectively have:

(i) vocational competencies and current industry skills relevant to the assessment being validated;
(ii) current knowledge and skills in vocational teaching and learning; and
(iii) the training and assessment credential specified in Item 2, or Item 5 of Schedule 1.

Industry experts may be involved in validation to ensure there is the combination of expertise set out above.

Scott Rogers • 1st
Director eSkilled LMS and E-learning
1y •••

Raelene.... this is incredible isn't it! I so wish I had considered this ridiculousness and raised it before the ASQA Review feedback closed... the only problem is that if ASQA has to audit with a panel under the full cost recovery charges by ASQA... a real Audit to the standards RTOs must meet would likely cost RTOs $100k for the pleasure of being audited.

Like · 2 | Reply

Fazluz ZAMAN • 1st
Tertiary Academic | Lecturer | VET Trainer | Education Quality and Compliance Administrator | Curricul...
1y •••

Direct CT or RPL .. need to know the volume of learning

Like | Reply

Nancy Pavlovic MAITD, MAIPM • 1st
Director - PAVLOV GROUP : ISO/RTO Lead Auditor, Project Mgr, Trainer, Writer, NLP Practitioner
5mo •••

Does David Garner former ASQA now promoting himself as an expert, know this?

Like | Reply

Raelene Bartlett • You
Founding Director at RTO Doctor
1y •••

And let's not leave out Australian Consumer Law on this one, after all, ASQA does provide a service, one which, as of 1 July 2020, becomes FULL COST RECOVERY!

From the ACL website...

...see more

Like · 4 | Reply · 19 Replies

Phillip Rutherford Ph.D • 1st
Training Systems Specialist
1y •••

Brett Hilderr is there any proof that they are actually providing this confidence? Not according to the media.

I am sure that if confronted in a court of law they would find many witnesses to back up their claim of success at this, but I feel confident that a parallel body could provide the community with an equal - if not better - level of confidence for a fraction of the cost.

Like · 1 | Reply

Geoff Sander • 1st
Team Member at The John Maxwell Team
1y •••

This is where we are referring to 2 different planets. Government and private enterprise. Government will never be able to climb to business standards because they don't need to and Business will never stoop to Government because they don't need to. It's a vicious stalemate.

Like · 1 | Reply

Phillip Rutherford Ph.D • 1st
Training Systems Specialist
1y •••

Brett Hilderr another difference is that ISO have competitors against which they have to compete for members' money. ASQA enjoys freedom of operations because no other organisation could be bothered competing.

Like · 2 | Reply

Geoff Sander • 1st
Team Member at The John Maxwell Team
1y (edited) •••

Blary fake news again Fssst! We will need more then just one because he'll just end up in #enoughisenough. No, in marketing we need something bigger, something Trump.

Like | Reply

Phillip Rutherford Ph.D • 1st
Training Systems Specialist
1y •••

Brett Hilderr especially if said organisation was run by members and not bureaucrats. AIM, AITD, IEAust etc all had their start when a few disgruntled folk got together and formed themselves into a member-based organisation, run by and for the .members.

??

Like · 2 | Reply

Geoff Sander • 1st
Team Member at The John Maxwell Team
1y ···

Brett Hilder No in marketing we need something bigger then just one journalist. Before you know it he's disappeared. We need something bigger, something Trump!

Like | Reply

Geoff Sander • 1st
Team Member at The John Maxwell Team
1y ···

No in marketing we need something bigger than just one journalist. before you know it he's disappeared. We need something bigger, something Trump!

Like · 1 | Reply

Raelene Bartlett • You
Founding Director at RTO Doctor
1y ···

An important perspective that others may not have considered is discussed in this article by Amanda Ryding and Laura Reisz
(Colin Biggers & Paisley Lawyers) in relation to vicarious liability and employers in Australia.

From the summary... ...see more

Like · 3 | Reply · 7 Replies

Phillip Rutherford Ph.D • 1st
Training Systems Specialist
1y ···

That's an interesting ruling. And in this world of competency-based training and assessment, any courses undertaken by supervisors which did NOT include duty of care to staff is one which should not be accredited. On the other hand, in cases where supervisors and managers have undertaken courses which DID include such competencies, then their liability is even more pronounced if they had been determined as competent during or at the course's comple ...see more

Like · 3 | Reply

Raelene Bartlett • You
Founding Director at RTO Doctor
1y ···

Would definitely make for the most interesting court case Phillip Rutherford Ph.D FAITD FAIM MAIPM MPD and how I would love to be a part of that one!

Like · 1 | Reply

Phillip Rutherford Ph.D • 1st
Training Systems Specialist
1y •••

Where I was called on as an expert witness I was able to show that the definitions of competence and competency-based assessment were taken totally out of context. In one case a project manager was dismissed because the owner claimed he had conducted an assessment of his competence and found him incompetent. I showed that the manager was neither trained in competency-based assessment, nor was competent at the task. The project manager won substantial damages.

I have been a witness in a few cases where the whole issue of competence has been challenged, and being one of the people who introduced these concepts into this country my expert testimony is listened to. (Being a Ph.D helps :-) LOL)

Like · 5 | Reply

Geoff Sander • 1st
Team Member at The John Maxwell Team
1y •••

Thank you Phillip on our friend's behalf. Most of the time these closures are over such trivia. It just takes someone with his head in the big picture to see the real story. We need more people like you.

Like · 1 | Reply

Phillip Rutherford Ph.D • 1st
Training Systems Specialist
1y •••

Geoff Sanderr any time. Happy to help.

Like · 1 | Reply

Geoff Sander • 1st
Team Member at The John Maxwell Team
1y •••

Phillip you are such an inspiration.

Like · 1 | Reply

Phillip Rutherford Ph.D • 1st
Training Systems Specialist
1y •••

Geoff Sanderr thanks Geoff.

Like · 1 | Reply

Raelene Bartlett • You
Founding Director at RTO Doctor
1y •••

Roman Gowor Office of the Minister for Employment, Skills, Small & Family Business - Senator Hon. Michaelia Cash Louise Pratt Christian Porter Independent Tertiary Education Council Australia Felix Pirie Andrew Shea Australian Skills Quality Authority (ASQA)

Raelene Bartlett • You
Founding Director at RTO Doctor
1y •••

IMPORTANT UPDATE...
Some of my followers may recall my horror in relation to ASQA's appearance at the Senate Estimates meeting late last year where I questioned the responses provided to Louise Pratt. Of course, some of these concerns were raised on the back of Andrew Laming's speech in parliament and Michaelia Cash's famous comments 'Mr Laming is a backbencher, backbenchers do what backbenchers will do' (I might add, Andrew is a very highly qualified 'backbencher' and far from being just a bencher, is also the Chair of the Standing Committee on Employment, Education and Training so Michaelia's comments were incredibly condescending and out of touch).

None the less, the important issue related to this article is that ASQA had taken a Question on Notice from Senator Pratt in relation to the competency of ASQA auditors. It's not likely that people would have monitored or followed this up and I'm told that unless something is published publicly, that ASQA can claim parliamentary privilege on the information. Given this information was in the public sphere on parliament's website, I'm now making sure that ire remains inevitably public by adding it to this important article.

The Question on Notice from Senator Pratt was:
Please provide the following:
o The qualifications and experience requirements for ASQA auditors.
o Any arrangements under which ASQA auditors have contracted to ASQA and to
VET providers and the arrangements for managing conflict of interest.
o Measures in place to ensure ASQA follows international audit standards.
o Instances of ASQA not following legal and litigant process.
o Whether automated or computer assisted decisions are made following submission
of audit reports.
The responses are in and certainly support the findings in my article. I'm unable to upload a document to LinkedIn so have put a copy in my Dropbox. You can access the document using this link https://www.dropbox.com/sh/cdx1yuqy14btzk7/AADYVkGjud2JQoYEB2WAwD0ma?dl=0

I will add any other documents to this folder for future articles and posts. On that note however, I would like to remind everyone of another important video I did late last year and provide an update on some pretty critical findings. You may remember the video about unlawful directions and being required to sign a Stat. Dec. for CRICOS registration renewal that would require a provider to make a false Stat. Dec.? Well the video is here https://youtu.be/CKRZivOzSL8 There was also a range of supporting documents in a Dropbox folder (that link is posted on the Youtube video link). The update? 3 months later and as far as I am aware, there is still no update! If you're going through a CRICOS renewal, keep an eye out for the Stat. Dec. you're required to sign. If you find it has been updated, please let us know so we can all be updated!

Like · 3 | Reply

Anthony Barber • 1st
Radiation and Risk Management System Specialist
1y •••

We have never had a qualified auditor from a training regulator. We have to breach our own supplier and external auditor policies every time a training regulator sends us an unqualified auditor. We have been on the receiving end of thinly veiled threats after asking 'auditors' for copies of their auditing qualifications. Once we even had a ton of non conformances issued because we did not have a 'quality system' even though we are ISO9001 compliant. The 'auditors' (2 of them) did not know what ISO9001 was, t ...see more

Like · 4 | Reply · 11 Replies

Raelene Bartlett • You
Founding Director at RTO Doctor
1y •••

Anthony Barber That is absolutely shameful! Did you pursue it further?

Like | Reply

Nancy Pavlovic MAITD, MAIPM • 1st
Director - PAVLOV GROUP : ISO/RTO Lead Auditor, Project Mgr, Trainer, Writer, NLP Practitioner
1y (edited) •••

Anthony Barber perhaps you showed them the Guidelines according to ISO 19011 for auditors ?
https://www.iso.org/standard/70017.html

#ANAO #ISO19011ForAPSStaffwhoAudit

Guidelines for auditing management systems
iso.org

Like | Reply

Anthony Barber • 1st
Radiation and Risk Management System Specialist
1y •••

Raelene Bartlett yes. Our director was eventually invited to the office of the head of the (then state) regulator for a face to face apology and was promised we would never have another unqualified auditor.
We have had nothing but unqualified auditors from state and federal regulators ever since.
The 'audits' are monkeys with checklists. All our operational training staff are qualified a ...see more

Like · 6 | Reply

Anthony Barber • 1st
Radiation and Risk Management System Specialist
1y •••

Nancy Pavlovic MAITD, MAIPM they wouldn't know what it was

Like | Reply

Nancy Pavlovic MAITD, MAIPM • 1st
Director - PAVLOV GROUP : ISO/RTO Lead Auditor, Project Mgr, Trainer, Writer, NLP Practitioner
1y •••

Anthony Barber sad but true

Like | Reply

Raelene Bartlett • You
Founding Director at RTO Doctor
1y •••

Anthony Barber would you be willing to share with others who might benefit from your experience how you established that the ASQA auditors were not qualified?

Like · 2 | Reply

Raelene Bartlett • You
Founding Director at RTO Doctor
1y •••

I'll also bet that those 'State regulators' from Queensland (based on your company) neatly transitioned to higher managerial duties once ASQA was established?

Like · 1 | Reply

Anthony Barber • 1st
Radiation and Risk Management System Specialist
1y (edited) •••

Raelene Bartlett at the opening meeting, we asked for copies of their auditing qualifications as this is a requirement of our quality system to verify the qualifications of all service providers prior to a job commencing. We ask electricians for a copy of their electrical license and builders for their builders registration as well. It's a no brainer to ask an auditor the same question, we pay a lot of money and spend a lot of our valuable time for these audits, we want a good quality aud ...see more

Like · 4 | Reply

Raelene Bartlett • You
Founding Director at RTO Doctor
1y •••

Anthony Barber You are absolutely right of course! I'm sorry that your experience was so appalling for simply doing what your operational policies and procedures state.

Like · 1 | Reply

Christopher Bedwell • 1st
CEO at Safety Heights and Rescue (RTO : 52610)
1y •••

What I find most disturbing is that as a small RTO, I am audited far more intensively and with greater vigour than large company owned RTO's...
I've seen some of the training materials coming out of these places and it's shameful....
Pre-purchased materials that are significantly lacking in both substance and quality - yet if I attempted to present at an audit it would be torn to shreds...
The disparity between auditors is also widely ranging and is not driven on an SME level but by a guessed paperwork scenario...

Like · 7 Reply · 1 Reply

Raelene Bartlett • You
Founding Director at RTO Doctor
1y •••

And let's not leave out Australian Consumer Law on this one, after all, ASQA does provide a service, one which, as of 1 July 2020, becomes FULL COST RECOVERY!

From the ACL website...

Suppliers and manufacturers automatically provide guarantees about certain goods they sell, hire or lease, and services they provide to consumers. These rights exist regardless of any warranty provided by the supplier or manufacturer. A supplier includes anyone—such as a trader, a retailer or a service provider—who, in trade or commerce, sells, leases or hires goods or services to a consumer.

A manufacturer includes a person or business that makes or puts goods together, or has their name or brand on the goods. A manufacturer also includes a person who imports goods into Australia, where the maker of the goods does not have an office in Australia. In these circumstances, the importer bears the responsibilities of the manufacturer for the purposes of the consumer guarantees regime.

https://consumerlaw.gov.au/sites/consumer/files/2016/05/0553FT_ACL-guides_Guarantees_web.pdf

I genuinely can't wait to finish my law degree!

Like · 4 Reply · 19 Replies

Raelene Bartlett • You
Founding Director at RTO Doctor
1y •••

For more information on consumer guarantees -
https://www.accc.gov.au/consumers/consumer-rights-guarantees/consumer-guarantees

Like · 3 Reply

Geoff Sander • 1st
Team Member at The John Maxwell Team
1y •••

Boom! Raelene, Boom! Boom! Brett, Boom!

Like Reply

Like | Reply

Phillip Rutherford Ph.D • 1st
Training Systems Specialist

1y •••

But what goods or services does ASQA sell? None as far as I can see. All they do is charge RTOs a mozza of money to come down and beat them up. There are whole industries around that can do that for you, and much cheaper too!!

Like · 2 | Reply

Geoff Sander • 1st
Team Member at The John Maxwell Team

1y •••

See, this is why the new bill didn't even get a look see. While the Government, ACCC and the greater community see them as beneficial, we are seen as the cowboys doing justice injustice. So this begs the next question, how do we turn this trend around?

Like · 2 | Reply

Phillip Rutherford Ph.D • 1st
Training Systems Specialist

1y •••

Brett Hilderr is there any proof that they are actually providing this confidence? Not according to the media.

I am sure that if confronted in a court of law they would find many witnesses to back up their claim of success at this, but I feel confident that a parallel body could provide the community with an equal - if not better - level of confidence for a fraction of the cost.

Like · 1 | Reply

Geoff Sander • 1st
Team Member at The John Maxwell Team

1y •••

This is where we are referring to 2 different planets. Government and private enterprise. Government will never be able to climb to business standards because they don't need to and Business will never stoop to Government because they don't need to. It's a vicious stalemate.

Like · 1 | Reply

Phillip Rutherford Ph.D • 1st
Training Systems Specialist

1y •••

Brett Hilderr another difference is that ISO have competitors against which they have to compete for members' money. ASQA enjoys freedom of operations because no other organisation could be bothered competing.

Like · 2 | Reply

Geoff Sander • 1st
Team Member at The John Maxwell Team
1y (edited) •••

Blary fake news again Fssst! We will need more then just one because he'll just end up in #enoughisenough. No, in marketing we need something bigger, something Trump.

Like | Reply

Phillip Rutherford Ph.D • 1st
Training Systems Specialist
1y •••

Brett Hilderr especially if said organisation was run by members and not bureaucrats. AIM, AITD, IEAust etc all had their start when a few disgruntled folk got together and formed themselves into a member-based organisation, run by and for the .members.

??

Like · 2 | Reply

Geoff Sander • 1st
Team Member at The John Maxwell Team
1y •••

Brett Hilder No in marketing we need something bigger then just one journalist. Before you know it he's disappeared. We need something bigger, something Trump!

Like | Reply

Geoff Sander • 1st
Team Member at The John Maxwell Team
1y •••

No in marketing we need something bigger than just one journalist. before you know it he's disappeared. We need something bigger, something Trump!

Like · 1 | Reply

Raelene Bartlett • You
Founding Director at RTO Doctor
1y •••

An important perspective that others may not have considered is discussed in this article by Amanda Ryding and Laura Reisz
(Colin Biggers & Paisley Lawyers) in relation to vicarious liability and employers in Australia.

From the summary...
In Australia, the law regarding the extent to which employers are vicariously liable for wrongful acts by an employee has, until today, been unclear.

In its judgment delivered this morning in Prince Alfred College Incorporated v ADC [2016] HCA 37, the majority of the High Court1 considered the correct approach to be taken to the question of Prince Alfred College's (PAC) vicarious liability for the criminal acts of its employed housemaster, Bain.

The majority of the High Court held that an employer could be vicariously liable for criminal acts of its employee, and espoused what was referred to as the "relevant approach", which involves considering whether the employer has assigned to the employee any special role, and the position the employee is in as regards the victim.

https://www.cbp.com.au/insights/insights/2016/october/the-high-court-clarifies-the-law-regarding-employe#_ftn1?utm_source=Mondaq&utm_medium=syndication&utm_campaign=LinkedIn-integration

Like · 3 | Reply · 7 Replies

Phillip Rutherford Ph.D • 1st
Training Systems Specialist
1y •••

That's an interesting ruling. And in this world of competency-based training and assessment, any courses undertaken by supervisors which did NOT include duty of care to staff is one which should not be accredited. On the other hand, in cases where supervisors and managers have undertaken courses which DID include such competencies, then their liability is even more pronounced if they had been determined as competent during or at the course's completion.

As we all know, being determined as competent means that evidence has been produced showing that the person knows what to do and has the skills to do it. And, if done correctly, the assessment will also show that the person can replicate such performance in the future (remember that ideal??). If, at some time in the future, they do not demonstrate those skills and knowledge then we are deep within the realm of discipline. It was proved - through evidence they themselves produced - that they could do 'it' (whatever it is). If they then don't do it then .....

This has been an essential element of the VET system since we introduced it back in the 90s, and one that the unions were totally behind. Unfortunately it is also one that has been forgotten over the years.

Like · 3 Reply

Raelene Bartlett • You 1y •••
Founding Director at RTO Doctor

Would definitely make for the most interesting court case Phillip Rutherford Ph.D FAITD FAIM MAIPM MPD and how I would love to be a part of that one!

Like · 1 Reply

Phillip Rutherford Ph.D • 1st 1y •••
Training Systems Specialist

Where I was called on as an expert witness I was able to show that the definitions of competence and competency-based assessment were taken totally out of context. In one case a project manager was dismissed because the owner claimed he had conducted an assessment of his competence and found him incompetent. I showed that the manager was neither trained in competency-based assessment, nor was competent at the task. The project manager won substantial damages.

I have been a witness in a few cases where the whole issue of competence has been challenged, and being one of the people who introduced these concepts into this country my expert testimony is listened to. (Being a Ph.D helps :-) LOL)

Like · 5 Reply

Geoff Sander • 1st 1y •••
Team Member at The John Maxwell Team

Thank you Phillip on our friend's behalf. Most of the time these closures are over such trivia. It just takes someone with his head in the big picture to see the real story. We need more people like you.

Like · 1 Reply

Phillip Rutherford Ph.D • 1st 1y •••
Training Systems Specialist

Geoff Sanderr any time. Happy to help.

Like · 1 Reply

Geoff Sander • 1st 1y •••
Team Member at The John Maxwell Team

Phillip you are such an inspiration.

Like · 1 Reply

Phillip Rutherford Ph.D • 1st 1y •••
Training Systems Specialist

Geoff Sanderr thanks Geoff.

Like · 1 Reply

Raelene Bartlett • You 1y ···
Founding Director at RTO Doctor

Roman Gowor Office of the Minister for Employment, Skills, Small & Family Business - Senator Hon. Michaelia Cash Louise Pratt Christian Porter Independent Tertiary Education Council Australia Felix Pirie Andrew Shea Australian Skills Quality Authority (ASQA)

Like Reply · 1 Reply

Geoff Sander • 1st 1y ···
Team Member at The John Maxwell Team

One that did our audit last year, turned up tipsy after being at the bar, and blatantly made comments that were racially discriminating about staff in the business she was auditing. My boss recorded it in case he would need to use it. We did have to go before AAT and they came up with mutual agreement. I told him to take it further but he decided against it in case it 'rocked the boat' too much.

Like · 4 Reply · 6 Replies

Load previous replies

Geoff Sander • 1st 1y ···
Team Member at The John Maxwell Team

Aaah! What can I say! At least, thank you Brett. Solid makes us stronger!

Like · 2 Reply

Phillip Rutherford Ph.D • 1st 1y ···
Training Systems Specialist

I am surprised nobody has challenged the competence of auditors. After all, an RTOs registration can be cancelled if trainers are not competent. Why has nobody push back and questioned the competence of the person to make this recommendation?

Like · 6 Reply · 8 Replies

Tom Bourne • 1st 1y ···
Consultant / Trainer and Assessor at Various Registered Training Organisation

Would be a very interesting test case to run, to see if ASQA actually had the legislated authority to make recommendations to close an RTO, let alone act on them. Now, if that case was brought by an RTO who was forced into closing it's doors, I am thinking there is a very good case for compensation, and if that happened perhaps class action lawyers may come into play.

Like · 2 Reply

Phillip Rutherford Ph.D • 1st
Training Systems Specialist
1y •••

Tom Bourne true. What if it was proven that an auditor was not competent when making a decision, or was making decisions applying standards which were not part of their skills set? I have been called as an expert witness a number of times on similar cases, the most recent resulting in charges of manslaughter being withdrawn.

As you say, maybe it is time for a test case - if only to ascertain if they are applying the same standards they demand of others.

Like · 1 Reply

Joanne Cornelius • 2nd
Managing Director and CEO at L. P. COMMUNICATIONS Pty Ltd Trading as The Learning Professionals
1y •••

I have challenged ASQA all the way to the AAT, challenging auditors qualifications and competency. I highly recommend all RTOs being audited to use the FOI act to determine the actual qualifications held and experience of their auditors. I did 3 out of the 5 auditor did not hold the minimum qualifications as per the VET regulator standards. It cost me $150,000 to fight ASQA at the AAT. They picked on the wrong person to mess with. ASQA settled when senior m ...see more

Like · 7 Reply

Raelene Bartlett • You
Founding Director at RTO Doctor
1y •••

For those that missed the story of Joanne Cornelius there is a series of 5 videos (thanks to LinkedIn's 'live' function not being continuous after a 10-minute timeframe) available on my YouTube channel, the first of which is here https://youtu.be/I6M3qSShXbs

Like · 1 Reply

Scott Rogers • 1st
Director eSkilled LMS and E-learning
1y •••

Phillip Rutherford Ph.D FAITD FAIM MAIPM MPD the problem is to whom do you raise it? Who regulates the regulator? The commonwealth ombudsman knows nothing about VET, has no ability to demand ASQA do anything. We have been talking about these issues, raising them with MPs etc. How do we get the government to act?

Like Reply

Phillip Rutherford Ph.D • 1st
Training Systems Specialist
1y •••

Scott Rogerss well, if enough people stopped accepting what is being dished out then the government will have to listen. It was a strike by ITOs in WA back in the second half of the 80s that saw the changes introduced to the VET system in the first place. Perhaps it is time for another general strike.

Like · 4 Reply

Dr. Brendan Moloney • 1st
1y (edited) •••
Darlo and Coursewriter.com We write your courses, get your courses online, and get them registered with acc...

Great article again! It would be hysterically funny, if not so serious, the way in which education regulators operate. I'd argue that it is even worse at TEQSA. The agency is predominantly bureaucrats with little to no experience in the tertiary education sector. Where regulators have some experience, they come from self accrediting universities. These are sandstone unis and the staff have little really experience of the full weight of harassment of TEQSA. So in short there is a bunch of public servants - in the main - trying to assess higher education administration and teaching and learning. Unlike ASQA, there is no assessment of skills or even basic requirements of any staff member in private higher education regulation at TEQSA. Anyone can basically be employed to start reviewing and making decisions on higher education applications and courses. ZERO qualifications or set experience required. While ASQA auditors most definitely sound dodgy, there is no legislative requirement for TEQSA - isn't this even more circumspect?

Like · 6 Reply · 4 Replies

Raelene Bartlett • You
1y •••
Founding Director at RTO Doctor

Yes Dr. Brendan Moloney TEQSA and Higher Education most definitely have a set of rules all of their own. Universities developing courses that don't meet the requirements for registration and/or licensing...Don't even get me started on the College of Law who is a TEQSA provider! I could be here for a very long time!

Like · 2 Reply

Fazluz ZAMAN • 1st
1y •••
Tertiary Academic | Lecturer | VET Trainer | Education Quality and Compliance Administrator | Curricul...

Name and shame list does not exist in TEQSA

Like Reply

Dr. Brendan Moloney • 1st
1y •••
Darlo and Coursewriter.com We write your courses, get your courses online, and get them registered ...

Dr. Fazluz ZAMAN not sure what you mean name and shame list. However TEQSA, probably illegally, does publish the names of applicants

Like Reply

Neil Chapple • 1st
1y (edited) •••
Director Of Studies at Sydney Metropolitan International College

That a detailed and comprehensive article on a contradiction that the regulator does not have to have the equal qualifications if not higher then the Education Provider. Unbelievable and how embarrassing. That needs to be fixed to be fair for all.

Like · 3 Reply · 3 Replies

Dr. Brendan Moloney • 1st 1y ···
Darlo and Coursewriter.com We write your courses, get your courses online, and get them registered ...

Brett Hilder An alternative model is the US one, where a government agency accredits the accreditors. In this way they can assure subject matter expert is a specific accreditation agency and the accreditation body can operate semi-commercially. This would allow the establishment and review of independent quality agencies, and decentralise power and decision making. Centralising all regulatory systems under one government agency is problematic.

Like · 1 Reply

Nancy Pavlovic MAITD, MAIPM • 1st 1y (edited) ···
Director - PAVLOV GROUP : ISO/RTO Lead Auditor, Project Mgr, Trainer, Writer, NLP Practitioner

Raelene Bartlett brilliant assessment of the root cause of #VETRegulatorInDenialOfItsInadequateAccountability

Further you present some solid and reliable solutions that treat the root cause of the trust deficit in the regulators treatment of private training providers.

Below image could easily be adapted to read:

No Amount of Denial / additional powers could repair the deep seated flaws in the Regulators Performance Against the Standards they too must comply with.

#ASQATrustDeficit

Like · 5 Reply

Sukh Sandhu (MAITD, MAPEX, MITECA) • 1st 1y ···
ISO 9001, RTO, HEP, ELICOS & CRICOS Consultant and Lead Auditor | Risk management expert | Registered M...

Great article Raelene Bartlett

Like · 4 Reply

Lee Perlitz • 1st 1y ···
CEO Lee Perlitz Training Consultancy

Well said and well researched Raelene. I agree completely.

Like · 4 Reply

Marc Miles • 1st
Training and Compliance professional
1y •••

Great article.

Like · 1 Reply

Peter West • 2nd
Digital Learning Lab TAFE NSW | Author | Speaker
1y •••

Says a lot..."Just because a section of the ESOS Act (for the purposes of the ELICOS Standards 2018 for example) provides them with the authority to, does not equate to them being qualified."
A great article.

Like · 3 Reply

Again, the question must be asked. In what other regulatory system does such physical, psychological, emotional and financial harm occur where those responsible for the audit process and therefore findings were under such a cloud of validity and reliability, but the destruction occurred anyway? In what world would this be acceptable?

The Bill that Changed the Game While Peak Bodies Did NOTHING!

> "Privilege is when you think something is not a problem because it is not a problem to you personally."
>
> **- David Gaider**

On 13 and 24 January 2020, the CEO of a peak body contacted the author via email asking for my opinion and feedback on the *National Vocational Education and Training Regulator Amendment Bill 2019*. His exact words were 'The team here are assembling member feedback concerning the *National Vocational Education and Training Regulator Amendment Bill 2019* (Cth.) currently before the Senate. Although some of the changes are administrative in nature, others concerning changes to the regulatory powers of the Australian Skills Quality Authority (ASQA) require a detailed assessment. As the views of members have been mixed, given your interest in the matter I'd welcome your thoughts on Bill – those elements that are thought to be straight-forward and those which are problematic'.

While the writer did provide a significant amount of feedback to him on 28 January 2020, the writer never heard another word from him again. Likewise, the writer also approached various Ministers from both sides of politics and not one person raised an objection, despite the many objections that the writer had presented. Issues raised included (but were not limited to):

- Concerns about the subjectivity of some proposed additions such as for example:
    - Principal purpose must be education;

- Commitment and capability to deliver quality vocational education and training;
- All of ASQA's General Directions were to become Legislative Instruments despite the fact that they were badly written and based on poor policy advice;
- Concerns that ASQA's changes to section 26 would cause issues with ASQA using historical evidence in cases where traditionally a section 26 notice would;
- The current templates in use for applications for VET accredited courses were in breach of the Standards for VET Accredited Courses 2012 and had been for years. In fact, it is only with the most recent changes in March 2021 in the Standards for VET Accredited Courses 2021 that the changes made historically have now been formally made. The templates were based on the Standards for Training Package template format but the changes were only adopted legislatively in March 2021. For several years now, ASQA has been forcing applicants to comply with a template that was inconsistent with the VAC Standards at the time;
- ASQA can cancel certification issued by an RTO without first directing it to do so itself, the consequences of which could be fraught with danger where for example ASQA cancels the certification but the certification was also linked to High-Risk Work Licences or registration with other bodies including say nurses, pilots, massage therapists, construction, etc. The writer also raised concerns where the graduate who certification had been cancelled may have also been subject to an application for permanent residency or sponsorship or similar, the impact that just cancelling someone's certification might have. There were also concerns raised about the lack of procedural fairness and especially in light of errors in the audit process which are significant and have every right to be appealed prior to the cancellation taking place;

- Most importantly, as has been seen through the sector in the past 12 months at least, providers' access to merits review, while already significantly hampered as identified in *National Vocational Education and Training Regulator Act 2011 (Cth.): An Investigation into Access to Merits Review*, was about to be completely changed and ASQA had been completely and utterly silent on how and why. Ordinarily, the explanatory memoranda would clarify any changes for parliament as the Bill passes through its process but nowhere was it highlighted that the rules for accessing merits review were about to change significantly. It was not discussed anywhere, the change was proposed and it was left for people like the writer to identify it, bring it to the forefront, which she and other individuals did and NOBODY acted on any of the feedback provided. Just to be clear, the writer provided this feedback to a range of people whose role it was to provide the feedback including, but not limited to:
    - One of the alleged peak bodies of this sector;
    - Assistant Minister for Vocational Education, Training and Apprenticeships;
    - Assistant Advisor to the Assistant Minister for Vocational Education, Training and Apprenticeships;
    - Shadow Minister for Education and Training;
- Another big change that was swept under the carpet and made without any clarification provided was that of the ability to remove conditions. This change was never before available and suddenly it was and this required further explanation which had not been provided in the Explanatory Memoranda.

So why was this whole issue regarding reconsideration a game changer for VET Providers? What was the big deal and why does the writer say our peak bodies, let providers down?

As was predicted by the writer, the proposed legislative change meant that the entire process by which a provider could access merits review changed. Up until the passage of the Bill unopposed with **NO** objections, upon receipt of an ASQA decision, for the majority of decisions, a provider could apply to the Administrative Appeals Tribunal ("AAT") for a stay of the decision or decisions and a review of those decisions, effectively, an appeal to the Tribunal to review those decisions that had been made because the provider disagreed with the findings by ASQA.

What this change meant was that now, as is currently the case, a provider **MUST** apply for a reconsideration of the decision by ASQA ***within 28 days***. The decision or decisions ***come into effect within 35 days***. ASQA has up to 90 days to consider the application for reconsideration. You can apply to ASQA for a stay of the decision however it is entirely discretionary upon ASQA to provide a stay of the decision. If you are near the 28 days and need to appeal that decision in the Tribunal, that decision may come into effect in 35 days, or worse, if ASQA accept the application for reconsideration but deny the stay and the provider doesn't challenge the denial of the stay because they don't understand the implications (which in our experience has been the most common outcome of this change), the decision or decisions actually come into effect while ASQA is considering the application for reconsideration.

In other words, you can no longer just go to the AAT and seek a stay, you must apply for an appeal via ASQA's processes first and if ASQA says the stay is denied, the decision will come into effect within 35 days and ASQA has up to 90 days to review the application. If ASQA responds that they affirm the decision under review (which in our experience is most of the time), it's too late to seek a stay from the AAT because the decision has already come into effect 35 days after it was made. This change, that went unopposed despite warnings, requires an explanation just so that the consequences of this change are clearly understood and how the national peak providers neglected and let down the sector they are supposed to represent.

Example:

Sunshine RTO has just received a Decision to cancel their NVR registration and their ESOS registrations because subsequent to an ASQA audit, ASQA believes that Sunshine RTO remains critically not compliant (*believe it or not, this is a very common scenario*).

Sunshine RTO wants to apply to appeal to the AAT and get a stay and review of the decisions. It does so around day 23 after receiving the decision letter. (*It should be noted that several providers at this point did actually pay to have their applications heard by the AAT but they were denied because the AAT could not hear the case due to legislation which now meant that as the next step has not been completed*).

The AAT hears the application of Sunshine RTO around day 27 or 28. Sunshine RTO is advised that it can no longer apply to the AAT until it has applied for a reconsideration with ASQA and ASQA have affirmed the decision.

If there is time before the 28 days arrives, Sunshine RTO applies for a reconsideration by ASQA but doesn't realise that it needs to seek a stay from ASQA. The decision comes into effect on day 35. ASQA has up to 90 days to consider the application for reconsideration. As the decision has come into effect, the RTO would be cancelled and so would their ESOS registration unless ASQA overturns the decision after 90 days by which time, the damage is done anyway.

If 28 days have passed since the decision letter and Sunshine RTO has not yet been able to apply for reconsideration with ASQA, the decision comes into effect because the appeal needed to be lodged within 28 days. See Rabih's story for an example of what happens in these situations.

As per the feedback provided at the time the Bill was available for consultation[60] and upon which **NOBODY** acted:

60 This feedback will be made available to anyone upon request via the RTO Doctor contact page https://rtodoctor.com.au/contact

> A provider can go to the Tribunal and seek a stay and often fight for no or limited conditions. A provider should always be given the benefit of the doubt and the opportunity to exercise natural justice before having conditions placed on them and their right to a stay compromised. At no point should a provider be found guilty and then have to demonstrate their innocence, the foundation of Australia's legal system is innocent until proven guilty. Many providers do not get an opportunity to demonstrate their innocence before the decision is made.[61]

This legislative change was completely preventable; or at least, it had the potential to be substantially amended to ensure procedural fairness. The question that must be asked of the peak bodies and the relevant Ministers is, '*Why were there no objections submitted when they at least had the objections in writing from RTO Doctor on behalf of the #enoughisenough campaign at the time?*'

61 Email correspondence from Raelene Bartlett to various sources including a peak body and relevant Ministers, via email, 29 January 2020, 2:11pm AWST.

What is Merits Review?

> *"Injustice anywhere is a threat to justice everywhere."*
> **- Martin Luther King Jr.**

All NVR RTOs have the opportunity for external review[62] for certain decisions[63] made under the NVR Act, namely, those made under s 199. The legislative framework for a stay and a review of a decision by ASQA in the AAT is well documented through case law[64] and as has been documented previously, was the most common manner of seeking an appeal until the *National Vocational Education and Training Regulator Amendment Bill 2019* was agreed to in the Senate without amendment and received Royal Assent. The most common applications that were made at the AAT are applications for '*a stay of the decision*' and '*a review of the decision*'. A decision that is subject to review has full effect and operation unless the Tribunal uses its discretion[65] to make an order to stay the operation and effect of that decision.

What this means in practice for an NVR RTO who has been impacted by a Notice from ASQA is that, at least from a legal perspective, their registration continues until the substantive hearing has been finalised and a new decision made. The external review process at the AAT is a mechanism allowing for a review of the original decision to determine whether the correct or preferable decision was made in the circumstances

---

62 NVR Act s 203.

63 Ibid s 199.

64 For example, *Sydney Training Academy Pty Ltd and Australian Skills Quality Authority* [2018] AATA 3361 (7 September 2018) [18], '*Australian Trade Training and Assessment Pty Ltd (ATTA)*' [14], '*Business Institute of Australia Pty Ltd*' (n 32).

65 AAT Act s 41(2).

of that individual case.[66] For those RTOs who are impacted by the new system, what this means is that provided the decision has yet to come into effect (see the previous chapter, '*The Bill That Changed The Game While the Peak Bodies Did NOTHING!*'), the AAT can use its discretion to prevent the decision from coming into effect until it makes its own decision.

The Tribunal is open to receive new evidence, including evidence that was not before the decision-maker at the time the original decision was made.[67] The overriding concept that drives this mechanism is that the Tribunal '*stands in the shoes of the original decision-maker*' and is able to undertake a fresh review of the decision, a '*hearing de novo*'.[68]

The genesis of merits review comes from the Kerr Committee in 1971 who explained that people who have been negatively impacted by Commonwealth or Tribunal decisions will generally feel as though that decision was wrong based on the merits of the case.[69] The Kerr Committee found that it was appropriate to establish a mechanism that was '*accessible (cheap, informal and quick) and responsive to the needs of persons using the system*'.[70]

What the Committee also found amongst many other things was that merits review Tribunals in Australia were not operating coherently and in accordance with these objectives. The full finding in relation to this issue is reproduced next as it demonstrates certain points (*emphasis added)* that will be touched upon next:

---

66 Judith Bannister, Anna Olijnyk and Stephen McDonald, (n 15) 225, Sarah Withnall Howe and Michelle Evans, (n 87) 193-194, Administrative Review Council, *Better Decisions: Review Of The Commonwealth Merits Review Tribunals* (Report to the Minister for Justice No 39, 1995).

67 There is anecdotal evidence that both ASQA and Tribunal members are frustrated by providers who submit fresh evidence confirming compliance through this process but regardless of their dislike or frustration at this process, it is legally permissible (and expected) outcome of merits review in Australia.

68 Sarah Withnall Howe and Michelle Evans, (n 87) 193-194 [2.2], Administrative Review Council, (n 119) viii [1].

69 Administrative Review Council (n 119).

70 Ibid 28 [2.11].

> ...the system of review tribunals can no longer accurately be described as a coherent system. For example, there are major differences both between and within the different tribunals in such matters as:

- **the degree of formality of proceedings, including the physical environment and the level of representation**;
- the style of proceedings, including the use of techniques such as decisions 'on the
- papers', mediation, non-adversarial proceedings and **adversarial hearings featuring cross-examination**;
- the mix of skills brought to tribunal panels, including the use of single-member panels;
- the level of information and assistance provided by tribunals and agencies to applicants and to the broader community;
- the method of selecting tribunal members, their terms and conditions of appointment, and the level of professional development and support provided to them;
- the availability and style of internal review within decision-making agencies;
- the methods adopted to ensure that tribunal decisions are considered by agencies in the development of their policy, legislation and decision-making processes; and
- **the cost of the merits review process**.[71]

Those issues highlighted in the extract from the ARC report are emphasised to demonstrate current features of the merits review process in Australia in relation to stay applications for NVR RTOs pursuant to s 203 of the NVR Act and s 41(2) of the AAT Act.

[71] Ibid 8 [1.8].

From the 28 reported decisions that were reviewed[72] for my book '*National Vocational Education and Training Regulator Act 2011 (Cth.): An Investigation Into Merits Review*', regarding stay applications, 28 of those applications were with legal representation where the hearing was conducted (on review of the reports) in an adversarial manner and in certain cases, in a Tribunal hearing room and frequently with cross-examination. The exact manner in which ASQA conducts itself during these hearings is consistent with the excerpt from the ARC Report finding above from the moment they are notified by the Tribunal that an application has been made.

The Tribunal notifies ASQA who immediately allocates the case to an ASQA lawyer who in each of these cases defends ASQA's original finding based on the previous legal decision that was made. One of the many reasons that this is problematic is because as a Commonwealth litigant, in accordance with the *Legal Services Directions 2017* (Cth.), the

72 '*VETiS* ', '*Institute of Training Pty Ltd*'(n 31), '*Technical Education Australia Pty Ltd*' (n 31) [104 - 105]; '*Trades College Australia Pty Ltd*' (n 31) [16], '*Australian Institute of Technical Training Pty Ltd*' (n 31) [53-54], '*Sher-E-Punjab Pty Ltd*' [104-106] (n 31), '*Business Institute of Australia Pty Ltd*' 11 (n 32) [30], '*Metro College of Technology Pty Ltd*' [34], '*Trades College Australia Pty Ltd*' [27-28] (n 31), '*Australian Trade Training and Assessment Pty Ltd*', '*Sydney Training Academy Pty Ltd*', '*Australian International College Pty Ltd*', *Australian Institute of Trades Pty Ltd as trustee for the Institute of Hotel Management Australia v Australian Skills Quality Authority* [2017], AATA 2912 (1 August 2017), *Oztech Trade Training College Pty Ltd v Australian Skills Quality Authority* [2018] AATA 3741 (9 October 2018), *Sunrise Institute of Australia Pty Ltd v Australian Skills Quality Authority* [2018] AATA 3935 (15 October 2018), *Real Training Outcomes v Australian Skills Quality Authority* [2018] AATA 4611 (18 December 2018), *Australian Vocational Learning Centre Pty Ltd v Australian Skills Quality Authority* [2018] AATA 4725 (21 December 2018), *Pacific Flight Services Pty Ltd v Australian Skills Quality Authority* (n 35) *Menzies Institute of Technology v Australian Skills Quality Authority* [2019] AATA 343 (12 February 2019), *Darwin Human Resource and Computer Academy Pty Ltd v Australian Skills Quality Authority* [2017] AATA 738 (24 May 2017), *Gurkhas Institute of Technology Pty Ltd trading as Gurkhas Institute of Technology ('Gurkhas') v Australian Skills Quality Authority* [2017] AATA 1018 (3 July 2017), *Skilled Education Australia Pty Limited v Australian Skills Quality Authority* [2019] AATA 317 (4 March 2019), *Chemcert Training Group v Australian Skills Quality Authority* [2019] AATA 313 (4 March 2019), *Daily Update Pty Ltd v Australian Skills Quality Authority* [2014] AATA 118 (6 March 2014), *Western Institute of Technology Pty Ltd v Australian Skills Quality Authority* [2018] AATA 94 (25 January 2018), *Elite Academy Australia Pty Ltd v Australian Skills Quality Authority* [2019] AATA 79 (5 February 2019), *BJSB Pty Ltd (t/a The Imperial College of Australia) v Australian Skills Quality Authority* [2019] AATA 1053 (30 May 2019), *Sunrise Institute of Australia Pty Ltd v Australian Skills Quality Authority* [2019] AATA 1131 (5 June 2019).

Commonwealth's obligation to act as a model litigant, and the nature of that obligation are explicit.

Areas that are a frequent cause for concern in the Commonwealth's adherence to this obligation[73] include those areas highlighted below:

> The obligation to act as a model litigant requires that the Commonwealth and Commonwealth agencies act honestly **and fairly in handling claims and litigation** brought by or against the Commonwealth or a Commonwealth agency by:
>
> (a) **dealing with claims promptly and not causing unnecessary delay in the handling of claims and litigation**
>
> (aa) **making an early assessment of:**
>
> **(i) the Commonwealth's prospects of success in legal proceedings that may be brought against the Commonwealth; and**
>
> **(ii) the Commonwealth's potential liability in claims against the Commonwealth**
>
> (b) paying legitimate claims without litigation, including making partial settlements of claims or interim payments, where it is clear that liability is at least as much as the amount to be paid
>
> (c) **acting consistently in the handling of claims and litigation**
>
> (d) **endeavouring to avoid, prevent and limit the scope of legal proceedings wherever possible, including by giving consideration in all cases to alternative dispute resolution before initiating legal proceedings and by participating in alternative dispute resolution processes where appropriate**
>
> (e) **where it is not possible to avoid litigation, keeping the costs of litigation to a minimum, including by:**

[73] Legal Services Directions 2017 (Cth.) app B, s 2

(i) **not requiring the other party to prove a matter which the Commonwealth or the agency knows to be true**

(ii) not contesting liability if the Commonwealth or the agency knows that the dispute is really about quantum

(iii) **monitoring the progress of the litigation and using methods that it considers appropriate to resolve the litigation, including settlement offers, payments into court or alternative dispute resolution, and**

(iv) ensuring that arrangements are made so that a person participating in any settlement negotiations on behalf of the Commonwealth or a Commonwealth agency can enter into a settlement of the claim or legal proceedings in the course of the negotiations;

(f) **not taking advantage of a claimant who lacks the resources to litigate a legitimate claim**

(g) **not relying on technical defences unless the Commonwealth's or the agency's interests would be prejudiced by the failure to comply with a particular requirement**

(h) **not undertaking and pursuing appeals unless the Commonwealth or the agency believes that it has reasonable prospects for success or the appeal is otherwise justified in the public interest, and**

(i) **apologising where the Commonwealth or the agency is aware that it or its lawyers have acted wrongfully or improperly.**

Each of the areas highlighted is an area that has been a constant cause of complaint from providers who have journeyed through the merits review process. Examples include that many providers do not get to finalise their application for merits review because the financial cost of fighting the application is, or becomes, too onerous. They do not often have sufficient funds; and very few, if any, providers who have pursued and been successful in an appeals process against ASQA have for example received the apology referred to at (i). Every ASQA matter is managed at the Tribunal by an ASQA lawyer meaning that if the provider cannot afford a lawyer, they are required to self-represent making the process unfair and intimidatory.

It has often been said that RTOs almost need to have as a standard operational practice, a litigation fund just in order to survive. This author has been in a Tribunal hearing where the Tribunal Member made it very clear that any company that has been operating for at least 5 or 6 years in this industry (international education and VET) should expect to have set aside a bank account established purely for the purpose of litigation.

On this basis, it would appear that the concerns of the ARC Report from 1995 (24 years ago) are resurfacing in today's Tribunals, a factor briefly discussed in relation to the model litigant obligation.[74] Additional likenesses can be identified between the ARC Report and merits review proceedings in Australia in this area today however they are beyond the scope of this book.

One feature that is not so often discussed in relation to merits review in these hearings but often arises as a further challenge in this adversarial, costly and overly complex process is that while an NVR RTO can provide fresh evidence, so too can ASQA and it is becoming more and more frequent that it attempts to do so.

Either party is able to produce fresh evidence in merits review hearings to assist the Tribunal to ensure that the correct and preferable decision is made. It becomes problematic when the correct and preferable decision however is increased, and additional factors sought that were not initially presented to the provider as being a concern. Legal literature provides examples such as *New South Wales Thoroughbred Racing Board v Waterhouse* (2003) 56 NSWLR 691, 711, there is an example of this in case law related to VET and ASQA proceedings, that of *G Plus G Global Trading Pty Ltd v Australian Skills Quality Authority*[75] highlighting that '*everything is on the table*'.

---

[74] *Legal Services Directions 2017* (Cth.) app B s 1 ("Model Litigant Rules").

[75] Ibid 8 [1.8].

ASQA often uses options available to it under the NVR Act[76] to obtain further evidence to improve their case at merits review.

Such options include the use of s 26 notices (sometimes in close proximity to each other and for vast amounts of information, most of which is completely irrelevant to the issue/s being appealed), s 62 requests and, what is commonly known in the sector as 72-hour notices which was developed with the intent of effectively preventing an RTO from seeking a stay of the decision once it has been made. While the provider is battling to produce sufficient evidence to ensure support the Tribunal to make the correct and preferable decision regarding the legal decision that it was initially required to review, ASQA is often busy extending the basis for that legal decision by procuring additional reasons for the decision when the provider is least able to defend themselves appropriately.

These issues are beyond the scope of this paper but are highlighted as they are tools that are frequently used by ASQA in this adversarial,

76 *'VETiS '*, *'Institute of Training Pty Ltd'*(n 31), *'Technical Education Australia Pty Ltd'* (n 31) [104 - 105]; *'Trades College Australia Pty Ltd'* (n 31) [16], *'Australian Institute of Technical Training Pty Ltd'* (n 31) [53-54], *'Sher-E-Punjab Pty Ltd'* [104-106] (n 31), *'Business Institute of Australia Pty Ltd'* 11 (n 32) [30], *'Metro College of Technology Pty Ltd'* [34], *'Trades College Australia Pty Ltd'* [27-28] (n 31), *'Australian Trade Training and Assessment Pty Ltd'*, *'Sydney Training Academy Pty Ltd'*, *'Australian International College Pty Ltd'*, *Australian Institute of Trades Pty Ltd as trustee for the Institute of Hotel Management Australia v Australian Skills Quality Authority* [2017] AATA 2912 (1 August 2017), *Oztech Trade Training College Pty Ltd v Australian Skills Quality Authority* [2018] AATA 3741 (9 October 2018), *Sunrise Institute of Australia Pty Ltd v Australian Skills Quality Authority* [2018] AATA 3935 (15 October 2018), *Real Training Outcomes v Australian Skills Quality Authority* [2018] AATA 4611 (18 December 2018), *Australian Vocational Learning Centre Pty Ltd v Australian Skills Quality Authority* [2018] AATA 4725 (21 December 2018), *Pacific Flight Services Pty Ltd v Australian Skills Quality Authority* (n 35) *Menzies Institute of Technology v Australian Skills Quality Authority* [2019] AATA 343 (12 February 2019), *Darwin Human Resource and Computer Academy Pty Ltd v Australian Skills Quality Authority* [2017] AATA 738 (24 May 2017), *Gurkhas Institute of Technology Pty Ltd trading as Gurkhas Institute of Technology ('Gurkhas') v Australian Skills Quality Authority* [2017] AATA 1018 (3 July 2017), *Skilled Education Australia Pty Limited v Australian Skills Quality Authority* [2019] AATA 317 (4 March 2019), *Chemcert Training Group v Australian Skills Quality Authority* [2019] AATA 313 (4 March 2019), *Daily Update Pty Ltd v Australian Skills Quality Authority* [2014] AATA 118 (6 March 2014), *Western Institute of Technology Pty Ltd v Australian Skills Quality Authority* [2018] AATA 94 (25 January 2018), *Elite Academy Australia Pty Ltd v Australian Skills Quality Authority* [2019] AATA 79 (5 February 2019), *BJSB Pty Ltd (t/a The Imperial College of Australia) v Australian Skills Quality Authority* [2019] AATA 1053 (30 May 2019), *Sunrise Institute of Australia Pty Ltd v Australian Skills Quality Authority* [2019] AATA 1131 (5 June 2019).

costly and overly complex process. Considering the flawed foundation that these actions and legal decisions are based on however, one must question whether the objectives of the NVR Act[77] are being upheld by the VET Regulator and how they can consistently claim to have complied with the Standards for VET Regulators. Certainly, in the context of the testimonials in this book, there is an abundance of questionable behaviour that should never have occurred. With ASQA being quite literally a law unto itself though with complete independence as a statutory authority who reports to and is monitored by nobody, it's not hard to see how this occurred. It is for reasons such as these that the #enoughisenough campaign began and the ICEA established.

It is important to consider '***The Obligation***'[78] that ASQA has as a model litigant and the significant concerns being raised around the nature of this obligation,[79] particularly around the areas of:

dealing with claims promptly and not causing unnecessary delay in the handling of claims and litigation[80] (*this extends to merits review proceedings*);[81]

- not taking advantage of a claimant who lacks the resources to litigate a legitimate claim;[82]
- not undertaking and pursuing appeals unless the Commonwealth or the agency believes that it has reasonable prospects for success, or the appeal is otherwise justified in the public interest;[83] and
- apologising where the Commonwealth or the agency is aware that it or its lawyers have acted wrongfully or improperly.[84]

77 *Legal Services Directions 2017* (Cth.) app B, s 2.
78 *Legal Services Directions 2017* (Cth.) app B s 1 ("Model Litigant Rules").
79 Ibid app B s 2.
80 Ibid app B s 2(a).
81 Ibid app B s 3.
82 Ibid app B s 2(f).
83 Ibid app B s 2(h).
84 Ibid app B s 2(i).

One of the biggest challenges in relation to the obligation being breached by ASQA is the manner in which a breach of any obligation needs to be notified. For legal practitioners and experts who practice in this field on a regular basis, there are other areas of concern around the obligation that are equally worthy of investigation although further investigation is beyond the scope of this book.

Analysis of the stay applications referred to throughout this book appears to support the findings of this research. This is especially with regards to the culture of ASQA,[85] how it manages merits review and the prospects of success[86] in opposing unfettered stay applications, or even stays with conditions applied that can be detrimental to the NVR RTO's ability to continue to access merits review.[87]

It is also worth noting that the author of this book did also approach the Hon. Minister Christian Porter in relation to these issues in his capacity at the time of being Attorney-General as well as the author's local member of parliament. Early on in my attempts to even get an appointment, it became obvious how little interest there was in the Minister's eye regarding the VET sector. For example, if I were to see him as my local member, I saw him in his local office (almost impossible unless it was close to election time, I had previously written requesting meetings about the issue of small business in VET for which at the time he was also Minister and could not secure a meeting time). I was forced to therefore make time to meet with him as Attorney General in his Commonwealth office in the Perth CBD in a building that towers over the city, with the most exquisite views of Perth's waterfront I think I have ever seen. The office itself, the size of a studio apartment.

The meeting was, for all intents and purposes, an absolute waste of time. He had little interest in hearing about the issues I was raising,

85 For example, at least 1 ASQA lawyer listed their wins on their professional social media profile.

86 The prospects of success referred to in this statement are different to those referred to by Tribunal members when undertaking their discretionary powers.

87 See '*VETiS Consulting Pty Ltd*' (n 31) and *Success Fast-Track Pty Ltd v Australian Skills Quality Authority* (n 35).

which included breaches of the model litigant obligation by ASQA's legal team and effectively tasked me to make a formal legal submission to provide him with evidence of where it was being breached in 'his' Tribunals. A statement that will forever remain ingrained in my memory was '*I am the Attorney-General. I have access to any record in any court in the country. If you say that these lawyers are breaching the model litigant obligations, provide me with evidence and I will look into it.*' The problem is that the examples of these breaches will not be found documented in any case notes that he could get his hands on. What's more, with the funding of the Commonwealth at his disposal, surely he had an obligation to investigate these issues rather than rely on a law student to provide formal submissions to facilitate his research?

That meeting will go down as one of the most disappointing meetings and a waste of 17 minutes of my professional life. It did however demonstrate 2 things. The first being that it's no wonder the culture of ASQA is so toxic when you look at the way in which that meeting was handled. Very paternalistic, tokenistic and almost an air of '*I'm so important and your issue is a waste of my time*'. The 2nd issue it demonstrated to me was just how political the regulatory environment relative to ASQA and the Tribunals had become. It is a known and well-established opinion that the Tribunal is stacked with supporters of the Liberal party and the Chief Commissioner at the time, now CEO was also once a Tribunal member.

Education Issues Australia recently sent an email to a large number of stakeholders, including Ministers and Senators and the ASQA Stakeholder Liaison Group asking the following question that reinforces the above findings regarding the politics of ASQA and the Tribunal:

> Earlier this year, a Deputy President of the Administrative Appeals Tribunal was forced to recuse himself after finding that they had failed to consider the evidence and submissions of an RTO.

In 2020, the same Deputy President was responsible for affirming a decision to cancel that RTO's registration and licences against the *National Vocational Education and Training Regulator Act* and the *Education Services for Overseas Students (ESOS) Act*.

The Deputy President, recused for apprehended bias, conceded that they had failed to consider the RTO's evidence and submissions.[88]

The same Deputy President has been a member of the AAT since 2017, in which time the Australian Skills Quality Authority has forcibly shut down hundreds of businesses, with the AAT the only avenue of appeal.

Of concern, the current ASQA Chief Commissioner was a Member of the Tribunal in the same location and at the same time.

Deputy Presidents are more senior and experienced legal officers than their Senior Member or Member counterparts. There have been more than 800 RTO's forcibly shut down by ASQA and left with their only avenue of appeal being the Administrative Appeal Tribunal, with (as at this date) 45 RTO businesses in ongoing reviews before the AAT, and a further 17 considering that option.

The admission by an experienced and senior Deputy President of the tribunal that they had failed to consider the evidence and submissions of an RTO undermines the already jeopardised confidence in the Australian VET Sector and the impartiality of its regulator.

Despite numerous Government commissioned reports into the litany of failures at ASQA, the regulator remains able to cancel, suspend and reject RTO's on the findings of Audit Staff

[88] *Australia Institute of Business & Technology - International Pty Ltd and Australian Skills Quality Authority* [2021] AATA 36 (21 January 2021).

> who are not required to hold mandatory qualifications before commencing audit work. Further, these same audit officers' recommendations to impose the severest possible sanctions against RTOs can be approved by Commissioners, without having to stipulate exact non-compliances nor state what rectifications would be acceptable to the regulator...
>
> If a deputy president can so readily disregard evidence and submissions, what of the Members who have heard hundreds of AAT matters - particularly as a result of ASQA's approach to challenge all stay applications in the AAT? An approach adopted by ASQA after Saxon Rice joined as Deputy Chief Commissioner Risk Intelligence and Regulatory Support in 2018.[89]

Soon after this email was sent, the Attorney-General was '*temporarily stood down*' while his defamation case against a journalist and the Australian Broadcasting Corporation ("ABC") in relation to historic rape charges that they reported on in the media. This action took place after many people questioned the conflict of interest he had in his proceedings against the journalist and the ABC given his role as Attorney-General (*personally, I don't think merely stepping down temporarily removes that conflict of interest but that is not the purpose of this book*). His role as Attorney-General was taken over by the former Minister for Employment, Skills and Vocational Education, Senator Michaelia Cash. If there was little hope of being heard impartially under Christian Porter, there is even less chance of being heard impartially by Senator Cash, the new Attorney-General who was until this recent posting, the Minister responsible for ASQA.

In this context, the final question in the email correspondence regarding the Tribunal member's apprehended bias, is of course one of the most important questions to be asked of Australia's legal system and Attorney-General right now. If a deputy president can so readily disregard evidence

[89] Email correspondence from Education Issues Australia to Raelene Bartlett et al, 15 March 2021, 12:24pm AWST.

and submissions, what of the Members who have heard hundreds of AAT matters - particularly as a result of ASQA's approach to challenge all stay applications in the AAT? Perhaps just as important and challenging to get an impartial answer for is, do they even care?

Consideration of Stay Applications

Reference was made earlier to the prospects of success in seeking a stay of a decision from the AAT in relation to ASQA decisions. When Tribunal Members consider making a stay order,[90] all members referred to the prospects of success as relevant factors that informed their decision. The prospects of success as seen in *Scott v Australian Securities and Investments Commission*[91] are well documented in case law and include a consideration of the:

- Prospects of success in the substantive hearing;
- The consequences for the applicant of the refusal of the stay;
- The public interest;
- The consequences for the Respondent in carrying out its functions depending on whether a stay was not granted or not;
- Whether the application for review would be rendered nugatory if a stay were not granted; and
- Any other relevant matters.

What is becoming more and more frequent during these stay applications is in order to demonstrate proper consideration of the prospects of success above, Tribunal Members are engaging in what is commonly referred to in the sector as a 'mini trial'.[92]

As stated in *Menzies Institute of Technology v Australian Skills Quality Authority*:

> The Tribunal acknowledges that in considering whether to grant a stay, it is not appropriate to undertake a full consideration of the merits of the substantive applications...However, the Tribunal considers that it is able to and that it is appropriate

[90] AAT Act s 41(2).

[91] *Anthony Scott v Australian Securities and Investment Commission* (2009) 51 AAR 114.

[92] For example, see '*Gurkhas*' (n 125) [29].

> to take into account the information and evidence presently available to form a general impression as to Menzies' prospects of success.[93]

In *Snook and Civil Aviation Safety Authority* [2008] AATA 861; (2008) 109 ALD 122 [21] referred to in *Sher-E-Punjab Pty Ltd v Australian Skills Quality Authority*, we see another quote that is often referred to in case law, 'It is well understood that in considering an applicant's prospects of success for the purposes of a stay application, it is not appropriate to conduct a preliminary trial of the issue'.[94]

While the purpose of this book is not to discuss in detail the prospects of success, there are 3 matters that are considered as part of the '*prospects of success*' being considered by Tribunal Members that must be addressed, at least by way of an overview or introduction to the issues in order to get a better understanding of merits review as it applies to RTOs and the journey that some of those whose stories are documented in this book had to, or were expected to undertake. The first issue is in relation to the financial viability of the provider during the merits review process. The second issue is in relation to reputational damage of the RTO; and the third issue is in relation to the public interest.

Financial Viability

One of the most common components of the '*prospects of success*' argument is whether the RTO has the financial capacity to survive if no stay is granted or if a stay is granted with conditions. Typical conditions that might be imposed on a stay order include no new enrolments, marketing and/or issuing of certification.

93 '*Menzies Institute of Technology*' (n 125) [19-20].

94 '*Sher-E-Punjab Pty Ltd*' (n 31) [27].

Each of these factors has a significant impact on the financial viability of a provider.[95] Putting aside that the underpinning legal decision made by ASQA that led to the application may well be flawed, invalid and/or unreliable, there is an important issue that a provider must demonstrate; that of financial viability. An RTO must provide evidence that it has sufficient funds at its disposal so the substantive review will not be rendered nugatory because the provider has run out of money, and/or that the provider would not be able to sustain itself financially if a stay were refused. This in itself is a catch 22 situation due to the Financial Viability Risk Assessment Requirements ("FVRAR").

There have been occasions where a Tribunal has deemed that the provider has sufficient funds available that the imposition of conditions to a stay order would not cause considerable negative impacts to the RTO. Equally, there have been situations where the Tribunal has identified that to impose a conditional stay on a provider might cause the RTO to become financially unviable. There are issues with both scenarios. By demonstrating that a provider would not be able to sustain itself in these circumstances or suggesting that there are sufficient funds available, the provider runs the risk of not being able to meet one of its registration requirements, the FVRAR referred to earlier.

By falling foul of this in the process of trying to access merits review, the RTO is at risk of being issued with a new Notice because everything is on the table as discussed earlier and this would become new evidence. An example of how this plays out is also covered in Rabih's story.

The provision of financial evidence to support the prospects of success is thus inextricably linked to those circumstances where the Tribunal finds that the provider has sufficient funds available to sustain itself. As part of the consideration of financial viability prior to and at the stay

95 In the context of normal business, the impact was destructive. In the context of the global COVID-19 pandemic which has already extended over 18 months and will continue to cause significant financial impact for at least another 9 months or so (at least until Australia's international borders are reopened), financial viability for many RTOs is already critical.

hearing, the RTO provides a copy of all financials to ASQA and is often cross-examined on its contents.

In doing this, ASQA is then empowered to use those new opportunities for finding evidence by way of issuing new Notices[96] such as a section 26 or section 62 Notices or 72-hour Notices as previously discussed. Having supported many providers through the preparation of such evidence within the usually short timeframes required by the Notices, it is this writer's experience that it is almost impossible to gather all required evidence in the required timeframe.

Often requests for information are so cumbersome that it requires significant additional resources to accommodate them and at a significant cost that was never budgeted for. Timeframes are often unreasonable, usually dating back to the first day of the provider's registration (if it was registered by ASQA to begin with) or, alternatively, from 1 July 2011 when the VET Regulator was established for those who transitioned to ASQA upon its establishment.

It is also the writer's experience that the requests can also be accompanied by unexpected audits and monitoring visits.

These additional circumstances are usually ways of generating more evidence and draining the financial resources of the provider before the substantive hearing forcing them to withdraw. In other cases,[97] the cost to the provider's ongoing financial viability of not obtaining an unfettered stay order is so significant that they are forced to withdraw and accept the decision by the Regulator. It should also be noted that the provider cannot obtain compensation for business loss due to the conditions placed on them by the tribunal and often requested by, or even offered[98] by the Tribunal Member, even if they eventually win their case.

---

[96] NVR Act.

[97] As of 1 July 2016.

[98] Case name withheld, professional correspondence and attendance in AAT hearing held on client's file.

Reputational Damage

ASQA changed its approach to the notification of sanction decisions some time ago now, although, in recent months, legislative changes as referred to earlier mean that even more information is made public.[99] ASQA publishes decisions in accordance with ss 209 and 216 of the NVR Act. Section 209 of the NVR Act provides for the release of information to the public if the information '*would reasonably inform a person's choice to enrol as a VET student with a registered training organisation*'. Section 216[100] provides for the publication of certain information on the national register[101]. ASQA revised its policy regarding the publication of regulatory decisions so that information about decisions is published soon after they have been made but before all avenues of appeal have been exhausted.

The details included on the decision table are significant[102] and remain on the ASQA website indefinitely (*although one benefit of those legislative changes discussed earlier in this book now allows RTO's to apply to have conditions removed*). Considering there is evidence to question the basis upon which those legal decisions have been made, it is strongly recommended that this policy be reviewed. The impact of such information being published before any avenues of appeal have been exhausted is not only potentially damaging to the future viability of the provider, but also to the personal reputation of those individuals identified on the ASQA website. It is rare that a Tribunal acknowledges

99 NVR Act.

100 The national register of Vocational Education and Training available online at <https://www.training.gov.au>.

101 Provider name (legal entity and trading names), provider number, all Higher Managerial Agents of the provider are identified personally, the type of decision, details of the decision, date of the decision, effective date, the status of decision and the status of the review.

102 *Greenfield Education Pty Ltd v Australian Skills Quality Authority* [2018] AATA 4210 (9 November 2018) [13].

such impacts[103] although one recent case demonstrated this awareness is growing.[104]

The Public Interest

Much has been said within reported cases in relation to the public interest, indeed, it is ASQA's favourite argument[105] for a refusal of a stay order or to support a stay order that has crippling conditions attached. A good overview of how most Tribunal Members approach the consideration of '*the public interest*' in stay hearings relevant to the VET sector is best summarised in *Australian Vocational Learning Centre Pty Ltd v Australian Skills Quality Authority:*[106]

> In the view of the Tribunal, the public interest is best served by not allowing the Applicant to continue to operate, as it is, in a way which is non-compliant with the Standards and in the absence of immediate and effective remedial action having commenced.

Additional comments include '... the tribunal held that the public interest in having a registered provider meet the required standards and conditions laid down in legislation outweighed any disadvantage to an individual non-complying provider'.[107]

Further commentary that is often relied upon in Tribunal proceedings in relation to the public interest is that of Senior Member McCabe in *Metro College of Technology*:[108]

> But there is also the question of the public interest. The regulatory system was devised to protect consumers of these courses, and to protect the good name of Australian educational

[103] '*Business Institute of Australia Pty Ltd*' (n 32).

[104] For example, see '*Western Institute of Technology Pty Ltd*' , '*Pacific Flight Services Pty Ltd*' [38].

[105] '*Australian Vocational Learning Centre Pty Ltd*' (n 125) [40-42].

[106] Ibid [41].

[107] *Metro College of Technology Pty Ltd and Australian Skills Quality Authority (Unreported).*

[108] Ibid.

> institutions overseas. Many students travel long distances from overseas [...] The regulatory regime assumes there is a public interest in ensuring these programs are properly run according to recognized(*sic*) standards. Failures to adhere to standards – particularly where those failures suggest systemic problems, poor judgment(*sic*) or an unwillingness to comply with the law – must be taken very seriously.

Considering the issues highlighted in this paper, it is imperative that the public interest is considered far beyond what Senior Member McCabe initially meant and that perhaps, it is in the public interest that these same issues should be considered with ASQA '*in the hot seat*' as opposed to alleged non-complying RTOs. One can only ask the following questions...

What happens when, as has been demonstrated through this research, the very basis for legal decision-making '*in the public interest*' is potentially erroneous and based on an unqualified foundation? Is that in the public interest?

The more critical consideration for the public interest would be '*Are these decisions being made by ASQA legally sound*'?

The writer is confident that like the public, Tribunals have an expectation that the legal decisions that come before it are based on sound and valid legal reasoning and would concur that it is in the public interest that the VET regulator critically review its approach to legal decision making under the NVR Act before seeking further sanctions of this nature in a merits review process.

Senior Member Puplick stated that:

> Regulatory bodies are established, in part, to ensure that the public interest is protected in the areas of their competence and the Tribunal should be cautious about taking steps which may derogate from the protection of the public interest by failing to

> give due regard (although not unqualified deference) to their assessments in such matters.[109]

It is the contention of this book that Puplick's comments could not have been more appropriate. While his intention was not meant to question the competence of the VET Regulator, it is suggested that his comments should now be considered in this regard, particularly given the substantial taxpayer dollars being absorbed by ASQA in this process.

109 '*Australian Vocational Learning Centre Pty Ltd*' (n 125) [42].

National Vocational Education and Training Regulator Act 2011 (Cth.): An Investigation into Merits Review (The Aftermath)

> *"You want the truth? You can't handle the truth!*
>
> **- Jack Nicholson**
> **in 'A Few Good Men'**

It should be of interest to readers that from an academic perspective, the research conducted that formed the basis of this international best seller was part of a Bachelor of Laws at Murdoch University in Western Australia. Supervised by the Academic Chair (at the time, now retired) of the Faculty of Law who was herself considered an expert in Administrative Law, the research received a result of Distinction. From the College regulations[110] of Murdoch University, an Academic Chair has significant responsibilities with regard to academic integrity and learning outcomes within the qualification in particular. From the perspective of lawyers and Barristers who specialise in RTO law, the book was very well received and highly praised. From the perspective of RTOs and those whose careers are in the VET sector, the feedback was overwhelmingly positive with many people expressing immense gratitude and appreciation that finally, someone was telling the story of how RTOs were being exploited in the AAT or in the lead up to proceedings in the AAT.

---

[110] Murdoch University, 'Academic Chair', (Web Page, 4 April 2021) <https://www.murdoch.edu.au/TNE/Roles-and-Responsibilities/Murdoch-Staff-Members-and-Departments/Academic-Chair/>.

From the regulator's perspective, the reaction was very different. While some auditors were very positive in their feedback, there were others whose behaviour was telling. One staff member purchased a copy and left it in the staff room for other staff members to read and the book allegedly did the rounds with most staff in that office. For some others, staff were (I'm advised) quite hostile towards both the book and the author. Others again found it an opportune time to clean up their social media profiles (including removing the trophy cabinet), while others contacted me privately to let me know that they supported the important work that I was doing and to keep up the good work. For one person though, the feedback was quite damning and at the same time, telling of what impact the publication would have on ASQA's regulatory performance.

Feedback from ASQA (at the time) included:

- That they found some of our arguments and reasoning a little hard to follow and that there may have been some misunderstanding of the relevant legal issues and principles in particular.
- They disagreed with a number of arguments and contentions including that they do not believe that it is only those who come from the VET sector who make the best auditors.
- They also didn't agree that it is necessary for ASQA's auditors to be VET experts in order to properly understand and apply the RTO Standards or to identify and assess a provider's compliance against those Standards.
- They believe that, consistent with the findings of the 'Rapid Review into ASQA' published on 30 April 2020 that rather it is imperative for auditors to have a thorough understanding of good regulatory practice and ASQA's expectations regarding how providers demonstrate compliance. Some of the qualities the review recommended ASQA auditors should have include integrity, critical thinking, sound judgement and strong communication skills though also accepting they should be

trained in relation to the VET sector, assessment methodology, interpretation of the Standards, documentation of evidence and report writing.

- They believe that overall, it was difficult to see that the contention of a flaw in ASQA's legal decision-making was supported by the discussion of the relevant legal principles and law.
- In relation to model litigant obligations, that no concerns or issues as to ASQA's conduct or behaviour of the kind referred to have been brought to ASQA's attention. ASQA was not aware of any occasion where it has been found to have breached the Model Litigant Obligations nor had the Office of Legal Services Coordination, the office responsible for administering the Model Litigant Obligations, referred any complaint or allegation.
- While the so-called Scott factors in the context of stay applications were correctly identified, ASQA found that the prospects of success is a separate factor in itself and it is not an overarching consideration and denied that as a general proposition, the factors of financial viability, reputational damage and the public interest are considered as part of the prospects of success. In particular, "the public interest" is a separate factor and does not form part of the consideration of the prospects of success.
- In relation to the discussion regarding "Ghost Colleges", ASQA said that while the book noted media reports that ASQA's Chief Commissioner expressly denied using the term in her meeting with Ian Callinan as part of his review of the AAT, the subsequent discussion in the book '...seems to proceed on the false premise that I did'. The book also claims that ASQA lawyers often use and refer to this "argument" in AAT proceedings. ASQA did a search of the 28 decisions referred to and could not find that term anywhere in the decisions and nothing attributing it to ASQA in its submissions or arguments.

It's unfortunate that there is such a difference in understanding and perspectives of how ASQA's regulatory practices are implemented and that ASQA itself has no real understanding of the experiences of those providers it regulates. It's also disappointing that rather than be on the defensive, ASQA didn't take on board the feedback and use it, as it expects RTOs to continuously improve their operations. After all, someone doesn't just go out and conduct research that is so 'solid' as ASQA suggested if it is not true and there is no basis for it. While ASQA may believe that the book is only the author's perception, even if that were the case, surely such feedback warrants considering the veracity of it and attempting to improve practice and systems?

Don't Poke the Bear!

Just like the research that was the foundation of the book '*National Vocational Education and Training Regulator Act 2011 (Cth.): An Investigation into Merits Review*', opponents of ASQA's regulatory practice cannot simply make up the '*stories*' and evidence that continually unfolds and is regularly submitted to the Senate Estimates Committee for an explanation and when no response is provided (and the questions not even asked), VET stakeholders sign a petition demanding answers. When the petition is dismissed but the opportunity for submissions to the Australian National Audit Office are made, it's no surprise that some of the following issues are raised:

- Conflicts of interest;
- Potential corruption;
- Competency of ASQA auditors has been raised numerous times;
- Racism;
- Inconsistent audit practices;

For as long as Australia's VET sector has been regulated there have been cries of inequality in audit practices; TAFE and RTOs are supposed to be regulated under the same legislation with the same level of scrutiny and outcomes, yet consistently, time after time, we see this is not the case, that TAFE will always receive different regulatory treatment to its private counterparts. For example, the level of non-compliance at TAFE SA became a nationwide conversation. After an ASQA audit of 10 courses identified critical non-compliance and failures, the regulator considered suspending 14 courses. The Federal Education Minister for Skills at the time was quoted as saying that it was an "indictment" on the State Government that it was turning to private training organisations which it had "cut off" to "rescue them because of their failures in managing the TAFE system."

A further article from the ABC stated that the SA Government set aside $2 million for compensation claims related to the TAFE SA saga, in particular, the damning audit of the institution's aviation courses that did not comply with the external accreditation requirements from the Civil Aviation Safety Authority ("CASA"). From the **Education Issues Australia** archive, we see the following regarding the outcome of TAFE SA (to view these articles more clearly, visit the Education Issues Australia Twitter page www.twitter.com/edissuesaus:

Australian Government
Australian Skills Quality Authority

Evidence analysis

ORGANISATION DETAILS

Organisation's legal name	TAFE SA
Trading name/s	TAFE SA TAFE South Australia Sustainable Industries Education Centre Onshore Petroleum Centre of Excellence Regency International Centre Adelaide College of Arts Adelaide English Language Centre Adelaide English Language Services Mining Engineering and Transport Centre Australian Arts and Design Academy
RTO number (if applicable)	41026
CRICOS number (if applicable)	00092B

REVIEW DETAILS

Type of review	Sanction
Evidence review number	EVRREC0001506
Date evidence received	24/10/2017
Date review conducted	27, 30 & 31 October 2017 and 1 & 6 November 2017

REVIEW TEAM

Reconsideration officer	N/A
Review officer	[redacted]
Technical adviser/s	N/A

CRITICAL NON-COMPLIANCE

SCOPE OF REVIEW

Code	Training Product	Models of delivery/assessment*
AUR32412/ AUR32416	Certificate III in Automotive Refinishing Technology	Apprentices/Trainees
AUR30812/ AUR30816	Certificate III in Motorcycle Mechanical Technology	Apprentices/Trainees
SIT30816/ SIT30813	Certificate III in Commercial Cookery	Face to Face (RTO) premises
MTM20111/ AMP20316	Certificate II in Meat Processing (Abattoirs)	Face to face (workplace)
CHC33015	Certificate III in Individual Support	Face to Face (RTO) premises
CHC43415	Certificate IV in Leisure and Health	Face to Face (RTO) premises
SIR50212	Diploma of Visual Merchandising	Face to Face (RTO) premises
SHB30416/ SIH30111	Certificate III in Hairdressing	Face to Face (RTO) premises
UEE30811	Certificate III in Electrotechnology Electrician	Face to Face (RTO) premises
UEE42711	Certificate IV in Air-conditioning and Refrigeration Servicing	Face to Face (RTO) premises
CPC32413/ CPC32412	Certificate III in Plumbing	Face to Face (RTO) premises
CPC50210	Diploma of Building and Construction (Building)	Face to Face (RTO) premises

*Apprenticeship, Traineeship, Face to face, Distance, Online, Workplace, Mixed, Other (specify)

FINDING FOLLOWING EVIDENCE REVIEW

Finding as at 10/11/2017: Critical non-compliance

Australian Government
Australian Skills Quality Authority

4 December 2017

[redacted]
Chief Executive
TAFE SA
GPO Box 1872
ADELAIDE SA 5000

By email to: TAFESAregistrations@tafesa.edu.au

RTO ID 41026
Audit No EVRREC0001566

Dear Mr Murt,

Re: Direction to rectify breaches of conditions

I refer to the VET Quality Framework sanction evidence audit of TAFE SA conducted on 27 October 2017. The audit focused on the qualifications or units of competency listed in your organisation's application or scope of registration.

Following careful consideration of the information provided in your response, ASQA has determined your organisation is **not compliant** with the requirements of the *Standards for Registered Training Organisations 2015* (Standards for RTOs) which is a breach of Section 22 of the *National Vocational Education and Training Regulator Act 2011* (NVR Act).

The Australian Skills Quality Authority (**ASQA**), as the national VET regulator, has made the decision to give a written direction, under section 35A(1) of the *National Vocational Education and Training Regulator Act 2011* (NVR Act), requiring your organisation to:

- rectify this breach by addressing each non-compliance outlined in the attached evidence analysis for UEE42711 Certificate IV in Air-conditioning and Refrigeration Servicing and expired course 52689WA Certificate IV in Preparation for Nursing Education within 20 working days of the date of this notice; and
- retain evidence this written direction has been complied with for examination at a future regulatory activity, by retaining evidence that you have addressed each non-compliance outlined in the attached audit report.

You are not required to submit evidence that you have addressed the non-compliances in response to this notice. ASQA will review evidence that you have complied with this notice at a future regulatory activity.

ASQA considers that issuing a direction to rectify a breach of condition is a proportionate response to the level of non-compliance identified. The direction to rectify a breach of condition has been issued as an alternative to requiring rectification evidence or proposing a sanction be imposed on your organisation. A copy of the final audit report is attached for your reference.

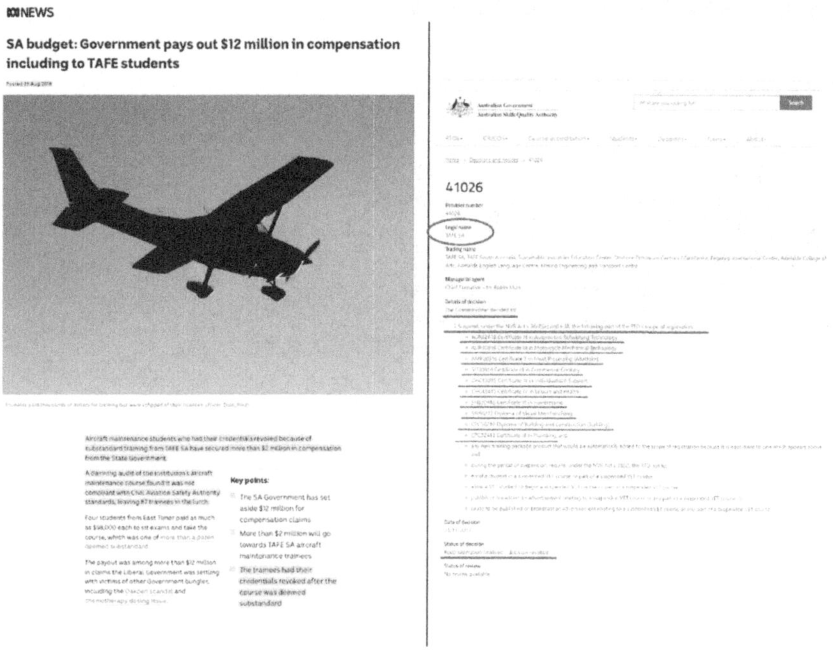

ABC NEWS

SA budget: Government pays out $12 million in compensation including to TAFE students

Aircraft maintenance students who had their credentials revoked because of substandard training from TAFE SA have secured more than $2 million in compensation from the State Government.

A damning audit of the institution's aircraft maintenance course found it was not compliant with Civil Aviation Safety Authority standards, leaving 87 trainees in the lurch.

Four students from East Timor paid as much as $98,000 each to sit exams and take the course, which was one of more than a dozen deemed substandard.

The payout was among more than $12 million in claims the Liberal Government was settling with victims of other Government bungles, including the Oakden scandal and chemotherapy dosing issue.

Key points:

- The SA Government has set aside $12 million for compensation claims
- More than $2 million will go towards TAFE SA aircraft maintenance trainees
- The trainees had their credentials revoked after the course was deemed substandard

Australian Government
Australian Skills Quality Authority

Search

41026

Provider number

Legal name

Trading name

Manager or agent

Details of decision

Date of decision

Status of decision

Status of review

Compare this result, also from the **Education Issues Australia** Archive to the furore surrounding another aviation program, this time at Box Hill TAFE in Victoria associated with a third party, non-RTO provider where a student became a paraplegic:

THE AGE

The Australian Skills Quality Authority began an audit into courses run in partnership between Soar Aviation and Box Hill Institute in November after complaints from students.

Emergency services at the scene of the crash.

The Australian reported the students' complaints centred around misinformation around their course, the aircraft they would be using, and also included allegations trainees were exhausting their loans before receiving their pilot licences after being made to repeat elements of the course.

Training resumed for Box Hill Institute students on November 8, after a suspension of six days.

Australian Government
Australian Skills Quality Authority

Search

About

4687

Provider number

Legal name

Trading name

Managerial agent

Decision type

Details of decision

a. AVI50215 Diploma of Aviation (Commercial Pilot Licence – Aeroplane)

b. Diploma of Aviation (Flight Instructor)

c. AVI50415 Diploma of Aviation (Instrument Rating)

d. Diploma of Aviation (Commercial Pilot Licence – Aeroplane)

e. Diploma of Aviation (Instrument Rating)

Additional information

Date of decision

THE AGE

"In light of the numerous complaints made by students, the writing had been on the wall for a long time, indicating there was serious deficiencies in the course construction and delivery," Ms Jones said.

A spokeswoman for the Box Hill Institute said following an intense audit and consultation, ASQA confirmed the college can continue to run its aviation course with Soar Aviation.

RELATED ARTICLE

UPDATED AVIATION

Light plane crash at Moorabbin leaves man seriously injured

"Student safety and wellbeing is a key priority for Box Hill Institute. We are committed to working closely with our partners to ensure the best outcomes for students," she said.

"Box Hill Institute is unable to comment on the legal proceedings as they are currently before the Supreme Court."

ASQA said it was satisfied, having regard to the risk posed to students and the quality of the sector, the most appropriate administrative sanctions have been imposed, with the regulatory authority issuing written directions to rectify breaches in training and resources.

Soar Aviation did not respond.

License this article AVIATION COURTS

Tammy Mills

Tammy Mills is the legal affairs reporter for The Age.

Similarly, in NSW, and also from the **Education Issues Australia** archive, a young girl is killed as part of a jillaroo course at TAFE NSW where the coroner even stated that the attention to risk management undertaken by the TAFE was not thorough enough contributing to the girl's death after she fell from a horse in Dubbo:

ABC NEWS

TAFE slammed over jillaroo student's death

By court reporter Jamelle Wells
Posted 23 Dec 2011, updated 23 Dec 2011

A coroner has described a New South Wales TAFE report on the death of a student in a horse fall as being 'not worth the paper it was written on'.

Deputy state coroner Sharon Freund said jillaroo student [redacted] died from head and neck injuries after falling from a bolting horse that was unsuitable for a beginner.

In March 2009 the 18-year-old from Newcastle was learning to ride as part of a TAFE jillaroo course at Dubbo in the NSW central west.

The coroner criticised TAFE for not being thorough enough in assessing horses used for beginner riders and said the ex-racehorse Dargo had been obtained for use just days after running in a race.

Australian Government
Australian Skills Quality Authority

What are you looking for

RTOs CRICOS Course accreditation Students Decisions

Home › Decisions and notices › 90009

90009

Provider number
90009

Legal name
TAFE NSW - Western Institute

Trading name
TAFE NSW - Western Institute

Managerial agent
Katherine Baxter - Institute Director

Decision type
Part suspension

Details of decision
On 11/01/12 ASQA decided to suspend with immediate effect the following units.

- RTE2130A Ride and care for horses and equipment
- RTE1104A Support horse work
- AHCLSK212A Ride hoses to carry out stock work
- AHCHBR101A Support horse work

On 11/01/12 ASQA decided to impose the following condition: the RTO must submit a change of scope application to ASQA (and not to the delegate) if it wishes to provide the above four units again in the future.

Date of decision
11/01/2012

Effective date
11/01/2012

The decisions in the cases above, where harm to the students and their families is of the highest order in some cases (*there is no worse harm than the premature death or disablement of a loved one*) is quite frankly beyond comprehension. Even more astonishing however is the inconsistency with which ASQA regulates in like circumstances between public and private RTOs which is demonstrated next. Consider the findings of the stay application for Pacific Flight Services Pty Ltd while seeking a review of an ASQA decision in April 2019 (**before** the Box Hill TAFE and TAFE SA incidents).

16. ASQA set out its findings as follows:—

> *15. The non-compliances included the following:*
>
> *• the Applicant has not provided evidence that it has implemented remedial action for four current students and one student who completed the Diploma of Aviation Commercial Licence —Aeroplane) in the past six months who may have been impacted by the non– compliance*
>
> *• the training and assessment strategies are not consistent with the requirements of the training package and the amount of training is not for international students; it is not evident that the students are engaged with the learning for 20 hours per week as required for international students and for the Diploma of Aviation (Commercial Licence– Aeroplane), the hours can be as low as 13.2 hours per week*
>
> *• the Applicant has allocated 320 hours of study but it is not evident how these hours contribute to the development of skills and knowledge as per unit of competency requirements*
>
> *• the Applicant doesn't have the trainers and assessors to deliver the training and assessment, and hasn't demonstrated that it has the learning resources that enable learners to meet the requirements for each unit of competency and that these resources are accessible at all times*
>
> *• the Applicant's trainers and assessors have been issued AQF qualifications by the Applicant in reliance on inadequate assessment.*
>
> *16. In addition, the Applicant admitted at audit that its current assessment tools did not meet training package requirements and yet failed to provide revised assessment tools.*
>
> *17. Other issues with assessment included assessment tools that contained insufficient performance benchmarks and assessment tools that do not guide the assessor as to the expected responses to knowledge questions.*
>
> *18. The Applicant did not provide an RPL assessment tool for the Diploma of Aviation (Commercial Licence — Aeroplane) and records sighted at audit for three students did not demonstrate that the competency requirements had been met or that their assessments had been conducted in accordance with the Principles of Assessment and Rules of Evidence.*

17. On the basis of these findings ASQA proceeded to cancel the Applicant's NVR and ESOS registrations.

If it was not clear previously, it should certainly be clearer now. Moreover, by the end of this book, and hopefully after the testimonials from those are amongst the most severely impacted RTOs under ASQA's regime, you will have a better appreciation for why #enoughisenough. In this context, wouldn't you think too that it would be in ASQA's best interest to at least consider an approach that is more reflective of continuous improvement than of dismissiveness?

Regulation in Australia

> *"Regulators have not been able to achieve the level of future clarity required to act pre-emptively. The problem is not lack of regulation but unrealistic expectations. What we confront in reality is uncertainty, some of it frighteningly so."*
>
> **- Alan Greenspan**

It may come as a surprise to many of my readers to know that from the time of settlement at least, Australia has always been regulated. When the English colonised Australia, they brought with them English law as it applied at that time. While there was undoubtedly some form of '*regulation*' amongst Indigenous Australians, not much is available in the literature that describes the regulatory practices of those times. What we do know though is that English law, brought by the colonists and deemed superior to all others, governed the colonists, the transported convicts that the colonists brought with them and Indigenous Australians at that time. There are still today substantial '*remnants*' of English law in our regulatory systems.

From an Indigenous perspective, the role of the influence and importance of Elders and implementing cultural lore continues but is becoming harder and harder to find due to many factors beyond the scope of this book. In saying that, many Indigenous Australians today suffer from the loss and breakdown of their culture, lore, customs and cultural practices; many are secondary and third generation victims of The Stolen Generation carrying the pain and loss of their ancestors.

It is widely recognised and documented that there are still too many Aboriginal deaths in custody and an overrepresentation of Indigenous

Australians in custody. As per the website '*Working With Indigenous Australians: First Nations People. Aboriginal and Torres Strait Islander people and their communities*':[111]

> The Aboriginal peoples of Australia had a complex system of law long before the establishment of British law in Australia, their system of law is often referred to as "traditional law"... it is also referred to as "the lore", however "rules of law and norms of politically appropriate behaviour were probably not distinguished" (Meggitt, 1962).
>
> There were no formal courts under traditional law, instead problems regarding traditional law were handled by elders - the oldest people in the community.

While it may be common in Australia, particularly in the legal system and regulatory space, the reality is that Law and Lore co-exist and are often used interchangeably. Depending on where they live though, Indigenous Australians experience law and lore differently. As the website says '*Traditional lore is connected to 'The Dreaming' and provides rules on how to interact with the land, kinship and community. Aboriginal children learned the law from childhood, by observing customs, ceremonies and song cycles.*'

On that basis, it's not difficult to see how the early regulatory practices of the British impacted not only Indigenous Australia, but also all of those people who would eventually call Australia home.

Perhaps the best known regulatory practice that came from the British colonial period in those times was what has become entrenched in Australia's history and known as 'The Stolen Generation'. For those who are unfamiliar with The Stolen Generation, the Australian Institute of

111 Muswellbrook Shire Council, New South Wales '*Working With Indigenous Australians: First Nations People. Aboriginal and Torres Strait Islander people and their communities*' (Webpage, 5 April, 2021). <http://www.workingwithindigenousaustralians.info/index.html>.

Aboriginal and Torres Strait Islander Studies ("AIATSIS")[112] describe The Stolen Generation as:

> Since colonisation, numerous government laws, policies and practices resulted in the removal of generations of Aboriginal and Torres Strait Islander children from their families and communities across Australia. Thousands of children were removed by governments, churches and welfare bodies to be raised in institutions, fostered out or adopted by non-Indigenous families, nationally and internationally. They are known as the Stolen Generations.
>
> The exact number of children who were removed may never be known but there are very few families who have been left unaffected – in some families children from three or more generations were taken. The removal of children broke important cultural, spiritual and family ties and has left a lasting and intergenerational impact on the lives and wellbeing of Aboriginal and Torres Strait Islander peoples.
>
> Affecting anywhere from 1 in 10 to 1 in 3 children, there is not a single Aboriginal and/or Torres Strait Islander community who has not been forever changed.

Arie Frieberg[113] (a well-respected Law Professor who is well published on regulation in Australia) suggests that there are three main periods or stages in the history of regulation in Australia. The first being from 1708 to 1901 which is known as the 'colonial period' and encompasses the establishment of the Commonwealth. The second period between

[112] The mission of the Australian Institute of Aboriginal and Torres Strait Islander Studies ("AIATSIS") include telling the story of Aboriginal and Torres Strait Islander Australia, creating opportunities for people to encounter, engage with and be transformed by that story and to help shape our national narrative; Australian Institute of Aboriginal and Torres Strait Islander Studies, '*Vision, mission and functions*' (Website, 5 April 2021). <https://aiatsis.gov.au/about/who-we-are/vision-mission-and-functions>, '*The Stolen Generations*' (Website, 5 April, 2021). <https://aiatsis.gov.au/explore/stolen-generations >.

[113] Arie Frieberg, Regulation in Australia, The Federation Press, 2017.

1901 and the late 1960's was one of strong protectionism which saw the development of much of Australia's legislation and government agencies, including further developing relationships with the States and Territories and local governments.

From around the 1970's until today, we have seen the emergence of what was, and remains, the third stage. Regulatory scholars refer to this as the 'regulatory state' or the 'post regulatory state'. The new regulatory structures reflected the privatisation, commercialism and contract development in relation to government functions. It has seen an increasing role of non-government and private commercial business in regulation, the emergence of concepts such as self-monitoring, co-regulations and process-based and performance-based regulation.

It was also during this era that market mechanisms and risk-based regulation first made their appearance.

When looking back at Australia's regulatory history and the '*definition*' of regulation, it's easier to understand how ASQA's regulatory construct and ambit has developed. Not only is Australia's regulatory history captured in ASQA's existence and 10-year history, but it really encompasses a whole gamut of relics of the past. We can see the colonial period and the reflections of British education systems in the way our schools and colleges are established and managed (especially the government schools and colleges). We can see strong protectionism that continues through Australia's vocational education and training sector and the international sector and we can most definitely see the impact that markets, privatisation and commercialism have had on the entire industry. What we also see in the regulatory history of ASQA is just how political its very existence is. There have been disjunctures throughout the history of vocational education and training ("VET") in Australia. In March 2015, I wrote about my concerns in relation to VET reform and regulatory performance. In the 6 years since that article was written, I don't believe that much has changed despite the disjuncture between:

- What the public wants;
- What the public needs;
- What industry wants;
- What industry needs;
- What the VET & international education sector wants;
- What the VET and international education sector need;
- What the regulator wants; and
- What the regulator needs.

Still, as I write this book, we are in the throes of VET Reform. As I wrote in that article in March 2015, there have been promises of reform since at least the mid 1980's when Australia was facing significant economic challenges including new markets, technology, high unemployment, significant retrenchments due to emerging technology and a global marketplace. To demonstrate this point, the article from 23 March 2015[114] is reproduced next.

[114] Raelene Bartlett, LinkedIn article, 'VET Reform and Regulatory Practice', (23 March 2015, accessed 6 April 2021). <https://www.linkedin.com/pulse/vet-reform-regulatory-performance-raelene-bartlett/ >.

VET Reform and Regulatory Practice - The Article

> "Reform can be accomplished only when attitudes are changed."
>
> \- **Lillian Wild**

As I sit here and contemplate why I am so disappointed in the achievements of the Vocational Education and Training (VET) Reform processes undertaken so far, I can't help but review where we've come from and where we're going, as well as where things are at currently as a result of the current VET Reform processes. Like many who are passionate advocates of a better system, I continue to shake my head in shame and at times, horrified at the way the system has been allowed to become not only the mockery of Australia but internationally also, where not too long ago our sector was amongst the most reputable in the world.

The Promise of VET Reform

As a sector, we were all so hopeful of significant change and strengthening of regulation and regulatory practice in Australia. We all, the Taskforce and respective Ministers *(how many have there been again? This in itself is representative of the perceived importance of this industry is the government's eyes)*, knew, even the old Labour government knew about the ongoing, unscrupulous, unethical practices that existed in the VET sector in Australia. Even the then Gillard government tried (however successfully or unsuccessfully) to placate the community (local and international) in response to the public outcry of 'shonky' RTO's.

These promises of reform have been consistent since at least the mid 1980's when Australia was facing significant economic challenges including new markets, technology, high unemployment, significant retrenchments due to emerging technology and a global marketplace, governments forged strong partnerships with large industry bodies, professional associations and unions in an effort to enhance employability, increase skill development and be better prepared for a globally and highly competitive marketplace. Sound familiar?

The Government effectively grabbed VET and used it as a band aid upon which to build policies and frameworks in order to equip the current unemployed and new generations of workers. It was also a measure that could be used to demonstrate the government's willingness and attempts at getting people 'off the dole' and into the workforce. The concept of continuous improvement that plagues the VET sector comes from the belief of governments that the workforce is dynamic, fluid and changes rapidly and therefore, the VET sector (the only sector) must remain current with those changes. The knowledge, skills, attitudes and capabilities that would fill this void would later become known as 'competencies'.

Additionally, in the mid 1980's, despite government intervention to attempt to make training accountable and produce the outcomes it needed, training reform did take place to focus on the needs of commerce and industry and ensure that certain individual abilities required in the workplace were personally attained by those involved in the training.

Various pieces of legislation were developed and enacted to force companies to spend a certain amount of money annually of training which also brought with it some flexibility in what type of training was permitted. All relevant and related legislation was finally repealed in the late 1990's as it became clear that the government was not achieving its objectives.

VET's presence in Australia has been mostly reflective of Government responses to economic issues and public outcry. As reported by the NSSC (2013, p14):

> *The AQTF 2007 review was in reaction to criticism of AQTF 2002 that the standards were too prescriptive. The standards were therefore re-focused to support continuous improvement and reducing the*

> *regulatory burden, as well as reflect outcomes-based objectives. The AQTF 2010 review was in reaction to provider collapses and concerns about low-quality providers in the vocational education and training market. Subsequent changes focused on financial management, governance and consumer protection.*

Fast forward to 2013/2014, the VET sector was waiting to see if the proposed Australian Vocational Qualification System (AVQS) were to be implemented or whether something else entirely would be determined. The AVQS of course was again developed based on Government's reactive response to the economic and political climate, public outcry that the system was too prescriptive and de-regulation should become a key feature.

New and higher-level skills, as well as certification for those skills was the supposed driver behind these reforms. It was suggested that the implementation of the AVQS would provide the integrity of the qualifications deriving from the VET sector that were missing and this will...

> *...support individuals on the career pathways, and ensures employers have the relevant and current skilled workforce to make them productive.*

This all of course sounds very familiar and a step back to the review of the AQTF 2002 standards that were too prescriptive, moving toward the AQTF 2007 which supported continuous improvement and reduced the regulatory burden.

So, upon returning to the VET Reform website this evening, wondering why we are no further advanced in this sad joke that our VET has become, it came as no surprise when I really read the (and I mean read as opposed to listened to) the main objectives of VET Reform:

Ministers agreed on six objectives for reform of the Vocational Education and Training (VET) system:

1. A national VET system which is governed effectively with clear roles and responsibilities for industry, the Commonwealth and the states and territories.
2. A national system of streamlined industry-defined qualifications that is able to respond flexibly to major national and state priorities and emerging areas of skills need.
3. Trade apprenticeships that are appropriately valued and utilised as a career pathway.
4. A modern and responsive national regulatory system that applies a risk-management approach and supports a competitive and well-functioning market.
5. Informed consumers who have access to the information they need to make choices about providers and training that meets their needs.
6. Targeted and efficient government funding that considers inconsistencies between jurisdictions or disruption to the fee-for-service market.

If we look closely, nowhere do I see amongst these objectives a commitment to ensuring that the effectiveness and strengthening of regulation in the VET sector in Australia (and offshore for that matter) would be closely examined and reformed. How did I not see something so obvious before now? The closest we get to achieving this is number 4 - *'A modern and responsive national regulatory system that applies a risk-management approach and supports a competitive and well-functioning market'*. Let's break that down a bit:

A modern and responsive national regulatory system...

Is it really that modern? While granted there are some areas of the RTO Standards 2015 that are newly introduced or completely redefined, there is really not much that is modern about these standards, they are for the most part rewrites, rehashing of past frameworks, reworded, reformatted and enshrined in legislation (for those who operated under AQTF as opposed to the Standards for NVR Registered Training Organisations 2012).

Responsive? Who have they been responsive to? They have certainly been responsive to the cries of many RTOs around the country who were overly concerned about the 'draconian' method of regulating, they were certainly responsive to the VET sector's cry for no AVQS, no accountable education officer, no requirement to be a company, etc. They were certainly being responsive in promoting to the public that they addressed the public's concerns about funding rorts, in particular about VET FEE HELP including the 'unethical' providers who are exploiting the disadvantaged by offering free iPads, etc. They've responded to VET providers' concerns about the ridiculous rate of change in highly unprofessional (in some cases) training packages and in some ways, they've even responded to mounting concern about the VET sector's participation in Australia's stock market. But have they really? *(Yes, I know one should never start a sentence with 'But').*

Draconian methods of regulating - in the interests of keeping the peace with RTOs around the country, it is our experience that the quality and performance of regulatory activity around the country has significantly decreased since the VET Reform process began. Many RTOs called this 'reducing the red tape', in fact, I'm pretty certain this is what the government called it to. Only there is a consequence of reducing the red tape and reviewing 'draconian regulatory practice', it was never going to benefit consumers of the VET sector; it would only favour providers, particularly those who the draconian measures were meant to identify, monitor and manage in the first place *(and most likely, the loudest supporters)*!

Exploitation and VET FEE-HELP rorts - responsive to the public? Absolutely! They've been told everything they wanted to hear! This government is looking out for you, we're getting rid of 'unethical providers' whether they be brokers or training providers, we've strengthened legislation, etc. What the public doesn't know however won't hurt them will it? The public doesn't really understand that many of the ads and companies responsible for this exploitation have been known to authorities for months (sometimes longer) and still nothing has been done to stop it (and in some cases, the lack of enabling legislation was not the cause of inaction). In terms of enhancing requirements for identifying providers and brokers, RTOID's, fees, charges and refunds, etc., all of this information was already required under the standards anyway! Examples could go on, but enough for this one for now.

That applies a risk-management approach...

A risk-management approach has been developed and implemented we are told however, with no transparency about how either of these actions occurred, it is difficult to analyse with any integrity whether the framework adopted is appropriate or adequate. It is my personal belief that if you are going to be risk-rated and your future regulatory oversight determined based on that risk-rating, you have every right to know how and why that risk rating was achieved and how, if at all, you can reduce the risk over time.

With this lack of transparency, it is questionable whether or not the risk-management approach that we've been told has been accomplished will actually be fit for purpose and fair and equitable to all providers.

And supports a competitive and well-functioning market...

It would appear that supporting a competitive and well-functioning market is in the process of being addressed however not as a result of enhanced regulatory performance but rather as an ongoing political football regarding competitive funding and the 'increased exploitation of funding by private providers at the expense of TAFE colleges around the country'. Who is the well-functioning market? Is the well-functioning market consumers and their needs? Having better informed consumers? Is it having better informed employers? Is it having more financially viable

TAFE colleges? Is it having less private providers accessing funding and a greater push for government funds to be returned to the TAFE sector?

When one looks at the break down of this particular subheading of the VET Reform '*Mission*', it is easy to see that very little of this really has anything to do with enhancing the quality and performance of regulation in Australia, it is, as always has been, about keeping the crowds quiet and voting at election time.

Effective Regulation

At the time of the consultation process regarding the AVQS, I personally and as the Founding Director of RTO Doctor was very vocal about some very significant benefits and drawbacks of such a system. I made it very clear that it wasn't that we necessarily needed a new system, we just needed a more focused system, more focused regulation with auditors who do the job properly, consistently and transparently. It was imperative that when the Taskforce reviewed policies in relation to the VET sector that it also considered the many other layers of legislation and policy guidelines (both State and Federal) that must be concurrently adhered to and they must not conflict with each other. Was this achieved?

It was also imperative that the Taskforce take into consideration some data from ASQA that may actually not be a true reflection of applications submitted that were deemed non-compliant. In many cases, the time frames for ASQA to process an application meant that in conjunction with the rapid transition rate of training packages, the materials being audited were always going to be non-compliant against the standards - ASQA were taking anywhere between 9 and 12 months to conduct an initial registration audit, an extension to scope of registration could take up to 9 months in some cases and there were numerous losses of applications and when clients have followed up the progress of those applications, they were advised that they had been lost.

While the duration for application processing times may in some cases have improved, the reality is there are many applications being approved that have left many observers completely gobsmacked with outcomes that are completely unjustifiable! The level of inconsistency in auditing performance in our opinion has worsened to a degree never seen before. It is our experience that the quality of auditing that has been taking place for the past 6 months at least has dramatically deteriorated and some providers are getting away with significant breaches. There is (and hasn't been for some time) a demand for compliance or quality from providers because there has been none from the regulators.

Such demands form a critical part of the regulatory landscape. If minimum standards of registration and performance by RTOs (public and private) are legislated, so too are the sanctions available to regulators. A good case in point is the national database training.gov.au who for the last seven months at least has had approximately 20 odd providers who as at 23 March 2015, have been suspended due to non-payment of annual registration fees! If regulators are going to enforce legislation, they also need to use the sanctions available to them otherwise the regulatory space will continue to be perceived by many in this space as a laughable joke. Some of the most commonly sighted companies on social media and supermarkets engaging in the highly discussed ads and recruiting practices exploiting prospective students have been known to authorities for so long, the ads and details provided to authorities and formal complaints been made however when those unethical providers see that they will not face any real action as a result of their activities, why would they stop?

Legislation currently provides ASQA for example to sanction providers for a significant range of breaches by financial penalty or jail and yet it is my experience that none of these actions have ever occurred. While it is understood that the one size fits all approach to regulation does not make sense, it seems the vast inconsistency in regulatory performance and quality has little rhyme or reason. Some providers get qualifications through in four days with and without an audit, others have to wait three or more months for a site visit.

Are current reform proposals the solution?

If the current reform efforts do not go back and look at the historical development of the VET sector, how it came to be and closely analyse the successes and shortcomings from the past, we will never end up with a reform effort that adequately addresses the needs of this country and our reputation internationally as a leader in the provision of education and training. What is currently being demonstrated is a real knee jerk reaction to a political issue that is not really addressing the fundamental flaws of the system by introducing changes that are heavily influenced by a political message that should never have been applied to Australia's education and training sector but it is in order to appease voters and protect the Prime Minister's election pledge of de-regulation and reducing the red tape.

If the government's commitment to our future is to provide a system that develops the skills and knowledge of our future country members (and those around the world), it is negligent in believing and promoting that a deregulated and/or self-regulated approach is the way of the future.

In a sector where people's lives are put at risk on a daily basis and will continue to get worse in the future, when the only time they consider 'self-regulation' is when there's an audit coming otherwise it is 'free for all and let's get away with what we can', our future generations are in trouble. Either the Taskforce really engages in genuine reform and makes the changes that need to be made as opposed to the changes that would equate to maintaining election promises or it has also been negligent and let down the current and future generations of our nation. The current proposals laid out to the sector are not fit for purpose, the current regulatory framework is not fit for purpose and the concept of de-regulation or self-regulation is not fit for purpose.

While it is understood and accepted that the Taskforce have done a great job so far of engaging with the sector, ensuring a more cooperative regulator in ASQA, encouraging ASQA to be a more capability building and customer service focused regulator, it needs to look much further and deeper than it is currently to really see the issues that are the most critical that need to be addressed.

Final Thoughts

In 2008, Tovey and Lawlor (p.3) wrote about training being "...frequently accused of being spasmodic, of little relevance to organisational, management and individual goals and very hard to measure...Many training programs were faddish in nature, swinging from one flavour of the month to another...Often training programs had been badly designed by unqualified individuals with insufficient experience." I would like to prose that Australia's efforts at VET Reform could just as easily be exchanged for the word '*training*'.

The Kangan Report (1974) states that relevance is the key factor in VET courses and that content must be relevant, that meaningless or underused knowledge and skills should be removed. Despite all of this historical knowledge, nothing has really changed since 1974 in course design (training package development for example) or in the regulatory space. As Tovey and Lawlor (2008, p.31) rightly state:

> *Governments, commerce and industry pay scant attention to the qualifications and expertise needed to facilitate the type and nature of learning required to deliver the results of which they constantly talk.*

Not much has changed. If they did, there wouldn't be such significant unrest in Australia's second largest export industry. Effectively, what it boils down to is that the purpose of VET will be different for different people. For the government it means one thing, for the community another. For TAFE it means one thing, for the private RTO it means another.

For the employer and the student, it can often mean something very different again. How can we develop a basis for a better system when we don't actually understand its true purpose? Maybe there is more than one purpose and it depends on whose needs we are trying to meet.

For now though, I will continue to be disillusioned (and saddened) by the ongoing neglect of our VET sector and the providers who continue to engage in intentionally non-compliant and/or unethical practices. For now, I will continue to shake my head in shame at the constant failures of our reform process to adequately manage the exploitation of consumers and to accept (read, in other words, not demand better) sub-standard performance for one of the most critical components of the sector, regulation.

References

Tovey, M., Lawlor, D. (2008). Training in Australia, 3rd Edition. Pearson Education, New South Wales.

Commonwealth of Australia. (2013). NSSC Standards Policy Framework - Improving Vocational Education and Training: The Australian Vocational Qualification System. NSSC, http://www.nssc.natese.gov.au/__data/assets/pdf_file/0005/75272/NSSC_Standards_Policy_Framework.pdf Accessed: 6 April 2014, 11.24am.

Commonwealth of Australia. (1974). TAFE in Australia: Report on needs in technical and further education, Volume 1: Report [Kangan Report]. Australian Government Publishing Service, Canberra.

Commonwealth of Australia. (1974). TAFE in Australia: Report on needs in technical and further education, Volume 2: Report [Kangan Report]. Australian Government Publishing Service, Canberra.

Pre-Publication Update

Since 23 March 2015, most stakeholders in the VET and international education sector would agree with me that nothing has changed; in fact, as I write this book, we are recovering from the global COVID-19 pandemic which globally has had an impact on VET and international education. Looking at VET and the international education sector in Australia, as well as that of ASQA's reform through the lens of regulatory history in Australia, we can better understand why history is just repeating itself and mistakes are not learned. Perhaps that too is a result of the challenge of scholars to provide a succinct definition of regulation; as long as ASQA's regulatory practices strive to achieve the balance between market driven needs and social control, the two main objects of the very definition, we will continue to see a cycle of repetitiveness in the way VET and international education is regulated in Australia.

If there are some things that we have learned about VET reform and ASQA's regulatory practice in the last 10 years that really does need to be incorporated into their future regulatory strategy, they are (and are not limited to):

- ASQA's approach to process-based regulation, meaning ASQA's focus on using powers of enforcement to ensure compliance is not as effective as it should be as a regulatory tool. Apart from the fact that ASQA really needs to adopt an approach that is multi-faceted and evidence based, one of the biggest disadvantages of this approach to regulation is that as a regulatory agency, it loses sight of what they are actually attempting to achieve, their legislated regulatory ambit.
- ASQA's one size fits all approach to regulation does not work for a whole range of reasons including but not limited to Federal, State/Territory and local government needs, market needs, public needs, industry needs, VET and international sector needs as well as global needs. What is needed is as

mentioned previously; a multi-faceted approach to regulation that includes authentic collaboration (recognised as authentic by all stakeholders as opposed to paternalistic, protectionist and tokenistic collaboration. It requires flexibility and acknowledgement that one size will not fit all providers if there is to be true equality and meaningful regulation. The provision of information, genuine stakeholder consultation and the provision of unbiased, authentic and non-manipulated information available to assist in the education of consumers.

- ASQA's current approach to regulation is data intensive; it requires the collection of a significant amount of information and then the analysis of that information. This process is not time efficient; by the time proper analysis has been undertaken, the issue of concern may well no longer be an issue due to the dynamics of human interaction and global economies. What's more, there are at least three additional issues that arise from the collection of so much data:
    - There is so much data that by the time ASQA has analysed all the data, they could lose sight of what they were actually looking for in the first place;
    - ASQA deals with many complex issues and it has admitted to not having the technical knowledge or resources to perform its legislated regulatory ambit. Therefore, what's the purpose of such an intensive gathering of data that is not able to be used efficiently, effectively or sufficiently to perform their role as a regulator? As a result of these deficiencies, ASQA are making qualitative, rather than quantitative judgements about the data they're collecting and in many instances, that data is being manipulated to 'tell' a story that the data potentially does not provide.
    - Thirdly, as I have detailed to ASQA on many occasions, and many RTOs around the country have also advised, the data that ASQA collects is not always relevant to the regulatory activities being undertaken. There is also the

fact that the questions that are being asked in the data collection process, need to be understood by everyone and be completely unambiguous. There is too much subjectivity in ASQA's regulatory practices and it all begins with the data that they collect. When there is such a significant disjuncture between what data is being requested and what data is being provided, there are bound to be gaps that negatively affect the meaning of the data being collected.

Risk-Based Regulation and ASQA's Risk Framework

> "Ethics is knowing the difference between what you have a right to do and what is right to do."
>
> - **Potter Stewart**

One of the most fundamental concepts to understand in risk-based regulation is that '*risk*' is defined and perceived differently depending on who is assessing that risk at any period of time. The following table demonstrates how the perception of risk changes depending on the assessor and the purpose of regulatory activity:

Issue	Purpose of Regulatory Activity	Risk Identified	Whose Perception?
Skill shortage - subsidies via government funding.	1. Accountability of government funds; 2. Consumer protection.	1. Exploitation of consumers; 2. Inappropriate use of government funds; 3. Too many students doing the same course, reducing employability.	1. Regulator; 2. Regulator; 3. Student.
Provision of quality education and training.	1. Education and training is fit for purpose; 2. Industry will have skilled employees;	1. The education and training provided does not align with industry needs; 2. The skills gap has not been filled;	1. Industry & Regulator; 2. Industry;

Issue	Purpose of Regulatory Activity	Risk Identified	Whose Perception?
	3. Students find the learning meaningful and are satisfied with their education and training experience.	3. Student perceptions will vary depending on what they're seeking, for example: • If the course no longer provides a pathway for skilled migration, the student perceives this as a risk; • If the student just wanted to undertake professional development, the risk is that they learn nothing that supports their professional skills and knowledge.	3. Student.

Issue	Purpose of Regulatory Activity	Risk Identified	Whose Perception?
The course is too short.	1. Accountability of government funds; 2. Consumer protection; 3. Meet industry expectations.	1. Government is paying too much for a course that isn't being delivered in the expected timeframe; 2. Student may not have sufficient time to learn; 3. Course doesn't meet industry needs.	1. Government & Regulator; 2. Regulator & Student; 3. Industry.

Issue	Purpose of Regulatory Activity	Risk Identified	Whose Perception?
Multicultural learning experience	1. Consumer protection; 2. Support inclusivity, diversity and cultural appropriateness.	1. A student comes from overseas to study a course in a school where they believed the cultural mix was multicultural but in fact the entire class is from one country. 2. Prevent discrimination or offence to the culture being represented through lack of information or engagement. E.g. Teaching about Indigenous Australians without confirming accuracy or appropriateness with Indigenous Elders.	1. Student; 2. Government & Regulator; 3. Indigenous Australians and the relevant community and Elders.

Apart from the perception of risk being open to interpretation, it is also important to remember that there are many characteristics associated with risk which also impact on regulatory activity and the lens through which risk is interpreted. These characteristics include:

- Future and potential risk (pre-empted potential risk that may or may not occur);

- Causation type characteristics (understanding the relationship between cause and effect of an activity or event such as loose gun laws and mass murders);
- Impressionable characteristics (no matter what type of intervention you put in place, the event or action is likely to occur anyway); and
- Double-edged (the risk presented could be negative but it might also bring new beneficial opportunities).

An analysis of ASQA's Regulatory Risk Framework has not been updated since Version 1.0 April 2016 and is not fit for purpose yet it is this model (and version)[115] that ASQA claims drives its implementation of risk assessment. It is this writer's opinion that the risk framework that ASQA claims drives its approach to regulation is critically flawed. In its '*Regulatory Risk Framework*', ASQA states that in relation to risk assessment relating to a provider and a case, the level of risk is determined based on the likelihood measures of the provider's past performance and the provider's conduct in this case as well as the impact on students, industry and the sector more broadly. These likelihood measures can then be combined and applied to the matrix and a level of regulatory response can be determined.

ASQA claims that it manages provider risk by continuously reviewing provider performance through a centralised report and also states that a provider profile '*...is fluid in nature and does not translate into a single score or rating of any kind*'. The principles underlying ASQA's risk-based regulatory approach state that ASQA:

- Efficiently uses resources to effectively identify and target the most serious risks and patterns of systemic non-compliance while minimising costs on regulated entities;

[115] Current at the time of publication; Australian Skills Quality Authority '*Regulatory Risk Framework*' (Webpage, 6 April 2021). <https://www.asqa.gov.au/sites/default/files/ASQA_Regulatory_Risk_Framework.pdf >.

- Seeks to minimise regulatory burden for proven high-performing providers with a history of compliance; and
- Applies procedural fairness in regulatory decisions and is transparent about frameworks that guide regulation.

In this writer's experience,[116] that ASQA is not complying with these principles in the application of risk management and managing the risk providers create for the regulator. The Regulatory Risk Framework refers to ASQA's requirement to apply a risk-based approach to regulation under the *National Vocational Education and Training Regulator Act 2011* (Cth.) ("NVR Act"). It also requires ASQA to implement proportionate, risk-based regulation that minimises impact on the regulated community, consistent with the '*Commonwealth Regulator Performance Framework 2014*' and in accordance with its requirements under the *Public Governance, Performance and Accountability Act 2013* (Cth.).

Despite being an independent statutory authority, ASQA is still bound by the Commonwealth's *Regulator Performance Framework* and the *Public Governance, Performance and Accountability Act 2013* (Cth.). The elements of the *Regulator Performance Framework* include that:

- Regulators do not unnecessarily impede the efficient operation of regulated entities;
- Communication with regulated entities is clear, targeted and effective;
- Actions taken by regulators are proportionate to the risk being managed; and
- Regulators are open and transparent in their dealings with regulated entities.

KPI 1 of the *Regulator Performance Framework* clearly states that '***enforcement activities only occur when there is a clear case for doing***

[116] Raelene Bartlett, (August 2019). Professional correspondence and confidential evidence on author's file.

so'. Page 19 refers to '*advice provided to regulated entities is consistent with communication policies*' yet, as was clearly demonstrated earlier, there is no consistency between the policies that ASQA communicates and its implementation of those policies.

KPI 3 of the *Regulator Performance Framework* clearly states that '*Efficient regulation takes account of the regulated activity, the nature of the regulated cohort, including its compliance history...and penalties are proportionate to both the seriousness of the breach and the risk being managed*'. One of the measures of '*good regulatory performance*' according to the Framework, is that '*regulators recognise the compliance record of regulated entities*' however, in this writer's experience, this is often not the case.

KPI 4 of the *Regulator Performance Framework* clearly states that '*Regulators minimise duplicative information requests...*', ...yet, in this writer's experience, not only are there often duplicative information requests, but often evidence that is submitted to ASQA is completely ignored and/or seemingly dismissed without consideration. This will also be demonstrated through the testimonials that follow.

In concluding this section on regulation, risk and ASQA, I offer these final thoughts. Ultimately, and importantly as far ASQA's regulatory practice is concerned, risk is a social construct that is driven by market and social changes. Risk is, and always will be influenced by how things are perceived and by who; all stakeholders have a different perception of the risk involved in regulating VET and the international education sector. Those perceptions are based on individual characteristics such as age, background, culture and even financial status. The market will always drive VET and international education in Australia and so ASQA needs to develop a regulatory strategy that caters for multi-faceted perceptions of risk.

Pre-Publication Update on ASQA's Regulatory Risk Framework

> **"One of the penalties for refusing to participate in politics is that you end up being governed by your inferiors."**
>
> **- Plato**

On 7 April 2021, ASQA's CEO announced ASQA's new Regulatory Risk Framework. Under the heading 'Legislative and regulatory practice context'[117] it is interesting to note that:

> The recommendations of the Rapid Review of ASQA's Regulatory Practices and Processes, 2020 (Rapid Review) aim to shift, over time, our regulatory approach from prescriptive and process-based compliance to a broader focus on self-assurance by training providers and excellence in training outcomes.

It is interesting to note this for two reasons in particular. The first reason this statement is interesting is because the *Rapid Review of ASQA* recommended that ASQA adjust its approach to performance monitoring in line with revised standards and a focus on provider self-assurance and references some of the key texts and modern regulatory tools in relation to evidence based, best practice regulation, it does not necessarily consider more broadly the operating context of the VET sector, adequately consider ASQA's cultural issues at various levels of the organisation or the multi-faceted concerns that impact the sector and the ability of self-assurance to remedy them, or the fact that technically speaking, the sector has been here before. The second issue related to suitability for self-assurance is slightly more complex and requires further discussion shortly.

117 Australian Skills Quality Authority, Regulatory Risk Framework, Version 1, April 2021, page 3.

Using ASQA's Strategic Reviews as the Basis for Systemic Risk Management

The Rapid Review refers to ASQA having, over recent years, conducting strategic reviews into the quality of international VET and English language education, unduly short training, and training for early childhood education and care. It is my experience, and I have widely communicated these views over the years, that the quality of research that was undertaken for these strategic reviews is not sufficiently evidence based to drive government policy (or reform) and that I'd be very surprised if there was a university that would approve the research undertaken for that purpose. The research is often flawed, incomplete, makes assumptions based on desktop reviews of evidence without ever testing the practices that stand behind the findings and those findings when they are made, are sometimes made by people who have limited (or any) qualifications or experience in the relevant sector and are therefore incapable of drawing such fundamental conclusions. I would add other strategic reviews that have impacted the sector just as significantly and riddled with the same issues including for example, but not limited to:

- Training in Security Programs in Australia, 2016;
- Targeted audits of VET FEE HELP Providers, 2015;
- Marketing and advertising practices of Australia's registered training organisations, 2013;
- Training for aged and community care in Australia, 2013; and
- Training for the White Card in Australia's Construction Industry, 2013.

Apart from the research flaws, it would be remiss of the researchers (and those making recommendations for the proposed changes to ASQA's regulatory practices) to neglect consideration or discussion about the many other multifaceted complex issues that underpin the challenges of regulating Australia's VET sector.

These issues include for example, the fact that the Standards themselves, while being a legislative instrument, are so frequently interpreted differently from one auditor to the next that it's very difficult to really say that the RTO is actually not compliant. This is even more challenging where:

- A large number of auditors are not sufficiently qualified (as admitted in parliament)[118];
- Training Packages that are funded by the Commonwealth government and supposed to be reflective of industry needs:
  - are not always reflective of what industry wants/needs;
  - are so poorly written and often have errors which, if a provider is compliant with clause 1.8, will have no choice but to be not compliant with industry needs or other regulatory or accreditation requirements;
  - Have been changing so frequently (or not frequently enough in some cases) that is impossible for providers to keep up;
  - Are so old but not maintained appropriately and are so difficult for providers to implement;
  - The purpose of training is being lost;
- Government funding doesn't cover the whole of the training and assessment process, only part of it and so there is a disjoint between what is required by one department and what is funded by the other under the guide that the government is making access free or equitable;
- Expectations of industry involvement are inconsistent with what industry expects to have to do.

These are only some of the issues/challenges but are identified to provide an example how the allegation of non-compliance against the provider is actually multifaceted in some cases (and not necessarily

118 Senator Louise Pratt, Education and Employment Committee, Employment, Skills, Small and Family Business Portfolio, Portfolio Question Number SQ19-001407, Question on notice no. 222.

that of the registered provider) and inconsistent with the intent of the legislation.

Unqualified Auditors

In addition to the concerns raised under this same heading in Chapter 2, this serious weakness of the regulator causes further concern for issues of VET reform and national VET policy. A brief reminder of the issues in chapter 2 is summarised below to put this concern into context. In addition to the previous question on notice regarding the qualifications and experience of ASQA's auditors in the Australian Senate, on 29 January 2019, **Education Issues Australia**[119] reported that:

> *Just last year ASQA enrolled 28 regulatory employees (30%) to acquire mandatory qualifications. Even if they did meet the requirements of ELICOS Standard P6.4 and held the Sch 1 requirements of the Standards for VET Regulators 2015, surely this loophole needs to be closed? Surely the person who is qualified under that Standard should be responsible for writing that section of the audit report where they operate in a team? (e.g. Just because someone is identified as a Lead Auditor, does not mean that they should be writing the entire report, making recommendations based on that audit report etc. where they are not qualified to do so). ASQA told @Louise_Pratt they had 93 Audit Staff and "on occasion ASQA employs staff that do not hold all of the mandatory qualifications.*

This finding from **Education Issues Australia** was also supported by the following evidence from the publicly available *ASQA Annual Report 2018/2019*:

The following questions summarise the concerns raised in Chapter 2 previously and set the foundation for the remainder of this discussion on unqualified auditors:

---

119 Twitter Account, Whistleblower for the Australian VET Sector <https://twitter.com/edissuesaus>.

1. How could an ASQA auditor who likely doesn't meet the Schedule 1 requirements of the Standards for VET Regulators 2015 validly and reliably audit any course? This is not the first time I have asked this question and I have never had an adequate response, yet hundreds of regulatory decisions have been made by ASQA on this basis since it was established and commenced operating on 1 July 2011. It should not be forgotten that a large number of ASQA staff then and now, were previously State-based employees/regulators.

2. How could an ASQA auditor who has done a quick and nasty auditing course (*remember those same short courses that ASQA sanctions providers for running which don't meet the AQF Volume of Learning?*) as identified previously in Chapter 2, validly and reliably audit a course?

3. How does an ASQA auditor conduct an audit on, report an audit outcome, make a recommendation of any kind (*let alone a sanction*) while not being qualified (*even remotely*) to do so?

For many years, ASQA has had a very difficult time securing suitably qualified auditors. The Standards for VET regulators are explicit about the qualifications and experience an ASQA auditor must have, yet far too frequently, there are auditors who are unqualified. When one considers the number of applications that make it to the AAT on the basis of these findings, it's quite extraordinary that nobody has interfered thus far. This is especially the case when questions have been raised on numerous occasions of the Senate in relation to the competency of ASQA auditors.

I personally also wrote an article on LinkedIn on this issue in February 2020 but the issue was also highlighted by Education Issues Australia via their Twitter page on 3 August 2020 when it highlighted that ASQA blamed '*auditor incapacity and inexperience*' for multiple reviews of the TAFENSW audit saga. These findings are not new for ASQA, they are endemic and have been since its inception. Once again, we have the regulator saying it is maintaining a standard of excellence amongst RTOs but it can't even meet its own legislative requirements – of course, it doesn't matter though, they're the regulator and untouchable, anyway right?

Yet, it is on the basis of findings from these '*strategic audits*' that national policy decisions are being made?

Training Packages

The concept and appearance of training packages have not got a significant history in Australia's VET sector. Around 1996 came an introduction to the concept and the first training packages introduced in 1997.[120] At that time, it was already widely acknowledged that Australian industry is 'constantly evolving'. Even back in 2007, we see that many of the challenges the VET sector experiences today existed back then:

> The skills needed to respond to this environment are well captured within industry's Training Packages, but as the national standards for workplace performance, they must continue to evolve if they are to identify and anticipate the skill needs of each industry, enterprise and the individual.
>
> Despite the name, they do not prescribe how an individual should be trained. Rather, they specify the skills and knowledge an experienced person needs to perform effectively in the workplace - simply put, they prescribe the 'outcome' or competency.

Some of the most common complaints in 2021 in relation to training packages remain:

1. They don't reflect industry's ever and rapidly evolving needs;

[120] Industry Skills Councils, 2007, 'Training Packages: A story less told', <https://www.voced.edu.au/content/ngv%3A22511 >

2. The skills represented in training packages cannot keep up with the speed of industry;
3. Those training packages that do attempt to keep up have changes to those training packages that are so frequent that the training industry can't keep up (*by the time it is endorsed, a new version is underway*);
4. Training packages do not (*nor have they*) really anticipated future needs, they are mostly reactive. Once upon a time, Industry Skills Councils were funded to complete an 'Environmental Scan' which attempted to anticipate future needs but again, the time between anticipation and actual endorsement - the horse had already left the gate and bolted!

There is one thing that many in the VET sector would argue though; training packages are NOT designed to specify the skills and knowledge that '*an experienced*' person needs to perform effectively in the workplace. Many (*if not most*) practitioners in the VET sector would argue that training packages are the minimum standard, experience is gained once qualified and deemed competent against the minimum standard. One thing everyone would agree on though is that Training packages do not describe (*or prescribe*) training outcomes but rather the standard expected upon assessment of competency against that minimum standard. How a candidate arrives at the point of assessment is not technically part of training packages. In recent years however, there have been attempts to include prescriptions in relation to training into training packages or '*prescribe*' its quality via other components of the VET Quality Framework such as the Australian Qualifications Framework.

Licensing and additional accreditation requirements were seen to be an integral part of training package development in those early days and in many respects, they continue to be. Their implementation however has not always been (nor is it still) been perceived as completely successful or integrated. There are many 'licensing' units who, despite having completed the unit of competency from the training package, still need to undergo a completely separate and additional assessment process. So if the intention of training packages was to provide an assessment framework for the minimum occupational standards, then where did all those licensing units go wrong?

A simple look at the various licensing units and the additional 'assessment' requirements demonstrates this point:

Licensing Area / Industry Unit of Competency	Additional Regulation / Licensing Concern
ASIC units of competency, for example, FNS Training Package[121]: • FNSASICV503 Provide advice in derivatives; • FNSASICY513 Provide advice in insurance broking; • FNSASICT503 Provide advice in managed investments; • FNSASICW503 Provide advice in securities; • FNSASICN503 Provide Tier 1 personal advice in general insurance; and • FNSASICT503 Provide advice in managed investments. **Training Package Implementation Information** All of these units have been written at Diploma level and represent the ASIC identified generic and specialist knowledge areas that were required to satisfy licensing obligations at the time of their release.	**Australian Securities and Investments Commission (ASIC)** **Training Package Developer** PwC's Skills for Australia (a branch of PricewaterhouseCoopers who was established as a Skills Service Organisation to support the work of Industry Reference Committees in their development of modern and relevant training packages). Recent industry consultation[122] demonstrated that while these units of competency may well be designed for the VET sector, KPMG acknowledged that they would not employ any VET graduate for these types of advisory roles; they would only look at university graduates and are not interested in liaising with RTOs. KPMG is of course a global financial services firm and network providing professional firms in audit, tax and advisory services. **Registration Requirement** Financial adviser (an Australian financial services licensee; or a representative of an Australian financial services licensee). ASIC Regulatory Guide (RG) 146 compliance.

[121] FNS Financial Services Training Package, current at time of publication.
[122] KPMG Sydney, professional correspondence held on file, 18 January 2021.

High Risk Work License (HRWL) units of competency, for example, RII Training Package[123] • RIIHAN211D - Conduct basic scaffolding operations; • RIIHAN208E - Perform dogging; • RIIHAN209E - Perform basic rigging; • RIIHAN210D - Perform intermediate rigging; and • RIIHAN201E - Operate a forklift. **Relationship between licensed and non-licensed units of competency**[124] Non-licensed units also exist for the areas of work listed in the previous table. Licensed units are to be used for training and assessment for licensing purposes, whereas industry units can be used for assessing workplace competence.	**State / Territory Based Regulators** **Training Package Developer** PwC's Skills for Australia (a branch of PricewaterhouseCoopers who was established as a Skills Service Organisation to support the work of Industry Reference Committees in their development of modern and relevant training packages). **Registration Requirement** The Model Work Health and Safety Regulations set out training and assessment requirements for a person performing high risk work, and the arrangements for issuing a licence to a person performing high risk work. These regulations recognise classes of licence for high risk work and require that all training and assessment for high risk work licences occur within the vocational education and training system. Unless otherwise advised by particular States and Territories, all training for licences must be issued against the relevant units of competency. Most units will include the following statement:

[123] RII Resources and Infrastructure Industry Training Package, current at time of publication.
[124] RII Resources and Infrastructure Industry Training Package Companion Volume, page 49.

	"The work required in this unit relates to the National Standard for High Risk Work but this unit does not provide the licence. Licensing, legislative, regulatory and certification requirements that apply to this unit can vary between states, territories and industry sectors, and must be sourced prior to application of the unit.

The following table from the Companion Volume[125] provides an example of where non-licensed RII units of competency cover similar content to imported licensed units of competency. With careful consideration of the content of both the matching licensed and the non-licensed units of competency, RTOs can cover off both units using a holistic approach to training delivery.

Unit Code	Unit Title	Unit Code	Unit Title
CPCCLDG3001A	Licence to perform dogging	RIIHAN208E	Perform dogging
CPCCLRG3001A	Licence to perform rigging basic level	RIIHAN209E	Perform basic rigging
CPCCLRG3002A	Licence to perform rigging intermediate level	RIIHAN210D	Perform intermediate rigging
CPCCLSF20001A	Licence to erect, alter and dismantle scaffolding basic level	RIIHAN211D	Conduct basic scaffolding operations
CPCCLSF30001A	Licence to erect, later and dismantle scaffolding intermediate level	RIIHAN302D	Conduct intermediate scaffolding operations
TLILIC0002	Licence to operate a forklift truck	RIIHAN201E	Operate a forklift

While the previous table provides a snapshot of the licencing and regulation issue and concerns, a much bigger issue (alluded to with the FNS ASIC unit of competency examples, has also appeared in recent years; that of the inflation of ANZSCO[126] Codes relevant to graduate outcomes of VET qualifications. Earlier this year (8 January 2021), the author published an article on LinkedIn that describes this issue in greater detail. For those who are unsure of what ANZSCO Codes are, the following information is provided by the government body responsible for them:

> The Australian and New Zealand Standard Classification of Occupations (ANZSCO) First Edition was the product of a

[125] Ibid.

[126] Australian and New Zealand Standard Classification of Occupations.

> development program undertaken jointly by a project team from the Australian Bureau of Statistics (ABS), Statistics New Zealand (Statistics NZ) and the Australian Government Department of Education, Employment and Workplace Relations for use in the collection, publication and analysis of occupation statistics. Subsequent revisions in 2009 and 2013 were undertaken by the ABS and Statistics NZ...
>
> Care needs to be taken when assigning information about particular jobs to ANZSCO classes because the same job titles can be used in different industries to describe different occupations (e.g. business analyst). Additionally, the titles used in ANZSCO are not an exhaustive list of all titles used by people to describe an occupation (e.g. brickie). To consistently and reliably allocate occupation information from responses in statistical collections to the correct position in the ANZSCO structure, the minimum information required is occupation title and tasks performed...
>
> ANZSCO is primarily a statistical classification designed to aggregate and organise data collected about jobs or individuals. The classification definitions are based on the skill level and specialisation usually necessary to perform the tasks of the specific occupation, or of most occupations in the group. The definitions and skill level statements apply to the occupation and not persons working in the occupation.

When qualifications are allocated to the national register, they are endorsed with an ANZSCO Code. For example, using the common BSB50420 Diploma of Leadership and Management, the national register includes the following information for the ANZSCO Code/ Identifier

Classifications

☐ Display history

Scheme	Code	Classification value
ANZSCO Identifier	111211	Corporate General Manager
ASCED Qualification/Course Field of Education Identifier	0803	Business And Management
Qualification/Course Level of Education Identifier	421	Diploma
Taxonomy - Industry Sector	N/A	Business Administration,Logistics,Purchasing and Procurement,Government Service Delivery,Warehousing and Storage,Local Government Administration,Automotive Manufacturing,Automotive Industry,Legal Administration
Taxonomy - Occupation	N/A	Transport Manager,Distribution Centre Manager,Information Services Manager,Manager,Corporate Services Manager,Public Sector Manager,Senior Manager (Public Sector),Office Manager,Legal Practice Manager,Operations Manager,Warehouse Manager,Business Development Manager,Production Manager,Business Manager

The way that the ANZSCO Code/Identifier[127] works in this situation is as follows:

Contents >> Major Group 1 Managers >> SUB-MAJOR GROUP 11 Chief Executives, General Managers and Legislators >> MINOR GROUP 111 Chief Executives, General Managers and Legislators >> **UNIT GROUP 1112 General Managers**

UNIT GROUP 1112 GENERAL MANAGERS

GENERAL MANAGERS plan, organise, direct, control and review the day-to-day operations and major functions of commercial, industrial, government and defence organisations through departmental managers and subordinate executives.

Indicative Skill Level:

In Australia and New Zealand:

Most occupations in this unit group have a level of skill commensurate with a bachelor degree or higher qualification. At least five years of relevant experience may substitute for the formal qualification. In some instances relevant experience and/or on-the-job training may be required in addition to the formal qualification (ANZSCO Skill Level 1).

Tasks Include:

- planning policy, and setting standards and objectives for organisations
- providing day-to-day direction and management of organisations, and directing and endorsing policy to fulfil objectives, achieve specific goals, and maximise profit and efficiency
- assessing changing situations and responding accordingly by issuing commands and directives to subordinate staff
- consulting with immediate subordinates and departmental heads on matters such as methods of operation, equipment requirements, finance, sales and human resources
- authorising the funding of major policy implementation programs
- representing the organisation at official occasions, in negotiations, at conventions, seminars, public hearings and forums, and liaising between areas of responsibility
- preparing, or arranging for the preparation of, reports, budgets and forecasts, and presenting them to governing bodies
- selecting and managing the performance of senior staff
- may undertake responsibility for some or all of accounting, sales, marketing, human resources and other specialist operations

Occupations:

111211 Corporate General Manager
111212 Defence Force Senior Officer

111211 CORPORATE GENERAL MANAGER

Alternative Title:

Chief Operating Officer

Plans, organises, directs, controls and reviews the day-to-day operations and major functions of a commercial, industrial, governmental or other organisation through departmental managers and subordinate executives.
Skill Level: 1

Specialisations:

Assistant Commissioner (Police)
Hospital Administrator
Kaiwhakahaere (NZ)
Managing Editor
Trade Union Secretary

As per the ABS website:

> **"Updating ANZSCO commences in March 2021**

127 Australian Bureau of Statistics, 'ANZSCO Contents', Webpage, <https://www.abs.gov.au/ausstats/abs@.nsf/Lookup/9F38DBF4AE58BAD9CA257B9500131004?opendocument >.

> On 25 March 2021, the ABS announced that a program of work to progress a targeted update of ANZSCO was commencing[128]."

It will be interesting to see what becomes of the revised ANZSCO Codes/Identifiers and the impact it has on training packages and the VET sector more broadly.

[128] Australian Bureau of Statistics, 'ANZSCO', <https://www.abs.gov.au/anzsco >.

The Mystery of ANZSCO, Australia's General Skilled Migration Program and VET[129]

I wonder how many others are unaware of the relationship between ANZSCO codes, immigration (GSM in particular) and VET qualifications?

I was explaining to some colleagues that it's unrealistic to deliver the BSB50618 Diploma of Human Resources Management or the new qual BSB50320 because the requirements for assessment and certification are completely unrealistic when you consider the level of employment a person with a Diploma of Human Resources Management might have in an organisation.

I explained just by looking at the core units in the superseded qualification...manage human resource services, manage recruitment, selection and induction processes, manage workforce planning, manage employee relations, manage rehab & Return To Work programs.

[129] Also published on LinkedIn, 8 January 2021, 'The Mystery of ANZSCO, Australia's General Skilled Migration Program and VET', <https://www.linkedin.com/pulse/mystery-anzsco-australias-general-skilled-migration-program-bartlett/ >.

Let's take a look...

Qualification details

Export summary to PDF
Notify me of changes

BSB50618 - Diploma of Human Resources Management (Release 3)

Summary

Usage recommendation: **Superseded**

Mapping:

Mapping	Notes	Date
Is superseded by BSB50320 - Diploma of Human Resource Management		18/Oct/2020
Supersedes and is equivalent to BSB50615 - Diploma of Human Resources Management		26/Sep/2018

Release Status: **Current**

Releases:

Release	Release date	Compare
3 (this release)	**30/Aug/2019**	☐
2 (View details)	21/Feb/2019	☐
1 (View details)	27/Sep/2018	☐

Companion volumes:

- Companion Volume Implementation Guides are available from VETNet

Delivery: Find RTOs approved to deliver this qualification.

Training packages that include this qualification

Code	Title	Release
BSB	Business Services Training Package	5.0-6.1

Units of competency

Code	Title	Essential
BSBHRM509	Manage rehabilitation or return to work programs	Elective
BSBHRM511	Manage expatriate staff	Elective
BSBHRM512	Develop and manage performance management processes	Core
BSBMGT516	Facilitate continuous improvement	Elective
BSBHRM513	Manage workforce planning	Core
BSBRKG502	Manage and monitor business or records systems	Elective
BSBRSK501	Manage risk	Elective
BSBWRK520	Manage employee relations	Core
BSBHRM501	Manage human resource services	Core
BSBHRM510	Manage mediation processes	Elective

I don't know about you but I don't know too many employers who would allow someone who has graduated with a Diploma of Human Resources Management to manage those things in their business let alone allow a student studying it to gain valuable work experience!

So, I went on and explained the value of ANZSCO Identifiers! Have you ever wondered about them? When was the last time you looked at how training package developers INFLATE these codes? It's no wonder industry doesn't trust what's coming out of the VET sector!

ANZSCO codes are what are used to communicate skill shortages on the GSM migration list. Let's take another look...

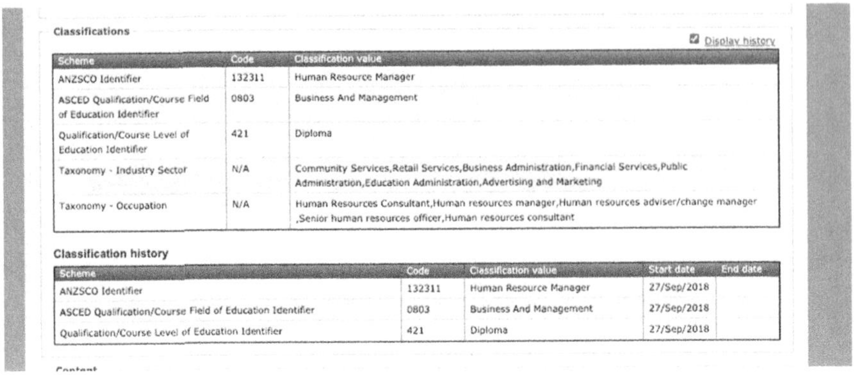

Classifications

Display history

Scheme	Code	Classification value
ANZSCO Identifier	132311	Human Resource Manager
ASCED Qualification/Course Field of Education Identifier	0803	Business And Management
Qualification/Course Level of Education Identifier	421	Diploma
Taxonomy - Industry Sector	N/A	Community Services,Retail Services,Business Administration,Financial Services,Public Administration,Education Administration,Advertising and Marketing
Taxonomy - Occupation	N/A	Human Resources Consultant,Human resources manager,Human resources adviser/change manager ,Senior human resources officer,Human resources consultant

Classification history

Scheme	Code	Classification value	Start date	End date
ANZSCO Identifier	132311	Human Resource Manager	27/Sep/2018	
ASCED Qualification/Course Field of Education Identifier	0803	Business And Management	27/Sep/2018	
Qualification/Course Level of Education Identifier	421	Diploma	27/Sep/2018	

Now, if you go to the Department of Home Affairs and look through all the legislative instruments that relate to skilled migration, you'll find this job role there. Alternatively, you can go a quick Google search and you'll find PLENTY of ads from migration agents and law firms promoting this as a visa pathway. Still not convinced? Here's one from my Google search (I am not affiliated with this firm in any way, and I am not suggesting they're doing anything wrong, I merely use it as an example of many).

HUMAN RESOURCE MANAGER Immigration to Australia PR Visa ANZSCO 132311

Plans, organises, directs, controls and coordinates the human resource and workplace relations activities within an organisation.

Australian Visa Assessment Form

Alternative Title: Personnel and Employee Relations Manager

Skill Level: 1

Specialisations:

Occupational Health and Safety Manager
Training and Development Manager
Workplace Relations Manager

UNIT GROUP 1323 HUMAN RESOURCE MANAGERS

HUMAN RESOURCE MANAGERS plan, organise, direct, control and coordinate the human resource and workplace relations activities within organisations.

Indicative Skill Level:
In Australia and New Zealand:

Most occupations in this unit group have a level of skill commensurate with a bachelor degree or higher qualification. At least five years of relevant experience may substitute for the formal qualification. In some instances relevant experience and/or on-the-job training may be required in addition to the formal qualification (ANZSCO Skill Level 1).

Tasks Include:

- determining, implementing, monitoring, reviewing and evaluating human resource management strategies, policies and plans to meet business needs
- advising and assisting other Managers in applying sound recruitment and selection practices, and appropriate induction, training and development programs
- developing and implementing performance management systems to plan, appraise and improve individual and team performance
- representing the organisation in negotiations with unions and employees to determine remuneration and other conditions of employment
- developing and implementing occupational health and safety programs and equal employment opportunity programs, and ensuring compliance with related statutory requirements
- overseeing the application of redundancy and other employee retrenchment policies
- monitoring employment costs and productivity levels
- may train and advise other Managers in personnel and workplace relations matters

Occupation:

132311 Human Resource Manager

Book Appointment Now!

You can book appointments with us simply tap/click above button.

Information in these articles are general in nature and may not apply to your specific situation. For more detailed/specific legal advice for you, we recommend proper legal advice from lawyer.

FIND OUT NOW !

Australian Visa Assessment Form

For more information, please read our articles:

[+] Family Law (8)
[+] Criminal Law (11)
[+] Commercial Law (6)
[+] Employment Law Australia (2)
[+] Powers of Attorney & Statutory declarations in Victoria (2)
[+] Conveyancing (4)
[+] Wills and probate in Victoria Australia (7)
[+] Migration (340)

I also used this example because it neatly explains how the ANZSCO codes work. If you look closely at the screenshot, you'll see something that is identical on the website of the Australian Bureau of Statistics (ABS), specifically in relation to the indicative skill level. See if you can see the similarities.

This one, from the ABS website...

Australian Bureau of Statistics

Statistics | Census | Complete your survey | About

> By Catalogue Number

1220.0 - ANZSCO - Australian and New Zealand Standard Classification of Occupations, 2013, Version 1.3

LATEST ISSUE Released at 11:30 AM (CANBERRA TIME) 05/11/2019

Summary | Downloads | Explanatory Notes | Related Information | Past Releases

Page tools: Print Page | Email Notification

- What's New
- Contents
- About this Release
- Expanded Contents
- Search ANZSCO Titles

Contents >> Major Group 1 Managers >> SUB-MAJOR GROUP 13 Specialist Managers >> MINOR GROUP 132 Business Administration Managers >> UNIT GROUP 1323 Human Resource Managers

UNIT GROUP 1323 HUMAN RESOURCE MANAGERS

HUMAN RESOURCE MANAGERS plan, organise, direct, control and coordinate the human resource and workplace relations activities within organisations.

Indicative Skill Level:

In Australia and New Zealand:

Most occupations in this unit group have a level of skill commensurate with a bachelor degree or higher qualification. At least five years of relevant experience may substitute for the formal qualification. In some instances relevant experience and/or on-the-job training may be required in addition to the formal qualification (ANZSCO Skill Level 1).

Tasks Include:

- determining, implementing, monitoring, reviewing and evaluating human resource management strategies, policies and plans to meet business needs
- advising and assisting other Managers in applying sound recruitment and selection practices, and appropriate induction, training and development programs
- developing and implementing performance management systems to plan, appraise and improve individual and team performance

Hold on a second! Did I read that right? No Way! Surely not! What have we here?

Indicative skill level:

In Australia and New Zealand:

> Most occupations in this unit group have a level of skill commensurate with a bachelor's degree or higher qualification. At least five years of relevant experience *may substitute for the formal qualification. In some instances relevant experience and/or on-the-job training may be required in addition to the formal qualification (ANZSCO Skill Level 1).*

It's little wonder then that industry is so demoralised about the quality of VET! Many would have you believe it's Registered Training Organisations who are at fault for not providing the training and assessment necessary to align with industry's expectations. Would it be more accurate however to say that RTOs have always been set up to fail with the inflation of ANZSCO codes going on for so long? Yes, that's right.

You see this issue has been going on for a VERY long time. I personally contacted personnel at IBSA and the ABS initially in April 2015. I contacted them in relation to another qualification that is misapplied as part of the GSM and would appear to have been a deliberate inflation of ANZSCO codes by what was then IBSA. My enquiries at the time were in relation to BSB51105 - Diploma of Management. The ANZSCO Code at the time was 132000. A quick glance at the qualification that followed BSB51107 is below BSB51915 - Diploma of Leadership and Management):

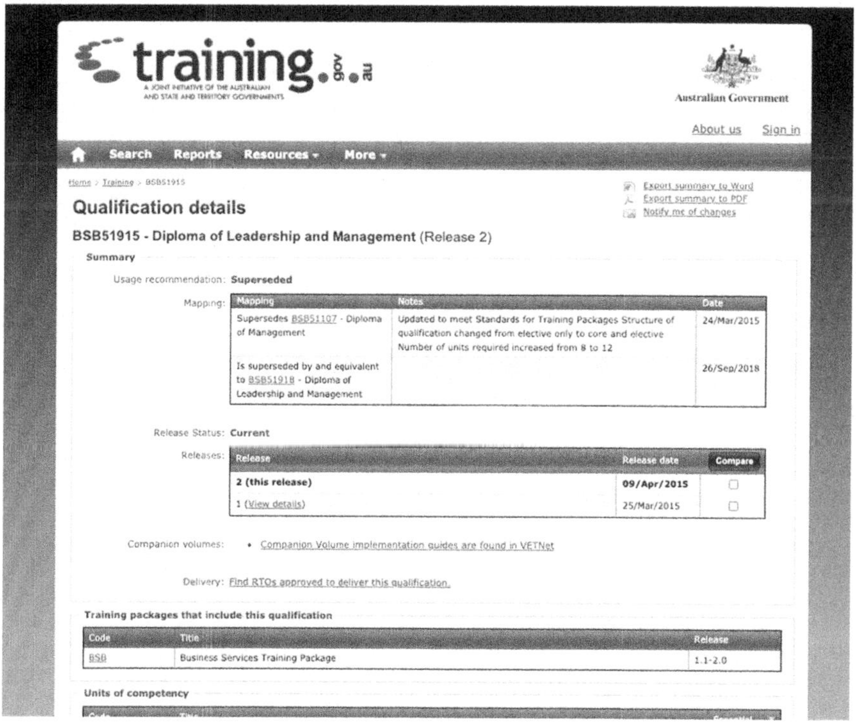

training.gov.au

A JOINT INITIATIVE OF THE AUSTRALIAN AND STATE AND TERRITORY GOVERNMENTS

Australian Government

About us Sign in

Search Reports Resources More

Home > Training > BSB51915

Export summary to Word
Export summary to PDF
Notify me of changes

Qualification details

BSB51915 - Diploma of Leadership and Management (Release 2)

Summary

Usage recommendation: **Superseded**

Mapping:

Mapping	Notes	Date
Supersedes BSB51107 - Diploma of Management	Updated to meet Standards for Training Packages Structure of qualification changed from elective only to core and elective Number of units required increased from 8 to 12	24/Mar/2015
Is superseded by and equivalent to BSB51918 - Diploma of Leadership and Management		26/Sep/2018

Release Status: **Current**

Releases:

Release	Release date	Compare
2 (this release)	**09/Apr/2015**	
1 (View details)	25/Mar/2015	

Companion volumes: • Companion Volume implementation guides are found in VETNet

Delivery: Find RTOs approved to deliver this qualification.

Training packages that include this qualification

Code	Title	Release
BSB	Business Services Training Package	1.1-2.0

Units of competency

And the ANZSCO codes listed on the national register TGA.

Units of competency

Code	Title	Essential
BSBIPR501	Manage intellectual property to protect and grow business	Elective
BSBREL502	Build international business networks	Elective
BSBLDR504	Implement diversity in the workplace	Elective
BSBHRM511	Manage expatriate staff	Elective
BSBCOM503	Develop processes for the management of breaches in compliance requirements	Elective
BSBHRM512	Develop and manage performance management processes	Elective
BSBMGT516	Facilitate continuous improvement	Elective
BSBHRM513	Manage workforce planning	Elective
BSBMGT518	Develop organisation policy	Elective
BSBWOR502	Lead and manage team effectiveness	Core

1 2 3 4 Items per page **10** | 20 | 50 | 100 Displaying items 1 - 10 of 37

Classifications

Display history

Scheme	Code	Classification value
ANZSCO Identifier	111211	Corporate General Manager
ASCED Qualification/Course Field of Education Identifier	0803	Business And Management
Qualification/Course Level of Education Identifier	421	Diploma
Taxonomy - Industry Sector	N/A	Automotive Industry,Business Administration,Government Service Delivery,Purchasing and Procurement,Legal Administration,Logistics,Automotive Manufacturing,Warehousing and Storage,Local Government Administration
Taxonomy - Occupation	N/A	Senior Manager (Public Sector),Business Development Manager,Information Services Manager,Business Manager,Manager,Distribution Centre Manager,Legal Practice Manager,Production Manager,Operations Manager,Public Sector Manager,Office Manager,Warehouse Manager,Corporate Services Manager,Transport Manager

Classification history

Scheme	Code	Classification value	Start date	End date
ANZSCO Identifier	111211	Corporate General Manager	30/Jul/2015	
ASCED Qualification/Course Field of Education Identifier	0803	Business And Management	30/Jul/2015	
Qualification/Course Level of Education Identifier	421	Diploma	25/Mar/2015	

Content

I'm pretty certain those codes don't reflect a Diploma. Let's see...

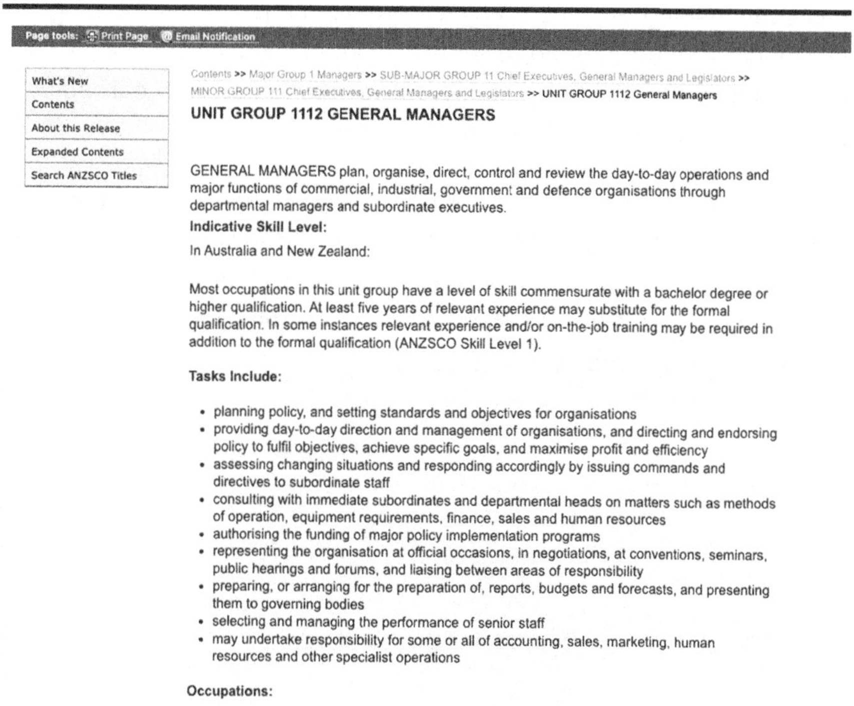

Page tools: Print Page Email Notification

- What's New
- Contents
- About this Release
- Expanded Contents
- Search ANZSCO Titles

Contents >> Major Group 1 Managers >> SUB-MAJOR GROUP 11 Chief Executives, General Managers and Legislators >> MINOR GROUP 111 Chief Executives, General Managers and Legislators >> UNIT GROUP 1112 General Managers

UNIT GROUP 1112 GENERAL MANAGERS

GENERAL MANAGERS plan, organise, direct, control and review the day-to-day operations and major functions of commercial, industrial, government and defence organisations through departmental managers and subordinate executives.

Indicative Skill Level:

In Australia and New Zealand:

Most occupations in this unit group have a level of skill commensurate with a bachelor degree or higher qualification. At least five years of relevant experience may substitute for the formal qualification. In some instances relevant experience and/or on-the-job training may be required in addition to the formal qualification (ANZSCO Skill Level 1).

Tasks Include:

- planning policy, and setting standards and objectives for organisations
- providing day-to-day direction and management of organisations, and directing and endorsing policy to fulfil objectives, achieve specific goals, and maximise profit and efficiency
- assessing changing situations and responding accordingly by issuing commands and directives to subordinate staff
- consulting with immediate subordinates and departmental heads on matters such as methods of operation, equipment requirements, finance, sales and human resources
- authorising the funding of major policy implementation programs
- representing the organisation at official occasions, in negotiations, at conventions, seminars, public hearings and forums, and liaising between areas of responsibility
- preparing, or arranging for the preparation of, reports, budgets and forecasts, and presenting them to governing bodies
- selecting and managing the performance of senior staff
- may undertake responsibility for some or all of accounting, sales, marketing, human resources and other specialist operations

Occupations:

Once again we see:

> **Indicative skill level:**
> **In Australia and New Zealand:**
>
> Most occupations in this unit group have a level of skill commensurate with a bachelor's degree or higher qualification. At least five years of relevant experience may substitute for the formal qualification. In some instances, relevant experience and/or on-the-job training may be required in addition to the formal qualification (ANZSCO Skill Level 1).

So next time you go out to industry and engage with them about the skills they need, maybe you could consider the ANZSCO code as part of the process of identifying the best fit for the student. It may just fall upon us to educate entire industries about how Australia's workforce has been inflated in some pretty common job roles for far too long. It's no wonder that our modern awards are not aligned with skill levels. It's no wonder that industry is crying out for graduates who can actually perform the role that their certification states.

It's no wonder that graduates are unemployable upon graduation from many common VET courses. The Australian Government has let them down. It's not the fault of RTOs at all. After all, RTOs are forced to deliver training packages. Yes, sure they can try accrediting a course but what's the first VAC Standard? Let's see...

GET LEGISLATION UPDATES **MY ACCOUNT**

Part 3 Course design standards

Applications for course accreditation that are accepted by the National VET Regulator will be accredited if they are assessed as meeting the following design standards. These are the course design standards that **must** be met for accreditation.

The accreditation of a VET accredited course may be cancelled under section 52 of the Act if these standards cease to be met.

VAC 6 Duplication

6.1 The course must not duplicate, by title or coverage, the outcomes of an endorsed Training Package qualification.

VAC 7 Course design standards

7.1 VET accredited courses are based on an established industry, enterprise, education, legislative or community need.

Oh that's right! The accredited course MUST NOT duplicate an endorsed training package qualification! So, forgive me for my pessimism but... REALLY? Who on Earth is responsible for making these decisions? It's time that VET Reform really got its act together and truly addressed industry needs instead of keeping people in high places in overpaid jobs and leaving industry without the staff it desperately needs!

What do you think? Do you agree that #enoughisenough and it's time the politicians listened to those experts who actually have an idea about the implementation of VET? People who have experience in the actual implementation and delivery of VET? I'd be interested in hearing your ideas on this.

It actually embarrassed me today to have to share such nonsense with industry colleagues. For a world-class system, we really do have some pretty ridiculous ways of doing things!

Want to know more? Check out the ABS website for yourself and compare the ANZSCO codes to the identifiers in qualifications on the national register of VET, TGA. You'll be surprised!

As mentioned earlier in this book, looking at the history of VET and the international education sector in Australia, as well as that of ASQA's reform through the lens of regulatory history in Australia, we can better understand why history is just repeating itself and mistakes are not learned.

The report 'Training packages: A Story Less Told' is also telling for a completely different reason and another that has not changed today:

> Looking back some 15 years, it would be fair to say that vocational education and training did not enjoy a strong status within industry or the broader community. Often seen as a poor relation to tertiary education, it was typified by courses developed by training providers in isolation from industry.

In 2007, 15 years ago, secondary schools would steer students in the direction of technical and trades (Tech School) or University students. There was almost a level of shame and failure to be identified as a '*Tech School*' graduate. In 2021, this is still no different!

We still have secondary schools separating students into tech or university streams and worst still, in many secondary schools across the country, there is little recognition that technical education actually includes more than TAFE. In visiting a number of secondary schools in recent years, many career 'teachers', VET Coordinators, Year Level Coordinators and Principals still equate VET with TAFE - three is very little recognition that private training providers exist. That tension between VET and universities also continues to exist - despite the many (mostly private) providers who desperately try to make this tension disappear.

Suitability of Australia's VET Sector for the Self-Assurance Regulatory Model

As is reported in the academic literature on best practice regulation, there are a number of factors to consider when contemplating self-regulation or what ASQA calls, self-assurance[130].

Providers invest a significant amount of time, money and energy into becoming providers who operate under a self-assurance regulatory model; just ask those delegates who did so a few years back at the last attempt at 'self-regulation'. There are very few (if any) private providers who continue to exist today under 'delegation', those that do, are primarily TAFE or government run organisations. There were a large number of private providers who invested heavily in becoming 'delegates' and despite many of them having an impeccable regulatory record, their delegate status didn't last long before regulatory change arrived. This is another example that risks occurring in ASQA's latest proposal to self-regulate.

Another issue that concerns me considerably is the change to the *National Vocational Education and Training Regulator Act 2011* (through that famous Bill discussed earlier in this book) that was amended to allow, for example, but not limited to:

- Increased capacity to use data collected under section 26 improperly (for example, the regulator currently uses these powers inappropriately by demanding in their formal notice that a vast amount of information, sometimes going back years, some protected by privacy laws, etc. be produced within a very short time frame); and

130 Interestingly, ASQA was at pains to explain in its Consultation Paper 'Working Together Towards Effective Self-Assurance' Version 1.0, July 2020' that 'self-assurance' is not 'self-regulation'. However, in the transcript of *Trades College Australia Pty Ltd and Australian Skills Quality Authority* [2018] AATA 1360 (24 May 2018), page 12 at [para 20], ASQA's legal team states '*This is a self-regulation model*'.

- Holding and storing that data for any use (while it may be listed on the notice for a specific purpose, the regulator can retain it to inform future regulatory activities). My concern around this issue is that already, ASQ auditors and investigators do not always apply the evidence in the way it is intended and therefore evidence interpretation can be quite subjective. Providers don't often get the opportunity to tell this story though until much later in the courts (many, however, will not even make it there).

Another issue of course is the cost of self-regulating only to find that ASQA is also engaging in its full cost-recovery process. In an environment where there is little transparency of costs already (for example, how does an ASQA audit of a first aid only provider ever get to say 48 hours of audit to be charged at $275 per hour but there is no itemisation of how that 48 hours was actually arrived at? We can get an itemised bill for our telephone bill, why can't we get one from ASQA?). The bigger issue though is if the agency is full cost recovery and there is no transparency around fee charging, there is no difference really to the current situation where auditors are self-interested in finding as many non-compliances (or at least suggesting that they have identified them) as possible because it means that there is more work for them. Where providers self-regulate and they have a full cost recovery regulator on top of that, those charges will only increase.

Further, the costs may be more amenable to larger organisations (such as TAFE) but small business and enterprise (let's face it, the majority of RTOs) might really struggle.

Another issue that can cause tension between the regulator and the regulated in a self-assurance/self-regulating world is that the perception of importance can be perceived differently not just between the regulator and the regulated, but also from one regulated party to another regulated party. Likewise, when the concept of self-regulation or self-assurance fails, who will get the blame? Of course it will be providers! It happened before - that's why the majority lost their delegation status despite the fact that they were excellent providers. The government engaged in regulatory reform of the VET sector and here we are, back on the merry go round.

One of the other things that need to be considered though in implementing a 'self-assurance' approach to regulation is assessing the likelihood of compliance and therefore whether or not the regulator will achieve its regulatory ambit. The Dutch Ministry of Justice[131] was one of the earliest 'bodies' to try and develop a framework for predicting the likelihood of compliance through what is known as 'The Table of Eleven'. It is called such because it is effectively a table of 11 factors or dimensions that, once separated into the categories of spontaneous compliance or enforcement in a table, there are a range of questions that we can ask about the regulatory environment that help us to predict the likelihood of compliance. This was revised by Parker and Nielsen to what is called 'the 14 compliance questions'. By expanding it beyond the spontaneous and enforcement options for predicting future compliance, the 14 compliance questions model is almost like a prompt to policy makers[132] that further divides the categories into additional categories of areas including economic, social, capacities of the target population as well as factors that promote deterrence and influence compliance.

The '*14 Compliance Questions*' are demonstrated in the table[133] as follows. Why reproduce the 14 compliance questions in a book like this? They are being reproduced to demonstrate that in recommending a self-assurance model as a part of ASQA's Rapid Review, such an important, evidence based regulatory technique does not appear to have been considered. If it had, the responses to some of these questions would have clearly demonstrated that this model is not fit for purpose.

131 The Dutch Ministry of Justice collaborated with Dr Dick Ruimschotel to develop the Table of Eleven to assist the government to predict whether the enforcement of new legislation would lead to compliance. The Table of 11 is based on 11 behavioural research indicated would influence compliance.

132 Christine Parker, Vikeke Lehmann Nielsen, *Regulatory Theory: Foundations and Applications*, ed Peter Drahos, (Australian National University Press, 2017), page 221.

133 Ibid, 221.

Spontaneous compliance factors	Enforced compliance factors
Economic, social and normative motives	**8. Respect for the regulator** *Does the target group respect the regulator and how it goes about its tasks? Do they have a relationship with the regulator? Do they respect the judgement of those responsible for law enforcement?*
1. Social and economic costs and benefits *Does the target group believe that it costs too much time, money and effort to comply? Does the target group believe that there are tangible advantages to be gained from breaking the rules? Does the target group see any advantage to them in complying with the rules?* **2. Degree of acceptance of this regulation** *Does the target group agree with the policy objectives and the principles that underpin the rules surrounding their licensed activity? Do they agree with how the policy and principles have been put into practice—for example, do they think particular obligations are unacceptable?* **3. Respect for the law in general** *Does the target group generally believe in abiding by the law; do they believe that complying with the law is a good thing to do regardless of whether they agree with a specific obligation?* **4. Existence of non-official influence over the targeted group's compliance** *Do industry groups and other regulatees, customers, investors, trading partners, local communities, industry groups, non-governmental organisations or other stakeholders facilitate compliance?*	**Deterrence factors** **9. Risk that any violations of the rules will be reported to the authorities** *Is there a high risk of violations being reported to the authorities, either by members of the target group's community or by the public? Is the target group deterred from noncompliance because they fear they will be complained about or reported if they do not comply?* **10. Risk of inspection** *Is there a low risk of particular businesses being inspected by the regulator, either by a physical inspection or by a records inspection? Do members of the target group perceive themselves as likely to be subject to inspection?* **11. Risk of detection** *Is there a high risk of any violations of the rules being detected if there is an inspection or some other monitoring (such as an audit)? What is the impact of factors such as an inspection only selectively examining records, particular violations being difficult for inspectors to detect or the ease of falsification of records? How does the target group perceive the risk of detection?*
Characteristics and capacities of members of the target population **5. Business model** *Is compliance relevant to the target group's business model or is it an 'afterthought', or even irrelevant?* **6. Knowledge of the rules** *Is the target group aware of their obligations? Do they know the rules that govern the particular activity? Are the rules comprehensible or are they too complex to understand?* **7. Capacity to comply** *Does the target group have the capacity to comply with the rules? Or do they lack the money, time, education or expertise to become aware of their obligations, decide to comply and implement compliance? Do they have good enough management systems to implement compliance?*	**12. Selectivity of inspection and detection by the regulator** *Is the regulator selective in identifying and prioritising targets for inspection? Do some members of the target group perceive themselves as falling outside the priority targets for inspection? Are they aware of how the regulator 'screens' for breaches when inspecting or investigating?* **13. Risk of sanction** *Is there a major risk of a violation, once detected, being sanctioned? Does the regulator have a practice or policy of dismissing charges or not enforcing charges? Does the target group believe that the risk of being sanctioned is low even if they are caught and the breach can be proved?* **14. Severity of sanction** *Does the target group believe that the sanction they will face for a particular violation is severe, that it will be imposed quickly and will have other tangible disadvantages for the person concerned? For example: does the person suffer a loss of reputation from being sanctioned that has a negative impact on their business activities?*

By contemplating the response to some of these questions from a broad, private provider perspective, it appears that this seminal work by Parker and Nielsen was not considered in a review that cost the Australian taxpayer an extraordinary amount of money[134]. While Parker and Nielsen state that not all 14 compliance questions will apply in all situations, on a broad scale, it is possible to consider how such questions could be answered by Australia's VET sector.

For example:

Economic, social and normative factors

Social and Economic Benefits

Does the target group believe that it costs too much time, money, and effort to comply?

Most private providers would argue that it does cost too much time, money and effort to comply in a sector that changes its regulatory response and strategy at the drop of a hat depending on political and media pressure. As Claire Field[135] famously stated recently, 'Governments must commit to long-term national VET policies'. Alarmingly, Claire provides the following analysis:

> Thanks to the NCVER's VET Knowledge Bank we now have data on 21 years of VET reforms.
>
> What the data shows is that governments have made 465 different changes to the VET system in the last 21 years. That's an average of one every two and a half weeks, every year for more than two decades.

134 Based on information from the Australian Government Tenders website, the ASQA Rapid Review cost an amended amount of $224,480 (original amount was $138,270). The implementation of the ASQA rapid Review cost an amended amount of $493,518. ASQA Rapid Review Report - Australian Government *Aus Tender* (Web Page) <https://www.tenders.gov.au/Cn/Show/?Id=03ba8d23-c015-45ea-ba8b-bdc14ce37595>; Implementation of the ASQA Rapid Review - Australian Government *Aus Tender* (Web Page) <https://www.tenders.gov.au/Cn/Show/?Id=280e5ba3-3b1f-4f90-8be5-ee3eb67ad785>.

135 Claire Field, '*The VET Reform Merry-Go-Round*' (Web Page) <https://clairefield.com.au/the-vet-reform-merry-go-round/>.

On this basis, one can clearly appreciate that the Australian VET sector could and should validly argue that it costs too much time, money and effort to comply. In fact, as I write this book, there is yet another movement (or more) encouraging providers to join a new system that does not require ASQA.

Degree of Acceptance of this Regulation

Does the target group agree with how the policy and principles have been put into practice?

As referenced earlier, there were a large number of private providers who invested heavily in becoming 'delegates' and despite many of them having an impeccable regulatory record, their delegate status didn't last long before regulatory change arrived. The whole delegation saga began over a political knee-jerk reaction to a media frenzy and ended much the same way. Given these regulatory reforms have occurred in much the same way, it's not likely that the Vet sector trusts in the process or actually agrees with it. As far as the author is aware, the majority of providers do agree that a regulatory framework is necessary and they agree to being regulated, it is simply the manner in which this takes place that is a serious area of concern for a sector that has endured too much regulatory change in a short period of time. For a system that endures 465 different changes in the last 21 years, an average of one every two and a half weeks, every year for more than two decades is more than most industries would ever face and far more than they should for an efficient regulatory system.

One more...

Respect for the Regulator

Does the target group respect the regulator and how they go about their tasks?

If you read ASQA's rhetoric about its surveys, it will tell you it's doing a great job. If you read their Annual Report, it will tell you they're doing a pretty reasonable job. If you ask the stakeholders of the VET sector if they respect the regulator, you need look no further than ASQA's Rapid Review, the Braithwaite Review or the Joyce Review (as well as a few petitions to Parliament along the way). ASQA is one of the least respected regulators in the history of Australian regulation yet it continues to have millions of dollars thrown at it in an attempt to salvage it. As the following stories will demonstrate, there are more than enough reasons why they are so poorly respected by industry. The question remains though, after more than half a million dollars, how did this get ignored?

In principle, the new regulatory risk framework could be promising however, unless the issues raised previously (at a minimum) and the subjectivity and toxic culture of ASQA is eliminated and trust regained, it is unlikely, in the author's opinion, that this *'revised'* regulatory risk framework will change anything. Time will tell.

The Human Toll

> "Behind every scar is an untold story of survival."
>
> **- Unknown**

On 1 July 2011, ASQA will have been with us for a decade. It's hard to believe that it's been 10 years since that first year where we heard some of the biggest promises and threats this sector has probably ever experienced. For many, it was an opportunity for hope that finally, VET Reform was going to make a difference and the sector would go from strength to strength and finally get back the first-class reputation it had around the world. For others, they would see ASQA's promise of 'closing down as many private RTOs as possible' as one famous ASQA Chief Commissioner once stated, come true.

As part of that journey over the past decade though, I personally have witnessed some truly horrifying stories and I know that there are many more that I'm unaware of. There are also those who are too ashamed or embarrassed to tell their story, although many, many more who are too afraid. In fact, several of the people who have bravely volunteered their journey for this book have done so with a real fear that they will be identified and they will be pursued again. There have been a lot of backwards and forwards moments in the lead up to them telling their story pending legal advice but in the end, they wanted their journey to be on the record so that people know that this really happened and that despite the pretty wallpaper and false facades, there really is a force of destruction behind those walls that is far greater than you ever imagined.

Trauma, Vicarious Trauma, PTSD and Anxiety: More than in the Mind

> "Others will never truly understand your journey."
>
> **- Dr Nicole M Eastman**

Dr Gail Crossley-Craven (Dr CC)

We change our world by changing and developing ourselves. With a rich background both experientially and educationally speaking, and qualifications in education, business and mental health, I bring an eclectic wealth of expertise from the educational, counselling and business arenas. There is a common thread that I've found that weaves its way through each of these disciplines; people are uniquely individual. Life's experiences affect each of us differently which means that some people can develop illnesses as a result of the way they react and cope with situations whereas other people can be barely affected by the same situations. It could be said that it's all in the mind and it depends on the attitude and personality of the person as to if "the glass is half full or half empty". In part, I guess this saying has some validity, nonetheless, there are people who are genuinely suffering and ill from the effects of trauma, vicarious trauma, PTSD and anxiety. For these people, all aspects of life can be affected and the severity of that influence is dependent on the unique individuality of the person affected and the measures that are employed to address trauma, vicarious trauma, PTSD and anxiety.

Trauma

> **"When fear is the dominant emotion in a flashback, the person feels extremely anxious, panicky, or even suicidal."**
>
> **- Pete Walker**

What is Trauma?

A trauma can be any distressing or upsetting event which include accidents, disasters or being hurt deliberately by other people. The trauma can be experienced by the individual person or it can be observed or overheard; the latter is vicarious trauma and can be equally problematic as if the trauma was experienced first-hand. Traumatic experiences can be overwhelming, threatening, frightening or out of our control. While some traumas are isolated one-off events that are not expected, other traumas are frightening as they are expected, anticipated and dreaded. Some careers expose people to trauma in the daily routine of the job, for example defence or emergency service personnel can experience or witness distressing events ongoing. It is normal to feel overwhelmed when confronted by a shocking experience however, people react differently because of natural coping abilities. Recovery time is very individual with some people requiring intervention.

Reactions to Trauma

Sadly, trauma is commonly experienced. Post-trauma symptoms can be physically and emotionally powerful and can feel particularly disturbing when the affected person does not understand why it's happening. Reactions to trauma can be linked as well as escalate to other reactions. Re-experiencing or re-living the traumatic experience can be equally confronting as the trauma itself when the person experiences repeated memories of the event unexpectedly. These unwanted memories where it can feel as though the trauma is happening again are commonly known as flashbacks and the physical reactions associated with them are as real as when they first occurred. Trauma memories are vivid and re-experienced in any of our senses of sight, sound, smell, taste or touch. Feelings of fear and anxiety can be natural and helpful responses to threatening situations and can continue over a period of time after the trauma. This increased arousal is not only a reminder of the trauma, but it can also be due to unexpected triggers which instil feelings of, and expresses itself as jumpiness, difficulty to concentrate, affecting sleep leaving the person exhausted and restless.

Further physical sensations might be nausea, fatigue, headaches or change in appetite. Many people use avoidance of people, places or situations that remind them of traumatic experiences to help manage their upset as this is the mind's way of avoiding strong feelings. This avoidance can be a conscious or a subconscious strategy. After experiencing traumatic events, a person's perspective of themselves and their surroundings changes dramatically. These changes in beliefs could include finding the world a more threatening place, blaming themselves, difficulty in trusting people which can impact on personal and professional relationships, disillusioned with life and its meaning, concern of losing control and questioning normal thought processes.

Trauma can expose people to many strong emotions such as anger and irritability often due to being stressed and insufficient sleep. It is common for people to blame themselves for their action or inaction and think that they will be judged by others which can lead to guilt and shame. Grief and depression can follow the experience of loss and feeling sad about the changes which have occurred.

Dissociative reactions are often associated with experiencing trauma as well as during periods of stress and high anxiety. Dissociation is a defence mechanism that can assist people to survive imminent threats. During trauma, people have automatic coping strategies associated with the sympathetic and parasympathetic systems. The 'freeze', 'flight' and 'fight' responses are associated with activity of the sympathetic branch of the autonomic nervous system whereas, the 'fright', 'flag' and 'faint' responses are associated with activity of the parasympathetic branch of the autonomic nervous system.

These six responses are further explained for a deeper understanding of what happens to a traumatised person at the time of the traumatic experience and at later times in their life. As an initial response to something scary, the freeze response is being on guard, watchful and ready to respond. The person's heart rate decreases and there is less movement as staying still reduces the chances of being seen to allow more time to assess the situation.

When something is perceived as a major threat, the flight response is an attempt to flee, escape or avoid a situation that could be threatening. The heart beats faster and the person breathes quicker to support the person's escape from the danger with little effort. However, when something is perceived as a major threat, yet escape is not possible, the fight response attempts to confront or overcome the person's opponent.

Similar to the physical response of flight, the fast beating of the heart and quicker breathing, reduces awareness of pain which makes the person appear more ready to 'win' making the eminent danger dissipate or allow the person to escape the danger. The fright response renders the person unable to move or scream as they are engulfed with fear which occurs when the perpetrator is close, and it is not possible to escape from the danger. The person is very physically activated with the heart beating faster, breathing quicker thus reducing the awareness of pain and suppressing anger. This response is often common in physical assault as submission can reduce perpetrator violence; 'holding still' can reduce the risk of damage; 'playing dead' can increase the chance of escape.

The flag and faint responses result from extreme trauma and are a result of or can produce unresponsive immobility and loss of consciousness. If a trauma is prolonged and there are no immediate opportunities to escape, exposure to such situations trigger a 'disgust' reaction whereby the body becomes unresponsive and immobile.

The surroundings might 'fade' along with any emotions or the situation might feel 'unreal' and the person's body may feel unresponsive so as to protect itself against heart failure during an inescapable attack.

When experiencing the freeze, flight, or fight stages, people have a sense of what is happening which is helpful, enabling them to consider possible options out of the threatening situation. However, people who experience the fright, flag, or faint stages tend to disassociate as they feel powerless to help themselves in the traumatic situation. It is thought that dissociation is a survival response when no other options are available.

The Impact of Traumatic Stress on Workers and Organisations

Psychologically traumatic workplace events are commonly known as critical incidents and occur in various work environments and workgroups in specific industries that are vulnerable to multiple incidents. These events include, but are not limited to, workplace intimidation and bullying, discrimination and inequity, workplace harassment and assault, workplace accidents and deaths, workplace audits and significant workplace changes without notice. It is interesting to note that even with legislation, policies and procedures, critical incidents still commonly occur. Workers who are exposed to critical incidents frequently experience emotional, cognitive and behavioural symptoms that compromise functioning in the workplace. Symptoms can include restlessness, insomnia, anxiety, detachment, intrusive images, poor concentration, social withdrawal or hypervigilance.

Within any workplace, a small percentage of workers will display symptom clusters of sufficient significance and duration to suffice the criteria for acute stress disorder (ASD) or a post-traumatic stress disorder (PTSD) diagnosis, with the majority of workers displaying higher than normal stress responses. Even when no symptoms are evident, problematic patterns can emerge in the workplace as absenteeism, poor attention at work (attending work, but in a highly distracted state), job avoidance, increased conflicts, accidents or loss of motivation. This not only indicates human resource wellbeing issues, but also results in loss of productivity and, in turn, decreased profitability for the organisation. Employees may socially isolate to avoid attention or discussing the stressful incident.

Productivity and employee motivation decreases due to anxiety, fear, sadness and dissociative symptoms impairing the employee's cognitive functioning and work skills.

Arousal symptoms will often enhance the worker's difficulties with sleep, resulting in poor concentration, irritability with peers, tardiness and absenteeism. As the workplace is a constant reminder of the event, an employee may become distressed at the thought of physically going to the workplace each day thus creating more anxiety. The employer might observe the worker as being distracted or unmotivated which can lead to workplace disruptions through sick leave, missed deadlines, compromised work quality, worker conflicts and decreased productivity. Furthermore, the employer is at financial risk of increased worker compensation claims, increased insurance claims or legal liability. Due to the operational, wellbeing and financial risks of traumatic stress from critical incidents, human resource practitioners develop and implement employee assistance programs (EAPs) and maintain pre-incident and post-incident procedures to mitigate risks and guide the organisation through critical incidents.

Post-Traumatic Stress Disorder (PTSD)

What is PTSD?

Many people will experience trauma during their lifespan and over time; most people recover from the traumatic experiences without requiring professional assistance. However, for the remaining people who have been significantly affected by trauma, the effects of the trauma last much longer and can develop a condition called post-traumatic stress disorder (PTSD). PTSD is a serious condition that can develop after a person experiences or witnesses an extremely traumatic event.

It is believed that approximately 5% of people will experience PTSD yearly in Australia. Even though being affected by traumatic experiences is normal, the person affected might feel shocked, scared, guilty, ashamed, angry, vulnerable or numb. However, the effects of trauma can last and may develop into PTSD which should only be diagnosed by a mental health professional or a doctor.

PTSD is caused primarily from being exposed to traumatic, life-threatening or frightening events. Not every person who experiences trauma develops PTSD; it depends on several factors. Therapists have concluded that people who have a high level of social support following a trauma are less likely to develop PTSD as the affected person uses their social network as a 'protective shield'. Memories in PTSD are more vivid and intense than those of regular events. The person's thinking replays the trauma as if it is happening again even though years might have passed.

It is believed that the brain encodes, stores, and retrieves trauma memories which means that some people are more likely to develop PTSD depending on their brain's encoding process. Some evidence suggests that genetic and biological factors can influence who develops PTSD following a trauma as the hippocampus is believed to influence whether memories of the trauma cause the development of PTSD.

Reactions to PTSD

People who develop PTSD experience vivid unwanted memories of the trauma, so much so that it can feel that the person is in the trauma in the present moment. Consequently, people with PTSD often feel nervous and experience a heightened awareness of danger. Some people can suffer vicarious trauma from witnessing or reading about other people's trauma which can develop the symptoms of PTSD. Generally, there are three main categories of symptoms which include intrusive, arousal and avoidance. Intrusive symptoms for people with PTSD include flashbacks and nightmares about the trauma which can be triggered by specific situations or discussions that are reminiscent of the trauma prompting them to relive it. People with PTSD may experience heightened tension and awareness of danger which is termed 'hyperarousal' and can present as insomnia, lack of concentration, ongoing fear or being easily startled.

Additionally, people with PTSD might dismiss their feelings about the trauma and shun people or situations that remind them of the traumatic experience. Loss of interest in enjoyable activities, feeling depressed, guilty or worried is common to feel along with being emotionally numb and aloof from friends and family.

It is a natural response to avoid things that are anxiety provoking and upsetting however, avoidance does not help PTSD long term. By avoiding memories of the trauma, the trauma itself stays 'unprocessed'. Therefore, nothing changes which leads to more negative beliefs. The misuse of alcohol and/or other substances to block out memories or feelings is employed by some people with PTSD which can lead to other conditions, illnesses and concerns. Although it can seem beneficial not to talk about what happened, avoidance is unhelpful on PTSD symptoms.

There are some unique qualities of the trauma memories of people who have PTSD. Feeling the trauma is happening in the present moment can be intrusive and involuntary as it is unexpected, unwanted and easily triggered by surroundings. The memories can be fragmented, vivid and detailed and prompted by the senses of sight, sound, touch, smell and taste. It is thought that if the brain has not had a chance to 'process' and store them properly at the time of the trauma, the person might continue to suffer from re-experiencing symptoms until the brain has completed 'processing' the trauma memories.

PTSD in the Workplace

People with PTSD may show various symptoms at work. These could include but are not limited to:

- Memory problems and difficulty retaining information,
- Lack of concentration on tasks and conversations,
- Fear and anxiety,
- Physical difficulties in performing the tasks of the job,
- Poor relationships with co-workers and management,
- Unreasonable reactions to situations that trigger memories,
- Absenteeism and lateness,
- Fatigue and lethargy,
- Panic attacks.

Strategies for Managing a Worker with PTSD

It is important to be flexible in managing a worker with PTSD. Like most situations, the more knowledge and information an employer has, the more assistance can be provided to retain a valuable worker for the benefit of the organisation and the individual. Communication is key and is often underestimated. Open communication is critical as people with PTSD may feel embarrassed to ask for assistance and support. Empathic listening gives the worker an opportunity to discuss any concerns which can be therapeutic in itself. If the worker is more comfortable communicating in writing, secure email invites openness and provides documentation of any concerns that the organisation needs to address. Inviting conversation about the changes that could be made to improve the work environment can be the catalyst for minimising future stress in the workplace.

Strategies to handle various issues and PTSD symptoms can be implemented to minimise distress to the affected worker, maintain workplace harmony and sustain productivity. An environmental analysis will identify possible triggers in the workplace that might cause flashbacks or other negative reactions.

If the worker experiences difficulty in concentrating, a quiet part of the office with minimal distractions can provide the worker with a more suitable workplace environment. Noise-cancelling headphones with the option to listen to white noise or soothing music while working can assist people with PTSD to focus with a relaxed headspace. Additionally, if participation in meetings is an integral part of the role, providing a note taker can alleviate added pressure to multitask when concentration can be a challenge. The worker is then able to focus only on what is happening in the meeting and revisit the minutes of the meeting at a later time.

As poor memory can be symptomatic of PTSD, written instructions for each task and daily lists can prompt the worker without workplace pressure. Electronic reminders to signal approaching deadlines are welcomed as there is less information that needs to be stored at the forefront of the worker's mind. To manage projects in a timely manner, large tasks can be broken into incremental goals. Checklists provide a means for a sense of achievement and increase the motivation and job satisfaction of the worker. Workplace mentors are a valuable asset for support and encouragement for all workers but particularly those with PTSD, as it allows for one-to-one discussions regarding their progress towards any assigned goals. To reduce pressure on workers with PTSD, breaks from work or extended work hours may allow for the necessary tasks to be accomplished. Positive reinforcement and constructive feedback engage workers and allows the consideration of possible job restructuring.

Where it exists, the organisation's EAP might need to be adjusted to reflect the day-to-day operations to accommodate counselling sessions within work time. If a worker with PTSD is startled easily, the office or desk might need to be moved to where they can see people approaching them. A flexible work schedule can minimise absenteeism and lateness as well as allowing them to work outside the regular hours if appointments and counselling sessions are conducted during work time. Raising awareness of PTSD and its symptoms in the workplace as part of a more comprehensive human resources program is likely to encourage workplace consideration and compassion rather than promote ostracization and discrimination. Being sensitive to all colleagues' needs can foster a better understanding of what workers might be going through.

Anxiety

What is Anxiety?

Anxiety is an unpleasant and uncomfortable feeling which could present in the form of worry, apprehension, uneasiness or all of these reactions and can be triggered in anticipation of something that is perceived as being a threat. Anxiety disorders are on the increase throughout the world due to the uncertainty, unknown and the stresses of everyday life. Unfortunately, some people who are experiencing and suffering from anxiety are too reserved to seek professional assistance for fear of being labelled or perceived 'damaged'. Most anxiety disorders present developmental symptoms in people between the ages of 5 and 24 and, if discovered early, can be treated effectively.

The cause of anxiety is dependent on the type of anxiety diagnosed. The thought processes and routines that create anxiety trigger unpleasant feelings within the affected person who often implements avoidance tactics. Both external and internal factors influence thought processes. These factors include:

- Genetics whereby a family history of anxiety disorders will have a higher chance for the family members to suffer anxiety due to the genes that are crucial to stress regulation and management of neurotransmitter systems.
- Environmental factors which affect our perspectives at work, relationships and family life, financial considerations and socio-economic issues.
- Substance use, misuse and dependence on illicit drugs, prescribed drugs and/or alcohol can cause anxiety or panic attacks and can amplify the effects.
- Brain chemical deficiencies and misalignments of hormonal and electrical signals may cause anxiety disorders.

- Medical factors such as medication, illnesses, stress from diseases/surgery of the individual or someone close (vicarious anxiety) are contributing factors to anxiety.

Reactions to Anxiety

The body and mind reactions are very similar to fear as to anxiety because fear and anxiety are interlinked even though there are subtle differences. Fear is an emotional response to specifics that might be linked to traumatic, identifiable situations from the past whereas anxiety is a reaction to an undetermined threat which is vague and undefined. By understanding the difference between fear and anxiety, an accurate diagnosis and effective treatment plan can be implemented for the affected person.

Anxiety disorders are considered to be a prolonged mental condition however, the emotional effects will often present as physical disturbances. Emotional symptoms of anxiety might include but are not limited to uneasiness, worry, feeling on edge, irritability, lack of concentration, depersonalisation, loss of control in thinking, feeling things are unreal and a feeling of impending doom. Physical symptoms of anxiety might include but are not limited to insomnia and on-going sleep disturbances, headaches, sweating or chills, muscle tension, quickening of heart rate, changes in breathing, ringing in ears, nausea and dizziness. It is important to remember that anxiety on its own is not physically harmful. However, if left untreated, physical and mental health problems can occur and quality of life can be inhibited.

What can be done?

Anxiety is a way to recognise that a person is under too much stress. It is important to be aware of the body's feelings and behaviours which disrupt the person's life so as to understand the changes that potentially could manifest into significant anxiety disorders. Prevention is always more desirable than the necessity to treat a disorder.

A simple and cost-effective method to manage anxiety is the practice of mindfulness and meditation; however, it should be emphasised that mindfulness and meditation are not cure-alls. They do not work for everyone, but they can allow the person to create a space between them and the cause of the anxiety. When a person creates a habit and patterns of specific reactivity, the tendency can create more distress which is why mindfulness is an important reaction rather than reacting with unawareness.

The main aim of meditation is not to dismiss any anxiety that the person may feel, but instead be more in tune with how they are feeling and what is happening in that moment. This results in anxiety reduction as meditation helps the brain to relax which prevents the person from becoming lost in their thoughts leading to feeling overwhelmed. Meditation helps deal with the unwarranted attention on the slew of worries.

Mindfulness helps the person to shift from negative preoccupations to an appreciation of being in the moment and having a larger perspective on life. The person allows themselves to feel and acknowledge their concerns, painful memories and other negative feelings without scrutinising or inviting them. This presence and openness of thought allows the person to safely realise the cause of their stress then helps them develop a sense of freedom and space naturally so that the anxiety does not consume them.

Cognitive Behavioural Therapy (CBT) focuses on the manner in which a person's thoughts, beliefs and attitudes affect their feelings and behaviours which can reduce stress thus help with anxiety disorders. CBT treatments aim to change a person's thinking patterns so that they can recognise their distortions in thinking, understand the behaviour and motivation of others, use a variety of problem-solving skills to manage difficult situations which, in turn, develops self-confidence in their own abilities. The focus of CBT is what is currently happening in the person's life rather than dwelling and ruminating on what has happened in the past. CBT is very structured as clients are encouraged to break down the thoughts, feelings and behaviours that are inhibiting them so that they can learn and apply skills and strategies in their everyday life to increase their coping mechanisms. Even though CBT is effective for many people, highly complex mental health issues and learning difficulties can pose problems as CBT is primarily focused on the client's ability to effect change in themselves and some clients find the focus too narrow.

However, it should be noted that cognitive restructuring in CBT can be effective as the person is encouraged to challenge negative thinking patterns that contribute to anxiety and replace them with more positive and realistic thoughts.

Some people have anxiety disorders with severe symptoms which can be treated through the use of medications in conjunction with other therapies such as CBT. To treat the psychological and physical symptoms of anxiety disorders, there are four main types of medications which include the non-habit-forming selective serotonin reuptake inhibitors (SSRIs), serotonin-norepinephrine reuptake inhibitors (SNRIs), tricyclic antidepressants (TCAs), and benzodiazepines which are recognised to have the potential of being addictive.

Alternative medications and supplements are not intended to be a substitute for prescribed medications however, they can be helpful in treating anxiety disorders. Important nutrients may be useful to obtain relief and manage anxiety symptoms; these supplements include Vitamin A, Vitamin B complex, Vitamin C, Vitamin D, Vitamin E, Fish Oil and magnesium. Furthermore, some herbs contain phytochemicals which might relieve some anxiety symptoms and come as an extract, tea, capsule or tincture. As with all medications and supplements, it is important and advised that a professional practitioner be consulted prior to treating the person. Some medications should not be taken in combination with some herbs, alternative medications and supplements as they have an adverse effect. Self-diagnosis, self-treatment and self-medication is not advisable.

Allied practices and techniques such as acupuncture, massage, yoga, exercise and a balanced diet, aromatherapy, acupressure, and art/light/music/play/journaling therapies to name a few, can also help alleviate the symptoms of anxiety.

Concluding Thoughts

Trauma, vicarious trauma, PTSD and anxiety affect people who are exposed to critical incidents and experiences which affect them emotionally, cognitively and behaviourally. Without recognition and treatment, the affected person's occupational and personal functioning can be significantly compromised. The effects of trauma, vicarious trauma, PTSD and anxiety is not a sign of weakness but rather the development of PTSD is closely connected to the person's neurobiology and occurs from the way the human mind processes memories. For these people, all aspects of life can be affected dependent on the unique individuality of the person. Trauma, vicarious trauma, PTSD and anxiety is far more than just being 'all in the mind'.

About the Author

Dr Gail Crossley-Craven owns and manages her own practice where she consults, coaches, counsels and mentors clients. She has clients throughout Australia and has worked with clients in Sri Lanka, Vietnam, Taiwan, Malaysia, America, UK and the Middle East. Gail is passionate about assisting people in reaching their personal and professional true potential with a transformational approach that is thought provoking and awakening.

"Everyone needs a Dr CC!" www.drcc.com.au (+61) 0419 764 796.

References

- American Psychiatric Association, DSM-5 Task Force. (2013). *Diagnostic and statistical manual of mental disorders: DSM-5TM* (5th ed.). American Psychiatric Publishing, Inc.
- Bolton, E., Holohan, D.R., King, L.A. (2004). Acute and Post-Traumatic Stress Disorder. In: Thomas JC, Hersen M, eds. *Psychopathology in the workplace: Recognition and adaptation.* New York, Brunner-Routledge.
- Brewin, C.R., Cloitre, M., Hyland, P., Shevlin, M., Maercker, A., Bryant, R.A., & Somasundaram, D. (2017). A review of current evidence regarding the ICD-11 proposals for diagnosing PTSD and complex PTSD. *Clinical Psychology Review*, 58, 1-15.
- Ehlers, A., & Clark, D.M. (2000). A cognitive model of posttraumatic stress disorder. *Behaviour Research and Therapy*, 38(4), 319-345.
- Grey, N., Young, K., & Holmes, E. (2002). Cognitive restructuring within reliving: A treatment for peritraumatic emotional "hotspots" in posttraumatic stress disorder. *Behavioural and Cognitive Psychotherapy,* 30(1), 37-56.
- Herman, J.L. (1992). Complex PTSD: A syndrome in survivors of prolonged and repeated trauma. *Journal of Traumatic Stress*, 5(3), 377-391.
- Howlett, S.L., and Collins, A. (2014). Vicarious Traumatisation: Risk and Resilience Among Crisis Support Volunteers in a Community Organisation. *South African Journal of Psychology* 44 (2), 180–190.
- Kahneman, D., & Egan, P. (2011). *Thinking, fast and slow*. New York: Farrar, Straus and Giroux.
- Lobban, F., & Barrowclough, C. (2016). An interpersonal CBT framework for involving relatives in interventions for psychosis:

evidence base and clinical implications. *Cognitive Therapy and Research*, 40(2), 198-215.

- MacLeod, C., & Mathews, A. (2012). Cognitive bias modification approaches to anxiety. *Annual Review of Clinical Psychology*, 8, 189-217.
- Robjant, K., & Fazel, M. (2010). The emerging evidence for narrative exposure therapy: A review. *Clinical Psychology Review*, 30(8), 1030-1039.
- Schauer, M., & Elbert, T. (2010). Dissociation following traumatic stress. *Journal of Psychology*, 218, 109-127.
- Shevlin, S., Hyland, P., Roberts, N.P., Bisson, J.I., Brewin, C.R., & Cloitre, M. (2018). A psychometric assessment of disturbances in self-organization symptom indicators for ICD-11 complex PTSD using the International Trauma Questionnaire. *European Journal of Psychotraumatology*, 9.
- Spence, J., Titov, N., Johnston, L., Jones, M.P., Dear, B.F., & Solley, K. (2014). Internet-based trauma-focused cognitive behavioural therapy for PTSD with and without exposure components: a randomised controlled trial. *Journal of Affective Disorders*, 162, 73-80.
- Watkins, L.E., Sprang, K.R., & Rothbaum, B. (2018). Treating PTSD: a review of evidence-based psychotherapy interventions. *Frontiers in Behavioral Neuroscience*, 12, 258.
- Whalley, M.G., Kroes, M.C., Huntley, Z., Rugg, M.D., Davis, S.W., & Brewin, C.R. (2013). An fMRI investigation of posttraumatic flashbacks. *Brain and Cognition*, 81(1), 151-159.
- Zalta, A.K., Gillihan, S.J., Fisher, A.J., Mintz, J., McLean, C.P., Yehuda, R., & Foa, E.B. (2014). Change in negative cognitions associated with PTSD predicts symptom reduction in prolonged exposure. *Journal of Consulting and Clinical Psychology*, 82(1), 171.

Possible Support Contacts

- **Heads Up** (www.headsup.org.au)

  Heads Up supports Australian businesses to create more mentally healthy workplaces.

- **The Mentally Healthy Workplace Alliance** (www.workplacementalhealth.com.au)

  A national approach by business, community and government to encourage Australian workplaces to become mentally healthy for the benefit of the whole community and businesses, big and small.

- **Beyondblue** (www.beyondblue.org.au)

  Information about anxiety, depression and suicide prevention, or seek support.

The Human Toll: Stories from Victims of ASQA's Regulatory Practices

> *"We realise the importance of our voices only when we are silenced."*
> **- Malala Yousafzai**

Disclaimer

The author provides notice that the stories that follow have been provided by victims of ASQA's regulatory behaviour.

In some cases, the victims have provided the stories themselves already written and, in other cases, interviews were conducted with the victim who detailed their experience verbally to the author.

In all cases, the stories below have been reviewed and approved by the victim for publication.

All stories were collected and shared under a Collaboration Agreement where the ASQA victim declared the facts of their stories and their experiences to be true.

The author of the book has not verified any facts, albeit, in some cases, the author was already aware of the experiences of these collaborators through professional interactions.

The important thing to remember is that these stories and experiences are being shared as victim testimonies. These stories are how these victims perceived their story to take place and the experiences and emotions that they went through and, in most cases, continue to go through.

That ASQA may have a different perception to their behaviour or the facts that led to the decisions that ultimately impacted these people's lives so greatly, while also important, is not really the focus of those sharing their stories.

The focus of course is that it doesn't matter whether the RTO was actually meeting its regulatory obligations, the focus is on the fact that:

1. Even the regulator has legal requirements it must abide by in executing its regulatory functions;
2. Each RTO and person affected was entitled by law to receive natural justice and to experience procedural fairness at every stage of their ASQA journey;
3. That there are model litigant obligations that <u>MUST</u> be followed by all Commonwealth lawyers, even at the AAT;
4. When the stakes are so high for a business, the regulator MUST only use qualified auditors and technical experts;
5. Audits should not commence while there is a conflict of interest that is not being appropriately managed;
6. The Commonwealth MUST be mindful of the consequences of their abrupt policy changes;
7. All RTOs are workplaces and ASQA auditors are in a workplace. Albeit, this needs to be tested from a legal perspective, if the auditors' workplace is considered to include the RTO, there needs to be recognition of workplace bullying and harassment laws and the accountability for breaches of this legislation if it applies. Likewise, if an RTO perceives that it is being bullied and harassed by ASQA auditors, it should be able to ask the auditor to leave the premises and exercise any other rights that they would normally have under relevant legislation. Furthermore,

there should not EVER be a negative consequence (such as, but not limited to vengeance or coming back for another bite at the cherry) for exercising your legal rights in this regard.

Most importantly however, the focus of sharing these stories is on the fact that all of these people are human beings. They deserve to be treated in an empathetic way. Everyone has inherent biases, admit to them and manage them. ASQA staff might benefit from training in being more sensitive to other people. Sensitivity training in this context is focused on making employees aware of their attitudes and behaviour toward others. Other forms of training that should be considered on an ongoing basis are around ethical decision-making, identifying bias, cultural sensitivity training (there has long been a feeling by many in the VET sector that ASQA as an agency is racist) and training in microaggression in the workplace.

According to Dr Derald W Sue from Columbia University[136] microaggressions can be perceived as everyday verbal, non-verbal slights, snubs or insults, whether intentional or unintentional, that communicate hostile, derogatory or negative messages to people based solely upon being members of a marginalised group.

136 Dr Derald W Sue is a university Professor at the University of Columbia who has published several books on microaggressions. Dr Derald Sue has put together a YouTube video explaining microaggression in everyday life at the following link <https://youtu.be/BJL2P0JsAS4>.

#1 Philippa's Story

> "They tell lies, and we're too scared to speak the truth out loud."
>
> **- Philippa**

Writer Note: All names and locations have been changed to protect the affected parties.

People in the Story

- **Philippa** - CEO of the RTO;
- **Vince** - ASQA auditor;
- **Amanda** - Contract Consultant who worked for a State regulator;
- **Kate** - Consultant for the CRICOS application;
- **Nadine** - One of the country's biggest experts in this industry who was a trainer and assessor with the college;
- **John** - Innovation College of Australia Staff Member assisting with the closure;
- **Shadow College** - one of the colleges that agreed to take students as part of the managed closure;
- **Julie** - the trainer who was on prolonged worker's compensation; and
- **India** - the final Consultant who assisted with the managed closure.

Complete Chaos & Destruction

This is the story of a multiple award-winning college in Australia with specialist trainers and the passion of one woman to help underprivileged people have a better life for themselves and their children. Originally registered in 2005, this college was one of the standout, best practice innovators in its State. It was widely renowned by the State regulator and funding bodies as being an outstanding provider. This college celebrated for providing an outstanding contribution to the community, even won awards for innovation in VET in Schools, providing those students who struggled with mainstream education models a chance at completing their year 11 and 12 studies with a qualification that would help them become employable the most they left school in areas of severe skill shortage.

Through its success, the college grew significantly in its early years and to support their ongoing commitment to quality and compliance, they engaged a Consultant who was also an auditor for the State regulator at that time. The Consultant remained with the company for five years as a contractor, with the purpose of ensuring that the College remained compliant with its registration and funding obligations. After a couple of years of continued, sustained growth, the college owner decided it was capable of duplicating its offering in other locations that have the same or similar community needs. Its staff had also grown to include a Compliance Manager, internal accountant, IT Manager and was still outsourcing independent compliance advice from its contractor Consultant and an external accounting company.

They applied for VET FEE-Help like many of their competitors and this only cemented their value as a high-value, award-winning provider making a difference in the community, giving those who would normally not get a chance, the opportunity to turn their lives around.

Around this time, the success of the college was substantial. It had gone from being a small niche provider to being able to roll out some of the most specialist, award-winning courses the industry had seen. They had brilliant employment outcomes, students were extremely satisfied and industry, even happier. In the opinion of industry, this college was providing graduates that were far more skilled and had far better knowledge than the majority of those already working in that industry. The contractor compliance Consultant, let's call her "Amanda", suggested that it was time for the RTO to move away from being an RTO under State regulation and to transition to ASQA. They added some new specialist qualifications to their scope of registration and they were notified of a concurrent re-registration audit.

They passed their re-registration audit without any hiccups and the amendment to scope was also granted. Around this time, they also had campus launches occurring in the new delivery location areas. After securing leases and fitting out the premises as a simulated environment in at least 3 other locations around the State (with a total investment value of several million dollars), the college received an offer to purchase and take over the RTO for $A5 million. A Heads of Agreement was finalised, deposits paid and, pursuant to the agreement, another campus opened in the outer suburbs of Western Australia.

Later that year, the gradual, slow death and ultimate culling of the VET FEE-Help program began to take place. Until early February that year, the RTO could do nothing wrong and was widely respected, even by its competitors, for the quality of its graduates and the expertise of its staff. Then suddenly, there was a 50% reduction in all VET FEE-Help funded places, the college was required to make five staff redundant, restructure classes, rosters, changes to the business model and every facet of the business were inevitable.

Early the following year, ASQA changed its audit model. There had been an increase in student complaints around the sector amid concerns of what was now nationally known to be the '*VET FEE Help rorts*' and while Philippa's college had never had so much of a whisper of a complaint, Philippa, the owner of the college was encouraged by the fact that they had won so many awards, had great teaching staff and the feedback from industry about their programs was full of praise. The company owner, Philippa, felt very comfortable as she felt she had engaged the right people and was taking what appeared to be good business advice from her external accountants and contractor compliance Consultant Amanda.

A few months later, an ASQA auditor, let's call him "Vince", contacts Philippa and provides confirmation of new audit arrangements. Around this time, Philippa engaged another Consultant, let's call her "Kate") to help establish the college as a CRICOS provider. The CRICOS application was finalised and submitted by Kate while the college staff prepared for the audit.

The contract Consultant, Amanda, spent more time and hours helping to review and make sure that everything was still compliant and to provide some pre-audit assistance to gather evidence requested by the ASQA auditor.

ASQA's auditor, Vince, requested evidence for a training product that the college was not delivering. The training package had recently had an upgrade and this particular qualification, being an equivalent qualification, was an automatic update to the college's scope of registration. The qualification was subject to an 18-month transition period and we were only just four months into that transition when Vince requested the evidence. On the day of the audit, the ASQA auditor Vince (who had conducted the audit alone) appeared insistent that he was there to make the life of the college difficult. He said that there had been a number of complaints about the college and some of its staff. After the site visit, a college staff member went to the cafe next door to get a coffee after what was a stressful time with Vince. When the staff member arrived in the café, the owner told the staff member that there were a group of our students in the café talking with a man and yelling and screaming. The café owner said he had to ask them to leave because they were making so much noise and scaring away his customers.

I also spoke with Vince when he called me to confirm that he had received confirmation in writing that we were relinquishing our registration.

Immediately after he appeared to call one of the students who was downstairs and suddenly a big commotion started and she was yelling out things to the effect of 'They're closed! We did it!'. It later became known to us that there was something untoward going on in the café next door to the college the day of the audit and we have reason to believe it may have been Vince talking with the students in the café. We believe it was Vince who was leading a group discussion with the students before they dispersed when the café's management asked them to leave.

The college had arranged for an expert from the 'specialist'[137] industry to come and do some guest speaking to the classes about different opportunities in the industry. A couple of days later, Vince was emailing management asking for the experts TAE40110 Certificate IV in Training and Assessment[138] and other credentials. One of the consultants "Amanda" working with us decided the right thing to do was to lodge a formal complaint with ASQA, this behaviour was unacceptable and needed to be accounted for.

Like many colleges at that time, there were also a number of colleges who, as a result of redundancies due to the reduction in funding available under VET FEE Help were starting to field complaints from staff and workers compensation claims for stress. This college was no different.

It had one staff member who was deliberately abusing the system and claiming workers compensation for stress while she was still working at

137 The industry area is too niche to name properly and so the term 'specialist' is provided to protect all parties

138 Which was current at that time.

other providers and doing the odd client from home. This particular staff member, let's call her Julie, was very disgruntled about the fact that some staff had managed to keep their jobs at this college but she was likely going to lose her job. So, she lodged a formal complaint with ASQA (the only reason we know is because she told us) and went on stress leave knowing that she couldn't be made redundant or terminated while on workers compensation.

A few weeks later, the college received its audit report and less than a week later, received another 5 complaints according to Vince (the auditor). By this time, Philippa realised there was something seriously wrong, she didn't understand what was going on. Nobody had ever lodged a complaint with her college. Students appeared to be happy, most staff were happy and industry were definitely happy. Nonetheless, Philippa began calling around looking for legal advice and an expert in this area. She'd never experienced anything like it so decided she needed help. She contacted multiple solicitors, all of them were contracted to ASQA in some capacity and therefore, presenting a conflict of interest. She eventually engaged a high-end law firm and was required to place a minimum of $A10K in their trust account.

The Consultants were still allegedly supporting her to provide a response to the audit findings. One Consultant (the one who was the auditor for the State regulator, Amanda), had been supporting management but it was becoming clear, her eyes were not focused on the RTO.

By now, it was also the end of the financial year, a particularly busy time for this type of RTO. They also had 2 partnership offers for the college with RTOs with similar qualifications; one at $A2.5 million and the other at $A2 million. These partnership offers were effectively to share facilities and resources across Australia.

Suddenly, more complaints started coming in, this time from the Department of Education. It seemed that ASQA had relayed their concerns to the Department and now they too were asking a lot of questions about exactly the same students that Vince had interviewed in the cafe and taken statements from. The original Consultant Amanda was now finalising and reviewing the college's response to ASQA and strangely, started following up her invoice. The college had never had payment problems and therefore was no reason for her to be questioning this. It would later become apparent that she was asking for her invoice to be paid because she received a tip-off that the RTO was being cancelled.

Around this time, the college's accounting firm was engaged to prepare the financials for the 2017 VET FEE Help program. In accordance with the program's contractual requirements, the accounting firm was required to prepare annual audited financial accounts/statements for review and approval by the Department. This cost the college a significant amount of money which ultimately, Philippa was required to personally pay back to the accounting firm. This is despite the fact that there were clear, fundamental errors in the accounts that the accounting firm submitted the financials without Philippa's consent.

Philippa had been trying to arrange a meeting with the principal accountant to discuss her concerns however, the firm was becoming frustrated and hit enter on the submission before obtaining her final approval. Furthermore, not only was this without Philippa's approval, but they unlawfully pressed enter on her behalf. They (the accounting firm) were only supposed to upload the financials and it was incumbent upon Philippa to hit send. Unfortunately, the financial information was ultimately submitted by the accounting firm before Philippa had a chance to review and approve it. In the liquidation of the company, she was still required to pay out a substantial sum as a personal guarantee, she felt completely betrayed by the accounting firm.

The other Consultant Kate and the lawyer worked closely with Philippa to understand the extent of her recommendations and findings. Philippa contacted another Consulting company at this stage as she was losing confidence in those around her. This consulting company was also not available so she was referred elsewhere. She engaged that Consultant, let's call her "India", after speaking with her. What made it worse at this time was that the original consultant, Amanda, suddenly became unavailable and booked out for the next 3 months. To this day she still finds that incredibly strange.

With a new advisory team in place, we began looking forward, responding to the audit report and managing the complaints. There were many long days and nights, a lot of questions and even more concern that maybe I wasn't doing the right thing, I didn't know who to trust anymore.

Students started bringing lawyers to the college with letters that had clearly been drafted by someone with intimate knowledge of the situation, demanding full refunds of their qualifications even though for many, they had almost completed. ASQA's decision hadn't even had an opportunity to be appealed yet, we hadn't even submitted our initial response to their allegations!

Philippa was beginning to experience serious problems at home with her husband and with her children. As a small family business, her children were all employed within the business and her now ex-husband was becoming concerned that this was going to affect their assets like their family home. Philippa says she was incredibly stressed, her staff were incredibly stressed. Philippa was also worried because her Mum had recently been diagnosed with cancer again and she thought she was going to miss being able to say goodbye to her if she died. It's fair to say, she was a nervous wreck and needed someone to just come along and fix it, take it away - she just needed to get away from the stress. Her blood pressure had gone through the roof, she was no longer sleeping, she couldn't eat and her closest relationships were falling apart. She now trusted nobody, not even her Consultant or her lawyer.

It was around this time that we had a discussion about bringing the sale of the business forward. I was introduced to a potential investor. An NDA was signed, and all relevant information was handed over to the potential investor. In the background, the Consultant India and the lawyer were continuing to try and mitigate risk and the severity of the situation with the complaints.

After some time, back and forth with information requests, while rectification and a response to ASQA was taking place, the investor, let's call her "Sally", had decided to proceed. It would begin with Sally coming into the role of CEO allowing me to walk away and for Sally to take over the management of the response to ASQA and the management of the complaints. They would take over the following week as CEO while all the paperwork was being finalised, just as a manner of keeping the ball rolling and not losing any time. A Deed of Arrangement had been entered into, the lawyers would do their thing and Philippa felt she could walk away and go and spend some quality time with her Mum. She had missed being around when her Dad passed away and she was determined to not have the same thing happen with her Mum.

It was around this time that our marketing had started to dwindle too. The news was starting to get around about ASQA and the student complaints that were generated by Vince (the ASQA auditor). We started approaching our marketing partners to review our enrolment packages in the hope that they could generate new enrolments for the college. Sally had prepared an email to go out to staff from me explaining that she would be taking over, explaining her background and her commitment to the college and getting it through this current hurdle. I was happy.

Even though the sale price was nowhere near close to that which had been offered only a few months before (this offer was only $A 1 million, I was satisfied that my vision would continue with someone whose long successful history in the VET sector would ensure the ongoing registration of the college, people wouldn't lose their jobs, students could finish their courses and I could spend quality time with my Mum before it was too late.

It was around this time we were also trying to get variations on our VET FEE Help contract. We had reached our maximum and needed to secure new availability for new students. The Department had been avoiding this issue for several weeks and we initially thought that it was related to the ASQA issues. It may well have been but nobody could have predicted what was about to happen. Sally took over on Monday as planned, the new agreement was being finalised amongst the lawyers.

Due to the inability to vary the VET FEE Help contract, the sale price was reduced even more significantly but we were ready to go by now and just wanted what was best for everyone. It became apparent that Philippa had got to the end of her tether and Sally was quite genuinely a great opportunity for the future growth of the college. We had also been granted an extension for our submission to ASQA previously and had sought another extension due to the sale. We received news overnight that ASQA had refused the extension. We also received news overnight, as did the rest of the VET sector, that Minister Simon Birmingham was making significant changes to the VET FEE Help program. This single announcement created a new wave of uncertainly about future viability and how much funding would be available for training. Philippa was done; she'd had enough, she had nothing left in the tank.

First, the rogue staff member lying about stress leave and being on worker's compensation, then ASQA, then the rogue auditor, then the fake student complaints that were indulged (and fabricated) by Vince (the ASQA auditor), the Minister now pulling the pin on the VET FEE Help program was more than she could bear.

In the space of a few hours, the value of the college had gone from $A1 million to $150K - at least that is what Philippa had been told; that $A150K was all the college was worth given all considerations now in play. Anyway, the day before, Sally had asked for the latest financials from the external accountant. Philippa forwarded them to Sally. The following day, Sally went to the office, did a big introduction to everyone, explained who she was, her background in the sector and how excited she was to be taking over such a great college. She took the Operations Manager out for a confidential meeting to discuss student numbers, the figures from the accountant and current issues. When they returned to the office mid-morning, Sally picked up any paperwork she had left in the office and walked out. Later in the day, Sally indicated that she felt we had misinformed her about numbers not being correct. At lunchtime that day, Minister Simon Birmingham scrapped the VET FEE Help program in its entirety.

The following couple of weeks were a bit of a blur as we tried to find an alternative buyer. We had notified authorities to advise them that we were still having ongoing issues with ASQA, the Department and now the scrapping of the VET FEE Help program had just made things a lot harder as we were trying to secure a buyer for the college.

We had secured tuition protection so we knew at the very least, if worse came to worse and the college had to close down, the students at least would be protected financially. Another buyer appeared but then changed their offer to the purchase of students as part of the closure or wind up. We had also had an interest in someone taking over the lease, etc. to enable the college to continue trading from the same premises. Unfortunately, despite everyone's best attempts, this also fell through. It's quite ironic really when something like this happens, you really do get to see the vultures come out to grab what they can. We had vultures coming from everywhere. There were more and more student complaints, the students had set up a little group encouraging everyone to apply for a full refund and their statement of attainment. There literally was no end in sight. It just kept compounding and was like an out-of-control cyclone coming through the college, picking everything up in its wrath and spitting it all back out again when it was done. It was exhausting.

After 2 years of fighting, we finally got to a point where we could no longer keep going. We submitted our decision to relinquish registration. We notified all relevant authorities, staff and students. Just over 2 weeks later, we received notices from ASQA saying that our registration was cancelled, our application for initial CRICOS registration had been rejected and was accompanied by an audit report. I still don't understand to this day how ASQA can cancel someone who relinquished their registration a few weeks prior.

Suddenly the alternative investor, let's call them "Discovery College", started playing funny buggers with me too and it was clear, the intentions of those behind Discovery College were never genuine. We started preparing the default data for the authorities.

The Default and Managed Closure

We prepared letters for relevant authorities and the students. This period of time in the VET sector was a chaotic time and colleges everywhere were collapsing as a result of the fallout of what turned out to be one of the Commonwealth government's biggest policy failures. The Commonwealth, to this day, blames everyone but itself despite the fact that its own policy failing and the government's mismanagement of that policy was the main cause of the issues. We tried so hard to do the right thing and manage student transitions and refunds in the best way possible because we had seen so many other providers in the weeks and months prior who had collapsed and the end result was absolute chaos for students, staff and the sector.

The media was having a field day sensationalising every RTO that collapsed under the failed policy saying it was the college's rorting of the system that was the issue. While I'm not saying that rorting wasn't happening in the system, this wasn't our situation. It's also not ok to just blame those RTOs for rorting the system; it is because the government failed in its duty to produce good policy and a program that didn't have holes as big as craters that enabled the program to be exploited. The Commonwealth was just as liable as those RTOs in my opinion.

That a government can allow all these students to sign up for these courses and just pull the rug out from under them is disgusting and should always be remembered as a shameful demonstration of Australian government policy.

We held meetings with staff to explain what was happening and we arranged for meetings with the students, their family and support people, and arranged for alternative providers to take on the students who wanted to continue with their studies. We were forced to get security to protect staff and Consultants who were assisting us because of threats that had been made against them, with many of them having a personal bodyguard to go to and from various premises. We arranged for 1 TAFE provider and 3 private providers for students to choose from, all of whom had the qualifications on scope and 1 of those providers had agreed to take on the current premises of our college, openly telling students that this is what they were going to do. You can imagine our surprise then when students who agreed to transfer to that provider (let's call them "Shadow College"), then told us that they were told after they agreed to transfer to Shadow College, that the CEO of Shadow College had advised them that they were no longer taking over the college premises! We later found out that other students who had agreed to enrol elsewhere had been approached privately by Shadow College trying to poach them and convince them to move across. This is just one example of the vultures that were parading around seeking to exploit the situation.

Another example of the complete and utter stupidity of what was happening is at this time, when we were holding the student meetings, we had a number of students approach the TAFE representative complaining that they did not receive a cash refund. The TAFE representative asked them if they had paid their fees in cash and they said no. To which he then asked them, if they had paid via VET FEE Help which was ultimately a student loan, why would they think for a second that they would receive a refund in cash? The students proceeded to advise the TAFE representative that they believed that they were entitled to a cash refund because that is what Vince (the ASQA auditor who was generating the complaints with students) had led them to believe. The

TAFE representative explained to the students several times that this was not a correct explanation of what happened. As the loan was to pay for their college course fees upfront, the government would recredit their VET FEE Help balance and there was no cash refund because the students had never paid any cash for the payment of their courses. They had signed up for a loan.

Relevant authorities gave in-person assistance with the managed closure but were pretty happy with the way in which we were handling the process. It's got to be said that managing the closure of an RTO is an incredibly stressful and time-consuming experience and nobody wants to do it. They were satisfied that we were collecting all the relevant details, managing student transfers, refunds, etc. appropriately and were happy to receive our records upon completion of notifying everyone and obtaining their choice for a refund or transfer.

Once this process was final, the students would receive their refund or have their VET FEE-Help loan re-credited. It was important to us that students be given a period of time to try and understand the situation, meet with the various providers and what they were offering, decide whether the location and delivery modes, etc. of the new providers was suitable for them, get independent advice and come back to us with their final decision in writing. We made ourselves available again for several days for students to arrange an appointment to discuss any questions they might have had and help them to make choices that were suitable for their needs. Not once did ASQA show up or even show any interest in trying to ensure that students were being adequately looked after.

After these meetings and the time we provided to students to make an informed decision about what they wanted to do, we notified the relevant authorities that the student records were available for collection. My recollection was that around 75% of students chose to transfer to another college and around 25% chose to receive a refund because they were too traumatised to finish their studies or didn't understand how they could continue their studies in another college under the VET FEE Help program when it had been scrapped by the Minister only a few days prior.

We had encouraged students to complete whatever units they were working on so that we could provide them with a Statement of Attainment or in many cases, some students were very close to completion with only a few assessments left to get their full certification. We updated all student enrolment records on HEIMS (the Department's database[139]), these details were changing daily. We booked a time for the authorities to come and recover all the student records in the manner in which they required. This took a lot of man hours and all student files were boxed up and ready for collection as agreed with the authorities. They were never collected.

Strangely, about 5 days after we had notified all relevant authorities, students and staff that we had decided to relinquish our registration due to the Commonwealth deciding to annul the VET FEE Help program, ASQA sent us a letter saying that they were cancelling our registration. We found this to be most peculiar. How could ASQA cancel an RTO that had already withdrawn its registration? On what basis had it been cancelled? We hadn't yet exhausted our appeal rights with the audit situation and it was, for all intents and purposes, validly still able to submit a response. **To this day, the national register and the ASQA Decision Table all hold an inappropriate cancellation decision about us.**

During all this chaos, and several days AFTER ASQA notified us that they had cancelled our registration as an RTO, they sent us yet another complaint and sent us another invoice for the audit they had undertaken. On the same day, we also received notice that the Department had launched the VET Student Loans program and we also received an application to apply to become a VET Student Loans provider during the transitional period.

139 HEIMS = Higher Education Information Management System.

Around this time, Julie, the disgruntled staff member who was on stress leave and getting worker's compensation whilst also working elsewhere and gallivanting around shopping centres threatening ex-staff of the RTO decided that she would lodge a complaint with Fair Work Australia for unfair dismissal.

Of course, with the college relinquishing its registration and closing, all staff had been made redundant and terminated because the company was closing down. The matter didn't proceed after we responded to the Fair Work investigation but it was just another example of vultures fighting for anything and everything they could get their hands on. Another example was the landlord of the Head Office. We even tried to negotiate sub-leasing the premises to another college but the landlord was insistent we had to maintain our lease, even though we were closing and there was not going to be any business left. This was another crippling factor by a stakeholder that, collectively, could have made a significant difference to the way in which this matter was handled.

By this time, most staff had moved on to other providers or had obtained work in industry again, they had lost all appetite to ever being a part of the VET sector again. For some other staff, they were so traumatised by the entire experience, they were unable to work at all. There remained a handful of loyal staff and contractors who even though they knew they were not going to be paid, remained on-site, going into the college every single day just to ensure that the students were going to be looked after, they received their certification and/or their student records were transferred to their new providers or authorities looked after them. We still had students calling the phone every day saying that they hadn't had their refunds processed yet, they wanted to change providers, the phone calls were constant. It got to the point where we couldn't keep up with the calls and many were being missed so we diverted them to message bank so that they could leave their details and we could call them back. When we called them back, the staff, now working voluntarily were being abused constantly. Even the Consultant working with us was still with us working to finalise everything knowing that she was not going to be paid. It really is in times like this that you see who is genuinely there for you and your college and who is just there to take advantage.

Life As We Knew It

Once the college was actually closed, all student records and certification finalised for transfer to relevant providers or relevant authorities, HEIMS updated and the liquidator appointed, those of us who had stayed until the end continued to struggle with most things on a day-to-day basis. We were burnt out physically and emotionally and although we didn't realise it at the time, severely traumatised. The staff member who stayed on voluntarily to help with the HEIMS updates, let's call him "John", would go to the local shopping centre and try to buy groceries only to be abused by students who were still trying to get hold of authorities who had not yet processed their refund. Other students would bombard him with abuse because while students had already been through the managed closure process and completed their selections relevant bodies present and contributing to that process, they were requiring students to go through the entire process all over again and they were angry! They'd stop him in his tracks, make threats saying that they knew where he lived and all sorts of things. It was a terrible time for him to the point where he was unable to go to the local shops anymore and would travel to neighbouring suburbs to buy groceries or get his wife to go instead. John now refuses to ever work in the VET sector again.

For one of our most experienced and prized trainers, considered an expert and one of Australia's best in her field by industry, she was crippled with trauma, self-doubt and a feeling of failure. While this was the perception of the industry of her skills and expertise, Vince, the ASQA auditor had insisted that she was not qualified or competent and didn't meet the requirements of the Standards. This trainer, we'll call her "Nadine", was one of the most qualified trainers in the VET sector in this particular industry and we had provided evidence of that but Vince insisted it was not sufficient, adequate and that every result that she had issued was invalid. Despite being one of Australia's most industry recognised experts, she is still unable to work at all either as a trainer or in her industry because of the trauma she experienced.

As Philippa recounts, for me personally, this period of my life is something that I still struggle with today and is a period of time I wish could just disappear from my memories forever. While the entire experience has left me incredibly traumatised, this period of my life will always be one of crippling fear and trauma.

Each night during the closure when I returned home, my ex-husband and I would argue about the impact the college closure was having on our lives and our family who were mostly all employed by the college and how their lives were being completely destroyed.

Consequences

Family Violence, Addiction & PTSD

Philippa continues to share her painful journey...

One particular night though after everything had been finalised, he bashed me to within an inch of my life. I was so badly assaulted that an ambulance had to be called; I could barely breathe, I could barely walk. I was so severely bruised that I didn't look anything like myself. It took weeks for me to recover physically and emotionally, I am still suffering from PTSD. I am still taking anti-depressants regularly, I am still taking anxiety medication, I still see a counsellor and am not able to work at all. Like John (the previous Operations Manager who stayed back to help with the HEIMS data), I would go to the shops and be abused and threatened by students and their parents and having been assaulted so severely by my husband, I became so scared that I couldn't stay in my house, I couldn't stay in the area so I escaped interstate. My adult children were so traumatised by everything that had happened; they had also been employed by the college, lost their cars and any income despite all of them having mortgages on their homes, also suffered terribly with one of my children becoming an alcoholic and drug addict who is still in and out of rehabilitation today, some five years later.

I also used to develop many of our training and assessment materials. I assisted in the development of the online Moodle lessons and videos. I was also a trainer for one of our short courses. I tried to get work as a contractor writing assessments, helping develop Moodle materials but I was so traumatised by everything that had happened with ASQA that I had lost all confidence to be able to produce anything that would be considered by ASQA to be compliant. Therefore, I constantly said to myself I have no right to ask for payment for something that the regulator says I did so badly. As a result, I started doing those jobs for free just so I could get more experience and learn what I was doing wrong. I was writing assessments for 2 of the colleges who had taken some of our students, both accepting all my work for no charge but demanding more and more. I soon realised that again I was being exploited and just went into hiding. I, too began drinking and just sat inside, effectively becoming a hermit in my new home, sleeping, drinking and pretending that none of this happened, I just wanted the memories to disappear and the more I drank, the easier it was to manage the trauma and forget about it all.

As the liquidation was being undertaken, there were questions and more questions about what had happened and why. I was forced to relive the trauma over and over again to try and explain to a liquidator how the knee jerk policy changes and ASQA's rogue auditor could cause something like this to happen. How several Consultants, including one who worked for a regulator as well as the accounting firm, could effectively get away with their part in this tragedy. Much of this time is a bit of a blur and occasionally, I get triggered by something and have vague memories of the months where the liquidation took place. I lost my house, my car, all the assets that I owned. I had to start all over again, it was such a terrible time in my life, my psychologist tells me that my mind has blocked it all out as a protection mechanism. I do believe however that those students who requested refunds did eventually receive them.

Five years later, I am still triggered by the smallest thing. It brings me to tears, cripples me and I immediately become extremely anxious and fearful that people are coming to hurt me. I still struggle to go to the state where my college was and where everything fell apart. I'm afraid that people will find me and assault me. I worry that even though the company was liquidated and technically speaking, it should all be over, I'm afraid that ASQA, the Department or someone else will still pursue me. I was incredibly afraid to share my story in case people come after me. As much as I truly believe that my story needs to be told, I still live in fear for my life and the lives of those who were a part of that whole tragedy.

One thing we all agree on is that people need to be aware of the absolute destruction that ASQA has caused in people's lives. As a previous CEO of a company, if I or any of my staff bullied and harassed my clients, stakeholders or staff the way that ASQA did, we would be held accountable. There are laws against workplace bullying and harassment and nobody gave ASQA permission for one of their staff to come into my workplace and bully and harass me, my staff or my students. I will never understand why Vince felt it was ok to behave the way he did. Only he knows the reasons behind that. While ordinarily, you could say that they will have to go to sleep at night knowing what they did, I truly believe that ASQA and Vince, in particular, have no empathy, are narcissistic and actually thrive on destroying people.

Then feelings and memories overwhelm me, I still drink myself to sleep and take all my medication to drown out every little trigger. There are still times I drink too much and call India, the Consultant who stayed with me to the end, knowing she wasn't going to get paid but because it was the right thing to do. In these times, I ask her in tears why she couldn't save me because she saves businesses all the time. I feel guilty for days afterwards because I know it's not her fault and that she did the best that she could at the time. She stood by me when many walked away and it's not her fault. The alcohol forces me to either mentally escape the pain or to focus on it to the point of harming myself and the relationships I have with people around me. All my family remain in my hometown and I rarely see them because I'm too afraid. I'm soon to become a grandmother for the first time and I am terrified of going back home to meet my first grandchild.

I hope that by telling my story, people will understand how ASQA can monumentally change your life and cause so much destruction, some of which you may never recover from. I don't know whether the Chief Commissioner is aware of what these people are doing, although to be fair, the current Chief Commissioner was not in place at the time this incident occurred, it occurred under the watch of a different Chief Commissioner. I have heard though, far too often, that these types of things continue. I'm not sure how ASQA cannot know or understand what some of its employees are doing. If I were in their shoes and these were my staff in an RTO, I'd be accused of not adequately monitoring my staff and their compliance with their rights, responsibilities and obligations under legislation that impacts their employment.

ASQA would consider that I am not '*fit and proper*' enough to run an RTO. How is it that these things occur under the watch of the Chief Commissioner, that their staff go out and do this to people and not only do they get away with it, but their fit and proper is never affected? How would ASQA management fare under their own Fit and Proper legislation? They're forever going around making allegations that people in the VET sector are not fit and proper but they really need to look in the mirror and take a closer look at their own staff and their actions. Their conduct is unconscionable but worse, we are actually paying for them to behave that way! That they can continue to run around being accountable to nobody is an absolute disgrace and something that the Commonwealth needs to be accountable for.

I don't know that I will ever recover enough to have a normal life again. What I do know is that I live a very isolated life with very few people in it because I have massive trust issues and have lost everything. I can't go through something like that ever again. I don't trust many people. Even providing my story in this book has been a seesaw of emotions and permission. Ultimately though, the story needs to be told for the betterment of the sector, so that ASQA knows and can no longer say that they never knew. I'm also hoping that by telling my story and the journey we went through, that it will help me and others who were impacted by our journey to finally begin to heal.

There's no happy ending here, just hope that eventually, we will have some sort of life where we're not sitting in trauma, fear, depression and anxiety and drinking ourselves to death but can actually enjoy the simple things in life once more. I hope that by telling my story I will at least have the courage to visit my soon-to-be-born first grandchild. I hope that by telling my story, the Chief Commissioner wakes up and starts managing her staff and contract auditors appropriately and that what was once one of the best VET sectors in the world, can become truly great once more. We owe it to future generations to fix this blackspot in Australia's education history.

~ END ~

Disclaimer:

Reader discretion advised. The following chapter may trigger people. It includes discussion of suicide.

If you need someone to talk to:

Lifeline 13 11 14

Beyond Blue 1300 224 636

#2 Greg's Story

> *"The dead cannot cry out for justice. It is a duty of the living to do so for them."*
>
> **- Lois McMaster Bujold**

When Australia's VET sector gets to the point where the mental health (and physical, psychological, spiritual health) of its workforce is being critically compromised as a result of regulation, it's time that the highest levels of government start to pay attention.

In October 2020, I wrote an article on LinkedIn called *Ring Around the Rosy...Part 1*. The article was designed to be a series but due to threats of litigation, I was minded to delay any further publications that I had hoped to write for the series. The article, however, was based on a post that I had read by a member of the VET sector in Australia and a newspaper article about how he was being held responsible for another man's suicide after ASQA made adverse findings. At that stage, all of the information was (and remains) publicly available.

I was issued with a notice requesting that I remove the article or heavily edit it as it was subject to legal proceedings. I am unable to reproduce the contents of the notice due to the law firm who issued it expressing that publication of the email is not authorised. What I can advise is that apparently this case remains subject to legal proceedings.

We prepared for the audit as we have done previously and the thing that sticks in my mind the most is the first comment made by the Auditor, and I won't give you his name, but I don't believe he's at ASQA anymore, and there was no, "*Hello, nice to meet you.*" It was, "*I'm here to close you down*". He came in and said, "*I come from a background of procedural fairness*." And I'm thinking OMG how dare somebody say that to me about my organisation and immediately in my mind I'm thinking about issues of bias. Thinking '*what's this about*' and the rest of it. When I challenged that statement *"I'm here to close you down"*, he intimated that one of my competitors had made a complaint about our practices and I said that I welcome any challenge and any opportunity to improve. I explained to him that as an industry association, we're here to do that. I always said and did all the right things at the right time and I was quite taken aback by the statement - '*We're here to close you down*'.

Despite everything and the way in which the audit commenced, we just went through the process and I had two of my staff in with this gentleman for what felt like 2-3 weeks *[a long audit]*. I'm not sure if that's correct, but it felt like 2-3 weeks. I'm probably dealing with the rectification side as well which could have been even longer, but the upshot of it was they were fine with everything. Honestly, you just wouldn't imagine that something so unbelievable as this would, or could, happen. There were two things that concerned this gentleman - 1) one of the main trainers had never been a real estate agent in his life and so we had to demonstrate to him that, whilst he hadn't been a real estate agent, he had been instrumental in the vocational education side of real estate training and the development of the training package and that in fact, he had been the lead in drafting the legislation that impacted on real estate agents. So we got through that one.

The next one we couldn't get by and I've done a little bit of research on this when it first happened. The way in which the real estate qualifications and units of competency had been written in the training package were poorly written. The core units required a formative and summative assessment. So, in short, I had to find an example to use when explaining this outrageous situation to my Board (because you need to understand, they too were still in complete disbelief). There is a requirement for something to be completed in a simulated environment before you can do it in a real-life final assessment. Part of this issue of course is that real estate and property management are regulated, licenced industries and those requirements change depending on the jurisdiction. Ultimately though, it is unlawful to do some or rather most of these things in a simulated, formative assessment environment anyway!

The example that I used to demonstrate this to my Board was to show them what we have to do when teaching someone how to use a mobile phone; the problem was the explanation I had to give was not what is actually expected of a competency-based training environment. In a competency-based training environment, if someone has demonstrated competency, they just have. You shouldn't have to go over and over more assessments. You might have completed the summative assessment but there was no formative assessment.

Why should we expect learners to do more than they have to in order to demonstrate competence? If someone can use a mobile phone, they can!

Anyway, to explain to the Board this concept of this gentleman's expectation, I explained in the easiest manner possible... Here's how we hold a mobile phone, here's how we press the buttons, then we have to put the phone down for a little bit, go on and teach something else like maybe how to charge the phone...you plug the charging device into the power point, you plug the other end of the cable into the mobile phone, you turn on the power point, make sure the charging symbol comes up and leave it until it says 100%. Then you go back to the phone. Here's how we hold a mobile phone, here's how we press the buttons, pick up the phone and teach them how to press the buttons again, then we have to put the phone down for a little bit, go on and teach something else like maybe how to charge the phone...you plug the charging device into the power point, you plug the other end of the cable into the mobile phone, you turn on the power point, make sure the charging symbol comes up and leave it until it says 100%. It's only then can we deem someone 'Competent' at using a mobile phone.

So that meant for our course, in order to demonstrate that '*process*' on paper, we effectively had to double the length of our course. Double the length, double the cost, double the time, all of those sorts of issues. When we were challenged on that basis, it was just, "This is the way it is.

This is what you need to do when simulating a work environment and the units of competency basically insist on a formative and summative amount of competence. I just don't understand who writes these training packages in such a way that legislative requirements are not considered in the assessment conditions (although at the time it was the methods and context of assessment)? Who signs off on the quality of the training package being suitable? How do these training packages get endorsed in this manner? Why doesn't ASQA see the genuine ridiculousness of what they're expecting when the industry evidence clearly stipulates that it is and would be unlawful to do certain things?

From there, I knew it was going to be quite a while doing all of this, so I went and sought some legal advice and the quick conclusion that we came to was that fighting ASQA is equivalent to fighting the ATO - you'll never win! On top of that, we engaged with another RTO around town that was similarly audited by this gentleman and they came to the same conclusion and they battled their way through making sure that every little nook and cranny that this gentleman insisted on could be met.

I'm probably giving some things away here, but things like a mechanics pit was 12cms too shallow according to the ASQA/VET world, in the mechanics world it was fine and perfectly acceptable and common. It was little things like that became a major issue and they had to just fight their way through it. It was the formative and summative requirement for us in a world where practice is so far removed legislatively from being able to produce that but we just set about making that happen, demonstrating the formative assessments - here's how we're going to train it again - and then do the summative assessment. That meant that our course went out to 12 weeks. Meanwhile, one of our competitors had been operating and doing the course in a shorter time, well and truly under our 6 weeks. I had spent the last 8-10 years fighting the fact that everyone is going to our competitor because it's shorter, sharper and shinier and it's easier. My mantra all along was that not only did we have an RTO but, as an industry association, we were representing real estate agents and the real estate industry and our vision and mission was always enhancing the reputation and relevance of real estate agents in the transaction. The level of professionalism and commitment to a profession is just as important as how long it takes to get through a course. Knowing that somebody was effectively undermining it, it literally made my blood boil. Now this is what I can say...

With the new president coming into my organisation, he sternly made the point that '*...these guys are doing it quicker, easier and cheaper, why can't we? Get your act together*'. So I sent in a mystery shopper. Normally I wouldn't worry about a competitor, but when I have people on my Board saying do it better, quicker and cheaper, I thought that I had better lift the sheets, find out what's going on and be able to compete. So, as part of that process, I discovered a number of things that were incredibly concerning not just to me and my RTO but to the real estate industry in South Australia. The quality of real estate training from this RTO was of significant concern. Things such as students could find answers on the other side of the whiteboard and, at the end of a lesson, they would swap over and mark each other's work.

They're the two things that stick in my mind because we went to great lengths to make sure that none of that was actually happening here because not only do we know that all of that is completely in breach of ASQA regulations, but it completely undermines the capacity, quality and integrity of the real estate industry, the very thing we were trying so desperately to professionalise!

The mystery shopper gave me enough information and obviously when this chap came in from ASQA (this auditor is well known in the VET sector, particularly in Adelaide, although he is no longer with ASQA today), and effectively said those two things to me... In my mind, I was thinking to myself...well, I've only got one competitor so it doesn't take a rocket scientist to work out where that complaint has come from, and whether it's true or not, I have no idea and ASQA will judge things as they **interpret**[140] them anyway, it's a losing game. At the end of the day, we were going for 15 weeks and the competitor was doing it in far less time than that. He wasn't even doing it properly as he was only doing it for 4 weeks. Ultimately, even the parchments that he was issuing to these students were in error. So, the incompetence right from go to woe was quite staggering.

Getting a parchment right in terms of '*well...here are all the units that make up a Cert IV*', well, in my opinion, it's pretty black and white and just to get even that wrong is pretty alarming.

This concerned me greatly because one of the issues that I had was that this means that there had been a number of students who had gone to this competitor, marched out with this parchment, went and saw the Commissioner of Licensing of Real Estate Agents, and said, "*Look at me, I'm ready to go, here's my evidence. I've got this parchment...*", even though the parchment was wrong...and they got licenced! How does that even happen and here we are, I'm being required to respond to things that are nowhere near as serious but completely outrageous all the same! I mean we're not talking about making coffee here! We're talking about people's family homes, their life-long assets sometimes up to millions of dollars, it's not a $3 cappuccino!

Apart from my role in the RTO, I am also a lawyer. I'm also very acutely aware of the fact that if I'm in receipt of information that could devastate the real estate industry as well as the profession at large, I've got to do something about it. So that's when I basically said, "*Enough is enough, I'm being undermined.*" I would go as far as to say that the whole real estate training system in South Australia, because of this particular gentleman, was being undermined and, I wouldn't use the '*fraud*' word,

140 Emphasis deliberately added to demonstrate that effectively, that's all ASQA auditors do is interpret their understanding of something, even when they have no skills, qualification, industry experience or technical advice to support that interpretation.

but it was just so vehemently incompetent. I could understand why real estate agents were sending people there in order to..." *Well, don't worry about the answers. They're on the other side. Just get them and then...*" The whole process was...I want to use the term '*Kangaroo Court*', but it was just a joke and it was quite embarrassing.

So to have someone from ASQA come in and knock on my door and have a crack at us only training it once when we were told '*formative*' and '*summative*' and that we had to do it twice, even performing things in a simulated environment that were not lawful in some situations, forcing us to assess students again even though they had already demonstrated competency, knowing that it wasn't even trained once by the competitor, but rather, the students at the competitor's RTO were just told *'there's the answers*', it was all quite devastating. I can't help but feel an enormous amount of frustration with the ASQA leadership through this process. Obviously, students were already under enough stress, we had to go through that rectification process, and we're talking hundreds of thousands of dollars, making sure that every student that had been through in the last six months had been *'rectified and remediated[141]'* so to speak.

So, in a nutshell, that was the drama we went through with ASQA. As I said, fighting ASQA, and even having an auditor come in and say, "*I'm going to close you down,*" I find that quite staggering. How is that even possible? Permitted? ASQA want to have a go at how '*poor*' they considered us as a training provider but to be honest, with ASQA staff (*not panel auditors but actual senior management level staff*) going around behaving in this way suggests to me that their own practices require considerable review and they perhaps need to look a bit more closely in the mirror.

The writer shared a story about another provider in Adelaide who was exposed to the exact same behaviour from the exact same auditor and how that particular matter played out. Unfortunately, for the purpose of

141 Again, we use this word loosely.

this book, the writer does not have permission from the RTO to divulge the details of their matter in this publication and in sharing the story with this person, complete confidentiality was maintained.

I'm staggered to hear that, Raelene. All my career, I have considered that anyone working in the public service, I hold them to a higher standard than what you've just described to me, and I'm still absolutely pissed off that someone can come into my organisation and say '*I'm going to close you down*' is...I expect a lot more from the regulator, I expect a lot more from a public servant and I cannot describe how disappointing this whole process has been and, without going into further details, has been absolutely devastating to all and sundry in terms of all of this. It's been a disappointment from woe to go.

The writer discusses another matter of which she is aware in the real estate training industry, this time under a different regulator, albeit, while ASQA was in place. Again, unfortunately, for the purpose of this book, the writer does not have permission from the now defunct RTO to divulge the details of their matter in this publication and in sharing the story with this person, complete confidentiality was maintained. The writer explained that this particular RTO had been audited by this alternative regulator and advised that they needed to do the exact same things that Greg had been told to do.

Again, this interpretation, albeit consistent with the ASQA auditor's interpretation (this auditor was also an ASQA panel auditor), came from someone with absolutely no background in real estate, no consideration of the legislative requirements for being registered as a real estate sales agent or property manager and therefore, the things that the auditor wanted to see based on what was written in the training package was completely inconsistent with industry and legislative requirements. The writer asked Greg if his RTO was just delivering short courses that industry considered skill sets but the training package did not, or, alternatively, was he delivering full qualifications. His response is next.

We were delivering full qualifications because, once again, our mantra was enhancing the reputation and being an industry association, the relevance of real estate training in South Australia, so having somebody come in and just do the 18 units required the licencing and getting their certification We basically came to the conclusion that that's simply not good enough for a real estate agent and we're going to pitch the whole box and dice, we were a market leader and we believed we owed more to the industry than just peddling poor, inadequate and insufficient training. These future real estate professionals deserve to have a holistic learning experience and we provide that. Then our competitor up the road thought that if they're giving a parchment out, we better do the same. The difference between 18 and 26, from memory - it might have been a bit more, was quite minimal in terms of making all that happen. We made a conscious decision that a Statement of Attainment wasn't enough and we wanted to make sure that we were teaching to the full qualification.

Declaring a conflict of interest as well, and we were doing that on the basis that if and when, and on the odd occasion funding would be available, funding would be based on qualifications not on Statements of Attainment, so we were keeping an eye on the longer term basis as well that enabled us to provide a holistic training experience in real estate training that we as the industry association had an awareness of that other providers and the training package didn't provide.

A question was asked about the size of the RTO and a description of its operations prior to the ASQA matter occurring. Greg's response is next.

We were reasonably large. We were delivering training face to face, online and blended. We would have at any one time, up to 600-800 students going through and I'd like to think that this was reasonably sizable. Prior to this, we were travelling along quite nice financially, then all of a sudden we got hit with this outrageous audit. We had been given a choice basically to either spend a bucket load of money fixing it or spend a bucket load of money fighting it. Once again, I don't subscribe to what this particular auditor's interpretation was of the simulated work environment, but, and I repeat, you don't fight them, even if you win this time around, you won't '*win the long game*' and they'll just come back for another shot, you just have to fix it. As far as I'm concerned, as soon as someone is deemed '*Competent*' using a mobile phone, you don't come back and do it again because that's not only frustrating for the student's learning journey and assessment process (which according to the Standards and ASQA's rhetoric is supposed to be THE most important component of compliance, meeting the student's identified needs, but it's frustrating for the students as well, they consistently ask (and rightly so in my opinion), '*Why are we doing this again?*'

The writer suggests to Greg that this is not consistent with the basic premise of competency-based training. Greg agrees.

Yes, that's exactly right. So, once again, rather than fighting it, and after spending time with lawyers, we decided we were better off just doing the dance that this man required us to do and we did. We got through it, but it cost us a lot of money, a huge amount of turmoil for the real estate industry in South Australia and the student outcomes were compromised by ASQA's expectations that were inconsistent with legislative and industry requirements and importantly, the fundamental basis of vocational education and training, that is, competency-based training.

The writer then asks Greg to describe what the auditor's expectation of a simulated environment looked like, what this auditor was '*expecting*' to see. The writer reinforces that her experience with this other RTO delivering these courses in another jurisdiction is that this auditor had required them to complete tasks and that the simulated environment that they wanted those tasks performed in was not legislatively possible to provide. Greg responds.

Yes, and that's a similar issue here. It wasn't so much the simulated environment. The simulated environment...in fact let me...let me explain.

The simulated environment wasn't so much the issue. It was because of the simulated environment, because we had to do it in a simulated environment, he required the formative and the summative assessment.

I've gone back in almost 20 years with the units of competency for real estate training and I believe that the literal interpretation of that paragraph has been dangerously decontextualised. And it simply says, "Where the assessment is part of a structured learning experience, a simulated type of environment, the evidence collected must relate to a number of performances assessed. Not necessarily the same performance undertaken twice, but more than just one performance across a range of elements across a unit of competency at '*different points in time*'. It's the different points in time that caused the issue". In my research, I couldn't find any other example whereby that '*different points in time*' was required in any other units of competency. So effectively, that's all it says.

Greg was asked about what the audit team looked like; how many were there? Were there technical experts? Assistants? Observers? Greg responds.

No, it was purely the one auditor. It's hard for me to say he was courteous, professional or unbiased when the first thing he said was, "*I'm here to close you down*". The hairs on the back of my neck stood up. Throughout that process, one of my staff became reasonably close with him.

This is purely hearsay on my part because I never personally heard it, therefore it is only hearsay from my trainer but this auditor, he admitted that he had some mental health issues and was going through some difficult things. So when you said he was on long-service leave earlier, I'm not the least bit surprised to hear. The writer corrects the statement to make it clear that this auditor is not on long service leave now (and potentially never was) but he definitely no longer works with ASQA.

Well to admit to one of my staff, regardless of how close they became, that despite everything, here he was making a judgement as to... concerned me greatly.

The writer asked...This was a complex audit wasn't it? In terms of you've got the additional licencing issues on top of the standard VET course. So once you went through the audit process, you would have given your response to ASQA and they would have come back and provided you with an outcome. What happened after that and how did that impact the licencing of real estate agents and property managers in South Australia? Greg's response is next.

It didn't impact the licensing process at all. All we had to do was pay someone a great big amount of money to copy and paste a formative and turn it into summative and all of a sudden, the learner resources went from 36 pages per unit of competency to 72 pages per unit of competency. I'm exaggerating on purpose, but I don't want to diminish anything that this individual did for us, because we rectified according to what that auditor wanted and claimed he needed and we got through it all. We're talking multiples of hundreds of thousands of dollars later, and it's pretty hard to recover from something like that.

A question is raised about whether the RTO is still running. No, basically as part of this process, I put in a recommendation to the Board that we should get out of the RTO world because it's all just too hard, it's too inconsistent. I'll use the words I put to the Board - it's just not Australian with the way it's being done. It's not a fair go with this process and in order to keep things up-to-date, by the time we had finished with property management licencing because we had just lobbied to get licencing for property management, I put a proposal to the Board that we run away as far away as we can and just get ourselves involved continuing professional development that does not come under ASQA's jurisdiction and therefore escapes the absurd audit decisions and inconsistent auditors, but we are not in the RTO world.

The writer explains that this is the exact same advice she gave to the RTO delivering real estate training in another jurisdiction referred to earlier. Greg responds.

Well, I'm delighted because I've spent the last few years thinking was that the right decision? Just knowing that we're not alone with Mr Stent and how it all panned out in the end...I still feel bad, but it is what it is. It can't be undone. We lost our RTO for it, the real estate industry in South Australia suffers as a result of it and in my opinion, ASQA just gets away with it.

The writer explains that there are a number of similar real estate RTOs around the country currently flying under the radar. That in order to be able to demonstrate compliance with the training package at that particular time, they were at risk of doing something that was unlawful, they were at risk at running programs that were completely and utterly financially not viable, and they were competing with other industry bodies that were flying under the radar doing online delivery whilst regulated by a different regulator than ASQA, when they should have been, at all times, under ASQA. So when you've got a provider doing a 10-day course online, you can't compete with that delivering a compliant and financially viable course. As a result, my recommendation was to also close down that RTO at that time. The writer says she's not sure if Greg knows who she is referring to and he responds as follows...

Yes, I do and I am aware. I know that that particular provider is under a different regulatory regime, and all I can say is, and I can say this without breaching any confidentiality, all the other REIs had looked to see what ASQA had done to us and they were shitting themselves. Now I don't know if that means they weren't doing the formative and summative but, at the end of the day, when we outlined to them our experience with ASQA, I would be reasonably confident to say that they all went to have a look that there was some form of '*teach how to use the phone, break, phone again*.

The writer explained that she had a feeling that the RTO still teaches the course in the same way, but I haven't checked recently, to be fair, but as soon as you're registered with another alternative regulator and commence online delivery, you're supposed to transition to ASQA, but these guys were flying under the radar for years and nobody ever forced them to transition. And that alternative regulator knew they were delivering online, but never did anything about it either. So ASQA never came after them because it would have been their job to come after them, because they were their regulator. So I don't know if they would have been included, but they were definitely doing the wrong thing for a very long time and it severely impacted my client's ability to run this program.

That sounds very similar to my competitor over here, and I want to divorce myself from any comment on that RTO you're referring to because I know the person and I worked with them for a while. I don't know anything about how their regulator works, but from my perspective, the real estate training in South Australia was being substantially undermined. There were deliberate actions as far as I'm concerned to basically say, *"Hey, don't spend $4,000 with that RTO! Come to us and we'll only charge you $3,700 and we'll make sure you get your certificate."* Many years before, I'd made a statement on our website that said, *"If you want to do tick and flick, go somewhere else. If that's what you want to do, I'm not passing judgement on anybody."* I then got some nasty phone calls from this competitor and a friend of the competitor who had some influence around my sphere of business, and

I was told to take it down immediately, at which time I did because this is all part of a fight. It got to the point where I thought, 'why bother even having this fight'?

In the end, we had this fight because an auditor came in and basically said we were doing the wrong thing, even though, to this day, I say we weren't and comparing it to what my competitor was doing, I'm speechless! The fact that they knocked on our door and we had a competitor up the road doing what they were doing? And to hear from the auditor that it was a complaint from a competitor, I was going, "*WOW, this is a wonderful business tactic on his part*" or whoever's part it was, I should say. It was one of those things.

The writer asks about regulatory audits prior to this one and what they were like in comparison. Greg's answer follows...

Two words - <Insert the auditor's name>[142] was the only difference! Previously we had Jenny[143] and somebody else when we extended our scope. We extended our scope to Business skills generally, Leadership. We wanted to become a broader RTO and we went through that process of having them come in and here's those units here, there's those things over there...it was very amicable. Even prior to that, under the... old standards.

Were they previously respectful and professional? Yes, previously it absolutely was. And there was a recognition that continuous improvement was always what we were looking for and aiming to achieve. If there were any suggestions of how we could make the learner engagement even better, we were all ears. What was different with this auditor was that he came in, had a preconceived biased view, almost like a little power man, and basically saying this is what I'm here to do. Now, there was no need for it to be articulated in this manner and I guess that's why I've still got my back up against the whole ASQA process and the fact that, in my opinion, the whole ASQA team circled the wagons because that auditor was a reflection on the leadership of ASQA at that time. And when I saw extensions for the rectification to make sure...not the rectification, but making sure that the students could transition to the updated system, I was...

It was almost too easy compared to what had happened, but obviously there was the intervening event being that the competitor becoming deceased and therefore I think ASQA realised that a reasonable request

142 The name was provided however has been changed for the purpose of this publication.
143 Jenny is a pseudonym for the auditor in question.

shouldn't be knocked back unreasonably and so I managed to get some extra time for our students to complete the course, rather than having to stress them all and get it done by a certain time.

The writer asks Greg to explain what happened next in his journey with ASQA to the extent that is possible. Greg has recently signed Terms of Agreement in relation to a separate matter that prevents him from discussing certain things, although he is permitted to discuss the issues disclosed in this particular story. It was important to both Greg and the writer to be able to articulate his story in that context. Greg continues...

Effectively, we trained all the students out to completion, that's what we did because we were made to, we really had no other choice...we were only training in property management licensing at that stage. I know that I was vindicated by ASQA about a month after, or maybe it was three months after.

I'd raised some issues and those issues were then accepted by ASQA as my interpretation as being correct...I was vindicated...I don't have all the details. All I know is that around three months later, that other organisation had closed down as well, so I think you can read into that whatever you like. But I have to say, getting that email from ASQA saying, "*Whilst we don't agree with everything you're saying Mr Troughton, we do believe that there are some significant issues here and we're going to address them*" was a huge relief off my shoulders.

Understanding that we need to be careful about what Greg can and cannot say, the writer asks Greg if he can share that vindication notification. Greg notes that...

My fear would be that that would be confidential to my previous employer, but what I can say is it was, and I'm paraphrasing here, "*Dear Mr CEO, we acknowledge and agree with some of your concerns and we're taking action.*" So that was at least something. I've spent the last 8-10 years on a professional vision and mission that real estate agents need to be a whole lot more bloody professional than what they are.

Greg is not a real estate agent, he's a lawyer '*by trade*'. He continues... So I've spent the last few years trying to make real estate agents and training providers in South Australia live up to these higher expectations of professionalism and to have somebody undermine that training process...it was literally soul crushing... one of the issues that I just couldn't get away from was the provision of answers and the subsequent '*tick and flick*'.

It was simply a case of '*Come in here, pay me your $3,000, I'll give you the parchment, off you go*'. We heard a lot of those sorts of issues when it came to multicultural students in a lot of other areas and I couldn't help but feel that's what going on. When respected people in the profession were saying to me, "*Oh, it's a lot easier over there.*" I'm going, hang on, it's not supposed to be easy. You're about to list someone's million-dollar house and sell it to somebody. It's not meant to be easy and the units of competency demonstrate that you need to be able to do these things and not tick and flick. So that's why, well in advance of all this, I was staggered and stunned and I am still in disbelief that someone was knocking on my door when the competitor up the road had been engaging in these practices for a number of years. My Board had come to the conclusion, prior to us being audited, if that's the way he wants to do his business, then just let him. Let's just continue doing what we can do and that's the approach we took.

The writer then asks Greg what impact that has had on real estate training and the real estate industry in Adelaide now? Greg continues...

In Adelaide, Harcourts are training, so one of my ex-staff members is working there. Another ex-staff member has opened up his own (*The Real Estate Training Academy*) and I'm aware of another staff member of mine who's doing a little bit of on and off training; they hire one of the venues in the parklands here and when they've got enough students, they'll run the course. So they're the ones that I'm aware of. I imagine Kaplan would have done quite nicely out of all of this as well.

I don't know how Kaplan does their business because when I look at what I was told, and obviously they've got lots of money, they could fight something like this if it ever came to it. A 2-, 3-, 5- or 10-minute conversation with a trainer at the end of a course doesn't really satisfy the units of competency as far as I'm concerned. Forgive me Kaplan if I've got that wrong, but I've researched it enough to know that if you can get through on Kaplan, then anyone can get through. That's my view when it comes to online stuff.

I believe that the formative and summative requirements under the new package no longer exist so, therefore, I really can't comment on whether it's gone up or down or stayed the same. If I had to bet, I do know that the trainers at Harcourts and The Academy are very astute trainers and I have every faith in what they are doing. Maybe not to the standard that I was, (I was a little bit anal retentive in terms of professionalism and all the rest of it), but they would be training to what is required by ASQA right now, for sure. They would have been looking at our business and saying, "*Well, we don't want that to happen here.*" They would be making sure that they're '*dotting the I's and crossing the T's*'.

The writer interrupts Greg's train of thought for a moment and says... so just going back a little bit, you just said that the formative and summative requirements that were the basis of that auditor's determination of non-compliance that existed in the previous training package no longer exists in the new training package? Greg continues...

We went to great lengths to battle that little bit of rubbish out of the new package, and at the time that the auditor made that finding, we were only months away from the new package, so having to spend all of this money on a training package that was eradicating the very issue we were being sanctioned for...yeah, it was a bit of a joke. And, if I might say so, I believe that this is where I think there was a level of unreasonableness on the part of ASQA and, in particular, that auditor because we were only months away from the new package. Having gone through and been a part of the development of the new package, being through all the consultation process, there's none of this formative, summative, all of those sorts of things.

I do know that some of the consultants that have been doing some work for these REIs still couch it as summative and formative and I suspect they're doing that just to make sure; just in case the ASQA attitude towards audits goes back to the same methodology and mentality of THAT particular auditor, they've got themselves covered. I do believe though, this auditor was never going to be about reasonableness or what is procedurally fair, he made his intentions very clear the moment he walked in the door remember? *"I'm here to close you down"*!

The writer asked Greg if the new training package was pending endorsement then, did he still happen to have the case for endorsement and the units of competency that she could use to demonstrate that those things were no longer required in the new package and this was all such an unreasonable, unnecessary experience that has caused critical issues for a significant number of people in South Australia?

She explains that she thinks that by demonstrating that that case for endorsement was already done and only months away, it really does support your story in saying that ASQA was a bit unreasonable about this. Greg said he might be able to find them because we were obviously heavily involved with the consultant that was engaged down in Tasmania to go through that process. It feels like every six weeks there was another survey going out just to make sure.

He continued...My Training Manager was more directly involved in that and, as I said, I just knew that every time a survey came out, I would have to ring and email a number of the principals and say, "*Hey, this is an important survey. Can you do it for us please?*" Otherwise, if they didn't get a suitable response or enough response, it would get delayed even further. Yet, given all the REIs, as conflicted as they may well have been, worked very closely through this process, along with others, to make sure that training represented the '*real world*'. That's why we're all keen on the new package - very keen on it!

The Artibus Innovation Case for Change[144] supports Greg's story and a sample provided below:

Description of work undertaken and why

A technical review of the existing suite of the CPP07 Property Services Training Package real estate qualifications was undertaken, which identified:

- **duplication and overlap of content** across the qualifications and units of competency;
- obsolete qualifications, which **did not reflect current occupational roles;** and
- **a gap between the qualifications and jurisdictional licensing requirements**.

The work undertaken with industry, state/territory training authorities (STAs) and the Technical Advisory Group (TAG) focussed on:

- following the AISC requirements and consolidating qualifications and units of competency;
- **developing streamlined qualifications that reflect current occupational roles;** and
- **designing skill sets that align with licensing requirements**.

Drivers of change

This project is a result of robust industry consultation to address the following areas of industry need:

144 Artibus Innovation February 2019, Case for Endorsement, CPP Property Services Training Package Review Release 8.0, https://www.artibus.com.au/wp-content/uploads/2020/09/Case-for-Change-Real-Estate-2017.pdf Accessed 12 May 2021, 2:01am AWST.

- **eliminate ambiguity** around qualification outcomes;
- clearly define skills, roles, and career progression;
- **ensure qualifications reflect real industry roles**; and
- future proof qualifications by considering technology, industry and social changes.

The writer continued by suggesting to Greg that at the time that his RTO was having to do all the rectifications and remediations, you would have been dealing with consultants, maybe some lawyers and the Industry Reference Committee ("IRC"). She suggests that he would have been dealing with a whole range of different stakeholders. What was his experience dealing with them?

That wasn't a bad time. The consultant that I had on was my ex-Training Manager and she knew the stuff like the back of her hand. She was equally surprised as I was with the interpretation that the auditor came up with. We worked with the Board, explained what had happened. The use of the mobile phone was the best example because they were just in disbelief that it would double in cost and that meant we were out of the running in terms of the competitive sense. We just got the rectification done. It cost an arm and a leg and, as I said, in a simplistic way and I don't want to disrespect the Consultant, the ex-Training Manager of mine, but it just doubled everything up because we had to train it twice. I'm simplifying it, but that's effectively what it came down to.

When we submitted it back to ASQA and said this is what we are doing, we overcooked it and cooked it and cooked it again. Obviously, we knew we were going to be fine, but the next step was actually getting the work done and being prepared in case someone knocked on the door and said, *"OK you've said you've done all this..."*. There were suggestions that we didn't even need to do it and I've gone, *"No, my name is the CEO.*

We need to do this. This is what we've said to a regulatory authority and we didn't do it to make them go away. We're doing it because this is what they've told us to do. I disagreed with what they have requested, but that doesn't mean there's any less of a responsibility, so unless we *want to fight upwards of a million dollars in the AAT, this is what we're doing."* So that's what happened throughout that period.

The writer asked how the industry responded to what was happening at that time? Greg continued...

We kept it reasonably close to our chest, apart from the Board. We kept it reasonably close to our chest because there was a little bit of embarrassment on my part and, whilst I'd been beating my chest, at the end of the day, do we spend a million dollars fighting in court or do we spend a million dollars fixing things? In the end, after speaking to another RTO around town, they just went about fixing it and so that's what we decided to do as well because we didn't want to spend a million dollars (*and I use that number just for purpose*) fighting it and coming out the other side and having to spend another million dollars to rectify as well. It was all just too risky and our brand name was just too important to us to have that fight. So that was the decision that we made.

I think there were a lot of other people around the countryside that were in disbelief when I was telling them the story, in particular the other REIs.

They're going, "*Well, how is this possible?*" And I'm saying, '*All I know is this is not a bad dream. This is actually happening and in order to satisfy them, this is what we need to do and in order to satisfy them'*. We became inherently uncompetitive, unviable, and all the rest of it, but we had to do it anyway in order to run off those six months of students that we were required to do.

The writer then asks the same question that each participant has been asked and reiterates that Greg should just answer the next question in the best and most truthful way that he could because the writer knew there were going to be some issues around what Greg had just signed off on. The question was - What impact did this have on you, your family, your professional reputation, the RTOs reputation? She explained that for many participants or those who had initially expressed interest in sharing their stories, there were stories of Post-Traumatic Stress Disorder, Counselling, Anxiety and antidepressant medication, divorces, splitting or complete loss of family assets, bankruptcy...Greg interrupts and says '*Fortunately, I don't have any of those issues. I would just give you one word, Raelene - devastated! And I don't really want to go any further than that*'.

As far as my family goes, all of the above. They suffered enormously as a result of these issues and they weren't the only family to do so. Sadly, there were many families affected in very negative ways. To have a regulator do what they did and in the fashion in which they did it was devastating, and the end results are devastating.

The writer then asks Greg...who would you say has been the biggest loser out of what happened in your situation? Greg doesn't hesitate to respond saying '*I would have to say the poor gentleman that died and his family*'.

The writer explains to Greg that she needs to be able to somehow explain to readers how that gentleman died as part of what happened to him (Greg). She asks how she can link the poor gentleman's death without getting either of us into trouble? Greg's answer is a challenge for both of us.

OK. The only thing that I can suggest is, and I want to think about this a little bit more, if I make available to you the acknowledgement apology letter from the widow[145]. Now that's publishable. I made sure that's publishable. I can't make any commentary around that. It needs to sit there by itself. I'm not sure I'd be encouraging you to make any

[145] The letter is not being published in this book but would be made available by Greg if requested.

commentary around that either because the other side's legal team can be quite aggressive. Lives were lost through this process, and I think you can say that and that's not anyone...I can't really say any more than that as frustrating as that is for me. It's devastating, just devastating.

All I can say is there has been an enormous strain on me personally... enormous strain. I think it's going to be with me for a long time. However, having said that, if you had asked me that 12 months ago, I would say no, but here we are a further 12 months on, I would have to say I've learnt a lot. It is what it is.

The only thing I can do now is have this conversation with you Raelene on the basis that I do harbour some grave concern over the behaviour of ASQA and its officials and I would not want this to ever happen again, even to my worst enemy. A bureaucrat being able to sit in their ivory tower and not appreciate what's happening at the coal face is simply not good enough.

It was devastating and I'm only just recovering from it now - emotionally, psychologically and all of those sorts of things. There was a book that I had the pleasure of reading over the last 12 or so months. It's called *'On My Watch'* and it revolves around the lady who was the CEO of the airports in the USA where the hijackers managed to get through the system and what she went through. That's probably given me strength to appreciate that there are bigger and brighter things in life and, having recently had a very good mate of mine die of pancreatic cancer, has put all of this into perspective for me. At the end of the day, I could have a swing at ASQA and be upset, but I've got a healthy family and we're living and breathing every day, so I can't complain.

The writer asks Greg if he ever approached the Chief Commissioner of ASQA or Ministers or anyone who could have made a difference? Greg continues...

I had a conversation via email when we were doing the extension to scope. I went straight to the top on LinkedIn to the CEO of ASQA at that time, Mark Patterson.

And then I did go and speak to the Minister Simon Birmingham and express some concerns but his hands were reasonably tied because of ASQA and the ASQA processes, so it was limited to that. Once we made the decision to rectify the issues we didn't think needed rectification, we didn't pursue appealing to Ministers or Mark Patterson again because we felt at that time that there was no point in carrying on about spilled milk, it would only come back and hurt us.

The writer asked what Minister Simon Birmingham's response was when he was advised about what was going on. Greg continues...

I tried not to get into too much detail other than the fact that I think he was the Minister in charge at the time, but having worked in a Ministerial office, I understood the processes, but I felt it was necessary for him to hear it. I knew there was nothing he could do. I've actually got a lot of time for Mr Birmingham, but just knowing that we had been done over by ASQA and a competitor was allowed to do what he was doing, I was overwhelmed by a sense of unfairness and so I felt that I needed to go and talk to him about that.

Effectively, he said something along the lines of, "*There's not too much I can do about it. This is the job of ASQA, the regulator and as the Minister, I'm unable to get involved...*" I told him '*I'm just here to tell you the story and to make you aware that this is what's going on. We are incredibly frustrated and you needed to hear it from me*' and it was left at that. I didn't expect anything more from Mr Birmingham other than for him to listen and to hear what I had to say.

The writer describes her experience with her local Member, a VERY high-ranking member of the Morrison government and how disgusted she was with his poor behaviour and complete disregard for the issues she was bringing to the table (issues about the impact of ASQA's behaviour on small business, potential breaches of model litigant regulations, etc.) and that she felt too that the manner in which the way she was treated was terribly misogynistic and demeaning. Greg says...

Yeah, that's right. The only reason mine wasn't like that with Birmingham was simply because 20 years ago, he was a Minister of Advisory at the same time as myself, so we had both a personal and professional relationship and, at the risk of sounding arrogant, I understand the limitations both politically and pragmatically when it comes to Ministers delving into things. So after spending 3-4 years protecting a Minister from the things he did and didn't do, that's the whole idea of the Chief of Staff and Minister of Advisors, but I can understand your frustration. I went in there with very little expectation. Greg asks... '*Was his Chief of Staff there as well*'?

The writer responded that there was a woman. The writer explained that she didn't know if she was his Executive Assistant, Chief of Staff or what, but she was there as well. The writer then explained that when she got home, she actually sent this woman an email saying, "Thank *you very much for arranging the time. I'm sure that you were as disappointed by the Minister's behaviour as I was*!" The writer explained that she just wanted to make sure that it was on the record somewhere.

She explained that she quoted some of the things he said and how disappointed she was and that she was just devastated. She just kept repeating and couldn't keep it from her mind, '*He has no right to speak to anyone like that*.' Greg says...Some might say, '*Karma*' and I've got to leave it at that!

Well I'm unencumbered by all the VET sector politics and that said, I haven't shared anything with you that is confidential. At the end of the day, my motivation for having this conversation with you is to outline the fact that having...and this will sound ridiculous...but having a government department regulator do what they did is still completely unbelievable to me. Regardless of what all the consequences were, I'm a believer in a '*fair go*' and there was anything **but** a fair go here.

Greg was asked if he ever received an apology from ASQA from what they, as an organisation did to him. Greg says...

Oh no, not from ASQA. Nothing from ASQA. At the end of the day, there was absolutely nothing from ASQA. What I got from ASQA was a vindication of what I had stated about my competitor that was undermining the real estate industry and its professionalism and training in South Australia. That's what I got from them. The only other thing I did get from them was when I asked for extensions in order to make sure that our students were being catered for whilst we were transitioning from pre-rectification to post-rectification; this was being conducted over the Christmas period so we wanted to make sure there were no issues. ASQA responded very quickly obviously because of the circumstances.

The writer then asks...Did you have any students... I've got clients all over the country that go through this process, have been over the years and still are currently. They are required to go through a similar process and they're having to contact all of their students who completed in the last six months. I know for all of them, they get a lot of backlash from students, employers and other regulators. To the point where people are sending abusive emails, they are abusing staff on the phone. They're thinking about having to get a security guard to walk staff to and from their cars when they leave the RTO because of the threats being made against staff. Who would have ever thought we'd see such scenes in Australia's VET sector? As one of the leading vocational sectors in the world, this is the type of behaviour that ASQA has consciously or unconsciously encouraged through its poor management of regulatory requirements. Greg responds...

No, we didn't have any of that. We literally draped our arms across our students and basically said this is what's going on, this is what we need you to do whilst we're transitioning and went from there. We tried to make sure there were no unnecessary blips or hiccups and all of those sorts of things. Once you've taught someone how to use a phone once, it's very easy to demonstrate they know how to use a phone in terms of competency, so we went about it in that fashion.

And we've got paperwork galore to demonstrate that next time that auditor wants to see it in writing - because obviously he doesn't see what goes on in the classroom, although I think they should. He needs to see what it is - the learner resources, the marking guides for each of the units of competency. The five documents plus the PowerPoints, plus...you know, here's the formative assessment, here's the summative assessment. There were things that we did towards the end that I said had to be done face-to-face and we insisted that the students would come in for two days so that we could be satisfied that they were 'Competent'. We were very anal retentive over those things. Once bitten, twice shy I think is the answer. ASQA could have come and observed a class but they were never interested; remember '*I'm here to close you down*'.

Obviously, the end of the story I can't comment on, but I've said this to you previously. The unprofessionalism, the un-Australian way, the way that the leaders of ASQA either turned a blind eye or didn't really care what THAT auditor was doing and saying. He was going about his business in the way that ASQA operated. You need to remember, the culture of ASQA at that stage was, '*Let's get them and let's close them down.*' I think that story needs to be said. Now Raelene, I don't know if you're starting to find this now, but I'm starting to get the feeling at the moment that some of the culture in ASQA has changed under the new CEO - no, OK?

The writer nods her head to demonstrate that no, that's not been her experience or the feedback that she's received from the sector. She explains to Greg though that if that's his perception, then I will write that he sees ASQA's perception in the sector now. Greg notes...

Well, that is my perception and with the people I've been working with since in the RTO world. I expressed that perception of mine but, at the same time, I make it quite clear that you should never trust ASQA because, regardless of what my perception is, ASQA can come and destroy your life on a whim. That's all I wanted to say. In terms of the other stuff that happened at the backend, that was just icing really...bad tasting icing, but I won't comment on that.

The writer explained the process for review, approval of the story and publication from this point forward so that Greg understood our agreement and the timeframes. He continued...

Well, as I said, I will only be retentive over the backend because, as you've said, you've experienced that law firm[146] and thank you for your support by the way. At the end of the day, it's just the way it is and as I said, it's been settled to my satisfaction so I'm moving on. As I said, that whole issue...my conversation with you right now is about accountability or lack thereof; accountability by ASQA. All that other stuff was just very noisy, very frustrating, personally demeaning, all those sorts of things, but if ASQA had done their job and done their job properly, I'd suggest to you that all of that other stuff would not have happened and another man would most likely still be alive today. If I'm laying the blame on ASQA, then so be it. I'm more than happy to do that.

I'm not training anymore. What I'm doing is, obviously having been bitten by ASQA, I'm helping out a few people. I was just participating in the ASQA webinar on Online Learning because I was actually interested in it. Online Learning became such a critical factor in the VET sector once COVID hit Australia; Zoom, training online all of those sorts of things. A couple of people I'm working with at the moment, that's what they are looking at doing and are currently doing. Whilst I just said to you that my perception was that COVID has sculptured their review of the world.

[146] This reference is in relation to the law firm that pursued Greg Troughton in relation to some issues '*unrelated*' to his ASQA matter but for which a man subsequently died after completing suicide.

From what I've just seen now on the webinar, the lady that would have been that auditor's boss effectively, whatever her name was, she was very, well, how can I explain... '*Clause 1.2 of the Standards basically says you've got to...*' Once again, they're giving no guidance whatsoever, they're hiding behind the Standards and they just don't get it... At least the Australian Taxation Office ("ATO") gives some guidance through guidance notes and all of those sorts of things. ASQA, at best, has got splinters up their backside and people are crying out to basically say, "*Is this OK? If it's not, we'll do it right, but...*" So they're guessing until they get audited and that's going to cost them a bucket load of money, there's no guidance for them whatsoever. Add to that the inconsistent approach by auditors and it's just an ongoing mess and recipe for disaster.

This lady today said she'd spent 20 years doing training and blah blah blah and they made a big thing out of that and as soon as she went into the ASQA speak, I'm thinking, '*She's swallowed the Kool Aid here.*' She was once in the real world of training and RTOs and all the rest of it and now she's gone into ASQA and I'm still listening to her just going, '*OMG, if I want to read about Clause 1.1, 1.2, 1.7 and 2.2, I can do that*'. This was specifically a consultation with four people including ASQA about Zoom requirements and online requirements and making sure that competency-based training is appropriate. As I said, my belief was that with COVID happening, I think they are regrettably acknowledging there's a lot of training that needs to go online. They're regretting that, but they have to acknowledge it and yet they're still in this push and shove, it's not good enough, it's not good enough. So every single RTO that I'm aware of that does it online is spending nine months of the year second guessing themselves. The PowerPoint will cut you up. I have to say it was a waste of time.

The writer agrees and says that she usually finds that the ASQA webinars are a waste of time, but she watches them so that she can reference them later on. The writer then goes on to make the following point '*I think that today's webinar (and I have thought about this quite a bit), with them approving the whole online delivery issue for COVID delivery, with that happening and them announcing a couple of months ago that they're going to be doing a strategic audit of online learning, I think they were obliged to do this particular webinar at this point so they could be perceived to be demonstrating guidance*'. It was quite tokenistic really.

Raelene, I 200% endorse it. That's exactly what it was. It was a conversation they needed to have and, as the bloke said, '*we've got 1,000 people on today*'. The reason you've got 1,000 people on today, sunshine, is because we all want some guidance and you've given us nothin'!

~END ~

Commentary

> **"Change will not come if we wait for a smoother person or some other time. We are the change we've been waiting for. We are the change we seek."**
>
> **- Barack Obama**

It is always a tragedy when a life is lost and Greg's story was no different. May we continue to bless the family and friends of the deceased and send them our sincere condolences. No family should ever have to go through an experience like this. The #enoughisenough campaign is however aware of at least two cases where such an experience has sadly occurred. Let's hope that this never happens again.

Real estate is a proud and highly regulated professional industry and it is imperative that ASQA takes something from this tragic point in history and ensures that it never happens again. It's not just the real estate industry though is it? To be completely honest, it should be no industry. In Victoria, there is legislation that commenced in June 2011 (strangely enough, around the same time ASQA was established) called 'Brodie's Law'. Brodie's Law made serious bullying a crime punishable by up to 10 years jail. As per the Department of Justice and Community Safety in Victoria:

> *Brodie's Law was introduced after the tragic suicide of a young woman, Brodie Panlock, who was subjected to relentless bullying in her workplace...*
>
> *Brodie's Law applies to all forms of serious bullying, including physical bullying, psychological bullying, verbal bullying and cyberbullying.*
>
> *Brodie's Law applies to bullying occurring anywhere in the community, such as workplaces, schools, sporting clubs and on*

the internet including email or social networking sites such as Facebook and Twitter.

Bullying is often characterised by a course of conduct that can include behaviour such as threats and abusive and offensive words or conduct. Serious bullying may also include conduct or behaviour that is intended, or could reasonably be expected, to cause the victim of the bullying to engage in suicidal thoughts or thoughts or actions that involve self-harm.

Really, it's all of those industries where there are additional accreditation requirements. Industries where typically, lives will be at stake and that extra layer of accreditation is there to ensure the integrity and safety of those industries. It is hoped that ASQA will learn that and partner with industry to truly make these issues a blot in Australia's history to never be repeated.

As the VET sector is demand-driven, core activities such as teaching, learning and assessment do not occur in a vacuum, but are affected by factors in the overall VET environment. These factors include industry shifts, enterprise training demands, technology changes and customer requirements.

The author is aware of at least three colleges that were affected in a similar manner by this ASQA auditor. Complaints were lodged to the current Chief Commissioner, South Australian ICAC, Commonwealth Ombudsman, several Ministers and ultimately, it was also reported to the Australian national Audit Office who is currently undertaking a review of ASQA. This was standard behaviour for this man and he effectively got away with it because 'he is no longer employed by ASQA'.

So apparently, you can do whatever you like, treat people as badly as you like, be responsible for the cancellation of businesses that turn over millions of dollars per year, engage in behaviour that leads to fatalities and because you no longer work for the department, you have no case to answer. I can't imagine any RTO owner ever getting away with treating an ASQA employee the same way and getting away with it! That would be perceived as being a breach of conditions of registration!

The fact remains, everyone involved in these situations is human and they all deserve to be treated humanely and in accordance with their legal rights. The public service is expected to behave in a manner consistent with the Code of Conduct[147] in the Public Service Act 1999 (Cth.) which states (*the most important, relevant clauses as far as these stories are concerned are highlighted*):

13 The APS Code of Conduct

(1) An APS employee must behave honestly and with integrity in connection with APS employment.

(2) An APS employee must act with care and diligence in connection with APS employment.

(3) An APS employee, when acting in connection with APS employment, must treat everyone with respect and courtesy, and without harassment.

(4) An APS employee, when acting in connection with APS employment, must comply with all applicable Australian laws. For this purpose, *Australian law* means:

(a) any Act (including this Act), or any instrument made under an Act; or

(b) any law of a State or Territory, including any instrument made under such a law.

(5) An APS employee must comply with any lawful and reasonable direction given by someone in the employee's Agency who has authority to give the direction.

(6) An APS employee must maintain appropriate confidentiality about dealings that the employee has with any Minister or Minister's member of staff.

(7) An APS employee must:

(a) take reasonable steps to avoid any conflict of interest (real or apparent) in connection with the employee's APS employment; and

(b) disclose details of any material personal interest of the employee in connection with the employee's APS employment.

(8) An APS employee must use Commonwealth resources in a proper manner

[147] Public Service Act 1999 (Cth.), s 13.

and for a proper purpose.

(9) An APS employee must not provide false or misleading information in response to a request for information that is made for official purposes in connection with the employee's APS employment.

(10) An APS employee must not improperly use inside information or the employee's duties, status, power or authority:

(a) to gain, or seek to gain, a benefit or an advantage for the employee or any other person; or

(b) to cause, or seek to cause, detriment to the employee's Agency, the Commonwealth or any other person.

(11) An APS employee must at all times behave in a way that upholds:

(a) the APS Values and APS Employment Principles; and

(b) the integrity and good reputation of the employee's Agency and the APS.

(12) An APS employee on duty overseas must at all times behave in a way that upholds the good reputation of Australia.

(13) An APS employee must comply with any other conduct requirement that is prescribed by the regulations.

All those who contributed their stories agree that this is the bare minimum requirement that ASQA staff should be required to comply with and be made accountable for when they don't.

Vicarious Liability

> "No law or ordinance is mightier than understanding."
>
> \- **Plato**

Author Note: This chapter has been written by an Australian Legal Practitioner.

A Registered Training Organisation should be able to put its best foot forward whenever it goes before the Tribunal.

This suggestion comes up frequently in stay hearings at the Administrative Appeals Tribunal ("AAT") and was also the case for Trades College Australia Pty Ltd which you will read about in Rabih's story later in this book.

The premise of course is that when a provider attends the AAT for merits review and requesting that the Tribunal use its discretion to stay ASQA's decisions, therefore preventing them from coming into effect, the RTO should be able to put its best foot forward - or demonstrate its best at the hearing.

Rabih's story is an excellent demonstration of where vicarious liability played out in a somewhat extreme manner. One of the biggest issues was around assessment practices.

While Trades College ultimately won their case, due to the fact that the AAT refused their request for a stay of the decisions, those decisions came into effect when they presented to the AAT for their first and second stay hearing (with a Federal Court hearing in between). The decisions to cancel registration and refuse to renew registration came into effect before the AAT handed down its ultimate decision finding in favour of Trades College. Unfortunately, though, it was too late and they are now in a position whereby they must apply again to become an RTO.

To better understand the concept of vicarious liability and what it means for registered providers, a lawyer who specialises in RTOs has contributed the remainder of this chapter.

While members of the High Court recently found that vicarious liability is 'attributing to one person the wrongful *acts* of another[148]', as Dietrich and Field suggest:

> Vicarious liability, at its core, imposes strict liability on employers for wrongs committed by employees in the course of employment. The precise boundaries of that liability, and the tests that ought properly to be applied in determining it, are contested questions. For example, what is the nature of the relationship that activates liability, and ought relationships 'akin to employment' suffice? What are the appropriate tests to establish whether conduct is 'in the course of employment', especially where intentional wrongdoing is at issue?
>
> It is fair to say that courts have 'struggled' to explain the law and are in an 'uncertain position about the approach which should be taken'.

There is the potential for exceptions to this rule for Independent Contractors given there can be a significant difference in the relationship of contractor and employer versus employer and employee. These exceptions however are very strictly defined and applied in law and include for example, the level of control an independent contractor has over their role and conversely, the level of control the employee has over the independent contractor. As described by Hancy:

---

148 *Ancient Order of Foresters in Victoria Friendly Society Ltd v Lifeplan Australia Friendly Society Ltd* (2018) 360 ALR 1, 5 [5].

An explanation for the dichotomy between these relationships was given by Dixon J in ***Colonial Mutual Life Assurance Society Ltd v Producers and Citizens Co-operative Assurance Co of Australia*** (1931) 46 CLR 41 - in the case of an independent contractor although the work is done at the principal's request and for his benefit it is considered the independent function of the contractor and not as something done by the principal by his representative standing in his place and therefore identified with him for the purpose of liability arising in the course of his performance.

The independent contractor carries out its work not as a representative but as a principal: ***Hollis*** [39]. The difference between the relationships has been said to be rooted fundamentally in the difference between a person who serves the employer in the employer's business and a person who carries on a trade or business of his own: ***Marshall v Whittaker's Building Supply Co*** (1963) 109 CLR 210, 217; Hollis [40].

It is a common theme in ASQA matters, particularly where the Regulator has issued a cancellation or a less serious sanction, to see Registered Training Organisations ("RTOs") play the internal '*blame game*'. We have all seen a provider in trouble pass the buck throughout the staff that are '*to blame*' for the problems the RTO has found itself in. So, who do we blame when something goes wrong in a Registered Training Organisation?

The answer is as simple as it is scary. Trainers blame Training Managers, Training Managers blame Operations Managers, Operations Managers blame CEOs, CEOs blame Directors and Owners. The unfortunate reality is that this principle is fundamentally incorrect. Section 133 of the *National Vocational Education and Training Regulator Act 2011* (Cth.) (*"NVR Act")* reads as follows:

National Vocational Education And Training Regulator Act 2011 - Sect 133

Personal liability of an executive officer of a registered training organisation--general

(1) An executive officer of a registered training organisation commits an offence if:

(a) the organisation commits an offence covered by section 133A; and

(b) the officer knew that the offence would be committed; and

(c) the officer was in a position to influence the conduct of the organisation in relation to the commission of the offence; and

(d) the officer failed to take all reasonable steps to prevent the commission of the offence.

(2) The maximum penalty for an offence against subsection (1) is one-fifth of the maximum penalty that could be imposed for the offence committed by the registered training organisation.

(3) An executive officer of a registered training organisation contravenes this subsection if:

(a) the organisation contravenes a civil penalty provision; and

(b) the officer knew that the contravention would occur; and

(c) the officer was in a position to influence the conduct of the organisation in relation to the contravention; and

(d) the officer failed to take all reasonable steps to prevent the contravention.

> *(4) The maximum civil penalty for a contravention of subsection (3) is one-tenth of the maximum penalty that could be imposed for the contravention of the civil penalty provision by the registered training organisation.*

The *NVR Act* sets out with absolute clarity, that for the CEO of a Registered Training Organisation (with some overflow to other High Managerial Agents) there is underlying responsibility for the actions of that provider. For this reason, it is fair to say that there is a doctrine of vicarious liability for anything done by, or on behalf of the Provider by an employee in the course of their employment, that rest on the CEO.

It is equally appropriate then that we consider who is an 'Executive Officer'. An executive officer is defined under the NVR Act at section 3:

executive officer, in relation to a registered training organisation, means:

(a) a person, by whatever name called and whether or not a director of the organisation, who is concerned in, or takes part in, the management of the organisation; or

(b) if the organisation is a body corporate:

(i) a person who, at any time during a period for which the organisation is registered, owns 15% or more of the organisation; or

(ii) a person who, at any time during a period for which the organisation is registered, is entitled to receive 15% or more of dividends paid by the organisation; or

(c) an administrator, receiver and manager, or liquidator of the organisation (other than a receiver and manager, or liquidator, appointed by a court); or

(d) if the organisation is a body corporate—the administrator of a deed of company arrangement executed by an organisation; or

(e) if the organisation is a body corporate—a trustee or other person administering a compromise or arrangement made between the organisation and another person or other persons.

It is reasonable to conclude therefore that as Hancy indicated earlier, a true 'Independent Contractor', in other words, an independent contractor that meets the lawful definition of an independent contractor, may not be captured under vicarious liability and are therefore completely liable themselves.

Given, as described earlier, there can sometimes be some '*overflow*' to high managerial agents, it is also important to clarify the definition of a high managerial agent under the NVR Act. A high managerial agent is defined under the NVR Act as follows:

> ***high managerial agent*** of a registered training organisation means an employee or agent of the organisation with duties of such responsibility that his or her conduct may fairly be assumed to represent the organisation in relation to the business of providing courses.

Australian Securities & Investments Commission ("ASIC") v Australian Skills Quality Authority ("ASQA")

The *Corporations Act 2001* (Cth.) sets out between ss 180 and 183 four main duties for directors of a Company, these are:

- Care and diligence;
- Good faith;
- Not to improperly use position; and
- Not to improperly use information.

There is no provision in the Corporations Act regarding a CEO or any 'Principal' in the same vein as the NVR Act.

Breaches of Directors' duties are clearly set out in the old *'liquidator's bible'* and include criminal sanctions, civil sanctions as well as commercial consequences. Importantly the penalties for misbehaving as a director start with disqualification from acting as a director. Other regulators, (including the ASX), have adopted and added to the ASIC requirements and helped make the Australian company regulatory one of the most effective in the world.

Despite this, when ASQA as the national VET Regulator sought to broaden its appeal and its approach, it did not adopt the ASIC and Corporations Act model as one of the bases for RTOs. Instead, it sought to further define and extend the operation of the CEO as a unique actor, something that only exists in the VET world. At the Regulator level, and at the Regulation level, the CEO is 'the boss' of an RTO and holds primary compliance liability. However, the CEO does not need to be a director of the company. Indeed, the CEO (or Principal Executive Officer ("PEO") which is defined under the *Education Services for Overseas Students Act* 2000 (Cth.)), does not even need to be employed by the provider. It remains one of the great mysteries as to why the VET Sector did not simply insist that the CEO of an RTO <u>must</u> be a director of the company exercising managerial control. So many problems would have been avoided.

As part of the corporatisation of ASQA, the Regulator has sought to broaden its appeal and its approach both at the Regulator level and at the Regulation level. Providers have been focused on the delivery of training and, in recent years, in their survival through COVID-19. In some cases, it appears, they may have forgotten their responsibilities under the *NVR Act,* but also under the Corporate Governance Principles that have been discussed earlier. The principles of the Directors duties under the *ASIC Act* are very different than that of the duties of CEOs (or PEOs) of an RTO.

To reiterate, effectively, the principle of vicarious liability extends to the CEO of an RTO. Any actions, costs or outcomes that stem from the business of the RTO falls specifically on the CEO. The legislation surrounding vicarious liability is jurisdiction dependent, with the following example, from the New South Wales legislation:

> The *Law Reform (Vicarious Liability) Act* 1983 (NSW) states, to the extent a servant's act or omission is a breach of the servant's duty of care, performed in the course of the servant's service to his/her master, the master will be held vicariously liable for that act or omission.

The following three (3) scenarios where the details have been redacted provide examples of how the impact of vicarious liability and its implied use under the NVR Act is clear and plain for all parties. The Regulator is unambiguous in its approach to the liability of the officers, agents and particularly of CEOs of RTOs irrespective of the proof or otherwise of a liability by other actors within the business.

SCENARIO 1

In this scenario, the Provider operated in the Trades Sector. The college was a very successful national provider and offered over 20 funded and unfunded VET courses. During the time that the Provider was operating, it had trained nearly 15,000 people in various qualifications. Graduates of the college were running very successful businesses within their chosen vocational profession and they spoke strongly in favour of the practices of the Provider.

The problems began when some students began complaining that a few of the trainers of the Provider were not delivering correctly. In some cases, students transferred during their course to either TAFE or to other Providers and their training and assessment was not fully recognised by the new Provider for RPL. The main Provider, and importantly, its CEO, were well resourced and had the correct Training and Assessment Strategy (TAS), training and assessment materials, resources, trainers and assessors and also prided itself on maintaining compliance at all costs. The issues stemmed from poor training practices of individual trainers.

There was never any indication until well into the matter before the Tribunal, that the CEO of the Provider that has been referred to, was anything other than diligent in their approach to the compliance of the business. Unfortunately, what occurred was a significant problem because a cancellation decision made by ASQA.

The Tribunal initially rejected the legitimate evidence of the Provider which said that it was '*not poor practices but unsanctioned and inappropriate training by individual (rogue) trainers which caused the critical non-compliances*'. This did not prevent the cancellation taking place. It also did not prevent the CEO being held personally liable in various debt recovery matters of disgruntled students seeking to recover their fees.

SCENARIO 2 – CRICOS

The CRICOS scenario is what many of my clients call '*the horror circumstance*'. Often in VET, one is dealing with individual students who sometimes do not have their qualifications recognised appropriately in their mind. However, for CRICOS colleges, the *ESOS Act* is unambiguous on the obligations of the Provider and the subsequent obligations of the High Managerial Agents, and in particular, the CEO/PEO of the Provider with respect to the status of students and their visas.

In this scenario, the Provider's student agencies were recruiting students and making certain promises with respect to Australian visas. Effectively, the students were being offered work-related visas in Australia if they commenced courses with this Provider. Not only was that fundamentally incorrect, but it was something that was entirely unsanctioned and unknown by the RTO. The RTO was cancelled as a result of non-compliance and in the appeal, a swathe of student complaints emerged and the beginnings of a debt recovery claim.

There were claims in some cases, that students had been misled into coming to Australia on the promises that at the conclusion of their studies, they would be able to seek Australian permanent residency. Irrespective that the claims were made by agents of the RTO without the knowledge of the business, it was held that the RTO and more importantly the CEO, were liable and responsible for the impact of those statements.

SCENARIO 3 – WIND UP

What happens when an RTO is wound up? Not cancelled, but suspended or sanctioned by ASQA but actually liquidated? There are specific elements within the *NVR Act* that deal with this, but the appointment of a liquidator constitutes an event of default and effectively an immediate cancellation kicks in. In this scenario, the Provider had two business partners. One business partner (the Director but not the CEO), issued Confirmations of Enrolment (CoEs) for students while 'the business' was aware that it was going to close. The business was liquidated as a result of unviability and the Provider was faced with a huge outstanding debt to students. In certain circumstances, students sued the Provider, sued the CEO and sued the two Directors. It was found that both Directors were liable. This is irrespective of the fact that one of the Directors was completely unaware of the further enrolments until after the liquidation. It was found that the innocent Director knew, or ought to have known, of these enrolments and in any event, stood to benefit from it. Students affected in this way would be in a different category to students affected by the regular enrolment or otherwise of students of an RTO that believes it's going to continue operating.

For this reason, the question of vicarious liability in the context of registered providers is one that requires very specific attention. The RTO business is a business that is granted through its licence issued by ASQA's significant powers. The private training, assessment, certification, and qualification of students effectively acts as a giant billboard to the world that this person is trained according to certain standards and to a certain level of quality. The Executive Officers, and most importantly the CEO of the RTO business, are unable to fall back on Australian corporate principles to try to protect themselves in the event that something goes wrong. Responsibility (and liability) rests on them.

It is for this reason that it is strongly recommended that RTOs have adequate Directors and Officers Liability Insurance and/or Management Liability Insurance, as well as a good governance framework in place such as having a Board structure which meets regularly to try and address these questions. It is imperative that these matters are dealt with on a day-to-day basis in a way that is acceptable and that is recorded and known by all members of the business.

Good and open communication with ASQA is also vitally important for this purpose. The future of VET colleges in Australia will put even more onus on the CEOs, executive officers and high managerial agents. It is also likely that further reforms will extend the vicarious liability on those agents in a bid to close a long-practiced tradition of outsourcing the role of CEO to a shadow or interim foreman option.

The CEO of a Registered Training Organisation is a position defined under the *Standards for Registered Training Organisations (RTOs)* 2015. Specifically, this role is defined as:

> ***Executive officer*** *means:*
>
> *a) a person, by whatever name called and whether or not a director of the organisation, who is concerned in or takes part in the management of the RTO; or*
>
> *b) an administrator, receiver and manager, or liquidator of the organisation (other than a receiver and manager, or liquidator, appointed by a court); or*
>
> c) if the RTO is a body corporate:

i. *a person who, at any time during a period for which the organisation is registered, owns 15% or more of the organisation; or*

ii. *a person who, at any time during a period for which the organisation is registered, is entitled to receive 15% or more of dividends paid by the organisation; or*

iii. *the administrator of a deed of company arrangement executed by an organisation; or*

iv. *a trustee or other person administering a compromise or arrangement made between the organisation and another person or other persons.*

This position, despite the issues outlined above, remains one of trust, both in the student/college relationship as well as in the relationship between the college and its regulator; for this reason, it should be taken very seriously.

In addition to implementing a solid governance system which includes a Board, another way to mitigate the potential risks of vicarious liability for CEOs should be to compel CEOs and Executive Officers to undertake certain training courses so that they properly understand their responsibility and their liability. These should be part of any future reforms going forward.

#3 Jane's Story

> ***"Justice will not be served until those who are unaffected are as outraged as those who are."***
>
> **- Benjamin Franklin**

We're a niche RTO in the southern area of Sydney, New South Wales. We've been running since 2005 and have always been highly respected by industry, the community, the regulator and the funding body. We had never had any complaints or been identified as not compliant and as far as I recall, in 16 years of being registered I only remember 3 face to face audits (one for initial registration in 2005, one for post initial 12 months later and another when we transitioned from delivering BSZ40198 - Certificate IV in Assessment and Workplace Training to TAA40110 - Certificate IV in Training and Assessment. We'd had other audits of course but usually desktop audits or audits from the funding body. We had never had any non-compliance identified previously, we were considered an excellent provider and amongst industry, a best practice and preferred training provider.

The college was running really well; We had full classes running twice a week (Mondays and Tuesdays and Thursdays and Fridays) and a full class for an evening group each intake. The majority of the time classes were full. We don't deliver to international students on a student visa, only domestic students and we never really looked to get into CRICOS[149] delivery, it just wasn't for us. We did our internal audits regularly;

we would implement any corrective action as soon as something needed to be rectified. If students made suggestions on their student evaluations about something and how it could be improved, usually, within 48

[149] CRICOS - Commonwealth Register of Institutions and Courses for Overseas Students

hours, the suggestion was implemented, likewise with suggestions from improving our work placements, making our courses better all the time. We spent countless hours identifying and implementing continuous improvements over our 16 years in business.

We were always engaged with industry, undertaking regular consultation and being so well respected by industry, we had a relationship where we were not only their preferred training provider, but also their primary source of current and innovative practice in the caring services and in particular, ways of providing best practice person-centred care. They were always the foundation of everything we did in our RTO and the patient care they delivered was considered as the building block and basis of the training and assessment we provided. Everything was built upon their accreditation and services that they provide; everything from our training resources, materials, handouts and equipment to our assessments, use of guest speakers, work placement programs and our overall Training and Assessment Strategies.

Even our trainers and assessors came from the very workplaces that we provided support to; it was almost like we were an extension of the care facilities themselves.

They were such an integral part of our delivery, assessment, resourcing and continuous improvement process and that was one of the things that was so unique about us was our very close relationships with our industry partners. We had so many sources of review and feedback on every factor that might have been relevant to care provision, even the residents contributed feedback and suggestions to help improve our courses ensuring that they like the services they received from the care facilities, our training and the services we provide were based on a comprehensive and holistic view of person-centred practice. Our students were not only introduced into the industry they needed to stay abreast of, but, if you go into any aged care facility in the southern region here, you will find that the majority of staff have undertaken some form of training with us.

While for many aged care providers, when the aged care standards came in around 2019, it was a monumental shift in the way training and assessment was delivered, for us, there was not much upheaval at all. If anything, because everything we did was already so integrated with industry and our industry consultation was such a significant part of our everyday operations, we were able to adjust our program to accommodate the new standards without as much as a batter of an eyelid. We always had brilliant reviews from both industry and students. I was going through some of our reviews just the other day because I often look back and ask myself how I got here.

One of the feedback forms we received recently that brought Jane to tears while preparing for this interview is shown next:

> The Holistic Carer Training Institute[150] has been built upon the foundation of the knowledge of experienced ethical nurses, who know exactly what is required to educate and develop staff in the science and art of caring. Their lengthy participation in the care/education system has enabled them to carefully screen potential students so that the 'right' people are chosen. Their no-nonsense practical approach to teaching is embellished by their ambition to ensure that quality care is the outcome of their input. 'Near Enough' just wouldn't be 'good enough' for the directors of The Holistic Carer Training Institute.
>
> I have been associated with The Holistic Carer Training Institute for many years and I have been very impressed by their hard-working and dedicated approach to their work. I would be very concerned if they did not continue in the training industry as the quality of new staff affects the quality of the care we are able to provide. Elders deserve the best care we can give them and the quality of worker's education is vital for this process. The Holistic Carer Institute knows what it takes to make a positive

[150] The name has been changed to protect the identity of the RTO as it continues its appeal against the National VET Regulator ASQA.

> difference to the life of a vulnerable person who is receiving care services. They have passion, the energy and the expertise to fulfill this need.

Another example of how valued The Holistic Carer Institute is by the aged care industry is reflected below:

> With over 30 years' experience in the aged care industry, and 28 years continuous service with this particular company which has facilities all over Australia, it provides me with what I believe to be in-depth knowledge and experience of the requirements for quality, competent staff for an aged care facility. My experience with this facility has consisted of being involved at the coalface; I have had hands-on involvement on the floor and in managerial roles. This has been complemented by my qualification in Training and Assessment which I have used over several years, specifically in my role as a care worker and providing significant on the job training.
>
> I have recruited many staff during my 13 years in management and planned, organised and conducted many staff on-the-job formal and informal training sessions. Over the years, I have mentored many staff and the results of our accreditation audits in the aged care industry, as well as resident satisfaction levels, reflect the high standard of care we expect from the care workers employed at my two sites; the majority of whom come from The Holistic Carer Institute.

With feedback like this, it's difficult to understand how Jane and The Holistic Carer Institute ever came to be in the situation that they're in. After all, is this the exact type of feedback that the public would expect to see of a training provider in the aged care industry?

Jane seems to slip away with her thoughts, she goes silent, sheds a few tears and then says:

I mapped the training and assessment process as best as I could. I thought everything was right, everything was being covered. Our facilities loved us; they have no hesitation telling us that we produce the best graduates this industry has seen for such a long time. Where did things go wrong? Because ASQA never came out, I wasn't aware that this isn't what they wanted; I didn't know that. How could I know what they want if they never come to see us? How can what they want be so far removed from what the aged care industry wants and needs?

I would attend so much professional development on compliance every year. When it came to submitting our annual declaration of compliance each year, I would go to the 5-session webinar for a highly respected and well recognised Consulting company in the VET sector in New South Wales where they would take us through the 5 phases of the student journey in exactly the way ASQA audits providers. I would take all the questions that came out of those and create internal audits according to those 5 phases of the student journey. I would conduct the audits. I prioritised the annual declaration of compliance each year because I knew how important it was. How is it that ASQA and The Holistic Carer Institute are just worlds apart on these issues?

It was like, during our audit, that even though we'd been operating as an outstanding provider (at least in the aged care industry's eyes). We were meticulous. We had planned and we were prepared with all the evidence they could have needed. Yet everything we prepared for and with was of absolutely no consequence and futile. The auditor had a list of things she wanted that we had been provided with at the last minute and we never really had the opportunity to demonstrate why we're the best at what we do. This continues to be the case today. Even in appealing ASQA's decision in the Tribunal, we have been unable to demonstrate this still. And now it's too late.

Even if I win my appeal, what's it all for? This industry is so competitive and our competitors couldn't wait to use the opportunity to kick us while we were down. For them, this presented a perfect opportunity to destroy our reputation, to create places for their own students to complete their work placements. They told our facilities that we had been cancelled, we weren't allowed to continue training, they told students they should enrol with them because we were closing down. They told our students and the facilities that even if they managed to get a qualification from us, ASQA would ultimately cancel their qualifications anyway and they'd be left with nothing. They told them we had lost our funding meaning that students couldn't benefit from the significant funding created during the global COVID pandemic to fill the skill shortage of aged care workers. We've been completely and utterly destroyed.

All that remains to this day is a lease, one of the best simulated aged care training facilities in the country and no students. I went to the accountant yesterday to go through the financials. The last year has been disastrous. Prior to that it was great, we never had a financial concern. We haven't had any enrolments for 2 weeks. Everyone knows, our region is so small. Everyone knows everyone and with competitors behaving in this way and ASQA doing everything possible to drag out the appeal process unnecessarily, the impact on the company's finances is just disastrous. They just keep going and going; it never ends.

I thought I was doing everything I had to do. Apart from those, I'd go and do validation webinars, mapping webinars with that same company; every time 1 came up, I'd go and do one. I have all the certificates, resources, templates and things that come with it. I was doing the absolute best I could. I was on the mailing lists for ASQA, TGA, VELG, Insources, all the big companies; I did everything I could think of. I was a follower of many groups on LinkedIn. I was a member of the RTO Assessors Group, another

> few that are very big, where I kept track of what was going on in VET, who was getting rubbished, etc. I was keeping abreast of what was going on, particularly in areas of VET Reform, training packages that are constantly changing and updates for the sector during COVID. I didn't personally comment, I didn't feel confident enough to get involved in the conversations (I'm an introvert); I watched the ASQA webinars, read their User's Guide prolifically. I followed them all to keep abreast of what was happening.

When Jane started out as an RTO in 2005, she commenced with aged care and business administration. As time went on, she added leisure and lifestyle courses and of course first aid. She also had TAA40104 - Certificate IV in Training and Assessment and TAA40110 - Certificate IV in Training and Assessment on her scope of registration but when TAE40116 - Certificate IV in Training and Assessment came out, she decided to relinquish it and focus on what she does best, aged care training and related courses. She initially had BSZ40198 - Certificate IV in Assessment and Workplace Training on scope, completed the transition to TAA40104 Certificate IV in Training and Assessment and again, transitioned successfully to TAA40110 Certificate IV in Training and Assessment. Jane recalls that time:

> An auditor did come out at the time of the BSZ to TAA transition to make sure I had everything in place and that the training and assessment I was offering was of the highest standard. Interestingly, one of the auditors in that office in charge of that project is still involved in my appeal today as an auditor; but under ASQA this time instead of being a State based regulator. I was fine, I passed without any issues at all. It was the State based regulator then, things were so different to being regulated under ASQA. You need to understand, we had been registered for 6 years when ASQA came in and we've been operating now for 16 years. It's not like we're a fly by night company that has opened up to exploit students and do a runner. That's not us.

> We ran a few courses, mainly for the facilities we worked with but in the end, we had such a big response to our aged care courses, that I whittled it down to aged care, first aid, CPR and non-accredited short courses that are specific to the aged care industry such as supporting residents and their families when a resident has dementia, falls prevention, palliative care, PEG feeding and so on.

We talked a little about the difference between the various audit types and how this audit was so very different to those she'd always had. Jane repeats that she has not had many face-to-face audits since she was first registered and doesn't recall any under ASQA, they were all under the State based regulator. Every other audit, except this one, was a desktop audit. Even desktop audits you at least have a chance because the question was always 'show me how you comply with this...explain how you do that', the questions allow you to provide the evidence that you can identify in your RTO that best demonstrates your ability to be compliant. Not anymore though. The current approach is simply a list of give us this. They take it away and apply it how they like and come back and ask for something more. When you say you don't have that, they deem you not compliant. Now it may be that you have something else that demonstrates compliance and you don't call it by the name used by the auditor, but often throughout this audit, I was told if I didn't have it, I was not compliant and not given an opportunity to provide something different or even explain.

During all my previous audits, not only were they more understanding and accommodating, but they were impressed with what we did, they always said they had no issues. I remember one lady's name, it was Melanie, that's all she remembers. She was lovely to deal with, how you expect a regulator to be. Jane explains that with the face-to-face audits:

> Here again I can't remember exactly how it went now because it was so long ago and to be honest, since this audit and the trauma I've experienced, I struggle to remember things. They

told me what they wanted, I had it all laid out, they looked at everything, they asked questions, asked the trainers questions; it was really good and if it looked like something wasn't quite right or I didn't have the right thing out, they'd say, that's fine, can you show me x, y, z. It was a process and they were understanding, compassionate and asked, 'can you show me...'. As we went along, if there was something extra, I could get it. If I misinterpreted it, they explained it. Before the student journey standards came in, I always had everything organised and had no problems. I thought I still did. Even though the standards changed and I started going to all the webinars knowing we had to change with it, we did. (Jane again reminds us that they started doing all of the webinars on the Standards, set up the internal audits accordingly as she said, "Blah, blah, blah!").

She said she couldn't come out for the audit this time and we'd have to have it by phone. Our audit was moved around a lot because of COVID. At first she wanted it in March, then I had to call her and ask if we could delay it for a week. I explained that we didn't have to but that I'd had someone at the college that wasn't well and so as a precaution I thought that I'd call and see if it could be rescheduled. She changed the date and it got changed to several months later.

She said that she wasn't coming out, it was going to be an audit conducted over the phone because of COVID. It was originally scheduled for five days for one qualification and two units of competency (*CHC33015 - Certificate III in Individual Support* and *HLTAID001 - Provide cardiopulmonary resuscitation* and *HLTAID003 - Provide first aid*).

It ended up being June or sometime around mid-year before the audit ended up taking place. As it was a phone audit, she gave me a phone number I had to call her on after a specific time. She said it was going to go for three days now, not five days and that she was only going to audit two units from *CHC33015 - Certificate III in Individual Support* now. She said that it doesn't normally take that long but to keep three days aside just in case. She said that they would use the same evidence and delivery data they had collected six months prior. She sent me a form I had to fill out when the audit started, sign it, scan it and send it back so she had that in her hand because she couldn't commence the audit unless that was signed; it was the Audit Verification Form - Opening and Exit Meeting. It started at 9:00am and it was supposed to go for three days.

On the morning of the audit, I thought I was fully prepared. I again had everything that I thought she would ask for on the desk ready to go. When the auditor Sharon[151] rang, she gave me a list of things she wanted over the phone and waited on hold while I went to get what she asked for, scan and send it to her by email or Dropbox. At worst, she said she wanted it before the next phone call. Honestly, I gave her what I thought she wanted but it was hard to understand what she wanted. I thought I had given her what she wanted. She never told me it wasn't what she wanted, if she only had asked, I would have been able to just give it to her.

Sharon started talking and told me she wanted this and that and I couldn't understand what she was talking about. She said, 'I think we'll stop for lunch' at about 12:30pm and '... we'll get back together at 2:00pm'. I rang back at 2:00pm. She missed the call but rang back. I had decided in that time that I obviously wasn't giving her what she wanted or was expecting. So I just said to her when she called me back 'Look, it's pretty obvious I'm not giving you what you want and we've already identified that what I've been doing in the past is not right. We've already picked up these things that you're looking at in our own compliance activities and that's why we actioned them

[151] Name changed.

and made continuous improvements. We already transitioned to the new approach[152].

So the stuff we're sending you is not the stuff we're currently doing'. So the auditor said in frustration '*OK, I'll tell you what... you send me a copy of everything you're doing now. I want a copy of the learner guide, the assessments, the mapping and everything. I want to see exactly how you're planning on doing this'*. I contacted the resource developer responsible for our learning and assessment materials as what we were delivering now was online due to COVID-19. Under the licencing agreement, I couldn't just give the auditor a copy because it was all online and not printable. Because I couldn't just give her a copy, they sent me a sample. I sent Sharon (the auditor) a copy of the session plans, a copy of the learner guide, assessments, additional resources, I double-checked the mapping to make sure it was right. I wasn't going to send them something that was wrong and besides, we had made changes and contextualised our materials so they needed to reflect this. I went through it with a fine-tooth comb. That first day, the audit finished at about 4:00pm in the afternoon, apart from the lunch break between 12:30pm and 2:00pm, I had been on the phone since 9:00am!

The second day, it started about 9:00am. I explained to Sharon about the situation with approach[153] and sent everything to her. After that, there was nothing else. I was asked to sign the Audit Verification Form again for an exit meeting halfway through Day 2.

Nothing, nothing further on Day 2, nothing on Day 3. She never saw my resources, nor did she express any interest in seeing them. I have a world class simulated training facility; she didn't want to see anything that I had prepared for her. She didn't

[152] Jane did say explicitly what she had changed but to identify it here might risk identifying her and her RTO so it has been changed to protect her and her appeal.

[153] Ibid.

see the simulated aged care facility where students learn and practice day in and day out prior to attending placement.

She didn't look or even appear to be interested in the thousands and thousands of dollars of resources that we use to teach aged care. She was just not interested, it was like I felt when she said '*Ok, I tell you what, you send me a copy of everything you're doing now. I want a copy of the learner guide, the assessments, the mapping and everything. I want to see exactly how you're planning on doing this'*. At the time, I imagined her throwing her arms up in the air such was the way she spoke to me. I felt exactly the same now, that I was so bad and such a naughty, nasty provider that she really had made her mind up about me and The Holistic Training Institute. I've never felt so awful and ashamed.

The next thing I heard, I was emailed a report to say I was not compliant and that ASQA were imposing a sanction[154]. I tried to fix the things she said were not right. She said there were knowledge requirements in the unit that were not covered in our assessments.

I tried to fix those knowledge items she said weren't covered by including them more explicitly in particular questions, the case studies, they still said it was not compliant. I didn't receive any phone calls, nothing, just a report to say I'm not compliant. That's when I really started to think that despite being in the aged care industry for over 40 years and having my RTO for 16 years, I '*clearly don't know what I'm doing*' and I called for help. You know, just about every RTO in New South Wales uses the same underpinning resources we do? I understand that you have to go through it and contextualise and we did; we heavily contextualised our resources. I understood what they

[154] The sanction is not being identified so as not to identify the RTO involved but it was not a cancellation decision as per the rumours by competitors.

> were saying, they didn't give me a chance. Then I spoke to their senior auditor.

For the purposes of maintaining confidentiality, we'll call this senior auditor Tom[155]. The way it happened was they send you a report and they say someone is going to call you and discuss it. Tom rang. I knew Tom from his earlier days as a State regulator. While having never dealt with Tom, I heard, and felt on the phone after I spoke to him, that he was a good egg. I said 'Look Tom, are you trying to shut me down? He insisted, 'No, no we're not doing that! We have a risk system; it goes from 1 - 4 with 1 being not too bad to 4 being really, really bad and you're just over a 1'. I asked him, 'what happens if I get it wrong? I know I'm doing the right thing but you guys clearly can't see that so I'm afraid I won't be able to demonstrate that again'. Tom simply said, 'you'll get <*insert sanction*>'.

Jane finishes by saying 'that's when I called for independent help because I was terrified; I couldn't afford to get this wrong'.

I asked Jane that if she could give ASQA feedback about their audit process, what would it be? She says:

> "The advice I would give is that they wait until they could send someone out. They could even do a meeting like we're doing now over a video call. This auditor, Sharon, I don't know what she's like, she could be a nice person. She was very softly spoken, but half the time I didn't understand what she was asking me for. She'd ask me for something and I'd say, "But Sharon, I just sent it to you" and she said, "Yes, but what about this and what about that?" Why are there so many things across different days?
>
> What Sharon didn't realise because she was not qualified or experienced in aged care was that we can't teach students

[155] Name changed.

everything in one day; it's got to be over a period of time. It's hard for me to map everything we do in different sessions to the various units and practical activities but if she had said that to me, that she was looking for something like that, I could have shown her or created one that showed her how we're assessing over a period of time, but it was like she just threw her hands up in the air and gave up and said we were not compliant. I don't know. I didn't quite know what she was after and I don't...I don't understand now. If she had said that she didn't understand, I would have been able to show her and explain, everything was mapped here. Unlike many RTOs here, we do a lot of practical training and assessment. Instead of giving them a book to 'go and answer these questions and get your experience on placement', we take students through every part of the practical training and assessment right here in our world-class simulated environment - and it worked against me.

There's a part of Jane's story that in my experience in the VET industry, is not uncommon. In fact, I'd go as far as to say it can happen in any industry, not just the VET industry. I ask Jane to tell me about Sophie[156].

Before Sophie came to work for me as a Contractor, she was working for a nursing home. She was working in the nursing home that my mother was in, but she was sacked and walked off the property (albeit I didn't know that at the time). Then Sophie went to work for another home care agency. Sophie wasn't getting enough hours and I brought her on as a Contractor. I took her on because my own colleagues in home care asked if she could help. I took her on as an assistant in the training room to help set up the classroom before students arrived. She seemed like she knew what she was doing and claimed to have had a long history in aged care. I paid for her to do her TAE40116 - Certificate IV in Training and Assessment, I felt it was an important investment. I

[156] Name has been changed.

thought by investing in her, I would be helping her to start again and we'd be able to take on an extra class, we had a long waiting list.

I have to admit, despite everything, she was a very good trainer. But as well as being a great trainer she was really inappropriate in the classroom.

I started getting a large number of reports and complaints from students. I started getting evaluations from students saying it would be good if she didn't share so much of her personal life in class. Then I started getting reports from students saying that they were offended by things she was saying. Apparently, she had been asking students for *Endone*[157], some students gave her money because she made them feel sorry for her. She told them about the home care that she provided for one of her clients. She would tell students that she had two clients she worked with two nights a week. As she got to know the students better, she started disclosing things like she was sleeping with one of the other carers who looked after the client (the resident apparently had 24-hour care). Students said that she didn't actually tell them she was sleeping with him on the client's property, but I now know based on my investigations since then, that she was. She would tell them she would do 'overnighters' and take her washing and do all her laundry at his house, using his electricity, etc. to save herself money, all sorts of things like that.

In addition to the feedback I was getting from students about Sophie, there was another married couple who were looking after this particular client.

Once I received this feedback, I decided that Sophie could no longer remain as a Contractor at The Holistic Carer Institute. Ethically and morally, I didn't believe it was appropriate for her to remain under our

157 *Endone* is the brand name of a medicine containing the active ingredient oxycodone hydrochloride. Other brands of oxycodone include OxyContin and OxyNorm and are highly addictive. It comes in different dosages and forms such as tablets, capsules, suppositories and liquid.

roof. I couldn't really use these reports against her in the legal system because 1] it didn't happen in the classrooms at the Holistic Care Institute; and 2] unless I had absolute proof, it would just be considered hearsay evidence.

The married couple sent the management at the Home Care Agency a report saying they came on duty and found bongs and other 'inappropriate stuff' going on. The management of the Home Care agency scheduled a meeting with her on the following Monday. They advised her 'we need to discuss the report. That weekend, Sophie went into the office, hacked into the Manager's computer to get a copy of the report and resigned. I didn't know about this until very recently. The management of the residential care facility didn't know about it either until recently.

It's funny, you never really know what people are like until after everything has happened. I was still employing her as a Contractor and I had no idea all this was happening. How could I? I was horrified when the reports from students started to come in. When I was informed, I sent her an email advising her to resign because of what she did. I explained to her everything that I had become aware of and that she was only a contractor, not an employee. I explained that I didn't want to have to put in writing all of these things that I had become aware of and so it was in her best interests to just resign.

Since then, she has done every conceivable thing she can to destroy me. Why would anyone do that? She's the one that was doing the wrong thing, I was only doing the right thing by my RTO and my students. How do people like that go around destroying other people? I just don't understand it.

It also recently came to my attention that when she was a contract trainer for my RTO, that she also started a Facebook group. I've got copies of text and Facebook messages that students have sent me saying things like, '*Listen...if you don't know the answers, give me a call and I'll tell you the answers*'. I didn't know about this at the time either, I only found out after she resigned when a few of the better students told me but it has also started to unravel recently. I've since had to go back and conduct remediation on all these students.

Some students used to think Sophie was fantastic, I can only imagine that they thought that though in hindsight because she did their assessments and/or gave them the answers. When Sophie was asked to resign or be terminated, she started trying to get the students in that Facebook group to help her ruin me by telling them stories and making things up. She started doing everything she could to ruin me personally and professionally. She then started saying a lot of stuff on Facebook that was really negative about me and the RTO that has just got out of hand.

Sophie would get the students to send me emails saying 'What have you done? Why did you get rid of Sophie? Sophie's the best trainer we've ever had'. There was no way in the world I was going to explain to students why I had to get rid of her. It wasn't professional, it was confidential, she was a contractor. I told Sophie if she wanted to come in and meet with me, we could speak but my mind was made up, I have sufficient evidence to support the messages, emails and calls I had received about her. I just told her straight out, 'you can come and discuss the issues I've outlined in the letter if you want to or you can just resign'. She resigned in November last year. Sophie had been with Jane for three years. Jane looks down and starts crying again...

> All I know now is I've got texts and things where she has advised students to go to SafeWork, the police, to the courts to get a restraining order against me. I have copies of emails, saying to students I'm here to support you.
>
> Sophie stated in her emails that she was on Valium for 4 months because of '*that woman*' (Jane). Later on, a student, Bianca[158] started to realise she's not going to have a bar of this and sent

[158] Name changed.

me a copy of all the emails, etc. I've been very fortunate; many CEOs might never receive that sort of valuable evidence from their students.

I got a call from the police this week telling me I needed to go and respond to a charge. I went to the police station and they said that they needed to interview me in relation to an allegation that someone made that I assaulted them. They were investigating a prospective charge of assault against me. Can you believe it? I'm 64 years old and have been working in aged care for more than 40 years, have been an upstanding member of this community for over 40 years, and they are investigating an assault charge against me. They told me that I could contact my lawyer if I wanted to, but they needed to interview me in relation to the allegations that had been made against me.

When I got there I was told, 'You don't have to answer' and so forth. They said, 'You're going to be video recorded. You can say no comment, but if you do answer, we may use this in any proceedings that may result as part of this investigation'. But I felt like a criminal. They had a video recorder going the whole time. And while it might be normal practice, it was very confronting for me. I am already so traumatised by everything that has happened and here I was, I had to go into an interview room where they video and audio recorded everything I said, every movement I made.

I was petrified and felt like I was being treated like a criminal. Why? Why do people like this get way with things like this? I've never had so much as a speeding ticket in my life and here I am at 64 years of age being investigated on an assault charge? Sophie had knowingly encouraged these students to do this at a time when they were very vulnerable. For example, the main person who had claimed I assaulted her, let's call her Vicky, had just lost her mother and was grieving. She was very vulnerable.

I have copies of everything, text messages, emails, incident reports. I took copies of everything into the police station so they could do a complete investigation.

I remember during the police interview, I said to the policewoman while the tape was running... 'you're going to find this is all rubbish, but you're looking at someone whose business is gone, whose life and reputation is ruined. But the person who did this, they're going to walk away and get away with it. They can just destroy someone's life, their business, their personal and professional reputation and get away with it. The police were going to turn the video recorder off but I made sure all of this was on the recording. I said to the policewoman, 'you're going to forget about me in 5 minutes when I walk out this door. But she's ruined me and she's going to get away with it and it's true'.

The police rang some people who had written incident reports and one of those people rang and said she had just been called by the police and she told them what happened. She said I think you just need to relax, because at the end of the day, what they're saying happened did not happen and there are enough witnesses to prove this didn't happen. Be strong.

A few days later, I was on a video call and the police called my mobile. I didn't realise it was them of course because it came from a private number and I have had so many awful calls from private numbers of late, I just don't answer them anymore. It was only when I listened to my voicemail messages that I realised it was the police who had called.

When I returned the call, the police officer who left the message had finished her shift and was gone for the day.

I called back the next day. The policewoman said there's nothing in this, she's going to file the case because there's insufficient evidence. I asked if she had told Vicky, the student who told everyone I assaulted her and she said she had. The policewoman asked me if I felt better. I tried to explain to her that it doesn't make a difference. Sophie and Vicky have done the damage and the damage can't be undone. I was very distraught and crying on the phone, this was all just so unfair, how can this happen?

So that was it. I got a call yesterday to say that the charges had been dropped. Exactly like I said would happen. They all get to move on and it's like nothing happened, the people who made the false allegations got away with it but I have to live with the consequence of what they're doing forever. In 64 years, I have never been investigated by the police, I have never been charged or charged on suspicion, I've never had a need to go to the police station like that.

It didn't end there though. The people who made these allegations against me also made the same allegations to the local member of parliament. That member of parliament then stood up in parliament and identified me and my RTO personally and asked what sort of college owner can get away with assaulting students and firing staff unnecessarily? I was never approached by the member of parliament to confirm anything or provide any answers to any questions, they just took for granted that what these people had said about me was true. Yet, that parliamentary officer's office is right around the corner from my RTO. The member of parliament posted on Facebook multiple times about how she had stood up for the student who had been assaulted and the employee who had been unfairly terminated and that such people should not be able to operate not only an RTO but also should not be able to operate an RTO in the aged care industry.

The member of parliament is sensitive to anything to do with violence and abuse. They hold the portfolio that covers violence and abuse. They're well known in this area as being advocates against violence because their son was king hit in a pub 10 years ago and killed. They have started a foundation and now they're out to get anyone or anything to do with abuse. I think this time, they've gone too far because they didn't even check the facts before taking the actions they did. They just stood up in parliament and carried on. I understand that they have gone through a horrible time; they lost their son, it's awful. The reality is, this person is everywhere in the community and everyone thinks they're wonderful, but this is destroying lives.

Like I said, their office is just around the corner from me and not once have they called me to see if any of the allegations were true. The absurdity is that they are never going to know that I've been cleared of the charge and even if they do find out about it, they're never going to say anything. No politician is going to get up and say they were wrong. So they have got away with it, the damage is done, they're going to get away with it. I have to somehow pick up the pieces and move on with my life as though nothing ever happened. But it did. Really, really awful things happened to me. These people are in the wrong.

The police asked me if I'd been down to see the politician, I said no, I didn't want to stir up any trouble. But I've lost staff over it, nobody wants to enrol in my college anymore because of the things that have been said publicly about me and my RTO and even the aged care facilities that I had such a close relationship for so many years have now turned against me too. I understand why, if I was in their situation, I'd be the same. They are the primary carers for the elderly of many people in their community. If the community is being told that I assault my students and shouldn't be allowed to train aged care, they can't afford to have someone like that associated with their facility.

> One more thing about the police. I said to them, 'you guys are the first people to ask me for my version of events, the truth'. Can you imagine? The first people to ask me if any of this was true were the police.
>
> Even the journalist who wrote about it in the newspaper; they gave me less than two hours before publication to respond to her inquiry, I didn't receive it until after the two hours had passed and the journalist just took the allegations to print. I had to wait for the police to ask me. Even a member of parliament who was supposed to be there to look after the people in their community didn't give me a chance to tell the truth or respond to the allegations, so that's it. There's no point in fighting it. The member of parliament has gone on holidays like nothing happened.
>
> Jane stopped for a moment. She's been crying for a long time and she tries to pull herself together. All the evaluations I got back about Sophie were fabulous, she said that the students were doing well and all their assessments were great. I had no reason to believe there was a problem. Why would I? I'm the CEO and didn't get involved in hands on training anymore unless absolutely necessary. Trainers and assessors hand their student results to admin once all the checks and balances are done. But in hindsight, I realise that the students were doing so well because she was giving them the answers on Facebook as a group, I was horrified.

Jane says she doesn't really know how the politician came to be aware of this issue. She didn't know anything about the member for parliament who claimed to know about everything that was going on. All Jane knew was that someone came in and showed me a page in the newspaper about the incidents that had occurred[159]. She said had no idea where

[159] The incidents were actually explicitly detailed but to protect Jane's identity and her RTO, these have not been included in this testimonial of her journey.

it was coming from. She just received that email from the journalist at around 4pm telling her that certain things had been said about her and her RTO in parliament and that unless she responded to the journalist' questions before 6pm, it was going to be printed in the local newspaper.

Jane said she sent it to her lawyer, but of course it was too late, the journalist just didn't provide sufficient time to respond. The newspaper article mentioned that the politician had brought it up in parliament, mentioned my name, mentioned my RTO's name and mentioned that I had been charged with assault and that the RTO had a culture of bullying which had spread throughout my entire business. Apparently, Bianca (the student), was not alone in all this. Jane believes that Bianca and Sophie were in on this together, there's just no other explanation for it. Parliamentary privilege - it allows politicians to say whatever they like and get away with it with nobody ever questioning the accuracy of their allegations. Nobody had even told Jane that the issues were being raised in parliament; nobody. She thinks it was televised or at least online, only because she used to sometimes watch it. She's not sure if it was, she just doesn't know if that one was televised.

I think after everything, that Sophie is behind it all. I do think that Sophie is the reason why I was advised about an audit after Sophie was warned that she had to either resign or I would terminate her employment. I believe she contacted ASQA anonymously and lodged a complaint about it. In contemplating everything that Sophie has done since, it seems pretty obvious. It seems absurd that ASQA has just not been anywhere near my RTO for over 10 years and suddenly, this all happens. I know it was her, there's no other explanation for it. She was there, she was there the whole time and telling ASQA whatever it is she wanted and they've obviously believed her. She was still a Contractor at that time.

Jane says that Sophie knew about the first audit report and that we had until a specific date to demonstrate compliance or we wouldn't be able to continue operating our business despite the sanction. Sophie knew about that. She said she didn't know quite how she did it, but she got on to the journalist and told them that she was illegally enrolling people after that date when ASQA had written to me enforcing the sanction (which was completely untrue). The journalist has obviously been on the ASQA website because they asked me about certain things that ASQA have put on there about me and the RTO. The journalist wanted to know why I was enrolling students if the ASQA website said I was subject to a sanction from a date months prior and it was clearly stated on the ASQA website that I was not permitted to enrol students and that I was still running courses, that any certificate I've issued since the beginning of this year is invalid. None of that was true. None of it. I have an unconditional stay of the decision and have always had an unconditional stay of the decision. Did you realise that the way that the ASQA decision table is maintained misinforms the public?

Even though my lawyer sent her a letter to tell the journalist it wasn't true, the journalist printed their story anyway. They wrote the story they wanted, even though they knew it wasn't true and simply put a disclaimer at the end of the story saying that my lawyer had provided advice in writing that there is no evidence that we did anything wrong. Can you believe that? She put it at the end so people would read all those bad things about me and at the end, it was almost like an 'Oh and by the way...'. It was intentionally written in that way to influence people's perception about the situation.

Jane is crying heavily now. I let her be and say nothing. It feels like minutes go by. Then she says:

> I don't understand why this has happened, the vicious attacks, why? How can this journalist do this when they don't really know? How do they sleep at night knowing that they've written something that is not true and they have the power to influence the perception of so many people by what they write? How are people allowed to get away with things like that?

Sometimes I look at what and who I am, and I'm not blowing my own horn here but I'm the least judgemental person you will ever meet. It absolutely shocks me that people are not the same. I find it hard to understand people who are vicious. The good guy doesn't always win. All I want to do now is get out. I've been in aged care for 40 years. A staff member who does the wrong thing, you do what's right to protect the vulnerable. An ASQA auditor comes along, no experience in aged care and completely destroys my business.

My students go to almost every aged care facility in the south and they use me instead of advertising for staff because of the quality of training the students undertake. One of the trainers I had, she heard I was going to get shut down (which also is not true) and she moved to another RTO. Other RTOs are not really too worried about teaching them the real practical stuff. I have people coming to me because they've been at other RTOs and couldn't get any practical training because all they'd done was manual handling and first aid and the RTO couldn't get work experience so they couldn't finish their course. I'd retrain them and send them out under my name. It's sad that now, many of the RTOs in this area are just in it for the big bucks. They don't provide any practical training, they just give the student a theory workbook, tell them to take it home and complete it as self-study and expect the aged care workplace to do the rest.

The things I worry about, the people assessing those students in the workplace are not assessors. They're not qualified. We train students, we assess students all before they even go out in the workplace. We send them out to industry to get exposure to the real environment; we give them the opportunity to gain industry experience once they already have the theory and the practical training to support a work placement. I couldn't send students out who had no idea how to do things. Those

> poor residents that have to get looked after by students who have no idea what they're doing. We never sent anyone out on placement unless they were ready. Even if we felt that they were ready but they didn't feel ready, we wouldn't send them, they just wouldn't go out.
>
> The reason all of the aged care facilities used to use my RTO is because even though they're not supposed to, they use them as staff because they know exactly what they're doing from the word go. On paper of course they're not staff, but that's part of the reason why almost all of my students, at least 90% of them get employed before they're finished their training. One of the last things our students are told when they finish their placement is to put their resume in. These facilities need staff. There are so many skill shortages in the aged care industry and just not enough trained staff to fill the void. They don't place an ad on Seek for future staff, they call me. They refuse to take students from the local TAFE because their course is just so bad and the students so poorly prepared for the aged care industry. I had a great relationship with just about every facility out there. If you read that feedback I gave you earlier, that's the type of feedback I get from everyone.

I ask Jane about her comment in relation to the aged care facilities using her students as staff. She says:

> I probably shouldn't be saying this but it's true and people need to understand and accept that this is happening under their very noses and why. Australia is a leader around the world when it comes to the standard of care in aged care facilities. When the royal commission talks about all these problems, it's other states. In some states, aged care workers don't even have to be trained.

There is a severe skill shortage. Now, with the findings of the royal commission released, they've swung the pendulum in a completely opposite direction. It's only a couple of States that really require investigation into their aged care system and yes, elder abuse has been identified. But to put cameras in residents' rooms, carers feel intimidated by the scrutiny of their every action. People are getting scared. Would it not be a better option to increase the staff to client ratio to allow two carers to work together with the clients? Work gets done twice as fast and there's no need for cameras!

People need to remember, the aged care course itself is an entry level course, there is no pre-entry course. The people enrolling in these courses are people who are not academics, but the course IS very hard for them, they're being taught things they absolutely don't need. They're learning about complex anatomy and physiology, the stuff they don't need to know because it is not even close to being a part of their scope of practice, they would just never perform tasks that require such knowledge. We tell our students what a rewarding and satisfying industry they're going into, how they will make a difference in someone's life, ensuring their final days on this Earth are safe, enjoyable and that they are well cared for.

Then, these same students go out and earn $23 per hour. They go out and they're cleaning up people's excrement and vomit, showering them, brushing their teeth, keeping them company when their own families desert them, taking care of them when dementia sets in and they've forgotten who they are, making their beds, holding their hand in the middle of the night when they're afraid of dying and there's nobody else around. And they are cheated. A measly $23 an hour. Most people will not work for such low wages, they can't survive on it so they go where the demands are less and they can make a living.

I saw one student the other day who did our course and was working as a checkout operator at the local supermarket. She said it was less stress and more money. The things carers are expected to do, the responsibility they have, they're not paid or valued sufficiently. You can work at McDonalds and get paid more. They can go and work in aged care facilities but the accreditation for aged care is so rigorous, so demanding, they have ongoing professional development requirements too but can't afford to pay their rent let alone pay for professional development. Many of them will never buy a house because their salaries are so poor. They get too stressed, they get frightened and jaded and so after a while, they leave. And so for every new aged care worker you put out there, there may be another two or three whose jobs have just become vacant. There's always a skills shortage in this industry. T

tryhere are residents who don't want to be at home or can't be at home for one reason or another and they're afraid, then you have residents in aged care facilities who are also afraid and they want to go home but there's nowhere for them to go.

The royal commission falls short on addressing a request for mandating a reasonable carer to client ratio. However, the government refuses to mandate it because they know it's impossible, it's all about the $$$. In the end, it's too hard for the carers so they leave and our elderly again feel deserted and abandoned. As a carer, you could have 8 people to look after and that's not uncommon but it's already way too many. They spread their shift out knowing they have to get 8 people up out of bed, 8 people showered, shaved, groomed, clothed, 8 people fed, do this, do that...often they don't even have time to say hi to the residents and really ask them how they are. It's sad but it's almost like residents are on a conveyor belt. There needs to be a mandated and reasonable carer to client ratio!

> Somehow, despite all of this, I need to explain to my students, that it's a great industry where they really can make a difference in people's lives - but it shouldn't be at the expense of their own lives either and the government shouldn't expect this. Although students love it when they are on work placement, when they are finished, they just want to leave the industry, they're burnt out and struggling to survive.

I happen to know that during this ordeal, Jane also lost her own Mother. I ask her about how this whole ASQA situation impacted her ability to care for her own Mother before she passed away and spend some valuable final moments with her. Jane's response is just heartbreaking:

> I haven't finished grieving with Mum, it's still very much an open wound and she passed away before Christmas in 2020, over 4 months ago now. I still have her ashes here and I really want to go and put her with Dad as she wanted but I haven't had a chance to go over there because I can't be away from the RTO and my obligations for managing ASQA and the appeal in the Tribunal. COVID has also made it difficult of course but the borders have been open for a while now and every day I look at Mum's ashes and wish I could finally put her to rest as she would have wanted. I feel guilty and ashamed because I've not done as she asked me to do. After everything she has done for me throughout my lifetime, the one thing she asked me to do when she's gone and I haven't been able to fulfill it. It places a very heavy burden on your soul.
>
> Mum was in an aged care facility; in fact, she was in one of the facilities that hosted our students. She had dementia for a long time and progressively it got worse. In those last months, it became very hard because I was trying to manage all of these issues with the RTO all the while, my own Mother, a woman who I loved more than anything slowly began to no

longer recognise me, I was a complete stranger to her. She became unwell and went into palliative care.

In the end she wasn't herself, she didn't know anyone. Most of the time she wasn't awake. They moved her into a palliative care room, and she died peacefully in her sleep. They just went in one day and she was gone.

She passed away here in Sydney, she was in one of the facilities where I have students, she was just around the corner from me. She arranged many years ago to have a plot beside Dad and asked me to promise her that I would take her to be with him when her time comes, she said she just wanted to be near him again. I want to keep my promise to her and to take her to be with him but I still have her here with me, it breaks my heart that I've not been able to go.

Her health started to take a downhill turn while the ASQA matter was going on (it still is). Mum had been in care before that but things really started to deteriorate around December last year (2020) so a lot of these other issues, the reports from students about Sophie, the audit stuff and managing COVID changes to our delivery were going on. We weren't yet involved in an appeal at the Tribunal at that stage. I think it would have been around the time of the reconsideration. Actually, no I remember telling you, there was a period of time when I hadn't heard or seen you for a while. You asked about Mum and I said Mum had just passed away.

I'm pretty sure it was during the reconsideration assessment period because ASQA can take up to 90 days to make a decision with that and they did take almost up until their last day.

With all the newspaper things, parliament, ASQA, Sophie, Bianca...I was not capable of going anyway. I think realistically,

> because of all the trauma and anxiety I've experienced because of this ASQA matter, I wouldn't have been able to cope with finally putting Mum to rest too. As soon as all of this settles down, I'll take her on a plane to Darwin and finally place her with Dad as she always wanted and I promised but for now, that chapter isn't closed and remains an open wound too.

In hearing Jane's story, I ask her about the impact that this has had on her personally. I ask her too about the impact on her family and the industry given that she was such an integral part of it here in Sydney. Again, Jane's words just tear my heart open and remind me of why the #enoughisenough campaign began. Jane shares the following.

> The impact on my family has been dealing with me because I have been an absolute mess. Poor John doesn't know what to do with me a lot of the time. It has affected me mentally. I have had to take medication regularly. I have panic attacks now. I get upset every time I go past an aged care facility. I start shaking uncontrollably.
>
> Likewise, whenever an email comes through from ASQA, even if it's just an update, I shake uncontrollably and experience panic. I'm so frightened all the time. I can never have faith that my appeal to the Tribunal will be successful because so much has gone wrong. As much as I have confidence in those helping me, I know what I've been through. I'm half expecting one day that I'm going to get an email saying we lost at the Tribunal and I don't know what I'll do after that; I can't even contemplate what that might mean. I'm crying all the time, so poor John, he doesn't know what to do or how to help and to be honest, I don't know that there's anything that he can do to help. He feels powerless to protect his wife and watch her go through all this and there's nothing he can do.

He does his best to support me. We have almost decided that we're going to pack up and sell and move to Darwin because I can't go anywhere without bumping into people who know what's going on. They ask so many questions, and often innocently, and I can't stop the tears when I speak to them. We are thinking quite seriously about going to Darwin to be with the rest of my family when I take Mum to be with Dad again because I can't relax. One of my staff, Kim has been wonderful and helping to manage the RTO while I can't. I've only got one class now though. I can't even go into the office now because I can't bear it. I feel like something died. I've already had to get over one death.

I know that what I'm experiencing is grief and I know I'll get over it but I'm sad that I had such a love for the industry and now I don't like it anymore, I don't want to hear about it, I don't want to go into it, I just want a new life.

Kim knows that when all of this finishes that her job is gone too. I've had to tell my staff, which wasn't easy, I don't know who's going to buy it or whether anyone will even want the place. Whether, if I can sell it, they will want the remaining staff, the name, whether they don't want the name because of what's associated with it. I just try to go through each day thinking what should I do? Should I revise my session plans? Put things in their place? Prepare the financials? I just don't know what people will want.

We've just gone through all our enrolments. For the first few years, going back to 2005, we used to keep them in archive boxes and I've had to get Kim to save everything electronically because I'll have to hand it over. But I'm basically, I'm lost. I don't know what to do. I don't know what's going to be expected of me, I don't know what to get on with, to prepare, there's no more enrolments, I don't know, I just don't know what's happening.

It's definitely had an effect on John. He's so scared, especially the night when the ambulance came. I'd collapsed and fainted and was unresponsive.

I'd had a panic attack. That really frightened him. We work hard all of our lives so that we can hopefully retire with the one we love and share a decade or two enjoying each other in old age before it becomes your turn but that night, John felt like he had been robbed, he thought he'd lost me forever. I'm trying to hold it together when John and Kim are here, when my family calls but when they're not here, I start thinking of the loss and the viciousness, and I can't get over it. It's just so far removed from my mind that people would do that to others.

I've never come across anything like that before. The RTO is definitely finished, even if I win the appeal, I know that. I've had people who were booked in for training in the past few weeks whose parents have told them not to come to me because I've 'got a history of abusing students'. I've got trainers at the moment who are still employed but they will leave too. One of them is currently on hospital leave but I've got a feeling she's going to resign when she gets back. She's still in touch with Sophie, in a different sort of way.

She felt sorry for Sophie too. She parents her. You see Sophie's never had any parenting. Her mother was disabled, her father was an army guy, and often not around. I wanted to give her a chance to turn her life around because I knew she'd be a good trainer. I don't know. Jenny, my trainer, mothered her, took her under her wing.

Jenny is an older lady; Sophie has poisoned her mind and I've employed Jenny since the week I opened in 2005 yet Sophie has poisoned her. I can't believe it after all these years. She's very good this Sophie, she's very, very good. She's going to get herself into a lot of trouble though if she keeps living like this. When I learned about all these things about Sophie, I also learned she's got tax fraud issues. I mentioned it to her, and she said, "Yeah, yeah". I told my lawyer and he said I had a duty to report her. I didn't but someone else did. She's already been in jail for Centrelink fraud.

Jenny's been on leave because she recently had surgery but I think under the circumstances, she won't come back; there's nothing for her to come back to. It is sad though, I thought Jenny was a friend.

I've been for a mental health assessment and I have a counsellor that I see. I was already on some medication that I've been on for 20 years, however they increased that medication and I have the Valium also which was prescribed and I take if I feel that I'm going to have a panic attack, I take a half or a full one, depending on how bad I feel. They're getting milder now, not as bad, it could be because I don't go out as much. I see a counsellor who is doing her Masters at a university here. That's as far as it's gone, I'm happy with that. I feel comfortable with that. She's very good and at the end of the phone if I need her.

I went out yesterday to see the accountant and we were at a restaurant; I didn't handle that very well. I'm still struggling. Only because I knew I'd have to tell my accountant the story and I got a bit anxious over that.

I'm not having to take Valium all the time now like I was. It's there, it's my safety net if I need it. One of the things I won't do now that I used to do all the time is watch the news and read the newspaper. I have had to stop that. I used to watch the ABC news and read the newspaper every day. I don't do any of those things now, I won't let myself, I'm scared of what's going to be in the news. I know that sounds irrational but I don't want to look at it anymore because things have gone in there without me expecting it that are just not true. I don't know what they're capable of doing anymore, I don't trust the journalist or the politician anymore and what they will do. They've done it before, there's nothing stopping them from doing it again. That's why I want to go where nobody knows me.

Recently, a few weeks ago, I'd been shopping with my husband. We were in the large department store in our neighbourhood and he was at one end of the aisle, I was at the other. All of a sudden, I couldn't remember what it was I was supposed to get. I stood there, with the trolley, my hands were shaking, I didn't know what to do.

John saw it from a distance and came running up the aisle. He asked me if I was ok. I told him I didn't know what I was doing, I had completely forgotten what I was supposed to be doing there. He just pulled me close and said let's get out of here. A few days later, I had to get some bread and milk. He said, 'let me go'. I told him no, that he had to let me try to do this. I needed to do this. When I got back into the car, I started shaking uncontrollably, started crying and was struggling to breathe because it was just so hard to do. I forced myself to go down there, even if it was just to get one thing. I have to be able to move forward and not be crippled by fear and anxiety like this.

Just the other day, all I wanted to do was just get a coffee. I just wanted to stop at the office and see Kim. I went to get the coffee she likes. They gave me the coffee and I was shaking so badly; I couldn't hold it. I spoke to the doctor about it and the doctor said when I go out and I'm trying to do something like that, take half a Valium and as soon as I start feeling stressed, just leave. Sh1e said that gradually I'll be able to do a little more each time. I'm not an unintelligent person, I know this is so ridiculous but it doesn't seem that I can control it very well. I think I just need it to be over and then, when it's really over, I'll recover. But while it's still going, it just keeps going. I just know.

I've made up my mind, 100% that I'm finishing with the RTO, the VET sector, the aged care industry. I just don't know what surprises I'm going to get on the way out and that scares me. I keep trying to look at the worst-case scenario, if you can accept that, then everything else is fine. To me the worst-case scenario is the Tribunal won't accept the appeal and I'll just have to close. If that happens, then I'll just do what ASQA needs and somehow find the money to pay my debts that I've incurred through the appeal and I've accepted that. I don't have a choice. Then I just go from there. I don't know what it is that ASQA will expect; whether I will need to relocate any current students, but I won't even have any anyway so I don't even know why I think about that. When this group finishes, that's it, there are no more enrolments.

I'm paying rent on a building I can't use. I just don't know. All I know is I'm hoping that things go to plan and I guess I shouldn't even say this but I wouldn't care if I came out of it with no money. My entire life's work has gone in a flash, I'm grieving and I know that, on top of another set of grief, that of losing my Mum.

There's also been an impact on the aged care industry. There have been a couple of cases where an aged care facility had an elder abuse issue. Because we don't have a lot of elder abuse that happens here, the newspapers sensationalise it as much as they can because they need something to print, a bit like my story really. For one of these facilities, now, when they talk about elder abuse, everyone talks about that particular aged care facility. Carers are not being trained properly across the country and in my area, now my RTO is gone, I have real concerns over the quality of training that people will receive, I mentioned earlier what I know happens with other providers.

Now in some States, it would be absolutely correct to write that the lack of training increases the potential for elder abuse in some States. In my case, they needed an RTO to be able to link the story to put in the paper so they used me. I'm the only RTO they could find. So when people talk about elder abuse, they talk about that facility, when they talk about poor training, invalid certificates, they talk about me and my RTO. That's all they can talk about. To be fair, TAFE copped it recently too. People were halfway through apprenticeships and had to go and start somewhere else. TAFE stopped offering aged care as a result and they rang me and asked if they could refer students to me, there's a TAFE not far from me but TAFE didn't ever really have a good name in this industry. I said yes and things were looking pretty good there for a while, but now, like everything else, this situation has meant that I don't even get those referrals now.

To be honest, I don't know how the lack of students is affecting aged care facilities. They might be taking them from others now, but there's not many to take them from.

They used to take them from one RTO but they got cancelled, another RTO was suspended. I was the main one that would send students out in the northern region of Sydney. In the southern region it's different. In the north, we're not really a diverse community. In the south however, there are many culturally diverse populations; for example, new migrants, where women are in the home so they think they'll do a caring certificate here and they do these courses. In many of those RTOs, 70% of the classes are African.

Aged care facilities don't want to be discriminatory but they can't have people who can't speak the language. Residents need people who will understand them. In a lot of cases in the southern regions, the students just don't understand the cultural differences and so forth. In the north where I am, we have people from the Philippines and Indonesia. We may have some in the class but usually not many, maybe five maximum in the class. There is no problem with their English and they're just naturally caring, beautiful people, this is their general nature and culture. That's why the facilities here don't have problems accepting it, in fact, they'll often be amongst the first to get any jobs on offer.

So I don't know what will happen to facilities now, who's going to send them students now. I know one of my old trainers has started up this RTO, one of the ones you buy and find a pop up in each state, almost like a franchise.

She's running that so I guess she'll supply them. I know certainly there's nobody from TAFE so I guess what will start happening is like a friend of mine who has another RTO does. Even though his RTO is in the southern region, he's now got students from the north. He'll send someone out. Another friend in the city will try and pick up their pieces left behind in industry by our departure but they're in the city so a lot of their people are more multicultural.

In the northern region, they're going to struggle to find carers who are well trained. For someone who wants to buy an RTO,

> it's the ideal RTO to buy really once all this ASQA stuff is out of the way because the relationships are already established and you've got the northern region effectively tied up. All you have to do is rebuild it, not the relationships, but the confidence and trust in the brand and the people who don't know you.

A question has been bugging me as Jane has shared her story. Does ASQA even know what she's been through? What they've put her through? Jane reflects on the questions for a moment and says:

> No, I don't think so. There wouldn't have been a reason for them to know that. During the audit, I barely spoke to the auditor Sharon, and although that audit went for 2 days, it actually only went for a handful of hours. Yes we were on the phone the whole time and the only time we hung up was over lunch. But it was pretty stressful.
>
> It was just constantly one thing after another. Then when I explained the next morning about the resources, Sharon, the auditor just said OK, send it all to me, that's the last thing I heard from her.
>
> There was no offer to do any part of the audit via video call or anything else. That was when I had that conversation with Tom (the senior auditor) where I aid to him that it seemed like he was trying to close me down. In fact, Tom had said that there was nothing to worry about. Tom had said that ASQA got people here on level 4's and we're a level 1. That's why I was so shocked. I think Tom must have misled me because at the end of that call, I thought I was low risk but he did make it clear that if I didn't get it right, next time the sanction would come into effect and that stressed me. Besides, if I was that low risk, how can their actions justify the level of low risk? It just doesn't make sense. None of it makes sense.

I can't understand how it all happened. I have no idea. And I have no idea why ASQA hasn't taken some responsibility for the situation because they hadn't audited me for ten years. I had no idea that what I was doing was not what they wanted. To just send me a letter to say we've re-registered you for another seven years, like they did a few years back, I'm thinking, '*Sheesh, I must be good if they're giving me seven years*.' Then I found out that nearly every RTO got the same letter.

But seven years, how do you wait that long to check the pulse of something and then come back and say that there's something wrong and it's their fault.

The funding body had come out regularly and checked everything; they gave me the all clear. I contacted a friend of mine, someone who is a TAE trainer because 2 of the trainers that I was going to train to come in have backed out now. He said there's not an RTO that's not struggling with these issues right now. He said to me, they're really attacking the Certificate III in Individual Support, as well as anyone that runs it. It took him 12 months to get through his audit. He was with TAFE for a long time before he started his RTO at the same time as mine and it took him 12 months to get through. Even another RTO, they were held in such high regard, they got a suspension. Some people have said you know what, it's just not worth it, take it off scope.

I mean, I don't know, we've always had 5-star reviews on Google then right in the middle there's one that discusses how disorganised, how awful we are, and so forth. It had to be Sophie, it's only one but it's right in the middle. The 'name' of the student who completed the review, we never had a student with that name. I mean some of the complaints they made were just outrageous. They called SafeWork and said we didn't have any sanitary bins in the toilets.

SafeWork called me, I took a photo of them, they came out and a guy turned up from the council saying they'd received a complaint that there were no sanitary bins. I had to take this man to the female toilets to show him. This is the shit I've been dealing with. I really hope she gets what's coming to her.

Knowing Jane is also a Christian, I ask how this has affected her faith. Jane says the issues haven't affected her faith. She does say though:

But I've been angry to the point where I've said to God, 'what the hell are you doing to me? Why are you doing this? What are you punishing me for? It hasn't affected my faith as such. I'm reading Ecclesiastes in the Bible at the moment where Solomon is talking about what's the meaning of life, it talks about how wicked people are getting praised, and wicked people are being slandered. It was so perfect, I read the whole thing through.

The end result is that you have to keep going because there's a purpose. I don't know what the purpose is but I'm hanging on knowing there's a lesson and that when all of this is over, there'll be another purpose. I don't even know what I'll do. I have no idea what I want to do. I would like to volunteer in a hospice, that's where I originally did my training, I think my nature and knowledge is well suited, at least aligned with working in a hospice. I don't see myself able to work again because of my age, and it doesn't matter, I'll just take it as it happens.

I don't want to do anything where I have to report to ASQA or be responsible for staff, I just want to start living a normal life.

> We don't know how this will end. There's a number of things that need to happen. I don't know what the next step is. I'd like to think one day I'll get a letter from the lawyer to say, 'it's ok, it's over. You can now cross that off the list'. The next thing to do will be to sell it. It's all got to be in sequence. I have no confidence in any part of that sequence. I've just got to hang on to my faith that this is going somewhere and that I might have a chance at a bit of peace before I die myself.

I asked Jane why she decided to tell her story. Her reason follows:

> I decided to tell my story to highlight the unfairness of what's happening out there, how people's actions can destroy other people and there doesn't appear to be a way of defending yourself. I'd also suggest that people not believe what they read in papers, it's often untrue and/or sensationalised. I don't believe anything anymore. You can see police, news reporters and media people standing outside someone's door and they are so intimidating. They were outside my home, my office, they could have said anything (and they did) and I wasn't able to defend myself. I understand bad things happen. But to think that people are allowed to do this to others and no one seems to put in the checks and balances, it's so unfair. I think that politicians are allowed too much freedom to be able to say whatever they feel like under 'parliamentary privilege'.
>
> Reporters can write anything without any regard for who they're hurting along the way and not be accountable for the truth. It's been therapeutic too, that someone might benefit from my story helps make it easier.
>
> They've robbed me for the love of my industry and I've been part of that industry for 40 years. When I say they, I mean ASQA, the auditors, Sophie, Bianca, the journalist, the parliamentary officer, they all had a role to play.

I started in this industry in 1979 in a hospice. And I've basically worked in aged care ever since, in some form or another. I did my training in a hospital where people came to die, my children also worked in the RTO, aged care was the first job they ever had when they left school. Being involved in the aged care sector is now all they know. My kids are in their late 30's and early 40's now. It's all they know, and because of what's happened to me, their name is mud too. They used to come into the aged care facilities when they were little kids. As soon as they left school, they went straight into aged care, we've all been part of aged care. My mother used to entertain in aged care facilities, she used to sing, dance, do reviews for them for years. Before she became unwell, she'd be a real person in my bed for students to have actual experience working with an elderly 'client'.

The local funeral director said to me recently, 'I remember when your Mum would pretend to be a resident in the beds at the RTO. It was the first time many of us had seen an old person' up close and personal.

We're not a bad RTO. We really did do nothing wrong. We're an aged care family, we've spent our whole lives doing that.

I just want it to be over. I just want to be able to start a new life somewhere, do something else, give back somehow. I've got all this experience, this knowledge, surely someone could use it. I've just got to get this part over with. Even though right now I might be broken, I know what the industry's like out there and I know how much I know and what I have to give. There must be somewhere where all my experiences can be useful, there has to be somewhere. I don't want to give back though any sense of an obligation of giving back, but I'm not ready to be thrown on a scrapheap either or being told that I'm past my use by date.

All these young people are going to come in without experience and they're going to make all these rules. They won't have the back stories. That's what's happened with ASQA. I mean really, what sort of foolishness that an auditor audits an RTO without being or securing an industry expert is just ludicrous. The very few audits I've ever had have always had, as well as all my funding audits, there was always an industry expert there.

It's just ludicrous, aged care will go downhill before they see that they've swung the pendulum too far. They have to remember they are dealing with human beings.

You know, I received a call yesterday when I was with the accountant. It must have been one of the very few facilities that didn't know about what has been happening. They asked me when they're going to get another lot of students. She said we haven't had any students from you for ages. Everywhere I go around here, I see my ex-students. I have students in nearly every facility in Sydney's north. I was looking at an Industry Consultation Form we completed in 2016. My God, you should have read it! It was absolutely singing our praises, '*send us your students*', '*we only take yours*', '*we don't want to take anyone else's students*'. And now it's gone.

Jane bursts into tears and immediately apologises. She says, "*I think I'm grieving*" almost like she still needs to justify her tears. She finishes with, "*I got so much support from people in my industry over the years, but you can't run an RTO without students or staff. I'm done*!"

~END ~

Commentary

Jane's story is another example of where politics meets ASQA's regulatory regime on a greater scale than usual. To begin with, as a low-risk provider who never had a problem with the regulator previously and was considered a highly compliant provider with excellent graduate outcomes, industry begging for her graduates and an investment in the RTO's resources that led to her being one of the most State of the Art facilities in her jurisdiction, she should never have been in this predicament. Add a global pandemic that unexpectedly led to a 'new version' of auditing, a CEO whose technical skills were not great, ASQA using a phone conference to conduct an audit when it would have been far more appropriate to use video technology which it is perfectly capable of using and few personal issues such as the gradual demise of her Mother and this was at all times a recipe for disaster.

This was before anyone even considered the fallout from the Royal Commission into Aged Care that was released during Jane's audit journey. As can be seen throughout the history of the VET sector, politics and media frenzies are often the precursor to increased regulatory action and policy change. Sadly, these policies will also be influenced by research undertaken by the regulator that had poor research methodology, was not necessarily valid in its findings as a result of the flawed research methodology and based on findings and recommendations from auditors who in all likelihood, based on ASQA's own admissions in the Senate at the time, were more likely than not to be unqualified auditors.

The danger of course for providers like Jane is that Australia is already experiencing one of its worst skill shortages in a critical area of need. Australia has an ageing population and woefully insufficient facilities and carers to facilitate the care needs of its projected elderly population. There are insufficient careers and facilities now and if ASQA continues on the same trajectory, there will be even less providers, carers and facilities capable of taking care of our elderly in the years to come.

Of course, one of the other significant issues which is a factor in all of this is not just related to ASQA but rather the training package and developers of qualifications and units of competency, including those who insist that the volume of learning in the Australian Qualifications Framework is the only way a qualification can be delivered. Until such time as the fundamental issues and gaps of irrelevant and inappropriate training package materials (or training products as ASQA likes to call them) are addressed, RTOs will continue to experience these sorts of unfair, inappropriate audit decisions and outcomes because the training package itself, which ASQA must regulate against is fundamentally flawed! It is time that people who develop these training products and who sign off on them prior to the AISC endorsing them that is primarily the issue. Yet, it is the RTOs and people like Jane who are being hung out to dry for implementing training products that industry don't agree with and training products that are so flawed that they do the system a huge injustice.

Braithwaite & Joyce Reviews

> "We have had enough."
>
> - **Michael Jordan**

Lost Opportunities

Organisational Culture

One finding that has been consistently and systematically identified in ASQA's operations since the PwC ASQA Process Review in 2013[160] is the poor culture at ASQA and the impact it has on its ability to perform its role efficiently. ASQA maintained, even in the Braithwaite and Joyce reviews that it is committed to ensuring that RTOs maintain and are held to account to the highest standards enabling them to deliver desirable student outcomes. What Braithwaite found in her review was that '*changing legislation without addressing the culture driving its interpretation will not necessarily produce the outcomes expected*'. Joyce also found similar concerns in his review (see particularly page 39). It is my experience in dealing with the regulator directly and in conjunction with legal representatives on behalf of lawyers that there has been no change to the regulatory culture, indeed I would argue that the culture continues to worsen and that staff retention continues to be a problem.

There remains a toxic culture at ASQA and one where auditors (*and some permanent regulatory staff*) have made it their mandate to close down as many providers as possible or give providers as difficult a time as possible. In some ways, this behaviour and culture continues to be

160 PricewaterhouseCoopers, Department of Industry, 'ASQA Process Review: Final Report. Prepared on behalf of State, Territory and Commonwealth Governments', (Web Page), <https://www.voced.edu.au/content/ngv%3A63423>.

rewarded by senior management who continue to use contract/panel auditors who are incentivised to prolong the audit process because it means they get paid more and audits are no longer equitable. It's almost a game of Russian Roulette whereby if you're a small or large RTO and you get the panel auditor who hates private providers enough, they will drag the audit out unnecessarily and inequitably to be able to provide an invoice for an audit that was unnecessarily long, targeted to '*close the provider down*' and regulatory managers, in approving the audits and their invoices which go well and truly over what was initially intended, condone the behaviour of the auditor. This is also influenced by issues of auditor competence as will be discussed later in this submission.

An example of audits being dragged out and perceptions of conflicts of interest is located in a Question on Notice to Parliament number 152, portfolio question number SQ18 -000359 and one particular panel auditing company. The company was paid $134,580 over that financial year and with one audit which did not even proceed beyond an application for a stay at the Tribunal, the company claimed $7,440 for the initial audit, a further $3,720 due to '*increased complexity*', an identical claim of $7,440 for the initial audit and a further $3,720 due to '*increased complexity*' (this time for a not -for -profit RTO).

The company claimed $510.40 for travel expenses for an audit in their own State which would have been attended to by car as it is only a 2 hour and 49 minutes' (259kms) drive from the suburb where the auditor resides and the location of the RTO. That's either some very expensive kms being recovered or some very expensive accommodation. On another occasion on the same QON, purchasing document 4500112794 indicates travel expenses of $2,095.59. There are more that are also questionable.

Likewise, another VET Consultant/Company is recorded on the same QON as having received $127,894 from audit work while also being paid (according to QON 177, portfolio question number SQ19 -001385) $6,320 for building template wording for non--compliance in audit reports. Of interest and perhaps purely coincidentally, for the audit that the first company claimed $7,440 for the initial audit, a further $3,720 due to '*increased complexity*', the VET Consultant/Company in the second example was also engaged privately by the same RTO that the first company claimed further funds for to be the expert witness against ASQA that subsequently lost its application for a stay and therefore was unable to proceed with their application for merits review. It is noteworthy that ASQA, who has always claimed that they do not endorse any Consultants, actually have promoted a preferred Consultant list through their legal team and these two panel auditors are the only ones who are listed on it[161].

This QON also provides insight into just how much ASQA is paying panel auditors who are conflicted when it comes to undertaking these audits. It is clearly in their best interest to draw these audits out (*regardless of whether they have merit*) to ensure that they can maintain their '*income*'. As long as there is a perception of auditors who are rorting the system and changing the toxic culture of its auditors and regulatory managers, ASQA's organisational culture will not change and the reform expected will not be achieved. In other words, while ASQA's reforms are based on audits performed by auditors with a conflict of interest, and regulatory managers who condone such behaviour and perpetuate that same culture through threats of '*closing down RTOs*', then it really finds itself in a position of being the pot calling the kettle black; RTOs can only be held to account to the highest standards if its regulator is also.

Senate Estimates

One industry stakeholder collaborates with the #enoughisenough campaign to ensure that ASQA is held to account. This volunteer is the mystery person behind the **Education Issues Australia** Twitter Page (https://twitter.com/edissuesaus). Education Issues Australia receives a number of whistle-blower type emails, calls and evidence from a range of stakeholders throughout the country. It is a confidential service that

161 Professional correspondence held on file by the author.

has been provided by a concerned VET stakeholder since March 2019. It is not merely a Twitter account and the reader would be dismissing some critical evidence of ASQA's conduct by dismissing it. Considerable time and effort goes into researching and confirming the accuracy of whistle-blower claims and any evidence provided to the service, all for no fee, no benefit other than making ASQA accountable to the public because few others will or do. The following issues have at some point since March 2019 been raised by Education Issues Australia. The writer confirms that these claims have also been verified and that all information provided by *Education Issues Australia* is indeed accurate and correct (much to the writer's personal and professional distress).

Emails to Various Commonwealth Departments, Bodies, Senators

AAT Deputy President Admits Bias After Failing to Consider RTO Evidence and Submissions

The following information has been contributed by Education Issues Australia.

A recent email distributed to the senate by Education Issues Australia concerns a recent AAT decision[162] whereby a Deputy President of the Tribunal (Queensland Registry) was forced to recuse himself on the grounds of apprehended bias after the Federal Court found that he failed to consider evidence and submissions presented by the RTO in their AAT hearing. The same Deputy President has been a member of the AAT since 2017, in which time the Australian Skills Quality Authority has forcibly shut down hundreds of businesses, with the AAT the only avenue of appeal. Education Issues Australia reported that of additional concern, the current ASQA Chief Commissioner was a Member of the Tribunal in the same location and at the same time as the Deputy President, creating another '*perception of a conflict of interest*' that taints the regulatory process of Australia's VET sector.

Deputy Presidents are more senior and experienced legal officers than their Senior Member or Member counterparts. There have been more than 800 RTO's forcibly shut down by ASQA and left with their only avenue of appeal being the Administrative Appeal Tribunal, with (as at the date of the email submitted to Education Issues Australia) 45 RTO businesses in ongoing reviews before the AAT, and a further 17 considering that option. The admission by an experienced and senior Deputy President of the tribunal that they had failed to consider the evidence and submissions of an RTO undermines the already jeopardised confidence in the Australian VET Sector and the impartiality of its regulator.

---

162 *Australia Institute of Business & Technology - International Pty Ltd and Australian Skills Quality Authority* [2021] AATA 36 (21 January 2021).

Despite numerous Government commissioned reports into the litany of failures at ASQA, the regulator remains able to cancel, suspend and reject RTOs on the findings of Audit Staff who are not required to hold mandatory qualifications before commencing audit work. Further, these same audit officers' recommendations to impose the severest possible sanctions against RTOs can be approved by Commissioners, without having to stipulate exact non-compliances nor state what rectifications would be acceptable to the regulator.

If a deputy president can so readily disregard evidence and submissions, what of the Members who have heard hundreds of AAT matters - particularly as a result of ASQA's approach to challenge all stay applications in the AAT? An approach adopted by ASQA after the current Chief Commissioner joined as Deputy Chief Commissioner Risk Intelligence and Regulatory Support in 2018.

With no obligation of ASQA to identify all alleged non-compliances nor specify exact rectifications they would accept of an RTO before shutting them down, and the only avenue of appeal being a Tribunal whose most senior and experienced representatives have admitted to not considering evidence or submissions, it is incumbent on the Senate to ask further questions.

Senate Estimates: ASQA Annual Report Discrepancies

This particular email addresses some concerning contradictions to previous representations that ASQA had made to the Senate Estimates Committee as well as other authorities which, to some extent, has not been properly pursued.

On page 35 of ASQAs 2019-2020 Annual Report, ASQA state:

> "**ASQA's goal is that providers achieve compliance with their regulatory obligations. A provider that becomes compliant** during either the Notice of Intention stage, reconsideration stage, or

> **at the conclusion of an AAT review process is considered a regulatory success**".

However, in an Administrative Appeals Tribunal decision of 15 October 2019:

> *"**ASQA submitted** that there is some importance to be given to its authority as a regulator. **It said that the potential to entrench a view amongst some in the VET sector that the regulators can be feasibly challenged and as a result lessens the impact of decisions and weakens an RTO's commitment to ensuring the ongoing compliance at all times as is required by the registration.**"*

The AAT matter was heard as a result of ASQA challenging a Stay application of ASQA's previous decision to reject renewal, in which the RTO in question submitted:

> *"It is committed to continue to rectify its compliance issues with a view to satisfying ASQA that it is compliant, so the matter would not need to go to final hearing."*

Despite this and the Tribunal Member's consideration:

> *"If an applicant's prospects of success are ineluctable, there would be much to be said about granting a stay so as to avoid every possible adverse effect of an adverse decision."*

The Tribunal member further stated, in relation to the RTOs prospects to successfully achieve compliance:

> *"Whether (achieving compliance) involves a 'flurry of activity' to become compliant or is 'too little too late' as ASQA suggested, is really beside the point."*

A submission by ASQA that compliance is either too little too late or as a result of a flurry of activity, as a reason for rejecting an RTO's desire to continue to operate in accordance with its compliance obligations, directly contradicts the Annual Report claim that a provider who achieves compliance in the AAT are considered a regulatory success in the eyes of ASQA. This contradiction appears to be supported by a statement by ASQAs own Chief Commissioner to Senate Estimates in 2018:

> *"The AAT gave them an opportunity to continue, and we had to try and cancel them a second time, which we were ultimately successful in doing."*

This raises questions as to the extent ASQA could truly or impartially consider an RTO making it through the conclusion of an AAT review process as a regulatory success.

It is particularly egregious for ASQA to claim that granting a Stay application "*weakens an RTO's commitment to ensuring the ongoing compliance at all times as is required by the registration*" given the alternative would be an RTO no longer ongoing whatsoever.

In another statement to this Senate Estimates Committee in 2018, the committee was also advised that, in comparative terms, the rate of compliance demonstrated by TAFE SA was better than some TAFEs in other states and also better than the average compliance rate for non-TAFE providers.

Mr Mark Paterson, Chief Commissioner and Chief Executive Officer for ASQA explained:

> *In terms of comparison, TAFE SA's rate of non-compliance in relation to the audit was 66.67 per cent. Other TAFEs have been as high as 79.38 per cent and the average for non-TAFE providers is about 68.19 per cent. So, in relative terms, TAFE SA has not demonstrated the same rate of non-compliance as other TAFEs and is comparable to non-TAFE providers.*

There is a serious question to be answered as to ASQAs analysis of a '**rate of non-compliance in relation to the audit**', with the apparent allowance of substantially non-compliant providers to be renewed or to continue operating. This is despite repeated submissions by ASQA, in numerous AAT cases, that '***ensuring ongoing compliance at all times***' is a requirement of registration and that anything less warrants cancellation or rejection of renewal, and that any activity towards subsequently achieving compliance is 'too little too late'.

ASQA's statements are not only inconsistent, but they are also answers given before Senate Estimates Australia's judiciary and in accordance with reporting and transparency obligations of the public service.

Senate Estimates: Allegedly Drunk ASQA Auditor Hurls Racial Abuse Against Staff

Amidst a bevy of complaints against the behaviour of ASQA auditors, including allegations by a former ASQA auditor that ASQA's behaviour is driving honest Australian business owners to contemplate suicide, it was revealed last month that an ASQA auditor had arrived at a 2019 audit drunk and proceeded to make racist remarks towards the staff of the RTO. The very same auditor later recommended cancellation of the RTO – which was approved – before the RTO applied to the AAT and produced audio evidence of the auditor's comments, resulting in ASQA settling the matter:

> *"One that did our audit last year, turned up tipsy after being at the bar, and blatantly made comments that were racially discriminating about staff in the business she was auditing. My boss recorded it in case he would need to use it. We did have to go before AAT and they came up with a mutual agreement. I told him to take it further, but he decided against it in case it 'rocked the boat' too much."*

Ignoring for the moment that a petition calling for a parliamentary inquiry into the activities of ASQA was signed by over 1,000 RTO industry members; and ignoring that in September 2017 commissioners and ASQA senior executives, including the current General Manager of Regulatory Operations, convened a meeting to discuss how it should handle four online petitions that, at the time, were critical of ASQA; the facts and circumstances outlined in this letter should themselves warrant inquiry.

It should be noted that the writer, along with a well-respected RTO lawyer and barrister, have been present in an AAT Registry after a hearing for an Indian-owned RTO, where one of ASQA's long term legal officers made a statement to the effect of (I don't recall the exact wording, but it was not far off from...), *"He couldn't wait to get rid of all these Indian RTO owners that came out here as international students to undertake studies and all they did was drive taxi and become hairdressers and now they're taking over our precious VET sector."*

The writer tried to discuss it in a meeting with the Commonwealth Attorney-General and local Senator amongst a range of other potential breaches of model litigant obligations. Effectively, nothing would be done. The author was disappointed and felt that it was a most unsatisfactory solution to a member of his electorate, and a concerned Australian raising breaches of model litigant behaviour with the one person who can influence (and sanction) their behaviour.

Other Issues of Relevance in that Same Email

There has long been a discrepancy between international student graduates and domestic graduates of courses that 'require' that their courses receive accreditation or endorsement from the Australian Community Workers Association (ACWA). In fact, Australian (domestic) graduates have no need for their qualification to have been endorsed by or accredited by ACWA, it is only when an international student seeking permanent residence in Australia that they need the course to be accredited and endorsed by the same body who is assessing the qualification for the purposes of permanent residence. A completely contradictory requirement that international students are advised is for the purposes of employment but, as mentioned, a domestic graduate does not require it for employment. In addition to the issues of equity surrounding this issue is the following that was raised in the same email by Education Issues Australia:

> *"It should be a shock, then, to the senior executives of ASQA, that Box Hill has since had its accreditation to deliver a Diploma of Community Services program suspended by the governing professional body, the Australian Community Workers Association.*
>
> *The Association took the dramatic step after supposedly receiving numerous complaints from students and discovering that Box Hill late last year chose to slash the number of work experience hours community services students received from 400 to 100."*

This serves as one of the clearer examples of ASQAs prejudiced decision making and a cover-up culture in what many regard as an ongoing vendetta against a subset of those it regulates.

The reality is that ASQA and its staff have gone ungoverned for too long. Commissioners have all but publicly confessed that they do not read in any detail the audit reports recommendations of its auditors. This should come as no surprise, given ASQA Commissioners spend less than 15 minutes in considering whether to accept a recommendation to shut down an Australian business positively contributing to the Australian economy.

ASQA's lax governance is in clear contradiction to its claims that a "*process of escalating delegations and various quality checks ensure that recommendations are well tested before being acted on*".

The facts, however, are clear: 96 out of every 100 Commissioner cancellation and renewal rejection decisions are being overturned or varied when challenged.

The Administrative Appeals Tribunal 2018-19 Annual Report identified that a 12 per cent increase in the number of applications lodged with the AAT in the 'other' category of the General Division was "*largely due to an increase in applications to review decisions made by the Australian Skills Quality Authority*".

Further, the AAT Annual Report identified that ASQA decisions comprised of approximately 36 per cent of the 1,076 new applications lodged within that category last year.

The AAT also reported that the decision under review was affirmed in 58 per cent of cases in the AAT's General Division. In stark contrast, only 4.2 per cent of ASQAs decisions are affirmed by the AAT.

Given the lack of internal or external governance of ASQA, it should be of no surprise that between April 2018 and December 2019, of 242 cancellation and renewal rejection decisions that were challenged, only 11 of those decisions (4%) were affirmed by the AAT and ASQA.

It is a damning indictment, particularly when ASQA Commissioners aren't reading audit reports of the recommendations prepared by its auditors.

If ASQA are winning just 4 per cent of challenged decisions, how many small and family business RTOs who could not afford the costs of the AAT have been wrongfully shut down by this regulator? How is this conduct possibly in the public interest? How concerned would the public be if this type of information were to ever be released?

The same email then goes on to address the issue of competence of ASQA auditors, as raised earlier in this submission:

> In addition to gross governance failures costing RTOs and Australian Taxpayers millions, it begs the question – just how qualified are ASQA auditors?

The answer is conveniently tucked away on page 81 of ASQA's 2018-19 Annual Report. Of 93 audit staff, ASQA last year alone enrolled 28 (or 30%) into mandatory auditor qualifications specified as required before they can make audit recommendations.

The term *'enrolled'* however is used loosely, given ASQA have repeatedly been accused of flaunting the very standards it regulates, by allegedly issuing qualifications to its own auditors through a 3-day Recognition of Prior Learning process to attain both a Certificate IV in Training and Assessment (TAE) and a Diploma of Quality Auditing. While that may go some way in explaining why so many decisions are overturned, it doesn't explain how ASQA can so blatantly disregard its very own risk and regulatory frameworks:

> *"ASQA auditors approached my RTO for RPL; the standard was too low to confirm competence. I then informed ASQA that I was no longer willing to work with their staff and they should send them elsewhere. They went to tick and flick where they could get the quals in three days – they told me so."*

If 30 per cent of ASQAs audit staff were last year unqualified to conduct audit activities, how many were unqualified in each of the years prior, and how many cancellation recommendations did ASQA allow them to make which ASQA Commissioners approved?

In June 2017, ASQA tabled a *Strategic Review Report* into unduly short training, stating that, "*There is significant risk that in many cases the duration of training is not sufficient to enable learners to gain the competencies specified in the training, leading to loss of confidence in vocational education and training and long-term costs to industry, individuals, the community and governments*".

The very same review went on to highlight "*the special case of the Certificate IV in Training and Assessment*". In fact, ASQA stated that "*poor-quality delivery of the TAE has a compounding effect on the quality of delivery and assessment for all vocational training in Australia"*. ASQA considered that this presents a significant risk to the entire VET system:

> *"This additional regulatory scrutiny of TAE providers alone cannot fully address the risks of unduly short training across the system. Chapter 5 proposes better specifying the duration of this essential qualification as one component of a recommended strategy to support more effective regulation and greater transparency for industry and learners."*

ASQA Strategic Review

The irony it seems has been lost on ASQA, who have presented a 2020/21 financial year estimated cost of regulatory functions. The estimate identifies that of $23 million dollars, there is an allocation of nearly $7 million for court and tribunal expenses against its regulated entities.

Two federal government reports[163] since 2018 have identified serious concerns with ASQA. These concerns were serious enough to report on, even though ASQA have been outside of the scope and terms of reference of these reports. The *Joyce Report* released in May 2019 reiterated concerns about '*the inconsistency of audits and auditors*' identified in the January 2018 *Braithwaite Report*.

Whilst the competency of ASQA's Regulatory Agenda has gone somewhat unnoticed in the public arena, a ruling handed down by an AAT Member in January 2019 concluded that ASQA, in pursuing its regulatory agenda, had "*misconceived the scheme of the NVR Act*".

ASQA maintains this is about establishing and meeting minimum standards within the VET sector. Yet ASQA has, without audit and in the last two years, allowed over 950 Registered Training Organisations to have their registration renewed for a period of 5-7 years.

163 The Braithwaite and Joyce Reviews referred to previously.

It is irreconcilable that ASQA's Regulatory Agenda to lift standards can be or is being achieved when, in two years, ASQA have without audit renewed the operations of one quarter of regulated entities for another half decade.

The damage being caused by ASQA is not limited to providers, with trainers/educators across all sectors at risk of losing their jobs as a result of ASQA's cancellations and disastrous implementation of new Training and Assessment credential requirements. This process saw 90% of providers unable to deliver the new TAE credential, resulting in trainers and assessors, many who have been educating in the sector for decades, unable to update their qualification and fearing for their jobs until the skills ministers stepped in to delay the introduction of the requirements.

Regardless of your views on the vocational education sector and its proponents, it is of vital importance that the nation can have confidence in vocational education and its educators. To do so there must be confidence in the Regulator. It should come as no surprise then that the Joyce Review found employer confidence in VET was declining, and the number of students seeking qualifications declining.

The threat to this confidence is not confined to Australia, with the Nepalese Ministry of Education deciding to no longer allow Nepalese students to come to Australia to study a vocational education program without it being part of a higher education program. The reason behind the decision of Australia's third largest international education market was reported to be because "*students in diploma courses suffered following the closure of their institutes*".

There is no debate as to the intent and need to bring higher standards and more confidence to the VET sector. Regardless of one's political or personal views on contestability within VET, improving the reputation of the Australian vocational education and training sector should be the priority of everyone, and can only be achieved with the support of a competent regulator.

The current execution by ASQA is not creating this confidence and is damaging Australia's reputation, equally hurting TAFE and non-TAFE providers and impacting on every electorate of Australia.

The Lion, the Witch and the Wardrobe

> **"Justice will only exist when the truth is honoured."**
>
> **- Hina**

Around eight months ago, I got a strange phone call and it went something like this:

RTOD: *Good afternoon, thank you for calling RTO Doctor. How may I help you?*

Caller: *Thanks so much for getting back to me so quickly.*

RTOD: *What can I do for you, <enter name>?*

Caller: *We've finally just got our CRICOS registration and I was wondering if you could please provide us with some PRISMS training?*

Pause...

For the uninitiated, PRISMS stands for *Provider Registration and International Student Management System*. It is the system that provides a Confirmation of Enrolment (or CoE) to an international student studying on a student visa. For the purposes of this article, PRISMS is the wardrobe. You, the reader, get to decide who is the lion and who is the witch (*a reader's prerogative as there's got to be some benefit in reading such a long article surely?*).

Now, back to the article...

RTOD: *Congratulations! You must be so thrilled and excited to be starting on this journey. It would have been a long road! We can certainly assist you, what's your*

CRICOS registration number? That will give me an idea of your details.

Caller: *Well, that's actually part of it. All of our CRICOS scope is not showing and that's why we thought we must need training.*

RTOD: OK, *what's your CRICOS registration number and we'll take a look? What courses did you apply to have on scope?*

Caller: *We applied for <insert qualification> and that's showing, but we also have <insert short courses and/or skillsets> which aren't showing and we don't know why.*

I take a look at the provider's CRICOS scope and confirm that, like the caller suggested, the short courses they were asking about cannot be sighted on the CRICOS register before saying to the caller:

RTOD: *I'm not really sure why you are expecting to see single units of competency, skillsets or short courses on CRICOS though. Technically speaking, only full qualifications can be registered on CRICOS.*

This is the point where the caller then questions my professional knowledge and experience of CRICOS (*me being an ex-regulator and all!*) and they say quite strongly that:

Caller: *Yes, you can. I applied for CRICOS registration for these courses and have a letter right here in my hand saying that registration has been granted to these courses. They have a CRICOS course code and I paid <insert amount> to have them registered.*

At this point, I repeat to the caller:

RTOD: *While I have no doubt that you applied for, and you're looking at a letter that says you have received,*

CRICOS registration for those particular courses, the reality is that, technically speaking, under the current legislation, that is not possible.

Usually at this point, the caller believes I have no idea what they're talking about and they go somewhere else, although one particular caller went a step further and explained:

Caller: *The truth is, we actually don't care too much about the qualification that's been registered. Our entire business model is based around all of these international students on a student visa who come here to get a 'certificate' for short-term workforce entry courses such as first aid, white card and RSA. We really just need to be able to issue CoEs for those courses. We have them registered on CRICOS. I have the letter here from ASQA with the relevant CRICOS course codes. Can you help us? We can issue the CoEs for the qualification, but we don't know how to issue them for the short courses. Can you teach us?*

I respond as follows:

RTOD: *Look, I'm sorry. I understand that you might have a letter saying that you're registered to deliver these courses to international students on a student visa, but I don't know why or on what basis. There is no legislative provision for those courses to be registered on CRICOS. The legislative basis for registering a course on the CRICOS register is found in the ESOS Regulations and it doesn't allow for those sorts of courses to be registered.*

By now, the caller usually thinks I'm a fruit cake and they move on to the next Consultant who will no doubt provide them with PRISMS training, even though no amount of training can make those courses 'suddenly appear' allowing them to provide their students with a CoE!

After having a good handful of these types of clients approach me for PRISMS training for the same reason, and after assisting an even bigger number of providers through sanctions because of alleged breaches of section 8 of the Education Services for Overseas Students (ESOS) Act 2000 (Cth.) ("ESOS Act"), RTO Doctor decided that it was time to investigate this little 'phenomenon' further.

The Trial

I confidentially approach a very switched on, unnamed colleague in the sector who owns a CRICOS RTO and ask them if they were aware of any changes that allowed this to occur and, if so, why they weren't exploiting it. They had been managing it in a completely different manner. They were unaware that this change was taking place but were quite annoyed that it might be taking place - after all, only a few months prior, they had received a sanction for, amongst other things, issuing CoEs to international students on a student visa while they were concurrently enrolled full-time somewhere else. Had they been aware of this change, they say that they would have actioned this years ago because they knock back literally hundreds of potential enrolments per month for those same courses.

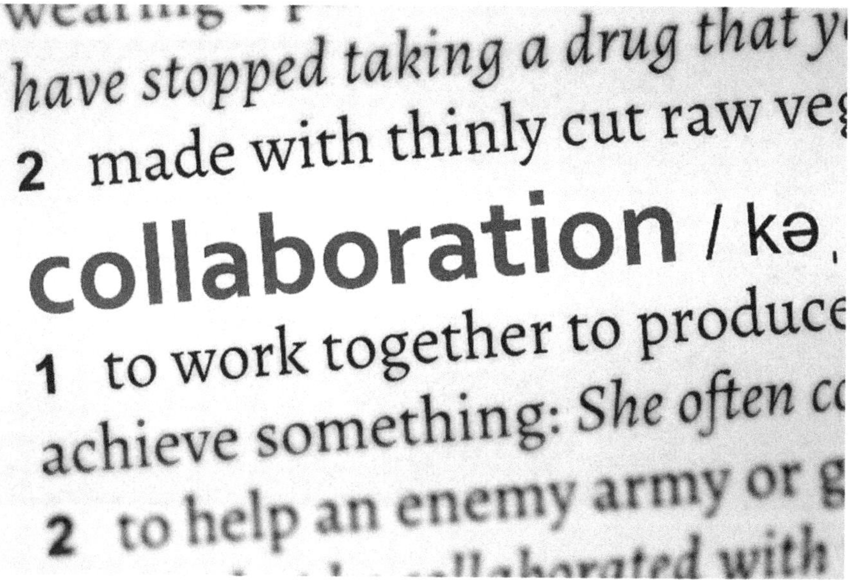

They decide to collaborate and, with the consent of some international students with a student visa who are onshore, the students approach these RTOs seeking enrolment in their short courses. The condition of participation in the trial? They must be able to secure a CoE for the short course. For the trial, we selected three short courses that are hot property on the international student market and all three courses that I know have been subject to the registration on CRICOS issue.

I approached another, well respected, CRICOS provider and asked the same question. They too were unaware of the changes and were quite understandably angry if that's the case because they have literally had a few thousand students over the years who could have benefitted from being able to pursue such courses with them, but because of the fact short courses can't be registered on CRICOS, these students either don't have access to them or they undertake them with another provider and lie about their eligibility to enrol.

This provider also decides to collaborate with us to get to the bottom of this mystery, with the same conditions as detailed above.

The Results

Both providers had a minimum of six students approach RTOs who allegedly had these three short courses registered on CRICOS, albeit those courses were not available for viewing on the public CRICOS register. Each of the six students from each provider sought enrolment into a single unit of competency course, but none were able to secure a CoE for the single unit course. There were various outcomes, including:

- Students were just enrolled as a domestic student would be;
- Students could be issued a CoE but it would be in a full qualification, not the single unit of competency sought;
- Others said, "Sorry but we're not offering these courses right now. Our next intake will be..."

Our trials were unsuccessful because our intention was to have an outcome of all students obtaining a CoE into these short courses.

Let's backtrack a little...

In early February 2017, I wrote to the then head of ACPET (now ITECA) expressing my immense concern over this issue. An extract of that email is provided below (some names have been removed for privacy reasons):

> Hi Rod,
>
> Sorry to disturb you on a Friday evening (I seem to be getting good at that, sorry :-( ) but I was talking with [redacted] this afternoon and she mentioned you were meeting with ASQA on Monday. I've been trying to bring this to the attention of law makers, ESOS regulators and ASQA without much luck and am hoping you might be able to have a bit more success. I've also got a meeting with Christian Porter (Liberal Senator, member for Pearce where I live) in the process of being scheduled and if necessary, will also try another politician I've been referred to.
>
> The issue is that ASQA auditors are curently going around finding providers critically non-compliant and in breach of the ESOS Act (and consequently the NVR Act) and, once it gets back to the Head Office, issuing immediate notices of intent to cancel registration for providers who are not registered on CRICOS but are not offering qualifications to international students but rather short courses (e.g. first aid, traffic management, taxi (not a full qualification but a group of units).
>
> I'm including my email **a discussion as an attachment with ASQA** as well as **my discussion with [redacted] (Barrister)**. I am aware of at least 2 providers in this situation, one who is about to go to the AAT and the other who is waiting for her audit report. Given the lack of definition of 'course' in the NVR Act and ESOS Act, VET Quality Framework and ESOS Framework, Migration Act & Regulations, ASQA are back to being in true form and interpreting it how they like. Clearly, if the intent of the legislation as being interpreted and implemented by ASQA auditors currently was for a course to be defined as a single unit of competency or anything other than a full qualification, we'd have a lot more CRICOS providers and a lot more CRICOS registered courses. There are a number of complicating factors with this that will affect providers (including TAFE) around the country.

Nothing eventuated from this discussion but more providers who became entangled in that mess. Around 6 months later, Rod left ACPET for greener pastures. I continued to raise the issues with anyone who would listen. After realising that nobody was taking the issue seriously, I decided to write an article that I published on LinkedIn on 13 December 2017, '**Section 8 of the ESOS Act: Are you at Risk**?' where I explained:

> *"One of the more common non-compliances we are seeing currently that is catastrophic for some providers is that the regulatory interpretation of what constitutes a 'course' has changed although there was little to no public announcement of this fact. What is fast becoming a greater risk for providers is the international student on a student visa in Australia who*

does not declare that they are an international student. We've seen a number of education providers who, during audit have produced evidence of trainer and assessor qualifications that were issued by a provider and yet that provider is not CRICOS registered! The stance by regulators on this issue is that it's your responsibility to ensure that the student is telling the truth and it is your responsibility to ensure that you are not enrolling international students on a student visa."

Let's refresh our memories on what section 8 of the ESOS Act is:

8 Offence: providing or promoting a course without a registered provider

(1) A person commits an offence if the person:

(a) provides a course at a location to an overseas student; or

(b) makes an offer to an overseas student or an intending overseas student to provide a course at a location to that student; or

(c) invites an overseas student or intending overseas student to undertake, or to apply to undertake, a course at a location; or

(d) holds himself, herself or itself out as able or willing to provide a course at a location to overseas students; unless:

(e) the person is registered to provide that particular course at that particular location; or

(f) the person does so in accordance with an arrangement that the person has with a registered provider for that particular course for that particular location.

Penalty: Imprisonment for 2 years.

Note 1: This means that, if 2 or more providers jointly provide a course, then only one of the providers needs to be registered.

Note 2: However, a provider of a course who is not registered must identify the registered provider in any written material promoting the course (see section 107) and must not engage in misleading or deceptive conduct in relation to the course (see subsection 83(2)).

Note 3: Chapter 2 of the *Criminal Code* sets out the general principles of criminal responsibility.

(2) The prosecution bears a legal burden in relation to the matter in paragraph (1)(e) (despite subsection 13.3(3) of the *Criminal Code*).

Note: A defendant bears an evidential burden in relation to the matter in paragraph (1)(f): see subsection 13.3(3) of the *Criminal Code*.

Defence: surveys etc. to assess demand for a course

(3) A person does not commit an offence under paragraph(1)(d) if:

(a) the relevant conduct was only for either or both of the following purposes:

(i) carrying out surveys or other investigations to assess the demand for the course; or

(ii) negotiating with another institution or other body or person in connection with designing or developing the course; and

(b) the person took reasonable steps to ensure that:

(i) overseas students and intending overseas students who were, or might become, interested in undertaking the course; and

(ii) any institution or other body or person who might also provide the course;

were aware that:

(iii) the person was not a registered provider for the course for the location; and

(iv) the relevant conduct was not carried out in accordance with an arrangement that the person had with a registered provider for the course for the location; and

(c) the person neither invited nor accepted any amount for the course from overseas students or intending overseas students, or from the students' agents.

Note: A defendant bears an evidential burden in relation to the matter in subsection (3): see subsection 13.3(3) of the *Criminal Code*.

Now, since that article was published, I can't even begin to contemplate the number of providers I have worked with who have been impacted by alleged breaches of section 8, some threatened with significant civil penalties and quite a few with the cancellation of their RTO. Likewise, I cannot even begin to contemplate how many providers have spent literally thousands of dollars on their enrolment practices and systems because of ASQA's findings as described in relation to section 8 of the ESOS Act or those trying to prevent it. While agreeing that investing in the improvement of business systems and practices is never a waste of money, it is when it was inequitably required and '*the system*' has been making '*a killing*' from applications on CRICOS for courses that were never eligible to be registered under the *Education Services for Overseas Students Regulations 2019 (Cth.)* ("ESOS Regulations").

In that article in December 2017, I discussed how the term '*course*' was being interpreted for the purposes of section 8 ESOS Act alleged breaches. This is repeated below to facilitate the continued understanding of this article:

> Whilst PRISMS, (Provider Registration and International Student Management System), the database that is used by providers, regulators and immigration and effectively is the backbone of the CRICOS register) is not designed to cater for '*courses*' in accordance with the current interpretation by regulators, make no mistake, there has been increased and quite significant scrutiny (some might even call it a witch hunt) on providers who are delivering '*courses*' without being registered on CRICOS to do so or without the course being registered on CRICOS. While some providers came to us for help to get them out of this mess and we have so far been successful in achieving it, there are many other providers who just cannot afford the cost of fighting the regulatory decision and accept the notice to cancel their registration and/or cancel statements of attainment and qualifications.
>
> While it is acknowledged that there are the occasional providers who knowingly enrol international students on a student visa and are in breach of Section 8 (they are certainly not our clients), there are increasingly more and more clients who have been impacted by this decision. Effectively, the regulator, specifically ASQA, has begun interpreting the word '*course*' in Section 8 of the ESOS Act to mean **any course of education and training under the Australian Qualifications Framework**. In other words, if it is a skill set but not a full qualification, you're in breach, if you're delivering a single unit short course, you're in breach of Section 8 of the ESOS Act, if you're delivering a first aid course and you're not CRICOS registered, you're in breach of the ESOS Act, the same goes for short courses including, for example, RSA (Provide responsible service of alcohol) and RSG (Provide responsible gambling services).

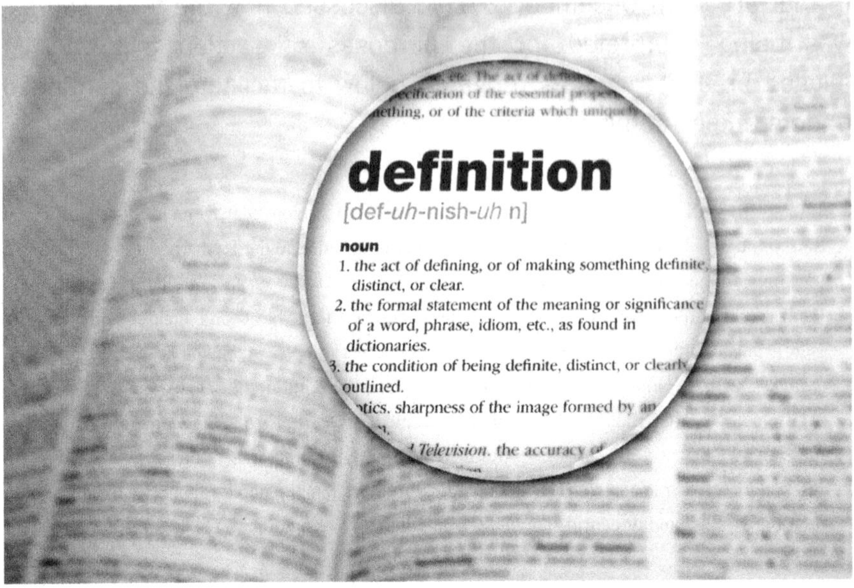

The power of a definition...and the money to be made from it!

Under the *National Vocational Education and Training Regulator Act 2011* (Cth.) ("NVR Act"), '*course*' is defined as '*...a course of vocational education and training*'. The term '*VET course*' is defined as:

> '*(a)* *the units of competency of a training package that is endorsed by the Ministerial Council; or*
>
> *(b)* *the units of competency or modules of a VET accredited course; or*
>
> *(c)* *the units of competency or modules of a course accredited by a VET Regulator of a non-referring State.*'

The ESOS Regulations provide the information that must be registered on the 'Register'. This is seen in the screenshot below:

8 Information to be entered on the Register

(1) For the purposes of paragraph 14A(4)(i) of the Act, the following matters are prescribed in relation to a provider's registration to provide a course or courses at a location or locations:

(a) the address of the provider's principal place of business;

(b) if the provider is a body corporate that is not a public provider—the address of the provider's registered office;

(c) the provider's postal address (if different from the address mentioned in paragraph (a) or (b));

(d) the provider's phone number and email address;

(e) the provider's ABN or ACN (if any);

(f) the provider's trading name or names (if any);

(g) if the provider is not a public provider and is not an individual—the name, phone number and email address of the provider's principal executive officer;

(h) the maximum number of overseas students, approved by the ESOS agency for the provider, to whom the course or courses may be provided;

(i) for each of the courses—the matters mentioned in subsection (2).

(2) For the purposes of paragraph (1)(i), the matters are the following:

(a) the level and field of study of the course (see subsection (3));

(b) the duration of the course, including any holiday breaks;

(c) the estimated total of the tuition fees payable for an overseas student for the course;

(d) the estimated total of the non-tuition fees payable for an overseas student for the course;

(e) whether the provider will only accept payment of tuition fees and non-tuition fees for the course in arrears;

(f) whether the course will be provided:

(i) by the provider; or

ii) by another registered provider, in accordance with an arrangement that the other registered provider has or will have with the provider for that particular course; or

(iii) by a person who is not a registered provider, in accordance with an arrangement that the person has or will have with the provider for that particular course;

(g) for each location at which the provider is registered to provide the course:

(i) the address of the location; and

(ii) the phone number and email address for the location; and

(iii) if subparagraph (f)(i) applies—the name, phone number and email address of the individual who is responsible for the day-to-day operation of the provider at the location; and

(iv) if subparagraph (f)(ii) or (iii) applies—the name, phone number and email address of the individual who is responsible for the day-to-day operation of the other registered provider, or the other person, at the location; and

(v) the maximum number of overseas students, approved by the ESOS agency for the provider, to whom the course may be provided at the location;

(h) if subparagraph (f)(ii) or (iii) applies—the matters prescribed by paragraphs (1)(a) to (g) as if the other registered provider, or the other person, were the provider mentioned in those paragraphs.

(3) For the purposes of paragraph (2)(a):

(a) the level may be, but is not required to be, one of the following:

(i) a level of the Australian Qualifications Framework, as existing at the commencement of this section;

(ii) non-award;

(iii) foundation studies;

(iv) English language intensive courses for overseas students; and

(b) the field of study must be:

(i) a detailed field under the Australian Standard Classification of Education, published by the Australian Statistician in 2001, as existing on 1 October 2019; or

(ii) English language study.

As can be seen, the requirements for registration of courses on the register is at subsections 2 and 3. What can also be seen very clearly here (*where the arrows are*) is that none of those criteria would be relevant to a single unit of competency.

The screenshot below is from the **Application Guide for Initial CRICOS Registration from ASQA** (17 August 2020) clearly indicating that someone can apply for single units of competency and skillsets:

Which scope items would you like to add?

This section identifies the type of scope items you would like to add as part of your initial RTO and/or CRICOS application. The scope items applied for in your application for RTO and/or CRICOS registration cannot be changed once the application has been submitted.

'Scope' means the nationally recognised training products (qualifications, courses and units of competency) and/or ELICOS courses that an organisation is registered to deliver and/or asse

Select the type of scope items you would like to add to your application—noting that you can o select ELICOS courses as part of an application for CRICOS registration.

It is advisable to limit the proposed scope of registration in the initial application, so that if the application is successful, your organisation can consolidate the quality of its operations before xtending its scope. This will also limit the establishment costs, as an applicant must have the quired resources in place for each product within the proposed scope. Availability and suitability of sources for **all** scope items sought will be examined as part of the process of assessing the plication.

Any nationally recognised training products (qualifications, courses and units of competency) applied for must be current. Refer to the national register (training.gov.au), maintained by DESE, for currency information and the correct codes and titles for each training product.

Please note: An organisation may only seek registration for a qualification or the 'Assessor Skill Set' from the Training and Education Training Package after it has held at least two years of continuous registration. This application **must not** include any qualification from the Training and Education Training Package, nor any of the following units of competency (or their successors) which comprise the 'Assessor Skill Set' from the Training and Education Training Package:

- TAEASS401 – Plan assessment activities and processes
- TAEASS402 – Assess competence
- TAEASS403 – Participate in assessment validation

Guide—Application for initial registration, updated 17 August 2020 Page 32 of 35

Fees & Charges

Of course, there's more! The **ASQA Fees & Charges Guide 2019-2020** includes the following fees and charges. I have provided screenshots but the link is available **here**. Why screenshots you ask? I have a burning question...

2.1 Initial CRICOS registration				
	Column 1	Column 2	Column 3	Column 4
Ref	Fee	Fee structure	Amount	Other matters
2.1.1	**Initial lodgement fee** The fee that may be charged when ASQA, as an ESOS Agency, receives an application from a provider that wishes to be registered to provide a qualification or qualifications at a delivery site or delivery sites to overseas students.	Per application	$500	Paid on application
2.1.2	**Initial assessment fee** The fee that may be charged when ASQA, as an ESOS Agency, considers a provider's application for registration.	Base fee includes: • Up to 4 qualifications • Up to 2 delivery sites Plus:	$8,000	• Paid on invoice • Total application fee (including lodgement and assessment) capped at $50,000
2.1.2(i)	Initial additional qualification fee	• each additional qualification	$155	
2.1.2(ii)	Initial additional Australian delivery site fee	• each additional delivery site	$1,640	

And for the purposes of providing a complete picture, changing CRICOS scope:

2.3 Change to scope of CRICOS registration				
	Column 1	**Column 2**	**Column 3**	**Column 4**
Ref	**Fee**	**Fee structure**	**Amount**	**Other matters**
2.3.1	**Change of Scope lodgement fee** The fee that may be charged when ASQA, as an ESOS Agency, receives an application from a provider that wishes to increase student capacity or add one or more qualifications at one or more delivery sites to its registration.	Add 1 qualification	$500	Paid on application
2.3.1 (i)	Change of scope- Additional qualification fee	Plus	$150 per each additional qualification	
2.3.1 (ii)	Change of scope – Additional student capacity fee	Additional student capacity	$1,640 per application	
2.3.1 (iii)	Change of scope – First additional delivery site fee	Additional (or replacement) delivery site,	$1,640 per application	
2.3.1 (iv)	Change of scope – Further additional delivery site fee	Plus: Each additional (or replacement) delivery site	$820 per additional delivery site	

Where does it say anywhere the cost and fee for a single unit of competency or a skillset? Yet, I know (*through contact with providers who have paid the fees*) that they do actually pay a fee. So how does ASQA even calculate the cost when its own fees and charges guide doesn't provide one for short courses that are not qualifications?

Now, subsequent to potentially getting an answer to that question, I have a whole lot more questions about what we're seeing here. In good old ASQA terminology, '*including, but not limited to*':

1. When of course did ASQA actually commence accepting these types of applications which are inconsistent with the ESOS Regulations?
2. How many applications has ASQA approved for single units and skillsets for CRICOS registration?
3. On what legal basis were those applications and their subsequent decisions made?
4. At what point did ASQA advise each of these 'applicants' that their very expensive courses would NOT appear on CRICOS and they would not be able to issue CoEs? In fact, were they at all advised?
5. Just how much money has ASQA made off these types of applications?
6. Did they EVER advise current CRICOS providers that they too could apply to have any of the single units that they deliver on the CRICOS register along with the rest of their CRICOS scope?
7. How many currently registered CRICOS providers would have applied to add single units of competency to their CRICOS scope had they been aware this was a legitimate practice that ASQA was engaging in?
8. Where did all the money go?
9. And the biggest one yet...why is there a Discussion Paper titled '**Improving regulation of supplementary courses to overseas students**'?

Is this really what it seems on the surface? An attempt to legalise a practice that has been going on for years despite the ESOS Regulations preventing it?

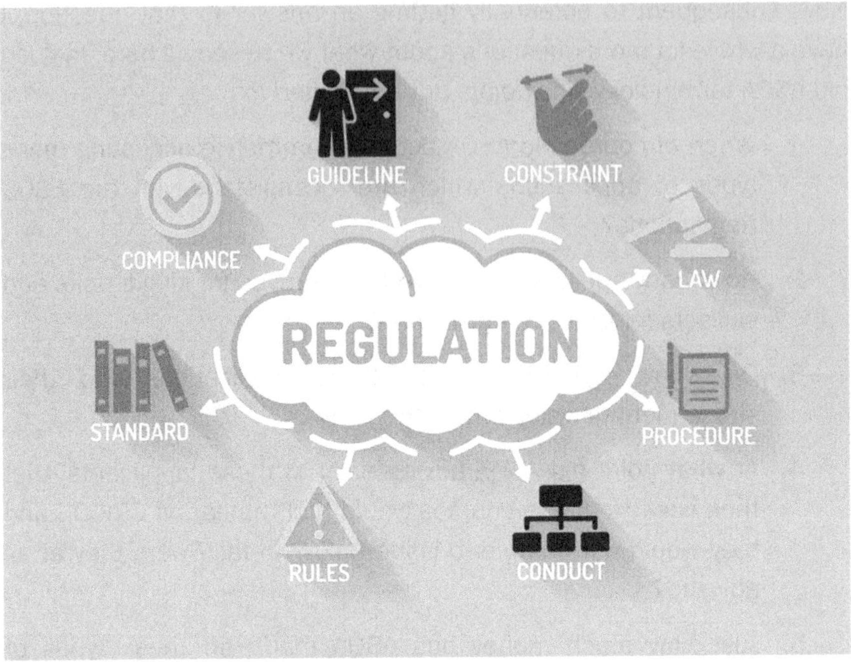

Improving regulation of supplementary courses for overseas students

The Discussion paper (*which is open for comments until 5 October 2020*), states that:

> *'...it is seeking to create new market opportunities for the education sector and support overseas students by expanding the delivery of supplementary courses and micro credentials to student visa holders.'*
>
> Now, don't get me wrong, under no circumstances am I saying this is not a great opportunity for international student visa holders. **What I am asking though is why would this even be a necessary discussion given ASQA has been accepting and approving these applications for years anyway?**

Historically, in other words, before ASQA was established, it was always known and accepted that any course under 12 weeks duration did not need to be registered on CRICOS. In fact, this is one of those anomalies and ridiculous gaps that occurs between the ESOS framework and the migration legislation. It was previously accepted by all State and Territory Regulators, and as far as I can tell, an '*unwritten rule*' that any course under 12 weeks didn't have to be registered (*actually, I think there was something documented by the Joint Committee on International Education but I don't currently have access to that document*). Of course, during those times, this led to a proliferation of international students undertaking a large number of courses that would facilitate their employability in Australia in jobs that Australian workers didn't want for a variety of reasons including low pay.

Those courses included but were not limited to for example the old Certificate III in Aged Care/Disability/Home and Community Care, the Certificate II & Certificate III in Security Operations and so forth. It was understood that international students come to Australia on courses that their student visas are aligned to; if they wanted to take additional courses concurrent with their student visa requirements, good on them. Is this part of the reason why some of those courses were designed to be less than 3 months? That's not for me to judge.

However, for the purposes of this article, ***it was an unwritten rule that anything under 12 weeks didn't need to be registered*** and provided international students did not breach their visa conditions, they could enrol in a first aid course, an RSA course or anything under 12 weeks. In comes ASQA, someone decides they would interpret a definition differently and here we are. Also of particular relevance here though is the fact that the **ASQA National Strategic Review into Unduly Short Courses** was also undertaken around the time the definition started being interpreted differently. Coincidence? Perhaps, but don't forget the courses that were being reviewed and which had the highest alleged '*unduly short durations*'.

So where does all of this leave us? Well, to begin with, we could all respond to the Request for Comment in the **Discussion Paper**, although I'm beginning to think that these changes are already in the bag to protect the money that has been collected and those applications that have been accepted and approved since at least early 2017. We could also demand that ASQA respond to the questions raised earlier at a minimum, although I suspect it won't. And besides, what's the point? They're accountable to nobody. Nothing will happen as a consequence of them engaging in this somewhat peculiar practice anyway. Maybe though if enough people put pressure on their local Members of Parliament to ask the questions in parliament, we might get some answers, although again, I highly doubt it. And what would it all achieve anyway?

My guess is that more than anything, there are going to be a significant number of infuriated CRICOS providers who have been undermined and who could have, based on the acceptance and approval of these single units and skills sets (*or, in ASQA's new fancy language, micro-credentials which is just another word for a Statement of Attainment*), could have made a significant amount of income by offering those same '*short courses*' or '*micro-credentials*' and they didn't even know it! I suspect too that there are a good number of CRICOS providers out there who have applied and paid to be able to register units of competency and skillsets on CRICOS, had them approved and have not been able to issue a single CoE since who are also very, very angry.

And on top of all that, there's a serious amount of money involved in the outcome. Either way, I think ASQA has some explaining to do!

#4 Jay's Story

> *"In any moment of decision, the best thing you can do is the right thing. The worst thing you can do is nothing."*
>
> **- Theodore Roosevelt**

Jay's story is an example of where ASQA have determined the outcome before they've even reviewed the evidence and that no matter what you provide, you can't change that perception. Jay's life was so completely destroyed by ASQA that, coupled with his own health problems and a failing marriage, it all became too much and he walked away, allowing ASQA to just cancel his registration. He was unable to continue the fight to save his RTO (or his reputation) because of the pressure mounting in other areas of his life.

Jay also experienced severe and complex health issues that nobody should have to go through. ASQA's usual pattern of putting the cart before the horse in complaint investigations and asking a provider to demonstrate their innocence after being judged guilty before any investigation has even taken place and re-registration audits that get re-labelled as compliance monitoring audits so that ASQA can recover an obscene amount of money via 'cost-recovery'. Combine this with auditors who haven't got the slightest clue about what it is you deliver because they are not even remotely qualified or experienced in the area; but you, as a provider are highly qualified and experienced. This auditor, though, treats you as though you know nothing! Here is Jay's story.

Like most RTOs in December of that year, it was a few days before business closure for the Christmas and New Year break. It was also 15 days before his wedding. Weddings are an important milestone for anyone but, in his culture and at his age, it had even more significance. It had been a busy year. An international expert in his field, Jay was well recognised throughout the world for his community work and community representation of minority groups. He is well known around the country for his work in charitable organisations around Australia. He is a member of numerous advisory boards and councils (both government and non-government) that have meant that for over a decade, he has contributed widely and significantly to the support and promotion of community development, cohesion and wellbeing. He has been for a number of years, a regular speaker on news and current affairs programs in relation to human rights issues and his areas of expertise. His RTO (and life as he knew it), was about to unravel faster than the speed of light. How does such an accomplished member of the community become involved in such a tragedy?

This story begins on one particular Thursday afternoon in late December with the arrival of a section 26 notice[164] from ASQA's office in that State. The email, short[165] and simple reads:

> *Please find attached NVR Act section 26 notice for your response and submission of the required information. I look forward to receiving your submission and response by close of business xxx December xxx.*[166]

A section 26 notice, in this case and many others, is usually an attachment on an email which, when you look at it, looks like the following:

It will include the CEO's details or may be addressed to 'The Proper Office' or something similar. This particular section 26 notice demanded that a significant amount of information for three (3) full years be produced within seven (7) days. The information included:

164 Notice to produce information.

165 A section 26 notice is a Notice to give information under the National Vocational Education and Training Regulator Act 2011 (Cth.).

166 Dates have been removed to protect Jay's identity and that of his RTO.

1. *Student enrolment and completion data for all students enrolled during the period xxx*[167] *and the date of this notice to include the following information:*

    - *Family name, first name;*
    - *Residential address;*
    - *Confirmation if you confirmed the student was not on a student visa;*
    - *Contact telephone numbers;*
    - *Date of birth;*
    - *Student ID number (if applicable);*
    - *Enrolment/commencement dates;*
    - *Code and title of qualification student enrolled in;*
    - *Codes and titles of units of competency completed and results;*
    - *Date testamur or statement of attainment was issued;*
    - *Source of funding for any completed units of competency;*
    - *Location where training and assessment occurred;*
    - *Name of trainer/assessor together with evidence confirming the assessor met compliance requirements relevant to NVR Standards clauses 1.13 – 1.16;*
    - *Confirmation of the assessment resources used for the student;*
    - *Details of how each student was referred, ie. via a broker, including the broker's name; and*
    - *Details of any third-party arrangements relevant to the individual learner.*

2. *Copy of the RTO's issuance register detailing the student's name, training product issued and date of issue for all AQF certification documentation issued in the period 1 January xxx to the date of this notice.*

[167] The date has been intentionally removed.

3. *Details of any third-party arrangements entered into in the period 1 January xxx*[168] *to the date of this notice.*

4. *Bank statements for the RTO for the period 1 January xxx*[169] *to the date of this notice.*

5. *Copy of training and assessment strategies implemented by the RTO for all training products on the RTO's scope of registration.*

6. *Copy of the last ten completed student files including all pre-enrolment communication, enrolment evidence, duration of enrolment (commencement to completion of training product), mode of delivery, location of practical training and assessment, all assessment evidence relied upon to form the assessor's judgement of student competency and a copy of the AQF certification documentation issued to the student on completion, ie. statement of attainment and or certificate.*

7. *If different assessment tools were used for any of the students listed above, copies of the completed assessment tools.*

As per the standard ASQA template, it is followed by:

> **Failure to comply**
>
> If you fail to comply with this notice ASQA may apply for an injunction in the Federal Court of Australia requiring you to comply with this notice.
>
> If you fail to comply with this notice ASQA may impose an administrative sanction under section 36 of the NVR Act against your registration.

168 The date has been intentionally removed.

169 Ibid.

LEGISLATION RELEVANT TO NOTICE

National Vocational Education and Training Regulator Act 2011

26 Condition—other information must be provided

1. An NVR registered training organisation must give the National VET Regulator such information as the Regulator requests, by notice in writing, for the purposes of this Act.

1. A notice must specify the period within which the information requested is to be given.

Criminal Code Act 1995

Division 137—False or misleading information or documents

137.1 False or misleading information

1. A person is guilty of an offence if:
    a. the person gives information to another person; and
    b. the person does so knowing that the information:
        i. is false or misleading; or
        ii. omits any matter or thing without which the information is misleading; and
        iii. any of the following subparagraphs applies:
            1. the information is given to a Commonwealth entity;
            2. the information is given to a person who is exercising powers or performing functions under, or in connection with, a law of the Commonwealth;
            3. the information is given in compliance or purported compliance with a law of the Commonwealth.

Penalty: Imprisonment for 12 months.

(1A) Absolute liability applies to each of the subparagraph (1)(c)(i), (ii) and (iii) elements of the offence.

2. Subsection (1) does not apply as a result of subparagraph (1)(b)(i) if the information is not false or misleading in a material particular.

Note: A defendant bears an evidential burden in relation to the matter in subsection (2). See subsection 13.3(3).

3. Subsection (1) does not apply as a result of subparagraph (1)(b)(ii) if the information did not omit any matter or thing without which the information is misleading in a material particular.

Note: A defendant bears an evidential burden in relation to the matter in subsection (3). See subsection 13.3(3).

4. Subsection (1) does not apply as a result of subparagraph (1)(c)(i) if, before the information was given by a person to the Commonwealth entity, the Commonwealth entity did not take reasonable steps to inform the person of the existence of the offence against subsection (1).

Note: A defendant bears an evidential burden in relation to the matter in subsection (4). See subsection 13.3(3).

5. Subsection (1) does not apply as a result of subparagraph (1)(c)(ii) if, before the information was given by a person (the ***first person***) to the person mentioned in that subparagraph (the ***second person***), the second person did not take reasonable steps to inform the first person of the existence of the offence against subsection (1).

Note: A defendant bears an evidential burden in relation to the matter in subsection (5). See subsection 13.3(3).

6. For the purposes of subsections (4) and (5), it is sufficient if the following form of words is used:

"Giving false or misleading information is a serious offence".

137.2 False or misleading documents

1. A person is guilty of an offence if:
    a. the person produces a document to another person; and
    b. the person does so knowing that the document is false or misleading; and
    c. the document is produced in compliance or purported compliance with a law of the Commonwealth.

   Penalty: Imprisonment for 12 months.

1. Subsection (1) does not apply if the document is not false or misleading in a material particular.

Note: A defendant bears an evidential burden in relation to the matter in subsection (2). See subsection 13.3(3).

1. Subsection (1) does not apply to a person who produces a document if the document is accompanied by a written statement signed by the person or, in the case of a body corporate, by a competent officer of the body corporate:
    a. stating that the document is, to the knowledge of the first-mentioned person, false or misleading in a material particular; and
    b. setting out, or referring to, the material particular in which the document is, to the knowledge of the first-mentioned person, false or misleading.

Note: A defendant bears an evidential burden in relation to the matter in subsection (3). See subsection 13.3(3).

It's not hard to understand why such a notice out of the blue might cause an upstanding and well-respected business owner to fly into a state of panic. Completely taken aback by the Notice and its request, Jay calls the number in the email signature and asks to speak to Jenny[170].

[170] Jenny's name has been changed.

For seven minutes, they discussed why such a notice had been issued as Jay had no reason to believe there was a problem. He is simply told because there is a need '...to investigate some matters of concern which requires appropriate testing and once that is done, you will be contacted further'. Jenny also stated that '...there will be a compliance monitoring desk audit in early January to look over the information provided and I dare say that it will result in further questions or actions or whatever happens....'. Jay asks if this has something to do with a complaint because he had no idea what it could have been from otherwise. Jenny simply advised that 'ASQA cannot confirm that it is NOT a complaint'.

The following day, Jay receives a Notice of Audit. It advises that there will be a desk audit in early January. A brief summary of a complaint is provided but nothing further, not even an indication of what clauses the audit will cover. Three months later, Jay receives his audit report with a Notice of Intention to Cancel his NVR registration with a response due on conflicting dates - the letter provided one date and the ASQAnet portal provided a completely different date. Amongst any rectification evidence, Jay needed to provide a response as to why he had enrolled an international student on a student visa in breach of section 8 of the Education Services for Overseas Students ("ESOS Act").

What followed was a year of drawn out back and forth responses to and from ASQA. Interestingly, Jay's RTO was subject to additional regulatory requirements as the qualifications he was delivering were from a training package where post course graduation licensing is required prior to being able to work in the industry. The licensing regulator knew of Jay's expertise in this area and considered his RTO amongst one of the best training providers in Australia in this particular industry area. They (the licensing regulator) had been in and audited his courses previously and found Jay's courses to be outstanding, producing some of the best graduates that their licensing body had seen in a very long time. They were more than satisfied. Jay's RTO was also the preferred provider for one of Australia's largest Commonwealth Government units, hailed around the world for their expertise in the areas that Jay trained them in.

Jay engaged a specialist consulting company to assist him to provide the relevant rectification material and response to each stage of the audit process and his application for reconsideration. It's at this point that Jay has, ever since, tried to warn other RTOs about the danger of not using the right consultants. It's so important that people ask others who have been through it; your Consultant can quite literally make or break your case. In Jay's situation, they were a contributing factor to what ultimately caused him to have to walk away from it all and say goodbye to his RTO. In trusting the consulting company he had engaged at that point to represent his best interests, the last thing he expected was for them to undertake an exercise to advise ASQA that not only was ASQA correct about '*assessment not meeting the requirements of clause 1.8*', but it was far worse than ASQA had identified and actually impacted in their opinion, many, many more students.' Regardless of whether this determination made by the consulting company was correct or not, if you are engaged as a consultant by a company to represent them and their company to provide evidence of rectification to the regulator, it is **<u>NOT</u>** part of your duty to then proceed to tell that regulator that the damage is far worse than they identified. **<u>Your responsibility is to the company that engaged you, not to the regulator</u>**! This single factor made the remainder of Jay's dealings with ASQA almost impossible, to the point where ASQA actually noted in their audit report that 'The RTO's independent audit findings appears to concur with ASQA's findings and go one step further to state that none of the students sampled by the consulting company had demonstrated competency when issued with their certification'.

Concurrent with this nightmare, Jay's marriage of 12 months was very rapidly deteriorating due to the pressure, including the financial pressure and his extended absence from home while trying to resolve these matters and trying to save not just his business but his reputation as well. ASQA had also raised allegations that because his RTO was in receipt of public funds, the audit findings suggested that he was not fit and proper and was acting against the public interest. Suddenly, everything he had worked so hard for was about to fall apart and his wife of 12 months was struggling. Not only was his wife struggling to deal with what was happening with her marriage as a direct result of what was happening with Jay, but she was also feeling very homesick.

She desperately wanted to return home to her family where she felt she had more support while he was going through this. As a newlywed couple, they had only just returned from their wedding when all this started with ASQA and 1 year in, they had still not been able to even go away for a weekend for their honeymoon. Their marriage became more and more vulnerable. Jay had stopped eating because of the stress, the financial pressure, the false allegations and combined with the trouble he was experiencing in his marriage now too, he had lost a significant amount of weight and was no longer sleeping either. He was becoming very unwell.

The pressure ultimately became too much. Jay withdrew his appeal to the Administrative Appeals Tribunal ("AAT") and allowed ASQA to cancel his registration. His wife had walked out on him, he had no money left and no desire to continue. Remembering how important marriage was to Jay, in his mind if he had lost his wife, was almost bankrupt and could never recover any costs for pursuing the damage caused by ASQA and was so ill from pursuing his right to natural justice, what was the fight for? The cost of everything he had lost was too big; some of that loss was not ever going to be recoverable anyway because it amounted to personal pain and suffering; the breakdown of his marriage, his loss of health, and his reputation. He had already lost everything that he had fought so hard for, and he had lost his wife. Rather than pursue an appeal that he was legally entitled to do and had an excellent potential of winning, Jay chose to walk away knowing that ASQA were going to cancel his registration.

While Jay ultimately lost a lot, he is the first person to tell you that he gained so much too from what happened. He gained a better understanding of how toxic the national VET regulator is and how certain individual employees of the national VET regulator are worse than most. In fact, Jay would tell you that Jenny is probably one of the most toxic ASQA employees out there - and he wouldn't be alone. The writer is aware of at least a dozen other providers in that State who would agree that Jenny is a narcissistic person whose sole purpose appears to traumatise people and destroy their lives. The writer is also aware of at least two national RTOs who have changed their Head Office address to reduce the risk of Jenny ever having an opportunity to try and destroy their business, they considered it a vital risk management strategy and if they've been able to do that, this writer certainly wouldn't disagree with them, in fact, she'd probably encourage it.

Jay subsequently was issued with divorce papers and went through the divorce process. What does he do today and where is he today? He has rebuilt his life as best as he can, albeit alone with no wife beside him, something that at his age and culturally is not common. He is continuing to work in the community where he adds enormous value that is respected and valued. He still has relationships in the VET sector with some people and from time to time will do guest speaking roles. Right now though, he's working on things much bigger than ASQA, things that will make a difference in this world and the Jenny's of the world cannot take away. There comes a time when those who are bullied are so tired of being trampled on, that they gather this enormous strength from their circumstances.

They develop the potential and the need to subsequently do good. When those feelings become overwhelming again, you are driven to keep striving to leave a legacy. For Jay though, this is just a part of his nature and always was, long before the ASQA chapter in his life came along like a cyclone destroying everyone and everything in its wake. ASQA might have given him a '*punch to the gut causing a technical knockout*' but they haven't beaten him. Jay's life is far happier today and he is doing what he does best, living a life free of stress and anxiety from ASQA and its bullies.

~END ~

Commentary

One of the biggest issues in Jay's situation was the ASQA Manager responsible for his audit. As mentioned earlier, the author is aware of a number of people who have been severely impacted by this person's narcissistic behaviour and approach to managing regulatory affairs on behalf of ASQA. Once upon a time, this was only relevant to those people who came under his jurisdiction; however, now that matters are sent all over the place, the writer has seen this man's signature on ASQA correspondence that is also outside his jurisdiction.

This man's behaviour has been implicated in Jay's situation, but I have also seen him implicated in recurrent miscarriages for another provider, a near heart attack in another and severe depression in yet another. This man is still in ASQA's employ as at the time of publication and continues to behave in this manner right under the Chief Commissioner's nose.

The second biggest issue in Jay's case of course is that of the somewhat well-known consulting company that for some peculiar reason, submitted documentation to the regulator that was not in his best interests. It is unclear why the Consulting Company had betrayed their client in this manner (after all it was Jay's company that engaged them) although what I can say is that they were incredibly lucky that Jay didn't sue them for at least negligence; he would have had every right to and in the author's opinion, should have. As long as these cowboy Consulting companies continue to engage in this sort of behaviour and worse, they will continue to be the cause of many other RTO provider's problems. This wasn't even a case of Jay not doing his due diligence - he did! The company came recommended, had been around for a long time and he'd heard good things about them. It's unclear how something could go so horribly wrong.

While it is true that Jay is fortunate in that he has reinvented himself and is enjoying his new career, it does not diminish what he lost - those things can never be replaced. And don't think he doesn't experience trauma related to what he went through still, you'd be fooled if you believed that to be true too. Jay still has flashbacks, deals with the fact that his wife left him, which is a cultural and religious taboo, he is incredibly empathetic and so when he learns that someone is going through something similar, he gives far more than he should of his time and expertise to assist them.

The VET sector and the industry internationally that Jay was involved in, as well as the Commonwealth government who used to engage him for his specialist skills are the ones who have missed out. Sadly, all because of the incompetence and ego of one man who undermines the entire ASQA jurisdiction he practices from.

#5 Cristina Anzellotti's Story

> *"Our problem stems from our acceptance of this filthy, rotten system."*
>
> **- Doris Day**

Cristina's story is tragic. Her story comes to us with permission from Cris prior to her death to ensure that there is an awareness in the sector of the toxic culture at ASQA and the harm it caused to Cristina, her RTO and her loved ones. Cris passed away approximately six months after this story was provided to Amy. She was found collapsed and deceased in her home. Amy believes she lost the will to survive and her serious health issues overcame her. Her heart was literally broken.

This email was also provided to the Assistant Advisor to Assistant Minister for Vocational Education, Training and Apprenticeships, the Hon. Steve Irons. Amy Boleszny has consented to her name being provided in conjunction with this email:

From: Amy Boleszny <email provided>

Sent: Friday, 9 August 2019 10:15 AM

To: 'GOWOR, Roman'

Subject: Cancellation of Registration for AHPTS

Dear Roman,

Many years ago, I helped a professional colleague, Cristina Anzellotti, set up her RTO training in Pathology Specimen Collection and Health Administration and Management.

I have acted as her Compliance Manager since then. She has successfully passed every audit and her registration was extended for seven years without audit as she was low risk and with a good reputation for quality.

She was a Smart and Skilled provider.

In the middle of last year a student made a complaint to ASQA trying to force AHPTS to give her a full refund on bogus claims. This student had completed all the training but failed to attend the mandatory practicum which was arranged with NSW Health in one of their regional hospitals.

The Refund Policy given to all students upon enrolment clearly states that no refund was possible under such circumstances.

Without giving the RTO an opportunity to respond to the claims, ASQA issued a complaint resolution with sanctions, forcing AHPTS to go to the AAT.

At the time, the CEO was critically ill in hospital so the matter was handled by the Training Manager, the partner of the CEO, was to attend the Tribunal, but she died suddenly thus leaving no-one to assist in rebutting the sanctions. Cristina, the CEO, gave ASQA permission to deal with me directly since she was still in the hospital.

ASQA gave a long list of documents they wished to see and I provided these by Dropbox. I then got an email claiming they had not received them and therefore was in breach, but I demonstrated that not only had they received them, but one of ASQAs officers had accessed them. I copied the documents again into a second Dropbox folder and again they were accessed by the same officer.

Meanwhile the family of the student was so abusive that Cristina paid them the full refund. Even that did not satisfy ASQA.

Then ASQA cancelled the registration and the lies started. Firstly they claimed they did not receive the requested documentation and promptly followed this with a statement that they could not open the documents (all MSWord and PDF documents). They then claimed they had telephoned the RTO office and got no reply. They had been told three months prior that the office was closed and given both my and Cristina's direct mobile number.

Next they claimed they had sent correspondence to the Parramatta office and because no reply was received, this was the breach that triggered the cancellation. Again, they knew that the office had been closed. In addition, had such a letter been received the building owner, being a long-standing friend, would have sent it on directly to Cristina.

He says no such letter was ever received and neither was a copy ever forwarded to me.

As a result of this, my seriously ill colleague lost the business that was her pride and joy, her best friend and might possibly lose her home. With no RTO she cannot claim the considerable amount of monies she is owed by Smart and Skilled. She has also lost the considerable investment she made in establishing and growing an RTO that had very high post-course employment records.

This is a shocking indictment of ASQA, in that they denied natural justice and ignored the evidence that the RTO had acted correctly, thus forcing a closure. The health industry has now lost a high-quality provider of Pathology courses at the time when it is needing to reskill workers because of facing so many nearing retirement age.

Kind regards,
Amy Boleszny
CEO

~END ~

Commentary

Cris' story has similarities to that of Philippa earlier. An ASQA auditor who takes it upon themselves to generate a range of complaints that never existed prior to their involvement, students had never lodged any complaints and the RTO had no record of any complaints. It is unclear why any staff member or contractor working on behalf of the national VET regulator might engage in such behaviour but one thing appears to be clear...in at least 3 of the stories in this book, ASQA auditors have been involved in the generation (and/or fabrication) of student complaints that did not exist prior to their involvement with the RTO.

Cristina's story is another demonstration of another life lost unnecessarily. The author can reveal that another provider of whom she is aware in the pathology collection space was audited a few years back, also nationally acclaimed for her expertise, multiple award winner, an incredible simulated training environment, outstanding industry recommendations and graduate outcomes. During an audit, the CEO was advised that they were critically not compliant and threatened with cancellation because their simulated environment did not have running hot water. The auditor was the same as Trudy Barlow[171] from Bronwyn's story next.

171 The name Trudy Barlow has been changed to protect all parties.

#6 Bronwyn's Story

> "When the whole world is silent, even one voice becomes powerful."
>
> **- Malala Yousafzai**

Dedication

Bronwyn dedicates the sharing of her story in this chapter to her husband, Alan Blencowe, because of his unwavering love and support during this dreadful time.

Introduction

The day that my life changed irrevocably in an instant was on the 9/10/2018 at 9:00am when Ruth Lonsdale[172], the Lead ASQA Auditor of our Compliance Monitoring Audit sat in my office opposite me and made the statement, "*You have such a large scope, how can you possibly manage this and all the students and meet compliance?*" I responded to her that we had great staff and systems and were highly compliant. She responded: "*Well we will see, won't we!*".

I instantly knew I was in for a fight. I just did not know how big a fight it was going to be and what a toll it would take on me personally.

That day was 2 years and 7 months ago and I am still reeling from the whole process that was to come.

Prior to this audit, VETiS Consulting Services had been audited by TAC and later ASQA every 12 months since we set up our business (January

[172] Ruth Lonsdale is a pseudonym. The actual ASQA auditor's name was provided but has been changed to protect all parties involved.

2012). By October 2018, we had "*survived*" seven audits and were ultimately found to be compliant in all except the last.

During this time, we provided a high level of customer service, high levels of compliance and all students had an exceptional "*journey*". We had an over 85% completion rate, 95% satisfaction rate and all internal and external audits were ultimately found to be compliant with all standards.

Over the seven years, many of my clients became good friends and we had a growth of over 300% during that time in our programs.

Our major work was in the VET in Schools Programs which offered vocational education and training to students in high school in over 80 qualifications.

Both my husband (who also worked in the business) and I wanted to provide these services for the benefit of youth in Australia and often said to each other when times were tough financially, "*We are doing this for Australia*"!

We had, in our last year, 18 full-time employees who felt the same as we did and wanted the company to survive past this audit, not only for us and themselves but also for our clients.

We were supporting the 18 full-time staff, 130 schools, 11000 students and whilst we were able to manage with a $400,000 overdraft, this was the cost of providing an excellent service in the industry.

As the meeting progressed with the Lead Auditor it felt like I was walking into a perfect storm where an especially bad situation caused by a combination of unfavourable circumstances was to occur. These circumstances are outlined below.

There I was, visibly distraught, in the wrong place at the wrong time with my future about to take me down a path I had never considered possible. Life as I knew it, would no longer be the same!

The introduction of the Standards for RTOs in 2015, was intended to improve the quality of Vocational Education and Training in Australia but in effect, from that day to this, we have seen 494 RTOs registration cancelled[173]. The reasons they say are they had critical non-compliances. This represented a staggering 1263% increase in cancellations prior to the introduction of the Standards in 2015. In many cases, like my own, as I understand, auditors stepped outside the standards to meet this agenda of shutting down RTOs for minor issues.

You might correctly think that all these RTOs should have been shut down.

Looking further, the reasons why the majority of these cases were shut down was for what we call *"Administrivia"*. This means that simple administration issues that arose prior to or during the audit which could have been fixed in 5 minutes. They were cited as critical non-compliances by auditors who were ill-informed, unqualified to audit, acted outside their own Standards for VET Regulators 2015, were potentially corrupt in their dealings, or had major conflicts of interest. Add to this the political agenda of shutting down private RTOs and it's a recipe for disaster in the most tragic of ways.

This catastrophic act for us has caused us to have to terminate 18 great staff, a huge impact on 11,000 (*yes, eleven thousand*) students through no fault of their own and 130 schools scrambling to find other RTOs that could service their needs as well as we did.

This had led to a massive human toll on the owners of the RTO, our employees, our students, our teachers and the 130 schools we were working with.

---

173 Bronwyn referenced the following article:
<https://compliantlearningresources.com.au/blog/shocking-stats-rto-cancellations-increased-by-1263-since-2014/#:~:text=This%20has%20culminated%20in%20the,as%20well%20close%20their%20doors>

When the news hit us, we notified our schools immediately and began the transition phase to locate other RTOs. I would have had about 300 emails from schools and teachers in those few days, supporting me personally and my RTO, stating they were gobsmacked by ASQA as we were so compliant with the standards and made the teachers compliant as well. They offered moral support, prayers, and encouragement which I greatly appreciated.

During the last week, two of my senior staff approached me with their support and told me that I had displayed great leadership to all staff during this horrible experience. This I greatly appreciated but still felt awful that I could not control the situation any further.

We tried everything we could given our financial situation. We appealed to the Administrative Appeals Tribunal ("AAT") but felt that our legal representation did not fully understand our situation nor the auditors and the conflict of interests we believed that they had. To this day, I firmly believe that two of the three auditors set out to shut us down because of a conflict of interest where they had gained employment with two of our competitors.

I feel that there were a few main reasons we were shut down, one of which was not related to our compliance. I discuss them next.

Firstly, a Political Agenda

During the Parliamentary Inquiry[174] in 2017, VETiS Consulting Services was personally verbally attacked by the Vice President of The State School Teachers' Union of WA Inc.[175] as well as the Chair of Sub Committee[176].

The Chair of the Sub-Committee, in her submission and her verbal presentation, stated that in relation to our company name 'VETiS Consulting Services Pty Ltd', it was "*no coincidence that the name blurs the initiative and the company*"; and that "*even more alarming is that there is a single biggest private provider operating VETiS programs to public school students, called VETIS Consulting*".

We raised our concerns over this statement and the fact that using the term VETIS throughout the inquiry gave our clients the impression we were being investigated. The Chair of the Sub-Committee stated to the Vice-President of the State School Teachers' Union of WA[177]: "*Clearly they have got a marketing aspect which they felt that we, as parliamentarians, were somehow doing something in that space, given that it is VET in Schools and that is what people call it. Do you have any concerns around their particular marketing aspects; or did you want to put anything on record?*"

The Vice-President of the State School Teachers' Union of WA replied:

---

174 Putting VET to the test: An assessment of the delivery of Vocational Education and Training in Schools. Education and Health Standing Committee, Legislative Assembly, Parliament of Western Australia. Report Number 3, November 2017. <https://www.parliament.wa.gov.au/publications/tabledpapers.nsf/displaypaper/4011022aac2755920d8d027a482581e9000e4ab3/$file/1022.pdf>

175 A specific name was provided however has been removed for the protection of all parties.

176 A specific name was provided however has been removed for the protection of all parties.

177 Education and Health Standing Committee, Inquiry into the Delivery of the Vocational Education and Training in Schools (VETiS) Program. Transcript of evidence taken at Perth Wednesday 6 September 2017. Session One: <https://www.parliament.wa.gov.au/Parliament/commit.nsf/(Evidence+Lookup+by+Com+ID)/AF6C23BED855EF9F48258199001C820A/$file/20170906+Transcript+State+School+Teachers+Union+FINAL.pdf>; The author of the chapter and the book acknowledge the incorrect grammar of the quote.

"I have to say that I am quite shocked that they believe they can own that sort of language. I am quite shocked. We have always had Voc-ed—vocational education—in schools, and the training aspect that comes in with it as well. I am quite shocked, to be honest with you.

I think that kind of goes to the heart and statement of private providers operating in the VET sector and this language and abuse of language with the general populace because it creates an assumption with general laypeople, if you like, who are not necessarily education bound, that the VET in Schools consulting group is actually what the VET in Schools component of the Department of Education is offering, so have made this unfortunate link between the two".

The Chair then went on to ask: "*So people believe that they are a public entity. And that is a significant risk?*" The Vice-President of the State School Teachers' Union of WA stated: "*They do. I think there is a risk not only just for the VETiS Consulting part, but I think there is a risk in a lack of understanding of what the private providers are all about and how they interact with the school environment. I am probably more comfortable saying that because I have not had very much interaction with VETiS Consulting*".

Then the Deputy Chair stated: "*I would have thought, just from a marking(sic) point of view, my gut feel would be that trading on that name, they would become the private provider of choice just because people would think that they are associated with the public sector*" to which the Vice-President of the State School Teachers' Union of WA "*Yes*".

The Vice-President of the State School Teachers' Union of WA stated '*I cannot, hand on heart, say that every private provider is completely dodgy.*

I am sure that there are some—I am sure that there must be some—that are doing the right thing but having a look at the list that was provided to us from the Department of Education about the names of the private providers that were operating in the system, VET in Schools—Vocational Education and Training Consulting—came up on every single page'. The Chair stated "*Yes. They are the largest private provider; we have just been told*". How appalling! Apart from the false allegations, they couldn't even get our name correct - VETIS Consulting Services Pty Ltd!

Interesting to note that the Vice-President of the State School Teachers' Union of WA believes "*a lot of schools would prefer to be going through the TAFE colleges, but it is the cost that has come with it as well. Fundamentally, I believe that a lot of schools would like to be going through TAFE*". Yet, as ITECA reported on 28 August 2019 in its media release titled *4.1 Million Students in Vocational Training - 71% With Independent Providers*, '*The latest data from the National Centre for Vocational Education and Training (NCVER) shows that it's the independent vocational education and training (VET) sector that continues to do the heavy-lifting when it comes to providing the workforce with the skills that it needs... The latest NCVER data is contained in a report entitled Total VET students and courses 2018 released on 28 August 2019*[178]*.*'

In the report '*Putting VET to the test: An assessment of the delivery of Vocational Education and Training in Schools*' from the Education and Health Standing Committee, we were cited again by the Training and Accreditation Council (TAC) and specifically via a letter from the now Director Quality Assessment at ASQA[179], Quality Assessment and Compliance, indicating that '*... while there were more than 40 [RTOs] were auspicing with schools, one was responsible for delivering more than half of VET to schools in an auspicing arrangement...The second largest in terms of student numbers was the largest in terms of qualifications offered (76) and the number of schools it delivered to.*'

---

178 4.1 Million Students In Vocational Training - 71% With Independent Providers, Media Release. ITECA, (Independent tertiary Education Council of Australia). 28 August 2019 <https://www.iteca.edu.au/UploadedFiles/MediaReleases/20190828_NCVER_Total_VET_students_and_courses.pdf>

179 The person is named in the original chapter provided however has been removed for the protection of all parties, page 20 of the report.

During the enquiry and in the report '*Putting VET to the test: An assessment of the delivery of Vocational Education and Training in Schools*', it was reported that the arguments often put forward in support of TAFE Delivery of VET in Schools are:

1. Its status as a public sector body, which means students are protected from private RTO failure[180]
2. Its close connection with industry[181]
3. The state training providers (TAFE colleges) have found it increasingly difficult to compete with private organisations and now provide only a small proportion of the training[182].
4. The Committee noted the demonstrated risk associated with private RTOs, coupled with a renewed commitment by Government to TAFE and recommends that TAFE play a greater role in VET in schools[183].
5. Multiple TAFE campuses across the state which students can access (in the event that the student moved schools or a campus closed, for example), but if a private provider collapses or the student moves schools the student needs to enrol with a new provider, which is disruptive[184].
6. TAFE colleges already had governance and management structures in place[185].
7. Regulations and auditing processes for TAFE colleges were described as 'highly stringent' which could give schools and parents confidence that the RTO was delivering to the standard required[186].

180 Ibid, page 35.
181 Ibid, page 35.
182 Ibid, page 38.
183 Ibid, pages 25 through 33
184 Ibid, page 35.
185 Ibid, page 35.
186 Ibid, page 35.

The State Training Board said in their submission that '*...where TAFEs are not achieving their delivery targets, they could be allowed to increase their VET in Schools delivery and this would also improve the quality and outcomes for industry*[187].

So finally, the hidden agenda has surfaced!

I felt extremely upset over these statements to the point that I complained higher up only to be told these people have '*parliamentary privilege*' and there was nothing I could do about the statements. Not only were the "*Marketing*" aspects incorrect, but they were also outright false!

When we were setting up the company, we had a brainstorming session with the staff to decide on a company name. One of my junior staff came up with the name and the logo. This was accepted by all staff and there was no mention of taking marketing advantage, nor was there any public sector vision that was even considered.

Not one of our clients saw us in either of these ways. We were a private company **AND** as a requirement by ASIC you MUST use Pty Ltd in your name at all times, which we did. No one EVER asked if we were the Department of Education's Registered Training Organisation!

Secondly, vengeance!

Vengeance is such an emotive word and one I do not use lightly. I claim that ASQA/TAC and in particular the Manager in Perth ASQA (previously TAC) has taken vengeful action again my RTO by using Auditors that would follow her directions, bully my staff and me, as well as lying in the AAT by saying we never passed an audit. She was caught out on this one when questioned by the Presiding Member.

---

187 Submission to the Education and Health Standing Committee Inquiry into Vocational Education and Training in Schools, Government of Western Australia, State Training Board, Page 12 <https://parliament.wa.gov.au/Parliament/commit.nsf/luInquiryPublicSubmissions/9F4426A98574266B48258198000D46E1/$file/20170807%20-%20VETiS%20-%20Sub%20-%20State%20Training%20Board%20and%20ITC%20network.pdf>

In my case, in particular, we (VETiS Consulting Services Pty Ltd) were under TAC for some years, prior to moving over to ASQA.

When we were audited under TAC in my new RTO VETiS Consulting Services Pty Ltd, I was exposed to this Manager when an audit was conducted on my RTO VETiS Consulting Services Pty Ltd.

From 16 April 2014 to 19 June 2014, Trudy Barlow[188] audited VETIS Consulting Services Pty Ltd and at the opening meeting, I asked the two auditors if they had any conflict of interest they wished to declare. They both said no.

One school they visited was in Perth's metropolitan northern suburbs[189] and interviewed the VET Coordinator. Upon their return to the office, the auditor Trudy Barlow declared that "*the co-ordinator hates you and has complained about the poor service she has received from your RTO*". I advised her this could not be true as we have a good relationship with the school, the teachers, and the coordinator. I rang the coordinator who was extremely upset that the auditor had lied to me. The Vet Coordinator said she complained about TAFE, not us and she would provide a Statutory Declaration to this effect. The Principal concurred. When I told the auditor Trudy what was said, she backed down and said she must have misheard!

Two students from a private school in the northern suburbs were interviewed by the Auditor who initially refused to allow my staff or the School VET Coordinator into the meetings. The VET Coordinator insisted, and we received confirmation from TAC that my staff could be present as long as they did not say anything. The student was interrogated and asked repeatedly if he had any complaints about us. Sadly, the student was autistic, and the VET Coordinator had to intervene and excuse the student from the meeting. I complained about this to the auditor as did the VET Coordinator, but no apology came.

188 The name of the auditor was provided but has been changed to protect all parties.
189 The name of the school was provided but has been removed to protect all parties.

In this audit report, there were many serious fatal errors that were made on a repetitive basis throughout the document which indicated to us at the time that it was either incompetency or malicious intent. In light of the failure on the part of TAC to discover these during the appeal and recognise the obvious conflict of interest of the auditor Trudy, was, in my opinion, indicative of incompetency or a conspiracy to cover up fatal errors. Because Trudy Barlow is an employee, albeit in a voluntary capacity with one of our colleges down South and her son Jamie Rogers[190] was enrolled with us, it is my opinion that she should have declared a conflict of interest. We were considering making a formal complaint to the Australian Competition and Consumer Commission at that time. Instead, though, I contacted one of the TAC Managers, who is now a Director at ASQA and asked for an investigation into the fatal errors and the serious conflict of interest. After several weeks of trying to find out what had occurred, I was promptly told there was no conflict of interest and when I asked how this was so, she told me she asked the auditor who said 'No'.

I approached a very well-known and respected independent auditor in the VET sector[191], explained the situation and he advised me that it absolutely was a direct conflict of interest and the auditor should have recused herself.

On each occasion of the audits (*remembering it was an average of one per year*), we were subjected to reports that had fatal flaws, procedural errors, administrivia and conflicts of interest.

The last audit with Ruth Lonsdale[192] and Prue Stevens[193] I asked if there were any conflicts of interest and they said NO.

Subsequently, after the final audit report was issued, I discovered that both auditors were now employed by two of my competitor RTOs. It was

[190] The name has been changed to protect all parties.
[191] The name has been changed to protect all parties.
[192] The name was provided however has been changed to protect all parties.
[193] The name was provided however has been changed to protect all parties.

interesting to note that Ruth Lonsdale advised me as she was walking out that I should employ a Compliance Manager. I indicated that I was about to advertise for one and as she walked out she told me to let her know when I was ready to advertise as she had someone in mind. On reflection, this was probably her or Prue!

This fear and hatefulness on the part of the Manager and the auditors was nothing short of a traumatic event for me which continues to this day.

Post Audit/AAT Hearing

The days that followed did not help. I had the AAT to contend with, collecting the evidence together again and dealing with my solicitor who was in Sydney and in different time zones, explaining why we were compliant and should get a "Stay". We even engaged a Lead ASQA Auditor, flew him over here to Western Australia from the other side of the country. He examined all our evidence and was shocked at the decision ASQA had made. He also found that we were highly compliant. He supported us at the AAT as well but ASQA outnumbered us and we lost.

During this process, we were threatened by the Department of Education with legal action if we did not find other RTOs for the students to transition to (Note: We had already done this), as well as perform other tasks that they wanted me to do. I could not deal with it anymore and my solicitor managed it and eventually, this went away. We also had the Minister for Education and Training in Western Australia[194] bad mouthing us on 6PR radio and when we tried to reply, they would not take our call.

When the AAT hearing was over and we had lost, once we knew our fate, I sunk into a deep depression. I held it together until the last minute

194 The name was provided however has been changed to protect all parties.

when the last staff member left the building and then I broke down. I sobbed and sobbed for hours.

The next few weeks were a blur. I could barely get out of bed, let alone shower, and get dressed. I wonder what would have happened to me if I did not have such a supportive family and husband. He often said to me, he would live under a bridge with me if it came to that. My poor husband has also suffered greatly (both personally and professionally) as a result of everything that has happened.

I had to pull myself together to get the business wound down, meet ASQA's requirements for closure, remit data etc. and then the final ASQA account arrived - $35,000! What a hide! Fail me, get more money, audit my evidence again, get more money!!!! I was being attacked all over again.

By this time, we already had to refund all our clients, transition our students to other RTOs we had found, finalise the collection of evidence and the issuing of certification before the cut-off date etc., all with only myself and my husband.

Then we had the process of selling our house to repay the business overdraft of $400,000 and then possibly looking for a rental to live in commenced. This was a long and tedious process but some months later we had managed to achieve this.

Then Depression

As the days flowed, and I had everything closed, I would sit and think about what had happened. Often, I would suddenly burst into tears and not even know what I was crying about. I had no spark anymore.

I could not connect well with family and felt that I had let them all down as well as my 18 staff members. I tried hard to find other jobs for them with other RTOs, provide glowing references for them etc.

I kept thinking about the staff and if they were OK. How were they feeling? Were they OK financially? Were they able to get another job? All are now employed elsewhere thankfully.

I kept thinking to myself, I don't know what's wrong with me. This is not me! I am normally a quick thinker, analytical and driven. I thought I was only tired and that it would pass soon.

But now I was just a shell that was trying to survive day by day. I eventually went to my doctor and he diagnosed me with depression. I was placed on anti-depressants and was on these for nearly two years. I have only recently come off them.

Two years, three months and ten days later, I am writing this story about the human impact, the human toll on me, my family, and my employees.

As the days flowed into months and my depression was getting better (a little), I looked into what I might do next. I applied for the aged pension (yes, I am now eligible believe it or not) and was successful. I am trying to keep my brain active by completing a few courses, two with private providers (who by the way were fantastic) and one small skill set with a TAFE College (who was shocking- subject to another story soon) as well as developing courseware for a Queensland University (who advised me this was the best he had seen ever!) and we have won a contract with TAFE NSW. We are about to commence marketing our courseware across Australia and looking forward to the future.

The perspective I have now is to share compelling experiences with the aim of them framing the way we need to treat each other, for the better.

Bronwyn Blencowe
"Survivor"
25/5/2021

~END~

Commentary

That retaliation should even be a legitimate fear in the sector for exercising your rights as a citizen and a provider is concerning and goes directly to this toxic culture that people speak of so openly and willingly in relation to ASQA. This culture was reported by both Professor Valerie Braithwaite in her review '*All eyes on quality: Review of the National Vocational Education and Training Regulator Act 2011 report*' and the Hon. Steven Joyce in his review '*Strengthening Skills: Expert Review of Australia's Vocational Education and Training System*'. As stated by Mr Joyce[195]:

> However, the Review is concerned about the quite surprising high levels of disquiet in the provider community about the way ASQA currently conducts its regulatory activity. There is always some tension to be expected between the regulator and the regulated, but it is apparent the issues expressed in this case go beyond that sort of healthy tension. The disquiet was also picked up by Professor Braithwaite in her review of the NVETR Act.[196]
>
> Many providers worry whether ASQA will treat them fairly and reasonably during the audit process.

After the Braithwaite and Joyce Reviews, ASQA paid an exorbitant amount of money to conduct an '*independent*' review of its processes. This led to the report '*Rapid Review of the Australian Skills Quality Authority's Regulatory Practices and Processes*' in March 2020. Despite some scathing findings in both the Braithwaite and Joyce reviews relating to

[195] Strengthening Skills: Expert Review of Australia's Vocational Education and Training System, April 2019, page 39.

[196] Professor Braithwaite identified a number of concerns, including 'the compliance burden on RTOs, the inconsistency of audits and auditors, the difficulty in making sense of ASQA's regulatory approach, and a disconnect from what RTOs considered important for regulation of the sector... [in short that] the sector's anxieties are increased by a lack of supportive regulatory conversations.'
Braithwaite, All eyes on quality: Review of the *National Vocational Education and Training Regulator Act* 2011 report, p 8

the toxic culture of ASQA, very little was discussed or offered in the Rapid Review. The chapter titled '*Chapter 4 - Overview of stakeholder feedback regarding ASQA's regulatory approach*[197]' only referenced the following issues:

1. Diverse expectations and understandings of ASQA's role;
2. Sector engagement and education;
3. Inconsistent audit practice;
4. Convoluted and unclear audit reports;
5. The severity and proportionality of regulatory actions in response to non-compliance.

By not capturing the main issues and concerns around ASQA's toxic culture, the rapid review failed to provide an accurate representation of the issues that concern stakeholders the most. Now, it is also noted that the rapid review report refers to 50 submissions being made. It is my personal and professional belief that the review did not receive as many submissions as it ordinarily would have because:

1. The timeframe for providing submissions was short and not during a time where most providers had the ability to submit anything of substance;
2. Stakeholders are so tired and burnt out from making submissions constantly in this sector that the thought of another was met with apathy.
3. There is a real feeling of not being heard, tokenistic responses from the government and for all the effort involved in preparing good submissions, people feel the time is absolutely wasted because nobody is genuinely interested in what they have today.
4. There were genuine concerns by stakeholders about the integrity of the independence of the rapid review.

197 Rapid Review of the Australian Skills Quality Authority's Regulatory Practices and Processes, MP Consulting, March 2020, Pages 22-23.

It is sincerely hoped that the review currently being conducted by the Australian National Audit Office will provide more detailed feedback and recommendations in relation to an issue that causes so much concern for the sector.

#7 Robert's Story

> "Our problem stems from our acceptance of this filthy, rotten system."
>
> - **Doris Day**

Robert provided a huge amount of information to be considered for inclusion in this book; information that demonstrates the fight he's been having for over two decades to address the rights of international students.

Robert is the founder of the Overseas Student Support Network ("OSSNET") based in Victoria.

I have personally known Robert for over 15 years, both of us working away independently (like so many of us do in this sector) to try and improve the lives of those who are most vulnerable. What many people in the sector (ASQA included) don't realise, acknowledge or appreciate, is that for many of us involved in the #enoughisenough campaign, we've been doing this for almost two decades, some of us even longer.

Robert and I first met at a time when I was working at Carrick Institute of Education in the Community Welfare department. We had been working collaboratively with ACPET, currently known as ITECA, who was a much stronger force than it is today. We also worked with many others in the sector, some of whom are part of the #enoughisenough campaign still today, and others who are no longer involved in the sector; one who is a lawyer specialising in migration and another who is doing a PhD in VET. Together, we all worked to achieve recognition in Victoria at least that work placements were a part of the enrolled courses of international students and recognition that this should not count towards the international students' rights to engage in 40 hours of work per fortnight while their courses were in session, a core condition of their student visas.

In Victoria at that time, under the occupational health and safety and workers compensation insurance legislation, any student undertaking work placement in Victoria had to be paid a minimum of $5 per day in order to activate their 'insurance coverage'. For international students, this became an enormous issue by virtue of the fact that they were being 'employed' and 'paid', this was taken to be included in their ability to undertake 40 hours work per fortnight. In some cases, this work placement meant that students were therefore in breach of their visa conditions, especially if the work placement had not been recorded on CRICOS (and some students had in fact been breached on this basis), while for others, it meant that their ability to work was being reduced by virtue of the fact that they were completing a mandatory component of their course.

This was an issue that caused considerable confusion and much frustration because again, some people, comfortably positioned in their ivory towers, thought they'd tweak the system without properly consulting the industry properly to actually understand how that 'tweak' would impact a significant component of the international education sector.

Robert continues to strive for justice, transparency in regulation and migration practices in Australia and best practice regulation in Australia's VET and the international education sectors. While much of what he had provided for consideration in the book will not specifically be included at this time, the fundamental issues are really the same. To address the detailed issues that Robert has provided to me would not be doing him or the work he has done, the justice it deserves. Robert has literally compiled decades of work, some of which could generate for both of us enormous legal concerns if we were to publish it at this stage.

Some of the contributions, but not all, that Robert has detailed involved the areas of:

- Visa fraud;
- Migration fraud;
- Exploitation of international students in the workplace;
- Exploitation of international students in their accommodation;
- Exploitation of international students by VET providers (public and private);
- International students losing money due to fake offer letters and confirmations of enrolment;
- Ghost Colleges as reported in the Callinan Review[198];
- RTOs threatening international students with being reported to 'authorities' or having their enrolment cancelled if they did not perform certain acts that they would not legally be required to do;
- Unpaid work experience that did not contribute to the courses of international students;
- Offers of guarantees of permanent residence (via cash, enrolment in certain courses, visa pathways, questionable future employment opportunities, etc.);
- International student suicides;
- International student sexual harassment;
- International students who had no trust in contacting the police or other authorities for fear of having their student visas cancelled; and
- International students who were afraid to tell their families and acquaintances about what was happening to them in Australia

[198] The Hon. Ian Callinan, 23 July 2019, Report "*Review: section 4 of the Tribunals Amalgamation Act 2015 (Cth.)*' <https://www.ag.gov.au/legal-system/publications/report-statutory-review-tribunals-amalgamation-act-2015>

> because they were ashamed and embarrassed at 'letting their families down'.

There were many other issues that Robert provided documentation about but they cannot be published at this stage as they could place both Robert and me as the author at enormous risk and compromise our personal safety. Some of these documents include transcripts of Federal Court Hearings and at the Victorian Civil and Administrative Tribunal.

Robert would be appalled if anyone thought for a second that these issues are unique to RTOs because they are not. TAFEs were just as guilty as was reported in The Age[199] newspaper for example.

Robert has been involved firsthand in traditional mainstream education, vocational education and training, university and the community education sectors and has not considered students' negative experiences to be simple oversights. He is also aware of many VET enterprises that have delivered, and are delivering, quality experiences and quality outcomes to international and domestic students.

This is just some of the work that Robert has been a part of and wants the sector to be aware of but the regulator to finally do their job properly and put an end to it.

Another thing that Robert feels very strongly about is the ongoing attempts at reform that are simply wasting taxpayer funds and reinventing the wheel. An example is provided in the submission he made to the Productivity Commission in June 2020. Robert is also the founder of

---

199 Farrah Tomazin, 27 May 2012, The Age newspaper 'Minister rages against rorts for courses'. The original link was <http://www.theage.com.au/victoria/minister-rages-against-rorts-for-courses-20120526-1zbzq.html>. It is referenced in the same manner by the NTEU <https://www.nteu.org.au/unsw/article/TAFE-Media-Stories%2C-26-29-May-12789> and by Leesa Wheelahan in Submission 77 of the 'Inquiry into the role Technical and Further Education system and its operation' <https://www.aph.gov.au/DocumentStore.ashx?id=e4b55f5b-0587-43ad-9556-d095a39c98f5&subId=206305>.

The Education Professionals ("TEP") and is closely associated with 'Life. Be In It.' on behalf of whom the submission was made:

> Many people currently holding positions of responsibility have little or no knowledge of the findings of the Karmel Report (1985), the Finn Report (1991), the Mayer Report (1992) and the Employability Skills for the Future Report (2002). These investigations and reports had our education offerings regarded as some of the best in the world - and must be revisited, TEP's suggested starting point is to revisit two of these foundation reports - there is no need for lengthy, costly and often fruitless philosophical discussions because the work has already been done (and already enshrined in legislation)

The Education Services for Overseas Students ("ESOS") Act 2000 (Cth.) also provides the basis for immediate action on basic compliance issues.

Robert believes that the VET sector in Australia needs a best practice regulator who has the capability, desire and motivation to address the issues that people and entities operating from inside and outside of the sector have raised. While some of the issues occurred pre-ASQA's establishment, Robert firmly believes that many have continued under ASQA's watch. As long as Australia has a national VET regulator whose regulation is fairly loose, focussed on the wrong, or distracting issues and doesn't have an audit workforce who is well qualified, highly experienced and works within the confines of a Code of Conduct and procedural fairness. One who can do so without bullying, harassment, intimidation and focussing more on its toxic culture than achieving the results it should according to its regulatory ambit, the types of issues that Robert has mentioned will not only continue but their perpetuation will increase the issues, the suffering and make them harder and harder to combat.

ASQA must change its industry-perceived focus and be seen to cooperate without resorting to bullying, harassing or using tactics such as intimidation. It must generate inclusive, quality outcomes that can help reduce its present-day toxic culture reputation.

Unless ASQA listens and positively responds to the types of issues that Robert has mentioned, its inaction will certainly increase the amount of suffering and the number of negative experiences of Australia's VET providers and of the international community.

We have so much more to tell!

~END ~

Vicarious Trauma

> *"The expectation that we can be immersed in suffering and loss daily and not be touched by it is as unrealistic as expecting to be able to walk through water without getting wet."*
>
> **- Rachel Naomi Remen**[200]

> *"Vulnerability is the core, the heart, the centre of all meaningful human experiences."*
>
> **- Brene Brown**

It was only recently that I was reading a newly published book on vicarious trauma that I realised that what I often felt and experienced while working on the types of matters that I do with clients was secondary and/or vicarious trauma. As I continued to read, I became more and more convinced that this was the case, not just for me but at least for some of the legal professionals that I work with on a daily basis, lawyers and barristers as well as the staff who work with us. Learning about the impact of vicarious trauma on myself and my own business, I have now integrated methods for managing vicarious trauma within my team and sought professional help for myself. I will discuss more about the impact of vicarious trauma on me personally and sanction management specialists generally in the chapters that follow. For now though, let's look at what vicarious trauma is.

While vicarious trauma is a relatively new area of study, there is quite a bit of research available about it, just not a huge amount of Australian

[200] Remen, Rachel Naomi Remen, 2006. Kitchen Table Wisdom: Stories That Heal, 10th Anniversary Edition. New York: Riverhead Books

based research. There are variations of the definition, but they are all fairly consistent in that they identify:

1. That it is something experienced by certain professionals and volunteers in their day-to-day work;
2. It usually affects people working or volunteering in the fields of law enforcement, victim services, emergency services and allied professions who support those in these fields;
3. It can occur from seeing, hearing, listening to or being exposed in any way to the trauma in the course of their professional or volunteer duties including, but not limited to, for example:
   a. Listening to individuals recount their own experiences of victimisation;
   b. Being involved in those traumatic events in some way (e.g. being help up in a compromising or unsafe environment);
   c. Looking at videos, reading testimonies reviewing case files, etc. of people who have experienced traumatic events day after day;
   d. Responding to traumatic incidents in the course of their professional duties;
   e. It is generally a negative reaction that presents as signs and symptoms, usually of a psychosomatic nature.

The Vicarious Trauma Institute[201] explains it in a very easy to understand way:

> Vicarious Trauma is defined as a transformation in the helper's inner sense of identity and existence that results from utilizing controlled empathy when listening to clients' trauma-content narratives. In other words, Vicarious Trauma is what happens

201 The Vicarious Trauma Institute, 'What is vicarious trauma' <https://vicarioustrauma.com/whatis.html>.

> to your neurological (or cognitive), physical, psychological, emotional and spiritual health when you listen to traumatic stories day after day or respond to traumatic situations while having to control your reaction. A transformation occurs to your inner-self as well as your perception of the world around you, that can cause serious impairment—depression, anxiety, addiction...Every time we interact from a position of compassion, controlling our empathic response with clients, patients, friends, congregants, strangers or neighbours, we are putting ourselves at risk.

The Vicarious Trauma Institute also suggests that vicarious trauma is underreported and widespread among the helping professions. This is potentially due to the fact that it's not a hugely known and accepted area or type of trauma but also, because those helping professionals who experience it, might also fear reporting experiencing symptoms for fear of losing their job or not being seen to be able to cope with their role.

One thing that is absolutely clear in the literature however is that vicarious trauma was added to the Diagnostic and Statistical Manual of Mental Disorders Manual 5th Edition ("DSM 5") after the events of 9/11.

Brene Brown is a well-known author whose talk on vulnerability is one of the most listened to TED talks in the world. Brene talks[202] about connection being the reason why we're here on Earth and that connection is what gives purpose to our lives. Importantly, Brene also talks about what was showing up early in her research and how this was really being understood by those in her research. She calls it '*...a fear of disconnection: Is there something about me that, if other people know it or see it, that I won't be worthy of a connection*'. She goes on to say that '*It's universal; we all have it. The only people who don't experience*

202 Brene Brown, The power of vulnerability. TED Talk <https://www.ted.com/talks/brene_brown_the_power_of_vulnerability>.

shame have no capacity for human empathy or connection. No one wants to talk about it, and the less you talk about it, the more you have it'. In many ways, people who experience vicarious trauma, experience their occupational or professional lives in this way too. As she says, '*we live in a vulnerable world. And one of the ways we deal with it is we numb vulnerability*'.

So what does vulnerability look like when we share ourselves with others? Perhaps one of the simplest definitions of vulnerability is provided by Mark Manson[203]

'*Vulnerability is consciously choosing to NOT hide your emotions or desires from others*'. While obviously there is a need for professional boundaries, being vulnerable in the workplace can look like something as simple as the following examples:

1. Speak your truth -if something is upsetting you, be honest about it to your Manager, Supervisor, Colleague/s. They will never know, understand or be able to support you if you don't.
2. Show that you care - When clients are explaining their stories, what they went through, your vulnerability allows you to empathise with them, to put yourself in their shoes. Likewise, if a colleague shares with you that they're experiencing signs of vicarious trauma or secondary trauma, show that you care.
3. Allow yourself to experience strong emotions - For many of us in these professions, we try to tell ourselves that our professional boundaries prevent us from getting too close to our clients. It is exactly our vulnerability though that helps us better understand and communicate to others the experience that they have suffered. We also don't allow the space for others to help or support us if we don't acknowledge or leave room for those big emotions either. We wouldn't do the work we do if we didn't

203 Mark Manson, 'Vulnerability in Relationships' <https://markmanson.net/vulnerability-in-relationships>. Mark Manson is the author of the #1 NYTimes bestselling books '*The Subtle Art of Not Giving a F*ck*' and '*Everything is F*cked: A Book About Hope*'.

care. Caring doesn't mean that you don't have professional boundaries. It simply means that you have made yourself vulnerable and this has allowed you to better understand your client and their needs.

4. Trust others and ask for help - Asking for help in the VET sector or the legal profession is almost asking the impossible. We live in such a world of fear that we might be found out to be not as good as we want others to think we are, or we don't want anyone to know what's going on. But one thing I do know is that asking for help and getting the support we need is always the better option. Too many people slip into further depression and anxiety, self-harm and suicide because they are too afraid to ask for help; don't let that be you. While it's easier to believe that if you don't tell anyone then you can't be disappointed, it is also in these times that we truly learn who we can trust.

So how does all of this talk about vulnerability and vicarious trauma relate to professional boundaries? According to Relationships Victoria, 'Professional boundaries are the legal, ethical and organisational frameworks that protect both clients and employees, or workers, from physical and emotional harm, and to maintain a safe working environment'. Of course, we all know that there are professional boundaries that must be maintained but that doesn't prevent us from being vulnerable and empathetic.

So what would symptoms of vicarious trauma look like? Janina Fisher holds a PhD in psychology and trauma and spends a lot of her time treating those who experience psychological trauma. She has designed the following diagram to demonstrate how trauma can present:

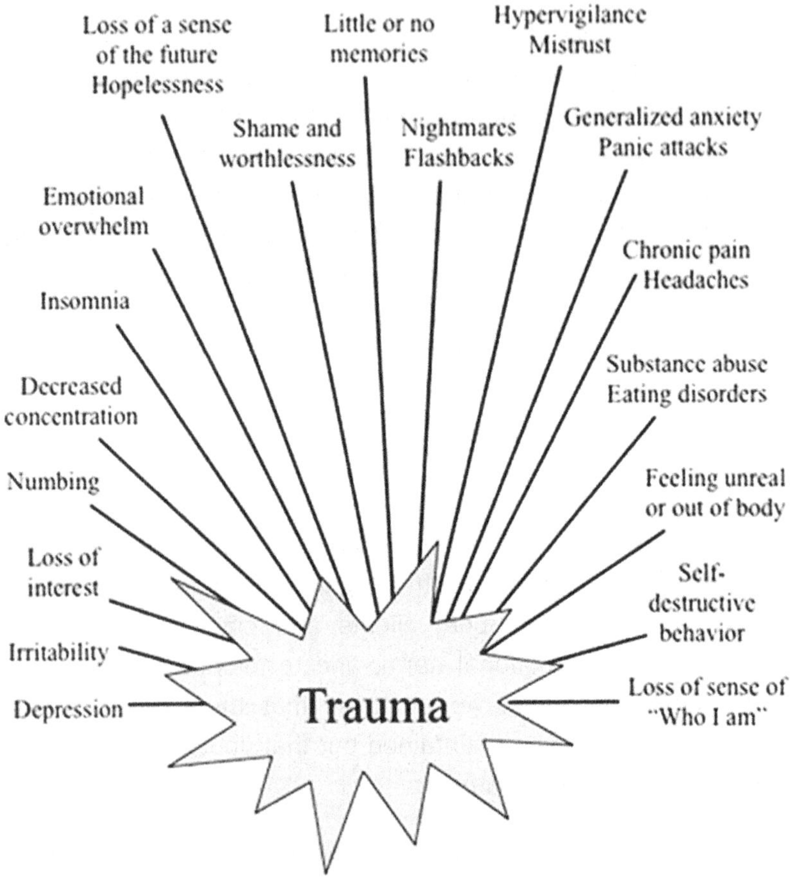

"Trauma survivors have symptoms instead of memories" [Harvey, 1990]

Adapted from Bremner & Marmer, 1998

Copyright 2007 Janina Fisher, Ph.D.

Other researchers[204] characterise the symptomatology of vicarious trauma in the following ways. There is a slide for personal and another for professional.

Examples of Vicarious Traumatization: Personal

• Physical	• Rapid pulse/breathing, headaches, impaired immune system, fatigue, aches
• Emotional	• Feelings of powerlessness, numbness, anxiety, guilt, fear, anger, depletion, hypersensitivity, sadness, helplessness, severe emotional distress or physical reactions to reminders
• Behavioral	• Irritability, sleep and appetite changes, isolate from friends and family, self destructive behavior, impatience, nightmares, hypervigilance, moody, easily startled or frightened
• Spiritual	• Loss of purpose, loss of meaning, questioning goodness versus evil, disillusionment, questioning prior religious beliefs, pervasive hopelessness
• Cognitive	• Diminished concentration, cynicism, pessimism, preoccupation with clients, traumatic imagery, inattention, self doubt, racing thoughts, recurrent and unwanted distressing thoughts
• Relational	• Withdrawn, decreased interest in intimacy or sex, isolation from friends or family, minimization of others' concerns, projection of anger or blame, intolerance, mistrust

(Adapted from J. Yassen in Figley, 1995)

Examples of Vicarious Traumatization: Professional

• Performance	• Decrease in quality/quantity of work, low motivation, task avoidance or obsession with detail, working too hard, setting perfectionist standards, difficulty with inattention, forgetfulness
• Morale	• Decrease in confidence, decrease in interest, negative attitude, apathy, dissatisfaction, demoralization, feeling undervalued and unappreciated, disconnected, reduced compassion
• Relational	• Detached/withdrawn from co-workers, poor communication, conflict, impatience, intolerance of others, sense of being the "only one who can do the job"
• Behavioral	• Calling out, arriving late, overwork, exhaustion, irresponsibility, poor follow-through

(Adapted from J. Yassen in Figley, 1995)

[204] Janet Yassen. 1995. "*Preventing Secondary Traumatic Stress Disorder.*" In Compassion Fatigue: Coping With Secondary Traumatic Stress Disorder In Those Who Treat The Traumatized, edited by Charles R. Figley, 1st edition, 178–208. New York: Routledge.

What these tables demonstrate is that vicarious trauma can present in a number of ways. The important thing now is to ensure that it is appropriately managed so that the impact is not duplicated unnecessarily. Joanna Fleck and Rachel Francis in '*Vicarious Trauma in the Legal Profession: A practical guide to trauma, burnout and collective care*' discuss that the first and most important part of managing the true extent of vicarious trauma in your workplace is to realise the prevalence and realise the impact that it is having, or has the potential to have, on your organisation. Other suggestions they recommend include:

- Incorporating mindfulness-based practices into your workday;
- Taking time for self-reflection;
- Self-care (including taking a mental health day if you need one);
- Reflective practice;
- Peer support;
- informal/formal support;
- Supervision;
- Trauma-informed supervision; and
- Individual therapy.

Of course, the biggest issue in all of those examples is that you must be vulnerable in order to benefit from them.

Something that we have recently implemented at RTO Doctor is like an orientation before we commence each project which gives each team member the ability to identify if something has a risk of becoming traumatic or re-traumatising. Then, once each project is complete, we conduct a debrief after each project.

These new practices are all part of becoming a more trauma informed small business and doing what we can to support each other and our clients better in what can be a very difficult and challenging time for everyone involved.

In closing, I would like to share the following recommendation, I found online[205]:

CARING FOR YOURSELF IN THE FACE OF DIFFICULT WORK

Our work can be overwhelming. Our challenge is to maintain our resilience so that we can keep doing the work with care, energy, and compassion.

10 things to do each day

1. Get enough sleep.
2. Get enough to eat.
3. Vary the work that you do.
4. Do some light exercise.
5. Do something pleasurable.
6. Focus on what you did well.
7. Learn from your mistakes.
8. Share a private joke.
9. Pray, meditate or relax.
10. Support a colleague.

For More Information see your supervisor or visit www.istss.org, www.proqol.org and www.compassionfatigue.org

For more information and resources or support for trauma informed care, service delivery, support and resources in Australia, a great place to start is the Blue Knot Foundation, the National Centre of Excellence for Complex Trauma on 1300 657 380 or https://www.blueknot.org.au/.

205 Professional Quality of Life Measure, website <https://proqol.org/ >, the original authors are reproduced in the image.

Impact on Sanction Management Specialists

> *"Tyranny is defined as that which is legal for the government, but illegal for the citizenry."*
>
> **- Thomas Jefferson**

Firstly, it's probably worthwhile explaining what a sanction management specialist is. A sanction management specialist is a role that has somewhat developed in recent years as a result of more and more public and private companies and private individuals appealing administrative law decisions. The administrative law decisions that this group of people specialise in is unique in that it is those decisions that are no longer internally appellable and can only be appealed using traditional court or Tribunal methods. In thé context of ASQA, this means people who support or assist those RTOs and private citizens who ASQA is pursuing with an administrative sanction which includes, but is not limited to for example:

- Reconsideration applications;
- Suspension decisions;
- Cancellation decisions;
- Written Directions;
- Conditions of Registration;
- Rejections of renewal;
- Rejections of initial registration (both NVR and/or CRICOS);
- Decisions to reject accredited course decisions;

- Infringement Notices;
- Cancellation of certification;
- Assistance with Expert Witness Reports; and
- Assistance with other legal matters (for example, defending allegations of breaches and offences under the NVR and/or ESOS Acts).

There are a range of matters that sanction management specialists will typically become involved in, ASQA matters, these are a good example depending on the qualifications and experience of the specialist. It is important to note that while many people might say that they can undertake this type of work, the reality is that there are a handful of people in the country who are truly qualified and experienced to undertake this type of work and most lawyers and barristers who work in this space know who they are. In fact, most of the VET sector knows who they are too, they don't yell from the treetops saying 'pick me', their reputations speak for themselves.

There are of course other areas where you will find sanction management specialists; basically any area where administrative decisions are made. Other areas include for example migration, citizenship, NDIS, Freedom of Information, Veteran's Affairs and Social Services. For the purpose of this book however, we will focus on sanction management specialists as they apply to the jurisdiction of ASQA.

Sanction management specialists who specialise in ASQA matters will usually spend the majority of their time working on matters that are in the Administrative Appeals Tribunal, the Federal Court or in conciliation usually within the jurisdictions of the two. A good sanction management specialist understands the importance of the role of a lawyer who specialises in ASQA matters and their role in supporting a lawyer, and/ or barrister to represent the client's best interests. It would be a very rare sanction management specialist (certainly none that the author is aware of) that would take a client through these matters without the assistance of a lawyer and/or barrister. They understand that each person has a specific role in the client's legal team that is engaged or retained to represent the client's best interests.

A good sanction management specialist knows their area of expertise and the areas of expertise of others. They know how each lawyer operates and they manage their projects and client expectations accordingly. If you are looking for a sanction management specialist and they say that you don't need to use a lawyer, that they can run the matter for you in the Tribunal, it would be fair to say that they probably don't have a whole lot of experience in these types of matters or, they do and are not that successful. Likewise, if you have a lawyer who says you don't need a sanction management specialist consultant, you should also run for the hills.

The important thing to know is that once you submit an application to the AAT, it automatically goes to ASQA's legal team to be allocated to a lawyer.

So, if your consultant is telling you that you don't need a lawyer, they're probably not doing you a great service and have an unrealistic understanding of what's involved. There are few people who can genuinely take on a qualified lawyer with no legal training and make no mistake - ASQA do not go easier on you just because you're not a lawyer! Furthermore, in a tribunal that is heavily influenced by ASQA as a regulator and often rules in their favour where applicants (providers) self-represent or use unqualified and experienced consultants, despite the fact that the Tribunal is supposed to be a jurisdiction where when a government decision falls short of what is required, the Tribunal has the power to set aside the decision, substitute the decision and/or make a correct and preferable decision.

The AAT operates '...largely without fanfare offering relatively convenient, informal and cheap processes whereby citizens can challenge adverse administrative decisions'[206]. Justice Kerr[207], also stated that 'The AAT has jurisdiction to engage in merits review only if an enactment specifically confers rights to merits review'[208]. The Federal Court however is a very different story. The Federal Court is a place for judicial review. As per the Federal Court of Australia website:

> The Court has jurisdiction under the Judiciary Act to hear applications for judicial review of decisions by officers of the Commonwealth.
>
> Many cases also arise under the *Administrative Decisions (Judicial Review) Act 1977* ("ADJR Act") which provides for judicial review of most administrative decisions made under Commonwealth enactments on grounds relating to the legality, rather than the merits, of the decision. The Court also hears appeals on questions of law from the Administrative Appeals Tribunal.

Regardless of which court or Tribunal you are facing, you always want to make sure that you have a team of people around you who are qualified and experienced in undertaking this important work that is often the last option for the provider. When the stakes are so high, the last thing you want to do is risk everything on someone who doesn't really know what they're doing.

Just as there are different sanction management specialists, they all have different and varying approaches in how they handle their matters. Some will just do what ASQA expects, others will review the evidence and make up their own mind, while others will challenge everything that has been alleged. Just as their approaches to managing their projects are different, so too are their personalities, likewise with their pricing! One thing is for certain though, the pricing of your sanction management

206 Justice D Kerr, 'The Intersection of Merits and Judicial Review: Looking Forward', 2013, University of Queensland Law Journal, Vol. 32(1), page 14.

207 The Hon Duncan Kerr Chev LH was appointed judge of the Federal Court of Australia on 10 May 2012. He also served as President of the Administrative Appeals Tribunal.

208 Ibid. Page 15.

specialist will always reflect the qualifications and experience they have and if ASQA are charging out their auditors at $275 per hour + GST, you can bet your bottom dollar that a good sanction management specialist will be worth every cent that you invest.

Just as each sanction management specialist is different, their experience with vicarious trauma will be too. For some they won't experience it at all because they really do not allow their professional boundaries to ever cross over into their personal lives. For others, while they do also have those professional boundaries, they do share some of that journey with the client and take on some of that trauma. For others, they did that once upon a time and found that it became too difficult on them personally and so they try hard to ensure that they keep their work at arm's length.

This doesn't mean that because they experience things differently that they don't empathise with their clients, that is not what I'm saying at all. It's more just a reflection of how some people's connection with others can impact their ability to experience vicarious an/or secondary trauma. It might also be a case of they are not aware of how vicarious trauma can present itself too or, for others, it might also be a case of it being something so personal to them that they would rather not disclose their experience with anyone else out of fear or shame. Whether a sanction management specialist (or lawyer for that matter) does or does not experience vicarious trauma and/or secondary trauma does not make them any better or worse at their job.

It might also be difficult to differentiate vicarious trauma signs and symptoms from what some sanction management specialists call 'side effects of the job'. If we review the signs and symptoms of how vicarious trauma presents itself again, this time using an image from Dr Colin James which he adapted from the one used earlier in Janina Fisher's model. Dr Colin James is a senior lecturer at the Australian National University School of Legal Practice and the Australian National University College of Law and was the Chief Investigator in a study that he undertook with Dr Nicola Ross, an Honorary Associate Professor at Newcastle Law School on how experienced lawyers respond to serious cases of domestic violence. The image that Dr Colin James provides regarding signs and symptoms of vicarious trauma is below:

Adapted from Janina Fisher

Based on the image provided by Dr Colin James in his presentation Vicarious Trauma in Legal practice,[209] the author can honestly say that she has experienced a large majority of the symptoms and behaviours shown over the years. It was only recently when the author was able to put a name to vicarious trauma that it truly explained a lot of things she had experienced over the years. You see the work of a sanction management specialist can be tough, in the paragraph that follows, you will gain an insight into what it is like.

Once upon a time, several years ago now, the writer would take on no more than four of these types of matters per year because of the physical,

209 Dr Colin James, 21 September 2017, Presentation, The Newcastle Club, '*Vicarious Trauma in Legal Practice*'.

emotional and spiritual havoc that it wreaked on her life. Soon however, the need for her services became so significant, that now she regularly is running anywhere between seven to nine of these cases concurrently and has been for the better part of around three years. Apart from going through the client's journey and experience and taking on all of that 'trauma', a sanction management specialist will usually pick up one of these projects when there are around 2-3 weeks maximum left for lodging an appeal. Within that time, they need to review any available evidence, come up with a strategy, provide the client with a cost estimate (where possible) and begin the preparation of the required evidence. Usually a client will have around 20 business days to file their applications and in order to demonstrate good prospects of success when seeking a stay of a decision, a reasonable amount of work needs to be provided at the time of those first hearings and conferences.

The deadlines for the remainder of the work will vary depending on what orders the Tribunal Member makes, when the appeal continues or whatever the case may be. There will be a specified period of time within which to submit further evidence and no matter what, come hell or high water, that evidence must be available and submitted to the Tribunal by that date. In many cases, this will lead to a huge amount of evidence between the sanction management specialist and the RTO staff being transferred and sometimes, filed at the very last minute. Then suddenly, it's a waiting game. Sometimes you feel like you and ASQA are holding the world at your fingertips which brings on those feelings described in the image above. Once everything is submitted, it's a waiting game again and nobody has any control of what period of time that might take. As the client continues to experience more and more frustration, the sanction management specialist also feels it. As the client waits with anxiety and trepidation for the final result, it is their sanction management specialist and lawyer that are usually there to support them through those harrowing days of waiting and waiting.

When the project's over, the results achieved, the client goes about their business and the sanction management specialist goes on; there's always another matter that is almost ready for submission and just like the last one, the long hours, lack of weekends and public holidays all commence again. Missing out on birthdays, nights out with friends, dinners and social nights are all part and parcel of dedicating your life to the sanction management process. You can literally spend a whole day at your desk (or night) without moving, and in fact that is probably more the norm! It can be challenging to get to the shops, do your grocery shopping or even cook a nice meal most nights; you live eating home delivered meals when you're in the dying days prior to submission.

Often the client does see the impact it has on your life, all they see is a constant barrage of emails requesting evidence of this, that and the other. Sometimes, they find it difficult to understand exactly what you're doing until they see the end product and then they understand. For the author, this always brings a sense of satisfaction because the penny finally drops and they realise what your value has been all along, up until that point, they were believing in reports from others, your word that it will be submitted on time, testimonials on your website and trusting in God, the universe or whatever their 'go-to' is, that everything will turn out ok in the end. Then when it is all over, you might take a day to just sleep, rest, go and do your shopping and catch up on what's been happening in the world.

For the team at RTO Doctor, as a result of identifying the potential for vicarious trauma to affect any one of us in the course of our duties, we have recently implemented a debrief after each project is submitted so that we can share and discuss the impact that the role has had on us. We've also engaged a counsellor to work with us on issues that cause us ongoing concern. Working so closely with people for so long and experiencing their sense of loss, powerlessness, trauma and anxiety on an ongoing basis usually leaves at least the author feeling the same thing.

What we identified was that if the author is experiencing signs of vicarious trauma, secondary trauma, compassion fatigue or simply burnout, then it's possible also that other team members have experienced the consequences of that or may have also experienced subtle types of secondary trauma. We've also incorporated into our orientation and induction a section on the type of work we do and how it might impact new staff members and basic information on vicarious trauma and secondary trauma. It doesn't matter whether you're the owner of the company, the sanction management specialist or the receptionist who takes the call, everyone has the capacity to be impacted and they usually are, even in some small, innocuous way.

It's our firm belief that if it's having this impact on us as a company that specialises in sanction management, there must be an even bigger impact on the staff and potentially the students of those RTOs going through the sanction management process. RTO Doctor is currently investigating ways of better supporting providers and their staff and students during this time, with new products and services coming soon! If you're interested, register your interest by completing the form on the RTO Doctor website at the following link https://rtodoctor.com.au/ under 'sanction management'.

#8 Sophia's Story

> "The time has come to put scaremongering to rest and to recognise that regulation can often support and advance efficient and more dynamic markets."
> **- Senator Elizabeth Warren**

Sophia's[210] story consists of an email that was provided to the writer to publish as a way of having her story '*on the record*'. This email was sent to the Assistant Advisor to Assistant Minister for Vocational Education, Training and Apprenticeships, the Hon. Steve Irons and the Chair of the Standing Committee on Employment, Education and Training, the Hon. Andrew Laming. Sophie is someone who is well known in Australia's VET sector and has an impeccable, long-standing reputation. This is her contribution:

From:	Sophia Emerson <email provided>
Sent:	Friday, 8 November 2019 9:25 AM
To:	'GOWOR, Roman' <email provided>
Cc:	'Laming, Andrew (MP)' <email provided>
Subject:	How ASQA treats RTOs under audit

Dear Roman and Andrew, just to keep you updated on my current experiences with ASQA.

Firstly, all RTOs undergoing audit are issued with this type of threatening letter before they are given the opportunity to respond and rectify any

210 Sophia's name has been changed upon request to protect all parties from retribution.

errors, omissions and defects. The shock this gave me triggered PTSD and I am struggling with that.

The audit report is full of errors made by the auditor in which she has made decisions which contravene long standing ASQA guidelines and accepted industry practice as previously confirmed by former audits of providers right across the nation.

Examples of this are:

- Claiming that units of competency and qualifications noted on training.gov.au as 'equivalent' are in fact not equivalent if there are any minor changes in the content of units, therefore the widespread and ASQA accepted practices in Credit Transfer are now a major non-compliance. If this is a change in directives from ASQA then millions of qualifications issued by providers (public and private) are in jeopardy.

- Disallowing the acceptance of a superseded qualification as proof that the student has met all the assessment requirements listed in the competency standards. This contravenes Standard 3.5 in that providers are legally bound to prima facie acceptance of qualification issued by other RTOs, with all that implies for attainment of the units and their contents.

- Finding a non-compliance that an assessor has not verified the authenticity of a testamur when ASQA itself has agreed this is not possible where the RTO is no longer registered. Formerly we used to do checks with ASQA but they could not cope with the work of checking records, so put it back onto the RTO to check that the provider had the qualification on scope at the time it was issued. We were also instructed that if the testamur looked genuine, then we could accept it.

There are also factual errors in the report that have occasioned a lot of unnecessary work for example:

"The RTOs practices are not compliant with the requirements of Clause 8.5 of the Standards for RTOs 2015 as it has not complied with Commonwealth legislation and regulatory requirements relevant to its operations; specifically:

- *Failure to notify ASQA of a material change or event can constitute a breach of the National Vocational Education and Training Regulator Act 2011. The RTO has not provided notification to ASQA of the commencement of offshore delivery as evidenced in the Training partner list 2018-2019 which makes reference to the approval of delivery overseas to industry clients in their home countries."*

I checked back on my files of notifications to ASQA and found the report form that was sent to ASQA in May 2018. The auditor has also stated that the individual delivering the training was not reported to ASQA. The notification form does not allow for inclusion of any details about who will be delivering the training. I queried the Manager of Compliance Brisbane on the ambiguous provider detail descriptions on the Third-Party Agreement notification form, and he confirmed that the reference to services to overseas students specifically applies to students who come to Australia to study under visas, not services to students where the RTO goes overseas to train.

I find it appalling that someone who claims to be a highly experienced auditor cannot know the pertinent facts.

The big imposition on RTOs resulting from ASQA auditing practice is if they find one thing wrong in a student file they issue a major non-compliance based on issuance of a qualification without evidence of proof of competency. If this results, the RTO has to check all student files for the preceding six months to confirm whether this relates only to the individual, whether it applies to the whole cohort or whether it is systemic across the whole system.

In cases where there are only a dozen graduates in a qualification in the time frame, this is not a problem. However the auditor found one faulty file amongst the selected students she requested for audit and we are now required to check the files of the 3,600 students who completed the unit in the six months prior. We have determined this is not a systemic error, but it is costing us $20,000 to gather the facts and compile the results.

While a large organisation taking in millions will shrug this off, for a small organisation like mine that represents half of my own annual salary. This practice is iniquitous.

Thank you both for your continuing efforts on behalf of beleaguered providers.

Kind regards,

Sophia Emerson

CEO

Sophia also recounted the time when she was in hospital following a minor heart attack. She received an email from a senior manager at ASQA telling her that she needed to provide certain information within the next 24 hours or she would be issued with a sanction for non-compliance with the *National Vocational Education and Training Regulator Act 2011* (Cth.).

The request for information was based on an ASQA auditor's request for Recognition of Prior Learning ("RPL") for the BSB551615 Diploma of Quality Auditing. Upon reviewing the ASQA auditor's submission, it became clear that there was insufficient evidence available to justify granting a qualification via RPL only. I had identified that due to the gaps in evidence I identified, that there was a need to conduct a reasonable amount of gap training and assessment before I could be satisfied as the qualified assessor under the Standards (and the owner of my RTO), that the ASQA auditor's evidence met the requirements of the training package and the principles of assessment and rules of evidence under clause 1.8.

Having received numerous applications from ASQA auditors previously for RPL for the Diploma of Quality Auditing, the Certificate IV in Training and Assessment, the Diploma of Training Design and Development, the Diploma of Vocational Education and training, the unit of competency TAEASS502 Design and develop assessment tools and TAELLN411 Address adult language, literacy and numeracy skills, there was sufficient evidence for me to make a determination that this 'gap' was evidence in the applications from all the unqualified ASQA auditors. It was clear that they didn't feel that they needed to complete the course because they had been auditing on behalf of ASQA unqualified for a sustained period of time. They felt that their 'experience' as ASQA auditors, albeit unqualified, entitled them to receive full RPL. I raised my concerns with the Commissioner because these unqualified and inexperienced auditors had the power of life and death over RTOs and I had a feeling that a complaint would be lodged against my RTO soon as a result of my professional assessment decisions.

My husband advised the senior ASQA manager, let's call them John Wayne[211] in writing that I was in hospital after suffering a minor heart attack and had no access to any data or RTO records while I was in hospital. John Wayne persisted, insisting that I supply the evidence he had requested within 24 hours or I would be issued with a sanction. Now, under normal circumstances, such threats would be enough to cause someone to experience severe anxiety, panic attacks, or, as it would have it, another minor heart attack.

I was already in hospital due to the stress but John Wayne just persisted and wouldn't accept that for medical reasons, I was unable to comply with his request while I was hospitalised!

[211] The senior manager's name has been changed to protect all parties; however, it should be noted that this person was an executive level senior manager.

I subsequently wrote to the Commissioner and explained what had happened, complaining about John Wayne's unethical behaviour. I received a very distressing response from the Commissioner in which John Wayne had advised the Commissioner that I was hysterical and untruthful. If I hadn't been so unwell in hospital, I honestly believe I would have sued him for defamation. From the tone of the person who wrote the reply, I could tell that the staff member was not happy to have to write such a letter. The author of that letter hinted between the lines that I should take the matter to the Tribunal. I didn't have the physical or financial capacity at that time to follow the advice of the author of the letter. I was genuinely very ill in hospital and my most important goal at that time was to try and regain my health so I could return home, be with my family and get back to work. In the end, ASQA let the matter drop, but not before it had caused me a great deal of distress.

~END ~

#9 Rabih (Rob's) Story

> *"When you believe in something, fight for it. And when you see injustice, fight harder than you've ever fought before."*
> **- Brad Meltzer**

The Story of a Resilient CEO and the Decisions That Rocked the Boat

The Trades College Australia Pty Ltd ("Trades College") story and that of Rabih Chamma are important in terms of the future of cases from the VET sector going through the court system. Although ASQA denies the meaning of what was, and are important findings by the Tribunal Members, the reality is that ASQA can deny its meaning all they like but the truth of the decision stands. Some of the most important findings were, and they are repeated in full in this story to demonstrate their importance and what one man and his college went through in what appears to have been an almost permanent battle since he was initially registered in 2012.

This story starts a little differently than the others by commencing with the end result. The author starts with the findings because there were multiple cases and literally thousands of documents produced for the hearing. If one was to read the story in the order it appeared, a perception would be created that is totally inconsistent with what the Tribunal Members ultimately found.

While this chapter is not the full story, it does capture some of the main themes and the ultimate findings by the AAT. In this current version of the Trades College matter, ASQA issued two (2) concurrent decisions. There was a complaint investigation in process and during that time, Trades

College's renewal of registration application was due and submitted to ASQA for consideration. As a result, ASQA's decisions were to cancel the NVR registration of the RTO and to reject the application for renewal of NVR registration.

Tribunal Hearings and the Federal Court

In the first stay hearing[212], the Tribunal refused the applications for a stay of both decisions which meant that the decisions came into effect while the case was under review. This meant that, based on the Tribunal's decisions on 24 May 2018, Trades College registration was cancelled and their application for renewal was rejected. It should be noted that as a result of these decisions, Trades College has not been able to operate as an RTO since May 2018 (three years now).

An appeal was lodged with the Federal Court for judicial review[213] and its decision was to send the applications for a stay of both decisions back to the AAT for consideration. The Tribunal makeup was different, however, this Tribunal member again, decided to refuse the applications for a stay of the ASQA decisions[214], meaning that the decision to cancel and the decision to refuse re-registration again came into effect.

What was therefore left to fight was the review of those decisions. So, what is stated next, are some of the most important findings of the Tribunal Members upon review of the decision to cancel and the decision to refuse renewal of Trades College[215].

212 Trades College Australia Pty Ltd and Australian Skills Quality Authority [2018] AATA 1360 (24 May 2018).

213 Trades College Australia Pty Ltd and Australian Skills Quality Authority No. NSD 893 of 2018.

214 Trades College Australia Pty Ltd and Australian Skills Quality Authority [2018] AATA 1703 (12 June 2018).

215 Trades College Australia Pty Ltd and Australian Skills Quality Authority [2020] AATA 812 (16 April 2020).

First, the most important decisions:

DECISION

Tribunal:	**Deputy President B W Rayment OAM QC** **Emeritus Professor P A Fairall, Senior Member**
Date:	**16 April 2020**
Place:	**Sydney**

The Tribunal decides that:

1. the decision to cancel the applicant's registration is set aside and the matter remitted to the respondent for further consideration with a view to its consideration of the applicant's fresh application.

2. the decision to refuse to renew the applicant's registration is affirmed.

The reason why these decisions had to be made was because the stay decisions had been refused. There was no longer an RTO registration to renew because the previous 2 Tribunal decisions were to refuse the stay decisions preventing the decisions from coming into effect. Once the RTO registration was cancelled, it could not be renewed or resuscitated. Therefore, this was the only decision the Tribunal member could make.

ASQA's Flawed Decision

The following screenshot makes it very clear that there were flaws in ASQA's decision-making. Had the previous Tribunal Members in the stay hearings agreed to use their discretion and impose a stay of the decisions, the Trades College case would have a very different outcome and it would still be training today.

FLAWS IN ASQA'S DECISION

7. The two reviewable decisions in issue are unusual in that the organisation has not traded for a long time. The considerations which led ASQA to cancel the registration of the

PAGE 4 OF 9

applicant are all historical and the evidence before us about alleged past breaches therefore had an air of unreality. There were significant problems about the conclusions reached by the auditor that led her to recommend to the Commissioners that the reviewable decisions be made.

8. In the first place, the audits conducted were desk audits only. The auditor did not visit the College's premises. Nor were interviews conducted with the assessors whose work the auditor criticised. The result was that the auditor knew nothing about the significant improvements, made by the College itself, to the premises it leases. It spent hundreds of thousands of dollars building and equipping areas and sites in its leased premises so that students could demonstrate their experience in various trades. In turn, the assessors recorded the work which the students displayed by videos which they retained. The facilities the applicant built and equipped in Punchbowl were described by Ms Bowler as state of the art facilities, and the work done by the applicant in their premises was unusual among registered training organisations. The building work done on the premises enabled students, including persons who were given RPL qualifications, to demonstrate their expertise to assessors.

The following demonstrates another critical finding for ASQA Commissioners and future matters where RTOs present at the AAT for stay hearings in particular:

> 13. Another problem about the way in which the case was conducted arose from direction made prior to the listing of the proceedings before us, at a time when we were not involved. We have concluded that in future cases where there is a contest about non-compliances, ASQA must start and do so without the assumption that its allegations of non-compliance are prima facie correct.

It is important at this stage to mention a key part of the 'Compliance Monitoring Audit' was allegedly due to a *'complaint'* from the Department of Finance (Department of Fair Trading NSW). This was also raised by ASQA during the stay hearing in May 2018[216]. The Tribunal Member questioned the legitimacy of this 'complaint' as is seen next.

The Tribunal Member asked whether they felt that the Department of Fair Trading in New South Wales was auditing ASQA itself[217]. The alleged complaint says in the transcript "*if no issues have been previously brought to your attention in relation to these particular RTO's that are the subject of this letter....*" The Tribunal Member then asked if there was any other correspondence from the Department of Fair Trading because what they were seeing seemed to be contradictory to the statement that there may have been a complaint. In confirming the Tribunal Member said do you think this is a complaint do you?

To which ASQA replied '...it was submitted as a complaint but that's our internal process'.

The Tribunal Member, in confirming that their reading of the alleged complaint seemed more like the Department of Fair Trading were seeking to identify if there was any evidence of these issues occurring or not in the past.

216 Trades College Australia Pty Ltd and Australian Skills Quality Authority [2018] AATA 1360 (24 May 2018), Transcript, page 58 at line 15.

217 Trades College Australia Pty Ltd and Australian Skills Quality Authority [2018] AATA 1360 (24 May 2018), Transcript.

Fit and Proper Person

Like many ASQA matters that have been pursued in recent times, ASQA sought to make a finding that Rabih Chamma (the CEO and sole director of Trades College) was not a fit and proper person. The allegation of not being fit and proper is one that causes significant issues for a person found 'guilty' of an ASQA breach of the fit and proper person requirements and therefore, any allegation of not meeting these requirements has serious repercussions. This part of the decision details to what extent ASQA will go to try and obtain a positive outcome. The fit and proper person requirements will be discussed in the next section under 'Commentary'.

FIT AND PROPER PERSON

17. The respondent sought to show that Mr Chamma is not a person who is fit and proper to lead the College. We are not satisfied that the respondent's allegation is made out. We find that he is a person who is fit and proper to lead the College.

18. The respondent relied upon the conviction of Mr Chamma for the offence of grievous bodily harm, for which he was given a two year good behaviour bond in 2011. Mr Chamma gave uncontradicted evidence about the circumstances of the offence at the hearing on 26 August 2019,[1] which we are satisfied to accept. Those circumstances do not suggest any propensity to criminality.

19. He also has a subsequent history of much important charitable work, including being in leadership positions both in this community and abroad. He conducted the College for some six years with apparent success, and has managed to keep the company afloat through difficult circumstances since May 2018. As a witness, we found him to be intelligent and apparently astute, and anxious to offer a good educational product. He should remain in charge of the College. The respondent accepted his leadership in consent orders made in previous proceedings between the parties in this Tribunal and we think that decision was correct.

20. We are not persuaded that any of the complaints against the applicant led by the respondent showed that Mr Chamma was not fit and proper to lead the College. For the most part, we were not provided with sufficient detail of the justification for those complaints. To some extent, the complaints may have stemmed from the difficulties of issuing certificates while unregistered.

The final decision clearly states that the new application to become an RTO should not be refused on the basis of the issues that formed part of this hearing.

DECISION

22. For those reasons, the respondent's decision to cancel the registration of the applicant will be set aside and the matter will be remitted to the respondent for further consideration with a view to its consideration of the applicant's fresh application for registration when submitted. The refusal of the respondent to renew the registration of the applicant in 2018 is affirmed. For reasons explained above, that affirmation does not entail that the applicant's new application for registration should be refused.

Current Situation

The current situation is that despite the fact that this decision was made just over twelve months ago, there have been several major events that have occurred since the decision was made that have impacted the ability of Trades College to submit a new application for registration. These issues include (but are not limited to):

The global COVID-19 pandemic. The ability to complete the application, prepare the required documentation, etc. has been significantly impacted by the COVID pandemic in New South Wales (which was one of the worst-hit states and territories in Australia. It has been impacted by multiple lockdowns and outbreaks causing significant challenges in preparing a new application.

1. **Training package changes.**

    - Since the decision was made by the Tribunal on 16 April 2020, there have been significant changes to both training packages. The CPC Construction, Plumbing and Services Training Package was replaced on 1 October 2020 with significant changes to many of the qualifications that Trades College had on its scope of registration. Had Trades College remained registered, it would have had until 31 December 2021 to transition to its new courses (around 18 months).

- The UEE Electrotechnology Training Package was also replaced on 12 August 2020 with significant changes to the qualifications on what was Trades College's previous scope of registration. Had Trades College remained registered, it would have had until 31 December 2021 to transition to its new courses (around 18 months). Now it has to apply for registration again, it must comply at the time of application with the new training package. Had Trades College remained registered, it would have had until 5 October 2022 to transition to its new courses (almost 2 years).

2. **Demonstrating financial viability.** Due to the stay decisions not being granted and Trades college not trading since May 2018, in addition to the global COVID pandemic, having to rewrite all of the training and assessment materials, continue to pay off loans for resources and equipment, pay rent, etc., the RTO must demonstrate at the time of applying for renewal that it meets the financial viability risk assessment criteria. This requirement was reinforced by the Tribunal reaffirming that Trades College will need to take into account current financial and economic challenges when reapplying for registration. This is shown below:

FINANCIAL VIABILITY OF THE COLLEGE

21. There is good reason to think that the applicant will show itself to be financially viable when its contractual arrangements are made to equip it to recommence trading. That evidence will need to be brought up to date when final plans are made to resume trading. It will need to take account of any economic difficulties which may arise because of matters such as the coronavirus infections, especially insofar as they may affect anticipated sources of finance available to the applicant for its operations. Those are matters to be dealt with in the future. The matters of disagreement between accounting experts called before us may well no longer affect the applicant when proper contracts are put in place with financiers and more detailed projections are available.

How did it get here?

Ultimately, while the original decisions were set aside and affirmed respectively, the Tribunal did, like many stories before, at least one of them published in this book, some of the issues around the Trades College case were related to complaints by staff members who sought vengeance after they had their employment terminated. Some of the other main issues that caused Trades College to find themselves in the Tribunal, Federal Court and then back in the tribunal (three times in total for this decision) were:

1. Pursuing a second bite at the cherry based on the Terms of Agreement struck in 2016 after a previous AAT threat to cancel;

2. Some of the main findings were related to students who were affected by the Terms of Agreement (in other words, they were again brought up in these proceedings, for a large majority of the hearing). As the decision record[218] states in paragraph 7 '*The considerations which led ASQA to cancel the registrations of the Applicant are all historical and the evidence before us about alleged past breaches therefore had an air of unreality'.*

3. Improper audit approaches and the fact that ASQA didn't visit the College premises, it only ever completed desktop audits. The auditor criticised a number of assessors but held no interviews with the assessors with whom the auditor criticised.

4. The audit took no consideration into account of the state-of-the-art facility that Trades College had costing hundreds of thousands of dollars to establish.

5. The use of section 26 Notices. We have seen in other areas of this book what a section 26 Notice to give information looks like and how ASQA improperly applies the findings it generates

[218] Trades College Australia Pty Ltd and Australian Skills Quality Authority [2020] AATA 812 (16 April 2020).

from conducting a review of evidence it collects via a section 26 Notice. This will also be discussed later in this chapter.

6. There was significant discussion of the Response Option Assessment Tool ("ROAT") and the role it plays in auditor decision-making and recommendations; it is also referred to in the decision as an algorithm and a spreadsheet. In reality it is an Excel spreadsheet that 'someone' has pre-populated algorithms in a template for auditors to use. Each of the sections is allegedly based on ASQA's risk assessment process.

Response Option Assessment Tool ("ROAT")

The ROAT has been the cause of discussion elsewhere in this book as a result of what appeared to be auditor manipulation of the data that went into the spreadsheet to produce a preferred outcome.

What is not well known is that ASQA auditors, when completing a ROAT, could inappropriately and subjectively calculate the ROAT scores and comments to produce a predetermined outcome. The ROAT underpins the administrative sanctions that ASQA chooses to use in each decision it makes. It is the author's belief that the administrative sanctions that ASQA applies, including the sanctions it places on providers as a result of the predetermined outcome, have a consequential fatal impact on a provider's registration. This is even more so IF the ROAT requirements have been incorrectly and subjectively calculated. There were a number of pages in the transcript[219] demonstrating the concerns that the Tribunal Members had with the use of the ROAT in the case of Trades College.

The Australian Government Solicitor ("AGS") says this is '*just a document given to the Commissioners*'. It's something taken into account and doesn't make *the decision. It takes into account the 'expert' auditor's input information...*'

219 Trades College Australia Pty Ltd and Australian Skills Quality Authority Transcript, No. 1994 of 2018, 16 December 2019.

The AGS says this is *'just a document given to the Commissioners'*. It's something taken into account and doesn't '*make*' the decision. It takes into account the ***'expert'*** auditor's input information. It would appear that this statement is inconsistent with ASQA's actual practices when it comes to recording and reporting audit outcomes and making recommendations.

One thing that must be brought up again at this point is the statement given to the Tribunal in relation to *'expert'* auditors. As we saw earlier in this book, the 'expertise' of ASQA auditors is highly questionable, an issue even reported to the Senate Estimate Committee on Education and Employment as recently as in the 2019-20 Supplementary budget estimates[220]. This finding was also made by the author in a published LinkedIn article, also included within this book. The issue of using technical experts in audits (as questioned by Counsel representing Trades College below) is also something that the author has been pushing for a lot in recent years, as demonstrated in the article the author published on LinkedIn that has also been included in this book.

While providing evidence the ASQA auditor was asked if they thought it might be important to have someone who has the ability to assess the Certificate III in Plumbing to confirm whether or not the assessment was in fact complied with given that they didn't have subject matter expertise themselves, to which the auditor replied, "No". They were subsequently asked by Counsel representing Trades College, "Why not?". The auditor replied because not all audits are conducted by auditors with subject knowledge. They have auditing skills and they have some subject knowledge of a 'qualification' but it's not necessarily the one that they're auditing.

The auditor's response is astonishing but standard as far as ASQA's usual response to such an issue.

220 Education and Employment Committee, Employment, Skills, Small and Family Business Portfolio, Question on notice no.: 222, Supplementary budget estimates.

The Use of Section 26 Notices

The use of section 26 Notices has unsurprisingly come up already in this book. Their use in the Trades College matter demonstrates again how ASQA's inappropriate use of any and all evidence gathered under a section 26 notice compromises the validity of the audit finding. One of the most basic issues with the improper use of section 26 Notices by ASQA staff is that they (ASQA auditors) don't ask a provider to demonstrate how it complies with specific regulatory criteria. An RTO cannot pre-empt (nor should it be expected to) how ASQA auditors will apply the evidence requested and as will be demonstrated next, best practice auditing approaches clearly and explicitly describe that auditors should not presume to know how evidence should be used to demonstrate compliance.

In their approach to managing section 26 notices, ASQA says '*here is the clause, you've provided this evidence as a result of a s 26 notice, we've applied that evidence against specific clauses and deemed you not compliant*'. It's an unreasonable situation where the regulator has put the cart before the horse. This is also inconsistent with auditing best practice approaches (*Standards for VET Regulators 2015*, clause 1.9) and has been a feature of the various VET Audit Handbooks over the years as per the screenshots below:

AQTF 2007

Evidence-based

Audit conclusions and recommendations about an RTO's compliance with the standards are based on valid, current, sufficient and authentic evidence. Findings are clearly based on evidence collected at the audit and, where non-compliance is recorded, the gaps in evidence are clearly identified.

An RTO must be given the opportunity to present to the audit team evidence that it has met the required outcomes. Auditors must not have preconceptions about the form that evidence may take.

The judgement about how evidence is related to compliance is guided by considering these questions:

Q: Is the evidence valid? Is it clearly related to the standard that is being audited?

Q: Has the RTO provided sufficient evidence for a judgement about compliance to be made?

Q: Is the evidence current or is it no longer relevant to the operations of the RTO?

Q: Is the evidence presented by the RTO authentic? Does it require further authentication?

Audit Handbook

AQTF 2010

Audit conclusions and recommendations about an organisation's compliance with the *AQTF Essential Conditions and Standards for Initial Registration/AQTF Essential Conditions and Standards for Continuing Registration* are based on valid, current, sufficient and authentic evidence. Findings are clearly based on evidence collected at the audit and, where non-compliance is recorded, the gaps in evidence are clearly identified.

RTOs

An RTO must be given the opportunity to present to the audit team evidence that it has met the required outcomes. Auditors must not have preconceptions about the form that evidence may take.

The judgement about how evidence is related to compliance is guided by considering these questions:

Q: Is the evidence valid? Is it clearly related to the Standard that is being audited?

Q: Has the RTO provided sufficient evidence for a judgement about compliance to be made?

Q: Is the evidence current or is it no longer relevant to the operations of the RTO?

Q: Is the evidence presented by the RTO authentic? Does it require further authentication?

As the audit progresses, the auditor must provide the RTO with opportunities to discuss the evidence provided and to provide more evidence, should it be needed. Clarity is critical here and the auditor should focus discussions with the RTO on the following points:

- 'This is the standard'
- 'This is the evidence you (the RTO) have provided'
- 'Here is a gap and it is for these reasons' (relating back to the principles of evidence, above)
- 'Do you have any other evidence that would close the gap?'

By using this approach, the RTO has reasonable opportunities to provide relevant evidence and help it clearly understand the audit findings.

While neither of these Audit Handbooks are *'currently'* in operation, they are consistent with the concepts expressed in the Standards for VET Regulators 2015[221] clauses 1.9 and 1.10 of the Standards for VET Regulators which clearly discuss that auditors should not have preconceived ideas about the form that evidence may take; that there are no preconceived ideas of compliance or lack of compliance. What these screenshots also demonstrate however is that this process that ASQA and its auditors are expected to abide by.

221 The Standards for VET Regulators 2015 (Cth.) are made under subsection 189(1) of the *National Vocational Education and Training Regulator Act 2011*.

The Standards for VET Regulators 2015 are very clear in clauses 1.9 and 1.10 about the expectations of an ASQA auditor:

1.9. The VET Regulator ensures that its auditors:

a) adopt contemporary best practice auditing approaches; and

b) exercise their judgement in a manner which maximises consistent interpretation of the Standards for RTOs, audit practice and findings across audits; and

c) from 1 January 2016, meet the national competency requirements for auditors specified in Schedule 1.

1.10. The VET Regulator makes decisions in a manner consistent with the principles of natural justice and procedural fairness.

In the matter of Trades College, ASQA are asked[222] how often they would ask for the entire set of student files as part of a compliance monitoring audit under a section 26 Notice to which the response was 'quite often'. When seeking clarification if that was the case even when there are hundreds of students, the answer was still yes. They then went on to confirm something that is well known in the sector; ASQA frequently uses section 26 notices to get assessment and other records.

I wonder why ASQA feels that it is necessary to use such force and threatening notices with such unrealistic time frames to request something that it could request in less forceful and intimidating ways.

The following issue goes in relation to the section 26 notices relates to the unreasonable nature of the request made by ASQA. It is the author's experience that such tactics are not unique to Trades College. This tactic is the same with almost every section 26 notice the author has seen. There is a considerable unreasonable amount of evidence required to be produced in a very short space of time and often, there can be issues of uploading, wrong page numbers, etc. that can occur when you are dealing with hundreds of records and potentially thousands upon thousands of pages of evidence to be scanned and uploaded to a Dropbox or similar or, alternatively, saved on to a USB.

[222] Trades College Australia Pty Ltd and Australian Skills Quality Authority Transcript, No. 1994 of 2018, 16 December 2019.

In some cases, the writer has experienced where ASQA has required the provider to print and manually paginate several thousand pages across 3 copies for ASQA and the Tribunal as well as provide a copy for itself to match. All of this evidence was due within a 2-week time frame. Obviously with so many records and in such a short time frame, there are bound to be errors and one would expect that a regulator might pick up the phone and ask for it to be sent through, or an email asking to submit it. Instead, what often occurs is ASQA will send a notice notifying the provider of a breach of the section 26 Notice and failure to comply.

Further, when there is a document missing amongst the evidence that the section 26 Notice was intended to provide, there were no phone calls or emails; alarmingly, they were accused instead of breaching clause 8.1(f) of the Standards for RTOs 2015 in relation to the archiving, retrieval and transfer of student records.

For absolute transparency, clause 8.1 of the Standards for RTOs 2015 states:

To be compliant with Standard 8 the RTO must meet the following:

8.1. The RTO cooperates with the VET Regulator:

a) by providing accurate and truthful responses to information requests from the VET Regulator relevant to the RTO's registration;

b) in the conduct of audits and the monitoring of its operations;

c) by providing quality/performance indicator data;

d) by providing information about substantial changes to its operations or any event that would significantly affect the RTO's ability to comply with these standards within 90 calendar days of the change occurring;

e) by providing information about significant changes to its ownership within 90 calendar days of the change occurring; and

f) in the retention, archiving, retrieval and transfer of records.

Counsel for Trades College continued and tried to elicit from the auditor if they understood the sheer number of documents that they were requesting within a very short time frame (bearing in mind that the auditor is the one who lists the number of students studying at the time of the audit on the report); the number was 417 student files[223]. The intention was to demonstrate the level of unreasonableness by the auditor in their expectations of volume of evidence in such a short time frame.

It is the writer's contention that there are far better, and less adversarial ways for ASQA to obtain evidence if it wants it. Further, there needs to be a level of reasonableness about the timeframes in which to produce such vast amounts of evidence and where a document is missing where there are such large numbers of documents, the first thought should not be '*they deliberately breached the section 26 notice*', but rather, '*let me contact them via email and see if they're aware that it's missing*'. This change of thinking is because the author's experience is that for every section 26 notice that she's been involved with (and there have been many), in 99.9% of cases, the missing document will not be intentional even if ASQA's initial belief is that it was a deliberate breach which is what the transcript suggests was the concern here.

Critical Non-Compliance

Another issue of significant concern that was raised by the Tribunal during this hearing was the concept of '*critical non-compliance*'. As will be seen through the transcript, the Tribunal was concerned that the term is not to be found anywhere in the legislation but its finding can have such severe consequences for a provider. What is perhaps less known to the Tribunal, is that the terms minor non-compliance, significant non-compliance and critical non-compliance for example were described in previous versions of the '2010 AQTF Audit Handbook' and the 'National Guideline for Managing Non-Compliance'. Since these are no longer in use though, there is no 'actual' legislative definition for a term that has caused so many RTO cancellations.

[223] Trades College Australia Pty Ltd and Australian Skills Quality Authority Transcript, No. 1994 of 2018, 16 December 2019.

In terms of previous 2010 Audit Handbook[224], the following definitions were provided:

Non-compliance	**non-compliance** The requirements of the *AQTF Essential Conditions and Standards for Initial Registration* or the *AQTF Essential Conditions and Standards for Continuing Registration* have not been met, based on the evidence reviewed. There are three categories of non-compliance, each explained below.
	Minor non-compliance The requirements of the *AQTF Essential Conditions and Standards for Initial Registration* or the *AQTF Essential Conditions and Standards for Continuing Registration* have not been met, based on the evidence reviewed, but there is no, or minor, adverse impact on learners and/or other consumers of goods and services produced in the training environment or the current (or future) workplace.
	Significant non-compliance The requirements of the *AQTF Essential Conditions and Standards for Initial Registration* or the *AQTF Essential Conditions and Standards for Continuing Registration* have not been met, based on the evidence reviewed, and there are indications of a significant adverse impact on learners and/or other consumers of goods and services produced in the training environment or the current (or future) workplace.
	Critical non-compliance The requirements of the *AQTF Essential Conditions and Standards for Initial Registration* or the *AQTF Essential Conditions and Standards for Continuing Registration* have not been met, based on the evidence reviewed, and there is a critical adverse impact on learners and/or consumers of goods and services produced in the training environment or the current (or future) workplace.

Audit Handbook | **47**

In the National Guideline for Managing Non-Compliance (2007)[225], the following definitions were provided:

224 Commonwealth of Australia, 2010. AQTF Audit Handbook, page 47.

225 Commonwealth of Australia, 2007. AQTF 2007 National Guideline for Managing Non-Compliance, pages 7-8.

Non-compliance

The requirements of the AQTF 2007 *Essential Standards for Registration* have not been met based on the evidence reviewed. There are three categories of non-compliance.

Minor non-compliance

The requirements of the AQTF 2007 *Essential Standards for Registration* have not been met based on the evidence reviewed but there is no or *minor* adverse impact on learners and/or other consumers of goods and services produced in the training environment or the current (or future) workplace.

Evidence indicates that:

- non compliance does not demonstrate a serious breakdown of the RTO's systems for the provision of quality training and assessment
- continuous improvement systems are in place
- data from the quality indicators or other sources shows that clients are generally satisfied with services and outcomes from the RTO.

Significant non compliance

The requirements of the AQTF 2007 *Essential Standards for Registration* have not been met based on the evidence reviewed and there are indications of a significant adverse impact on learners and/or other consumers of goods and services produced in the training environment or the current (or future) workplace.

Evidence indicates that:

- training and assessment systems are not sufficiently focused on quality training and assessment outcomes and meeting individual learners' needs in some areas of the RTO's operations
- systems to continuously improve the RTO's operations are inadequate
- data from the quality indicators or other sources shows that a range of clients have expressed dissatisfaction with services and outcomes from the RTO
- previously identified minor non compliance has not been rectified or evidence of improvement within the applicable period has not been provided.

National Guideline for Managing Non-Compliance 7

Critical non compliance

The requirements of the AQTF 2007 *Essential Standards for Registration* have not been met based on the evidence reviewed and a critical adverse impact on learners and/or consumers of goods and services produced in the training environment or the current (or future) workplace is occurring or has occurred.

Evidence indicates that:

- training and assessment systems are not achieving quality training and assessment outcomes and are not meeting individual learners' needs
- there is a breakdown in, or absence of, effective management systems
- there is no systematic approach to continuous improvement
- data from quality indicators or other sources shows that there is widespread or persistent dissatisfaction with services and outcomes.

In extreme situations evidence from audit may indicate risk of injury or death to people in the training environment or the current (or future) workplace. In such instances, the level of risk and potential impact on learners and/or other consumers of goods and services produced in the training environment or the current (or future) workplace warrants immediate rectification.

It is therefore unclear why the definitions of at least minor, significant and critical non-compliance can't be more clearly defined in the legislation. If a change is to be made, it should ensure that all terms of 'non-compliance' are included, for example, a common finding in recent months has been '*concerning non-compliance*' which has also not been defined. There was a reasonable amount of time allocated to the Tribunal's concern that there was no legislative definition of 'critical non-compliance'[226] and then the impact of and influence of such a finding on the ROAT (Response Option Assessment Tool). The concerns of the Tribunal regarding critical non-compliance and the use of the ROAT included the types of algorithms and weightings placed on various components of the ROAT and how these affected a regulatory decision or outcome.

The Tribunal Members were also very concerned about whether there is the capacity to balance the negative findings with positive findings. So for example, in the case of Trades College, that they had invested several hundreds of thousands of dollars into the training rooms and equipment, was there somehow, within this spreadsheet, the capacity for the auditor to provide positive feedback or points about the provider to provide the Commissioner in making their decision, to which the ASQA auditor replied, "No".

Of course, of significant concern was the AGS suggesting this is '*just a document given to the Commissioners*'[227]. It's something taken into account and doesn't '*make*' the decision. It takes into account the '*expert*' auditor's input information. This is problematic for two reasons:

1. By no stretch of the imagination is the ASQA auditor usually an expert.

[226] Trades College Australia Pty Ltd and Australian Skills Quality Authority Transcript, No. 1994 of 2018, 16 December 2019.

[227] Trades College Australia Pty Ltd and Australian Skills Quality Authority Transcript, No. 1994 of 2018, 16 December 2019.

2. It is not just a document given to the Commissioners. It has a far more important role to play in every single audit decision and not just those that go to the Commissioners!

There are many concerns that have been raised about the ROAT for many years but the findings in this hearing, particularly as they relate to '*critical non-compliance of assessment practices*', will certainly go on to make the difference in how the ROAT is handled in future audits.

There is another concern however over the ROAT, the Audit Outcome Decision Record and by the Commissioner, the materials that the auditor and subsequent manager send to the Commissioners when seeking approval of the recommended decision or decisions. The situation is not unlike the Immigration Assessment Authority ("IAA"). The IAA was established under the Migration Act 1958, and similar to ASQA, is an independent body with extraordinary powers. The IAA has the power to fast-track reviews of certain decisions made by the Minister for Immigration, Citizenship, Migrant Services and Multicultural Affairs[228].

The types of decisions that the IAA consider are those where the Minister has refused to grant a protection visa to people known as 'fast track applicants. Fast track applicants are identified in a legislative instrument which is maintained by the Department of Home Affairs[229] and updated regularly. The legislative instrument has a range of immigration identification numbers which align with a person and if your immigration identification number is on that list, you will not be eligible for a fast-track review.

228 The title was current at the time of publication. Incredulously, the title of Ministers changes on a very regular basis, particularly in the area of immigration and skills.

229 The name of the Department was current at the time of publication. Departmental names change on a very regular basis, particularly in the area of immigration and skills.

An example of what this looks like in reality is provided in the next screenshot from the legislative instrument itself[230]:

Schedule 1—Person Identification Digit

1 Department of Immigration and Border Protection Person Identification Digits

0048626968	0072515613	0088943716	0079207155	0089793020
0076738267	0038843674	0090127662	0037100586	0084063782
0052510824	0068749664	0077540957	0083687913	0093460090
0089049463	0089049536	0094794344	0094985241	0089469738
0078428848	0094841098	0036711520	0098804966	0051378523
0086434174	0098107590	0074204613	0076935693	0095947327
0089119794	0089119878	0088910373	0086892172	0090596427
0090596426	0090596442	0110379407	0083679499	0087198111
0087198146	0090131240	0101199676	0087244930	0086236821
0085123700	0087405247	0106389219	0087055395	0088549701
0089416837	0086134100	0089149055	0889149058	0087684358
0087019924	0087019984	0089416866	0086544929	0087405162
0087405199	0086550106	0087776673	0087776648	0086623478
0088532174	0088532072	0089194346	0088709529	0088800778
0089660694	0086766699	0089885444	0089885447	0089885449
0086134276	0090462882	0086967892	0086967919	0090085016
0096706891	0082363266	0085752375	0068868111	0087717423
0087717501				

Some fast-track applicants will not be entitled to a review by the IAA and the IAA does not receive applications for review from fast-track applicants themselves. The '*applications*' are automatically referred to the IAA by the Department of Home Affairs.

The role of the IAA is interesting in that it is somewhat similar to the internal reconsideration process at ASQA. The Department of Home

230 *Migration (IMMI 17/015: Person who is a Fast-Track Applicant) Instrument 2017*. This instrument is the *Migration (IMMI 17/015: Person who is a Fast-Track Applicant) Instrument 2017*. This instrument may also be cited as IMMI 17/015.

Affairs describes the type of decisions that the IAA can make in an 'information sheet' on their website[231]:

> The IAA can make two types of decisions. We can agree with the decision of the Department not to grant a protection visa, or we can return the case to the Department for further consideration because, for example, we find you are a refugee. The IAA does not have the power to grant protection visas.

While the IAA says on its website it is independent of the Department of Home Affairs, the concerning reality is that, like the ROAT and Decision record that the Commissioners receive, all of the evidence upon which the decision-maker will rely is selected only by the immigration officer managing the fast-track applicant's case.

How a review commences

When the Department of Home Affairs (the Department) makes a *fast track reviewable decision*, it will be automatically referred to the IAA. This must be done as soon as reasonably practicable after the decision is made.

There is no need for a fast track review applicant to submit an application to the IAA.

Information given to the IAA by the Department

When the Department refers a matter to the IAA for review, it must also provide a statement to the IAA that:

- sets out the findings of fact made by the decision maker
- refers to the evidence on which those findings were made, and
- gives reasons for the decision.

The Department must also give the IAA any material provided by the referred applicant to the decision maker before the decision was made and any other material considered by the Department to be relevant to the review.

In other words, there is the potential for the IAA (or in ASQA's case, the Commissioner) to receive biased evidence upon which to receive a predetermined outcome because the '*decision-maker*' or the immigration officer/case manager makes a determination about *what they consider is relevant for consideration*. This is just like the evidence that goes into the ROAT and that is subsequently sent to the Commissioner or Commissioners for approving the recommendation made by the auditor and/or the relevant manager.

231 Immigration Assessment Authority, March 2021. 'What you need to know about the Immigration Assessment Authority', <https://www.iaa.gov.au/guidance-forms/information-for-fast-track-applicants>.

Assessment Practices

The majority of the Trades College case was based around 'assessment practices'. Assessment practices that were only ever reviewed via desktop, no site visit was made (something that the Tribunal has been quite critical of) and the concepts of sufficient, authenticity and reliability as rules of evidence.

The Concept of RPL

The concept of Recognition of Prior Learning (RPL) took centre stage here and for all the wrong reasons. It would appear, based on the transcript at least, that they were concerned by ASQA that the evidence was not sufficient, reliable or authentic. One of the most damning findings from the Tribunal in relation to this was that even if the conclusions ASQA reached were correct, the decision to cancel was flawed.

9. The auditor did not even gather that the sites worked upon by the students were part of the College premises, and queried whether the students in question were indeed the students to whom the videos purported to relate. The means by which the College recorded their identities was by photographing their driver's licences and other identity documents. All of those problems were capable of easy solutions by making the processes followed by the assessors more transparent. We expect that since the applicant plainly desires to have its registration restored, it will take the appropriate steps with whatever expert advice is necessary to satisfy the regulator. All of those steps can be made clear to ASQA as part of a new application for registration when the applicant has its processes in place.

10. It seems to us that even if the conclusions reached by ASQA about the deficiencies of the RPL processes of the applicant were correct, the decision to cancel the applicant's registration altogether was flawed. That is because ASQA took no steps to satisfy itself about whether the face to face teaching (not involving RPL for the most part) could not continue. An alternative which was open to ASQA was to reduce the scope of the applicant's registration so as to permit the face to face teaching to continue. The

PAGE 5 OF 9

applicant's evidence satisfied us that the electro-technology course taught by Mr Limnos was conducted well. That teaching constituted a significant part of the services offered by the College.

Questions are asked about the RPL evidence collection process with discussions centres around third party reports, competency conversations, verification of evidence provided by the student and suggestions that this party verification after a competency conversation is called '...good practice'.

Likewise, questions are asked about whether ASQA provides a guide about how to conduct RPL and the auditor confirms that ASQA does not provide any such guide but does provide a good summary of what ASQA expects to see to meet the rules of evidence.

The student would go away, produce evidence and give that to the assessor, the assessor would go through that evidence, then they would have that competency conversation where they talk through what the candidate has done based on the evidence. The assessor would take copious notes or a recording of it and then they would go, and if they needed to, do any practical challenge tests or any observations they might arrange for that as well, and then the assessor would go and verify what the candidate has told them with the appropriate person. That would tick off the rules of evidence and then that evidence, that has to be all matched up to the unit to make sure that there is sufficient evidence here to be able to make that decision.

One of the concerns about the RPL evidence submitted to ASQA was that the RPL Observation checklists included a lot of checklists with ticks on them to confirm that the assessor had observed a, b, c. There was a lot of discussion[232] about how ticks were not sufficient as evidence of satisfactory performance of skills because it is possible that the RTO made up the evidence, the ticks don't describe what the assessor saw and anyone could write them, etc.

The Tribunal asked numerous questions[233] about the use of ticks by an RTO in its assessment practices, in relation to the concept of reliability that ASQA was so concerned about as well as whether the auditor had even been to the RTOs premises prior to making their decision to see the type of facilities that Trades College was using in conducting its assessment process. The auditor was very clear that at no time did ASQA visit the premises in relation to this audit, it was all conducted via desktop and through the use of section 26 notices to provide information.

232 Trades College Australia Pty Ltd and Australian Skills Quality Authority Transcript, No. 1994 of 2018, 16 December 2019.

233 Ibid.

The concept of reliability and the Tribunal Member's discussion of how it understood reliability to apply in relation to the use of ticks and the expectation that tradesmen across different colleges would provide copious written records of observations made for interesting reading and solid understanding of what actually happens in the real world of assessment. It was noted that the Tribunal Member raised the concern with ASQA about their expectations of observation checklists and reliability in assessment. It was suggested that if the assessor was to provide a full description of what the person showed them on an observation checklist, there was concern there would be industry problems because all the assessors would have to sit there having judged the expertise of the candidate for a very long time, writing it all out or typing it out so that the assessor from College 1 can be certain that the assessor in College 2 produces the same result.

The Tribunal Member put this into perspective and compared it with another education sector by saying that these assessors are tradespeople. They're experienced tradespeople. They're far more practical; they haven't got university degrees, they've got trade qualifications. The Tribunal Member suggests that you could end up having quite a bit of trouble if you wanted everything documented like that for the colleges and industry! It was suggested that if something like this happened in the university sector, it would treble or quadruple the amount of time spent marking one paper.

The reality is, there is no other education sector in Australia where such justification of assessment is required. In universities around the country, a tick is more than acceptable. In primary and secondary schools, a tick is more than acceptable. Why is it that VET is so special that you need qualified tradesmen, many who are experts in their field and know what competency looks like, especially if they have to meet the requirements of the Standards, why is their 'tick' not acceptable like every other sector?

Bear in mind, the Standards for RTOs 2015 actually require the following for someone to be even permitted to train and assess:

Trainers and assessors

1.13. In addition to the requirements specified in Clause 1.14 and Clause1.15, the RTO's training and assessment is delivered only by persons who have:

a) vocational competencies at least to the level being delivered and assessed;

b) current industry skills directly relevant to the training and assessment being provided; and

c) current knowledge and skills in vocational training and learning that informs their training and assessment.

Industry experts may also be involved in the assessment judgement, working alongside the trainer and/or assessor to conduct the assessment.

1.14. The RTO's training and assessment is delivered only by persons who have the training and assessment credential specified in Item 2 or Item 3 of Schedule 1.

If their professional judgement based on their qualifications and experience can't be trusted, why have the standards above in the first place? More importantly, if you're going to have an ASQA auditor, who may not even have an auditing qualification come and audit you and they don't have the first idea about the subject matter, how can their opinion honestly be superior to that of a subject matter expert? Remember, we say this in the transcript earlier, and this point is so critical that it is repeated below:

> While providing evidence the ASQA auditor was asked if they thought it might be important to have someone who has the ability to assess the Certificate III in Plumbing to confirm whether or not the assessment was in fact complied with given that they didn't have subject matter expertise themselves, to which the auditor replied no. They were subsequently asked by Counsel representing Trades College why not? The auditor replied because not all audits are conducted by auditors with subject knowledge. They have auditing skills and they have some subject knowledge of a 'qualification' but it's not necessarily the one that they're auditing.

The absurdity of this situation is beyond stupidity but this is the basis upon which hundreds of RTOs have had their registrations cancelled, including all of those whose stories you have read in this book. Is this really what is in the public interest? Is this really what you expect your taxpayer dollars to be paying for?

The Tribunal member continues but is concerned that the whole issue about RPL and credit transfer might just be a distraction when it is very clear the issue is with the rule of evidence 'reliability'. A discussion ensued between the 2 very learned Tribunal Members about what the meaning of reliability is under the Standards for RTOs 2015. It is the author's contention that, if we have 2 very senior Tribunal Members, one of them a university professor and Deputy President of the Tribunal, and they can't interpret the legislative term or basis for the term '*reliability*', then what hope have the almost 4000 RTOs regulated under these standards got?

It is also suggested that this additional information that ASQA says is necessary for reliability is actually only there to facilitate their audit processes because they do not have subject matter expertise and in many cases, are not even qualified to conduct the audit. Furthermore, even when this additional information is available, there is no reliability in auditor decisions. When ASQA auditors can look at identical evidence and come up with two completely different interpretations, that too is a significant reliability issue and something the sector has been screaming about for years. And they are absolutely entitled to when ASQA auditors don't even meet the Schedule 1 requirements under the Standards for VET regulators and are not even subject matter experts, or they have never set foot in an RTO for any other purpose than as a representative of the regulator! In contemplating the completion of the ROAT discussed earlier, the underpinning 'spreadsheet' that 'produces' the recommended regulatory action, there's not even reliability in its completion amongst auditors because it too is very subjective to a degree.

Perhaps the lowest blow in the proceedings came from the Australian Government Solicitor; it's unclear why the comment was made but there is no other justification for the comment that follows. The main issues in the Trades College case were around assessment (clause 1.8) and the issuing of certificates which ASQA claimed were deficient because they were not conducting RPL correctly. In fact, the argument between the link between clauses 1.8 and 3.1 is a long standing one that the writer, personally, can't wait to be decided by the courts because they've got away with it for too long. Nonetheless, the last straw was played by the AGS in the comment that they should win just on financial viability grounds[234]! Since Trades College lost its stay applications, it could no longer trade so it is a low blow and a clear, unambiguous demonstration of they were willing to pursue Trades College and Rabih and close him down no matter the cost.

Current Situation

Sadly, despite their win, Trades College has still not been able to lodge its application to become an RTO still due to the issues identified earlier; COVID, training package changes, etc. Rabih also received an invoice from ASQA for $14,000 for the audits it conducted.

In total so far, Rabih says this fight has cost him over a million dollars. He is committed to reopening an RTO and training and assessing students from his state-of-the-art premises in Punchbowl, New South Wales.

At the time of writing this book and while sharing his story, Rabih received another notice from ASQA. This time a '**Warning Advice**' after ASQA allegedly undertook an investigation in relation to Trades College in October 2020 after an 'alleged complaint'.

In typical ASQA form, they allegedly received an allegation and conducted their own investigation without EVER contacting Rabih or Trades College

234 Trades College Australia Pty Ltd and Australian Skills Quality Authority Transcript, No. 1994 of 2018, 16 December 2019.

to seek a response and made a finding without Rabih or Trades College even being aware that such a process took place.

Surely Rabih and Trades College have a right to respond to any complaint firstly, but secondly, any complaint that ends, as it has in this instance, with a formal warning advice of breaches of the NVR Act!

The letter makes significant threats of potential criminal prosecution and fines under the NVR Act being imposed and almost as an *'in passing'* comment at the end under '*Next Steps*', the ASQA **Director, Compliance** says, '*In this instance, ASQA will take no further regulatory action in relation to these contraventions*'.

Now hold on a minute! Trades College was **NEVER** contacted about any such alleged contraventions until this letter.

Again, if ASQA's senior management are going to run around writing warning advice letters which say in the subject line '***Breach of...***' (*not alleged, but breach of*), and then write that these are allegations with potential penalties which include criminal prosecution and then say *'oh, and by the way, we're not taking action at this time*'; ASQA needs to be very careful because some people will not back down and this is pure bullying and intimidation.

It is very clear that there is bad blood here after the final result at the AAT but Rabih would be well and truly within his rights to pursue this latest letter further.

This letter is a disgraceful demonstration of someone being deemed guilty before they've had a chance to prove themselves innocent which is 100% consistent with ASQA's toxic, predatory behaviour.

This letter was dated 11 May 2021 - at a time when ASQA is allegedly implementing the Joyce and Braithwaite reviews and being a very different regulator. This letter is evidence that nothing has changed.

Commentary

Of all the things that can destroy a person more than losing their RTO, it's losing their fit and proper status and it's something that ASQA are pursuing more and more.

The impact of an adverse decision from ASQA on a person's fit and proper can be crippling in terms of future repercussions and yet, despite this, there are incredibly, very few people in the sector who really pay attention to it. You must know though, that when ASQA comes knocking, if they're coming after your fit and proper, you better become aware of the impact it will have on your future! So just who does have to sign a fit and proper declaration?

The *Fit and Proper Person Requirements 2011* are a legislative instrument. They are part of the VET Quality Framework and are made under subsection 186(1) of the *National Vocational Education and Training Regulator Act* 2011 ("NVR Act"). Those persons who are subject to fit and proper persons requirements are shown below:

FPPR 5 Persons subject to Fit and Proper Person Requirements

A person mentioned in FPPR 4 does not meet the Fit and Proper Person Requirements if the National VET Regulator is satisfied that, having regard to the matters provided in paragraph FPPR 4 (a) to (k), one or more of the following people do not meet the Fit and Proper Person Requirements:

(a) an **executive officer** of the person referred to in FPPR 4;

(b) a **high managerial agent** of the person referred to in FPPR 4; or

(c) **any person** or entity **which exercises a degree of control or influence over the management or direction of the registered training organisation.**

Now over the years, the writer has been the brunt of a reasonable amount of flack from people who think that it is particularly unfair that they might be captured by this legislative instrument including, but not limited to for example:

- Training Managers;
- Compliance Managers;
- Stand-in CEO's (where there is another CEO who makes decision);
- Board Members (regardless if they are volunteers); and
- Some even say Consultants, although the writer argues that this is not always the case.

Each of those people is required to be able to sign the fit and proper declaration that ASQA provides confirming that they are suitably fit and proper to manage and/or provide advice to an RTO registered under the NVR Act. While the definition of executive officer and high managerial agent were provided earlier in this book, it is perhaps important to revisit them in light of the fit and proper legislation.

Fit and Proper Person Requirements 2011

executive officer has the meaning given by section 3 of the Act.

National Vocational Education and Training Regulator Act 2011

executive officer, in relation to a registered training organisation, means:

(a) a person, by whatever name called and whether or not a director of the organisation, who is concerned in, or takes part in, the management of the organisation; or

(b) if the organisation is a body corporate:

(i) a person who, at any time during a period for which the organisation is registered, owns 15% or more of the organisation; or

(ii) a person who, at any time during a period for which the organisation is registered, is entitled to receive 15% or more of dividends paid by the organisation; or

(c) an administrator, receiver and manager, or liquidator of the organisation (other than a receiver and manager, or liquidator, appointed by a court); or

(d) if the organisation is a body corporate—the administrator of a deed of company arrangement executed by an organisation; or

(e) if the organisation is a body corporate—a trustee or other person administering a compromise or arrangement made between the organisation and another person or other persons.

Fit and Proper Person Requirements 2011

high managerial agent has the meaning given by section 3 of the Act.

National Vocational Education and Training Regulator Act 2011

high managerial agent of a registered training organisation means an employee or agent of the organisation with duties of such responsibility that his or her conduct may fairly be assumed to represent the organisation in relation to the business of providing courses.

So Why Is It Such a Big Deal?

Under the criteria for registration as an RTO, there are certain requirements that must be met. Likewise, clause 8.1 of the Standards for RTOs 2015 also has a thing or two to say about it. According to the ASQA website[235]:

[235] Australian Skills Quality Authority, 'Fit and proper person requirements' <https://www.asqa.gov.au/standards/faqs/fit-and-proper-person-requirements>.

The *National Vocational Education and Training Regulator Act 2011* defines anyone who manages the RTO, or owns more than 15 percent of it, as an 'executive officer'.

All executive officers and the 'high managerial agent' of an RTO must satisfy the *Fit and Proper Person Requirements 2011.*

These people must make a 'fit and proper person' declaration, in accordance with ASQA's requirements, whenever their RTO:

- applies for initial registration or to renew registration as an RTO, or
- employs a new manager.

So, for all the new managers and Board members who are in an RTO, there's an expectation that you have completed a Fit and Proper Person Declaration and that you are considered suitable by ASQA to be involved with the NVR registered RTO.

The fit and proper criteria in the legislative instrument are quite long and in the author's experience, many people who are affected by it, have never seen it before. Let's take a look at this more closely. The criteria are also quite subjective, let's take a look. Emphasis is that of the writer.

Fit and proper person criteria

FPPR 4 Criteria for suitability for registration

In assessing whether a person, who is **an applicant for registration** as an NVR registered training organisation, **an applicant for renewal of registration** as an NVR registered training organisation or who is an NVR registered training organisation, meets the Fit and Proper Person Requirements, the National VET Regulator must have regard to the following considerations:

(a) **whether the person has been convicted of an offence** against a law of the Commonwealth or of a State or Territory and if so, the seriousness of the offence;

(b) whether the person has **ever had his, her or its registration on the National Register cancelled or suspended**;

(c) whether the person has e**ver had a condition imposed on his, her or its registration on the National Register**;

(d) whether the person has ever breached a condition of registration in Subdivision B of Division 1 of Part 2 of the Act;

(e) whether the person has ever become bankrupt, applied to take the benefit of a law for the benefit of bankrupt or insolvent debtors, compounded with his or her creditors or assigned his or her remuneration for the benefit of creditors;

(f) whether the person has ever been disqualified from managing corporations under Part 2D.6 of the *Corporations Act 2001*;

(g) whether the person was **involved in the business of the provision of courses by another provider who is covered by any of the above paragraphs at the time of any of the events that gave rise to the relevant prosecution or other action**;

(h) whether the person has ever provided a State or Territory registering body and/or the National VET Regulator with false or misleading information or made a false or misleading statement to a State or Territory registering body or the National VET Regulator, and whether the person knew that the statement made or information provided to the State or Territory registering body or VET Regulator was false or misleading;

(i) whether the person has **ever been found not to be a fit and proper person for the purposes of the *Education Services for Overseas Students Act 2000***;

(j) whether the **public is likely to have confidence in the person's suitability to be involved in an organisation that provides or assesses national qualifications**; and

(k) **<u>any other relevant matter.</u>**

As can be seen, FPPR 4 casts a very wide and a very subjective net. Many of the areas are somewhat straightforward, regardless of whether we believe they're appropriate or not. For example, there is an extreme amount of subjectivity in the clause '*<u>any other relevant matter</u>*'. This catch-all phrase allows the regulator to effectively find whatever they want and throw it in!

Other areas of concern under FPPR 4 include for example whether the person (remembering who is captured here) was **<u>involved in the business of the provision of courses by another provider who is covered by any of the above paragraphs at the time of any of the events that gave rise to the relevant prosecution or other action.</u>** In other words, every manager who has ever worked for an RTO that has had an adverse ASQA outcome is captured by this clause and technically, may have problems with ASQA in the future. This has important consequences for the individuals involved but also for the sector; after all, how many people will eventually get caught in this one?

And the subjectiveness of the next two:

(j) whether the public is likely to have confidence in the person's suitability to be involved in an organisation that provides or assesses national qualifications; and

(k) any other relevant matter.

How is (j) measured? Who determines whether the public is likely to have confidence in the applicant? And what about (k) and 'any other relevant matter'? Who is the judge of that? Who determines what might constitute a 'relevant matter'? And this **IS** a condition of registration. It is also considered at initial and renewal of registration. The mind-boggling thing is how did this ever get through Parliament?

Fit and Proper Person Declaration

Have you ever taken the time to read the front page of the declaration form? Have you noticed the statement that says...?

> If ASQA is not satisfied with an organisation or relevant people associated with its Fit and Proper Person Requirements, ASQA may:
>
> - Impose a sanction, including cancellation, on the organisation's registration as an RTO and/or CRICOS provider; refuse the organisation's initial application to become an RTO and/or CRICOS provider.

There's also a little statement there that ASQA can ask any RTO or CRICOS provider at any time.

There is a nice little explanation on page 2 of who must complete the declaration in ASQA's opinion providing examples of who they think you may need to get to complete a form. Confirmation of the types of people who are captured by this legislative instrument is referenced below:

Executive officer/s

An executive officer is any person who takes part in the management of your organisation or is partly responsible for the management or decision making for your organisation.

Examples of 'executive officers' where completion of a Fit and proper person declaration is mandatory include:

- a director of the company
- a secretary of the company
- a chief executive of the RTO
- a principal executive officer of the CRICOS provider.

Examples of 'executive officers' where ASQA may request completion of a Fit and proper person declaration include:

- a compliance manager
- a marketing manager
- a training manager.

High managerial agent/s

A high managerial agent represents your organisation in relation to providing courses.

Submitting an FPP declaration for 'high managerial agents' is not mandatory, unless specifically requested by ASQA.

Examples of 'high managerial agents' where ASQA may request completion of a Fit and proper person declaration include:

- a consultant or employee with an ongoing role related to regulatory compliance
- a consultant or employee who represents your organisation at audit
- an agent who recruits students on behalf of your organisation, or
- people who fulfil any of the roles described above on behalf of your organisation in a third-party arrangement
- people who provide training and/or assessment on behalf of your organisation in a third-party arrangement.

The consequences of the people in the above roles coming back with a negative or subjective fit and proper (based on what we saw earlier, e.g. any relevant matter) is very concerning. It means that your RTO is constantly on the chopping block as a result of the deeds, misdeeds or alleged deeds of others. In my experience, people don't usually get to provide their innocence in these matters until you're in the Tribunal, mostly because that's when ASQA will go clutching at loopholes and digging in dark corners you didn't even know existed.

There was considerable discussion amongst the Consultant community at one stage (quite a while ago now). If I recall correctly, it was just a general discussion along the lines of 'what will you do if you are asked to complete one'? The author has refused to complete one under any circumstances on the basis that questions 9 or 10 of the declaration would require me to breach the confidentiality I have with my clients. To be clear, the author refuses to provide the following information about any of her clients. See the questions referred to next:

9.	Do you or any related person, have a current or past association with: • a current or former RTO, CRICOS provider, higher education provider, other than the organisation outlined in Section B of this declaration. • any organisation that has applied for registration with ASQA or a state registering body. *('Association' includes but is not limited to business dealings, employment, contracting, endorsement and/or the provision of services as a third party.)*	☐ No *Go to Question 10* ☐ Yes *Provide details below*

Provide details of any current association:	
Name of person who has current association:	
Legal name of RTO/CRICOS provider/higher education provider (or applicant):	
Trading name/s:	
Describe your association with the organisation:	
Start of your association with the organisation:	Click or tap to enter a date.

Provide details of any past association:	
Name of person who has past association:	
Legal name of RTO/CRICOS provider/higher education provider (or applicant):	
Trading name/s:	
Describe your association with the organisation:	

Form - Fit and proper person declaration, updated 13 March 2019 Page 8 of 13

The previous screenshot clearly demonstrates how and why my client confidentiality might be compromised. Likewise, this also demonstrates how staff who were employed with another RTO who received a sanction, it's clear how it would potentially arise here. Question 10 of course as shown next is just as problematic:

As indicated earlier, based on the current legislative instrument and the manner in which these declarations are completed. There are real legal problems for consultants who might disclose client confidential details by completing one. Can you imagine losing your RTO registration because your consultant assisted a client in the AAT?

What About the Public Interest?

> *"Government alone will never be able to do it. It is only the people themselves who must utilise the law for the purpose of bringing justice at the doorsteps of the large masses of people of the country."*
>
> **- Justice PN Bhagwati**

ASQA argues in AAT hearings[236] that its regulatory functions under the legislation include:

- The processes and procedures required for the legal registration of VET providers and the accreditation of approved qualifications and courses of study;
- To regulate to ensure the maintenance of quality VET for the purposes of ensuring credible, value for money outcomes for consumers;
- To protect and further improve Australia's significant international reputation as a consistent provider of high-quality VET services;
- ASQA has a responsibility to regulate in the public interest to ensure the prudent and effective spending of scarce tax funded resources.
- Where the standards of delivery of VET are questionable, ASQA is required to place the public interest above private/corporate interests.

On the preceding points, it is difficult to see how ASQA can honestly claim to achieve all of these things based on what we have seen in this

[236] The following are submissions that are made by ASQA in Stay hearings at the AAT.

book. It is not possible for a national VET regulator to achieve those objectives when a significant portion of its decisions are inconsistent with the Standards for RTOs 2015 and the Standards for VET Regulators 2015 because they are:

- Poorly interpreted;
- Based on invalid or unreliable evidence;
- Inappropriately applied to the Standards;
- Biased or includes a conflict of interest;
- So procedurally flawed that it would not stand scrutiny;
- Do not use technical experts when there is clearly a basis for relying upon them;
- Use panel auditors who are conflicted in the performance of their role because they are able to increase or suggest areas of non-compliance in order to increase their future invoicing capacity;
- ASQA employees who undertake audits and either are not suitably qualified or experienced to do so and/or abuse their role in order to achieve outcomes that were never intended and in some cases, not even divulged to ASQA its employer.

If it is in the public interest for ASQA to achieve all of the things raised above, then it is equally in the public interest to be alerted to these critical shortcomings of a regulator who uses millions of dollars of taxpayer's money in achieving these shortcomings.

ASQA often argues in stay hearings that the objectives of the NVR Act best serve the wider public interest and that they (the objectives of the Act) contemplate the suggestion that the interests of the general community have precedence over private or individual interests. While there is no doubt that ASQA intended for this phrase to be used against private RTOs, it probably did not, in all likelihood expect that the same could be applied to its own actions as a regulator. Likewise, while the legislation serves the interests of students, the efficacy of quality VET and specifically the reputation of Australia as a provider of such training, it remains unclear how it can possibly achieve these in the public interest when it is so far off achieving its own objectives. Of course this not a new finding, there have been many concerns since the PwC review of ASQA in 2013, the Braithwaite review in June 2018, the Joyce review in March 2019, the rapid review in March 2020 and now, in 2021, the review into ASQA by the Australian National Audit Office. That's 1 review every year for the past 4 years at least on 1 regulator. How many millions of dollars of taxpayer funds has been invested into ASQA trying to learn how to do its job while cancelling hundreds of good businesses along the way? Surely that information is in the public interest to know?

Is it in the public interest to know that there have been, for a long time now, a sizeable number of ASQA auditors, responsible for making recommendations to managers and completing Audit Outcome Decision Records for management to sign off on and they're not even suitably qualified? Likewise, is it in the public interest to know that there are a number of ASQA employees who have gone around trying to get work on the side from the very RTOs they're proposing to close down?

Is it also in the public interest to know that there are senior ASQA managers going around threatening people that 'I'm here to close you down' or during unannounced audits, generating complaints from students where none existed previously, not even internally at the RTO and giving their mobile number to students telling them to call him so he can make sure they get a refund?

In *Hogan v Hinch*[237], French CJ stated that when 'used in a statute, the term [public interest] derives its content from "the subject matter and the scope and purpose" of the enactment in which it appears'. In April 2006, Chris Wheeler, the then Deputy NSW Ombudsman at a conference at the Australian Institute of Administrative Law[238] stated that:

237 Hogan v Hinch (2011) 243 CLR 506 at [para 31].

238 Chris Wheeler, April 2006, Australian Institute of Administrative Law ("AIAL") Forum No. 48, '*The Public Interest: we know it's important, but do we know what it means?*' <http://www5.austlii.edu.au/au/journals/AIAdminLawF/2006/2.pdf>

> 'Acting in the public interest is a concept that is fundamental to a representative democratic system of government and to good public administration. However, this commonly used concept is, in practice, particularly complex...'

He also states that:

> Acting in the public interest has two separate components:
>
> - objectives and outcomes - that the objectives and outcomes of the decision-making process are in the public interest, and
> - process and procedure - that the process adopted and procedures followed by decision makers in exercising their discretionary powers are in the public interest.
>
> The objectives and outcomes component is the aspect of the public interest most referred to in the literature. The process and procedure component appears to be less discussed but is just as important.

He goes on to say:

> This component would include:
>
> - complying with applicable law (both its letter and spirit);
> - carrying out functions fairly and impartially, with integrity and professionalism;
> - complying with the principles of procedural fairness/natural justice;
> - acting reasonably;
> - ensuring proper accountability and transparency;
> - exposing corrupt conduct or serious maladministration;

- avoiding or properly managing situations where their private interests conflict or might reasonably be perceived to conflict with the impartial fulfilment of their official duties, and
- acting apolitically in the performance of their official functions (not applicable to elected public officials).

The public interest also goes to the protection of Australia's reputation as a domestic and international provider of quality vocational education and training as well as the maintenance of confidence in the regulatory framework that operates in the vocational education and training sector. Based on everything we've seen in this book, it is questionable how much of what the national VET regulator does for the purpose of maintaining quality in Australia's VET sector. It is also questionable whether ASQA is maintaining confidence in the regulatory framework thereby protecting Australia's international reputation, that actually is, in the public interest.

The *Public Interest Disclosure Act 2013* (Cth.) is interesting in the context of the types of conduct it says might be subject to the *Public Interest Disclosure Act 2013*. This conduct includes, but is not limited to for example:

- a contravention of the law;
- corruption;
- perverting the course of justice;
- maladministration;
- an abuse of public trust;
- falsifying scientific research;
- wastage of public money, and/or
- conduct that is a danger to health, safety or the environment.

How many of these issues have we checked off the list in this book? Far too many! Sadly, only the following people can make a public interest disclosure:

> A current or former public official can make a disclosure. This includes:
>
> - public servants (ongoing, non-ongoing and casual);
> - parliamentary service employees;
> - service providers under a Commonwealth contract;
> - statutory office holders;
> - staff of Commonwealth companies; and
> - temporary employees engaged through a recruitment agency.

A public official also includes any other person deemed by the authorised officer to be a public official for the purposes of the Public Interest Disclosure Act. Of course, this is a concern for us in the sector because we've been raising these issues for several years now to politicians, public consultations and nobody appears to be listening. The author can also confirm that she personally has formally advised ASQA of some of the issues raised in this book.

A copy of this publication will be sent to the Australian National Audit Office (ANAO) as another mechanism for someone to ensure that ASQA's regulation is addressed and that where it is identified that there have been concerns of public interest breaches, hopefully, they will act accordingly and hold the relevant people accountable.

In discussing the public interest though, it's important to reflect on the legal journey of the Trades Colleges matter as the repercussions of this decision will have a lasting effect on the sector more widely. A discussion of that decision follows.

The Impact of the Trades Colleges Legal Journey for the Sector

The Trades College Australia decision by the AAT was an important decision for the sector. ASQA had issued Trades College Australia with a cancellation notice and refusal to renew registration under the *National Vocational Education and Training Regulator Act 2011* (Cth.); effectively two decisions, both which were appealed. Trades College Australia ("Trades College") lodged applications for a review and a stay of each decision to cancel. An initial hearing[239] was held before Member Maryniak QC at the Melbourne Registry on 24 May 2018. Trades College was represented by M Peter Doukas and Mr Travis Mitchell as Counsel. ASQA was represented by Mr Damien Cox who, at the time of publication, was the head of ASQA's legal team.

The facts of the decisions in this matter are important for a number of reasons but the main issues of the case are discussed next. The main reason however why this was such an important decision is it may just create a more equitable outcome for providers going through the Tribunal in future.

The initial request for stay decisions was refused by Member Maryniak[240] whereby, in his reasons for his decisions, a significant focus was placed on ASQA's allegations of current and historical (2016) non-compliance.

Curiously, at paragraph 11 of that decision, Member Maryniak refers to Trades College bearing an onus of self-regulation under the Standards. There are no RTOs (other than TAFE perhaps) who self-regulate under the Standards for RTOs 2015 so it is unclear on what basis Member Maryniak makes this extraordinary statement. There were some other

239 *Trades College Australia Pty Ltd and Australian Skills Quality Authority* [2018] AATA 1360 (24 May 2018).

240 Ibid.

concerning reasons provided in this decision record[241] which was ultimately appealed in the Federal Court of Australia[242] on 4 June 2018.

Ultimately, the two major findings in relation to the Trades College matter that will change future cases in the Tribunal and Federal Court are:

> 13. Another problem about the way in which the case was conducted arose from direction made prior to the listing of the proceedings before us, at a time when we were not involved. We have concluded that in future cases where there is a contest about non-compliances, ASQA must start and do so without the assumption that its allegations of non-compliance are prima facie correct.

The acknowledgement by the Tribunal that ASQA (and the Tribunal) must not start from the basis that they are actually correct in their findings.

And the other main finding was what ultimately happened when the AAT refused to stay the decisions of ASQA which we have seen in the previous screenshot, was based on a false understanding of the situation, was that a very good RTO with state-of-the-art facilities was closed down and forced to apply for a new RTO registration because the Tribunal got it wrong in the stay hearings.

Had the Tribunal used their discretionary power to stay the effective decisions, Trades College would not be in the situation it is today. Trades College had very good prospects of success in winning their case.

By refusing the stay decisions, the Tribunal rendered the Tribunal process nugatory. Even by winning its case, Trades College is still no better off because the decisions had come into effect and the only option left open to the Tribunal was to require ASQA to accept a new application for registration.

241 Ibid.

242 Trades College Australia Pty Ltd and Australian Skills Quality Authority No. NSD 893 of 2018.

It is hoped that in future, Tribunal Members will be reminded of this precedent and be more mindful of the outcome of Trades College before using their discretionary powers under the Administrative Appeals Tribunal Act 1975 to refuse applications for stay decisions.

Where To From Here?

> **"Good regulation should be conducive to business and to customer protection."**
> **- Jamie Dimon**

The Department of Prime Minister and Cabinet updated their '*Regulatory Impact Analysis Guide for Ministers' Meetings and National Standards Setting Bodies*'[243] in May 2021 after the *Conrad review*[244]. The opening statements of this document make it explicit that the role of a Regulatory Impact Analysis is critical. It explains[245]:

> Regulation is an essential part of running a well-functioning economy and society, but must be carefully designed so as not to have unintended or distortionary effects, such as imposing unnecessarily onerous costs on those affected by the regulations or restricting competition. Assessing the impact of regulation, including analysing the costs and benefits, is therefore important to ensure that it delivers the intended objective without unduly causing adverse effects.

In the context of what this book has discussed, it seems that the Regulatory Impact Analysis Guide has some fantastic options available to be explored if ASQA were to genuinely be motivated to address the issues raised. The Guide[246] includes questions to be considered for a

243 Department of Prime Minister and Cabinet, May 2021, '*Regulatory Impact Analysis Guide for Ministers' Meetings and National Standards Setting Bodies*'.

244 Peter Conran, 'Review of COAG Councils and Ministerial Forums: Report to the National Cabinet', October 2020.

245 Department of Prime Minister and Cabinet, May 2021, '*Regulatory Impact Analysis Guide for Ministers' Meetings and National Standards Setting Bodies*', page 6.

246 Ibid.

Regulatory Impact Assessment ("RIA") to be undertaken including for example:

- What is the policy problem?
    - Define the problem
    - Market failure
    - Regulatory failure
    - Unacceptable hazard or risk
        - Is the cost of regulating in proportion to the real-world risk?
        - Can risk be eliminated entirely?
        - Who should bear the cost?
        - What are the genuine consequences of no action?
        - Are there deficiencies in existing approaches?
        - Why does current regulation not properly address the identified problem?
        - Is it a problem of design or implementation, or both?
- Why is government action needed?
    - Have governments-Commonwealth, state or local-attempted to fix this problem before?
    - Is there an inefficient allocation of resources?
    - Are there equity issues?
- Is the market unable to deliver a much-needed public good?

In the context of the issues raised in this book and publicly, including through the Joyce and Braithwaite reviews, the rapid review and now the intervention of the Australian National Audit Office undertaking a review as the result of sector outrage, it would seem that these are critical questions to be answered. It's not enough in my opinion to offer Stakeholder Roundtables where the people on that Roundtable do not necessarily represent the views of the area of the sector they are perceived to. It's also not enough to provide a tokenistic Stakeholder Liaison Group who really don't have a huge say in what happens; I have it on advice that they are provided with an agenda set by ASQA, they have pre-determined policies, etc. that they are asked to provide feedback on but they don't really have any control over introducing new, key information and assist in producing meaningful change. It is my understanding they are there to create a perception that ASQA is taking into consideration the views of the sector but this is not really what happens is it?

The guide also has the following to say about 'Self-regulation'[247] (emphasis by the author):

> Self-regulation may consist of industry-written rules and codes of conduct enforced by the industry itself. Where industry participants understand and appreciate the need for self-regulation, this can be a good option.
>
> Any red tape resulting from self-regulation is usually minimal and often administered sympathetically by the industry. Self-regulation is a good option where the consequences of market failure are low and the market is likely to move towards an optimal outcome by itself.
>
> Self-regulation is not a viable option if an industry has no incentive to comply with its own rules. In some cases, self-regulation may create public concern, where, for example, perceived conflicts of interest could threaten safety, such as in food-handling, healthcare or aviation. **Self-regulation**

[247] Ibid, page 19.

> **should be approached carefully where previous attempts to achieve compliance or penalise non-compliance have failed.**

While ASQA has stated in its Consultation Paper that:

> Self-assurance is not the same as self-regulation. Self-regulation often involves industry taking responsibility for regulation, with government having a limited role. The concept of self-assurance requires providers manage their business to ensure a focus on quality, continuous improvement and ongoing compliance with standards set by governments. The role of ASQA, as the regulator is to promote this culture, to monitor each provider's performance against the Standards, to identify any non-compliance and to support providers to return to compliance (or to take necessary sanctions action where this is not possible).

There is little historical evidence that such an approach will actually work. Apart from the fact that the public consultation period was so ridiculously short as to ensue that limited responses would be received, this is something that has been tried and tested before and, in my opinion, should have been the subject of a Regulatory Impact Analysis rather than relying on a self-funded rapid review with just as few submissions! To be clear and transparent, the numbers of submissions for each are below:

- Rapid Review - 50 submissions[248]; and
- Consultation paper on self-assurance 65 submissions[249].

248 MP Consulting, March 2020, Report on the Rapid Review of ASQA's regulatory practices and processes, page 11

249 ASQA website, '*Self-assurance consultation feedback*' <https://www.asqa.gov.au/working-together/self-assurance/self-assurance-consultation-feedback> accessed 27 May 2021.

Now in a sector that has approximately 4000 RTOs, a workforce of approximately 40,796[250], I think my point is clearly made that basing implementation of such an important policy on 65 submissions is not only inconsistent with best-practice regulation but it also demonstrates that there is likely to be a real risk in complying with the recommendations of the Guide[251]. Such a critically low response rate for such an important regulatory decision is surely not what is in the public's best interest (especially for a regulator whose annual budget has been significantly increased) or for the improvement of the VET sector generally. Based on the workforce statistics from IBISWorld and the number of submissions to each of the reports, this equates to:

- Rapid review - Approximately 0.12% of the VET sector workforce; and
- Consultation paper on self-assurance - Approximately 0.16% of the VET sector workforce.

The Rapid Review report from March 2020 provides a chapter of 2½ pages on 'Aligning audit practice to focus on self-assurance' but doesn't really describe what that looks like. The Consultation Paper then is released for feedback some 8 months later with ASQA's own perception of what that looked like, a perception that, based on the 50 submissions received made it clear that '*Responses to this question reinforced the need for ASQA to provide more information on the concept of self-assurance*[252]'. The other main problem with this type of consultation however is that the questions, much like the audit by the Australian National Audit Office are pre-determined to ensure that only the feedback that directly responds to those criteria may be included.

250 IBISWorld, Technical and Vocational Education and Training in Australia - Market Research Report, Updated February 2021 <https://www.ibisworld.com/au/industry/technical-vocational-education-training/601/>.

251 Department of Prime Minister and Cabinet, May 2021, '*Regulatory Impact Analysis Guide for Ministers'* Meetings *and National Standards Setting Bodies'*.

252 ASQA website, '*Self-assurance consultation feedback*' <https://www.asqa.gov.au/working-together/self-assurance/self-assurance-consultation-feedback> accessed 27 May 2021.

Of course, one other major issue that needs to be considered amongst all this and reinforces the need for enhanced consultation and compliance with best practice regulation and the '*Regulatory Impact Analysis Guide for Ministers'* Meetings *and National Standards Setting Bodies'* is the fact that the ASQA has been pushing to become and opera as a full cost recovery agency for several years now. Some of the key questions that the Guide[253] references that must be considered include:

- What kind of businesses are we talking about? How many are there?
- What products or services do they deliver? What industries are they in?
- How many people do they employ and how long have they been in business? Where are they based?
- How likely is it any new costs will be passed on to consumers? Show both the direct cost to business and the anticipated amount to which this is likely to be alleviated by being passed on to consumers.
- How well prepared are the business owners to cope with new regulatory requirements? Are they represented by an industry association?
- Do any options require changes in production, transportation or marketing procedures?
- Are there regulatory compliance burdens imposed on businesses? For example, administrative costs associated with complying and/or reporting on regulatory requirements, or a costs associated with delivering the regulated outcome being sought.
- Are there cost recovery charges imposed by government on businesses (or community organisations or individuals)? What is the value of these charges?

253 Department of Prime Minister and Cabinet, May 2021, '*Regulatory Impact Analysis Guide for Ministers'* Meetings *and National Standards Setting Bodies'* pages 22-23.

- Are there special burdens on small business arising from the fact they often lack the required specialist legal, accounting or Human Resources skills in-house? Does the proposal disproportionately affect small business? Does the analysis adequately take into account the different impacts on small businesses of different sizes, types and locations?

Community Organisation Impacts

- What sectors do they operate in? Are they large or small?
- What kinds of activities do they undertake? Do they deliver services on behalf of government?
- Are they represented by a peak body?

Individual Impacts

- Who are the people or households affected? How many are there?
- Why are they affected? Will the burden fall on those who can least afford it?
- What type of households do they live in? Where do they live and work?
- How old are they? Are there cultural issues that need to be taken into consideration?
- What understanding do they have of the policy issue?
- Are they organised into any representative entity?

Community/Environment Impacts

- Does the proposal shift costs from one cohort to another?
- Are employment levels affected – will levels be reduced?
- Does the proposal reduce economic growth? How?

- How is the health and safety of individuals' or communities' impacted?
- What environmental assets are affected? Is there any degradation or pollution likely as a result?

Impacts on Government

- What is the cost to all levels of government of developing the regulation?
- Are education campaigns necessary to provide information to affected stakeholders?
- How will information be collected and collated?
- Will the regulation require enforcement? Who will do this? Will inspections be required?
- Does taking no action or eliminating regulation at one level of government, shift costs or risks to other levels of government or the community?

The last time an RIA was performed in relation to ASQA's full cost recovery efforts, it was postponed due to considerable backlash. It resurfaced not long before the global COVID-19 pandemic and was again put on the backburner. It is however likely to make an appearance again soon with news that TEQSA is preparing to implement full cost recovery also. This concept of full cost recovery has been floating around in the ethers for some time now and as PwC indicated in the Executive Summary of their 2013 ASQA Process Review[254]:

- If full cost recovery is interpreted to mean 100 per cent of costs, this cannot be achieved under the Australian Government Cost Recovery Guidelines. PwC observed that going forward the marginal cost of understanding ASQA's cost structures, in order to support fee based full cost recovery, would likely

254 PwC, 2013 ASQA process review: Final report, Prepared on behalf of State, Territory and Commonwealth Governments, page vii.

be disproportionate to the revenue that would be generated. Further, under a fee-based model, as an organisation moves toward full cost recovery there comes a point at which the organisation would have to incur costs driven only by the need to support a higher level of cost recovery. ASQA is not at this point at this stage, however moving to a higher level of cost recovery would require investment in systems that support efficient and effective regulation and clearer articulation of costs, but these systems are not currently in place.

- ASQA's costing approach was appropriate when initially developed. If, in the future a higher level of cost recovery is required, examination of fees should be undertaken at that point in time, and operations and available data to support any proposed changes.

The Joyce review[255] also had this to say:

> It is important that ASQA be adequately resourced to perform the guidance and educative role and to perform its role more generally. In many jurisdictions there is an understood difference between parts of the regulator's activity that should be directly funded by the regulated through cost recovery arrangements versus what are broader activities for the 'public good' and should therefore be government funded.
>
> There are clear activities where ASQA's costs can be passed onto the sector as part of the existing cost recovery arrangements. However, there is a range of activities that should be performed by ASQA that exceed the direct regulatory function and move into a policy assessment or system supervisory role including broad education and guidance. In the opinion of the Review, this broader range of activities should be directly funded by the government. These activities

[255] The Hon. Steven Joyce, Strengthening Skills: Expert Review of Australia's Vocational Education and Training System, page 40.

are part of ASQA's broader responsibilities in delivering a well-regulated and quality training sector as a benefit to wider Australian society.

For all of these reasons, it is strongly recommended that ASQA conduct a full, comprehensive Regulatory Impact Analysis before it proceeds to implement any further policies and that it only implements best-practice regulation strategies. So far, since it was first established in July 2011, ASQA has been the cause of much angst and problems, including the significant issues provided in this book and it should not be allowed to continue to regulate as an independent statutory authority and as the majority of the VET sector would agree, should no longer be unaccountable for their decisions, actions and behaviours.

ASQA needs to take a comprehensive look at the type of people it engages, their behaviour and conduct, their qualifications and experiences and ensuring that what it provides as a regulatory agency is fit for purpose. It is unreasonable to expect that the sector will continue to accept the poor behaviour of ASQA employees and contractors, especially when it borders on, if not is clearly demonstrative of conflicts of interest and unlawful bullying, harassment and intimidation.

ASQA also needs to be far more diligent in its monitoring of conflicts of interest with its employees, no matter what level of the organisation, including when it comes to the termination or departure from the regulatory agency. It is unacceptable that senior executives and managers at ASQA can go from being significantly involved in ASQA's management and the next day be running their own Consultancies supporting the very people they regulated just 24 hours prior. The Public Service Act 1999 (Cth.) makes it very clear that ASQA has a responsibility to manage such conflicts of interests, whether real or perceived.

In addition to the preceding issues, ASQA must manage its toxic culture for it is having a devastating impact on the sector. The stories and testimonies provided in this book are but a small cross-section of the VET sector and the author is aware of many, many more victims of ASQA's toxic culture and bullying behaviour. The author is aware of a large number of other ASQA victims who:

- Have had repeated miscarriages after having to deal with the narcissistic behaviours of one ASQA manager still employed by ASQA;
- Another who walked away from his appeal after losing his young daughter to cancer during the audit process and subsequently his marriage while also being diagnosed with cancer himself. The bullying and lack of empathy caused this internationally renowned expert to just walk away despite everything he lost in the process;
- An RTO owner who was the victim of ASQA doing numerous Federal and State based police searches against them and because it was a common name, presenting evidence that was not even relevant to them or their case;
- An international expert whose wife was so concerned that he was about to have a heart attack as a result of the of the pressure and behaviour being demonstrated by an ASQA manager that she forced him to walk away from the business;
- Another man who died of heart failure after having his RTO closed down when he was pursued for having non-compliant assessments when he was one of the most qualified people in the world in relation to his industry area;
- The ex-CEO of a large training provider who as a result of ASQA's bullying and behaviour, ended up homeless; and
- The RTO owners who have received medically diagnosed mental health disorders as a result of the stress and anguish caused by ASQA's behaviour.

The list could go on, but #enoughisenough. It is time that change occurred before anyone else dies unnecessarily.

Conclusion

> "When progress becomes barbarity, it ceases to be in the public interest."
>
> **- Paul Vega**

The public interest is not best served by having a regulator whose staff are not suitably qualified to perform their legislative objectives. This issue of unqualified auditors has been going on for far too long, as evidenced by the numerous questions about it to the Senate Education and Employment Committee, Education, Skills and Employment Portfolio.

There is absolutely no question that the public would be horrified if it understood the amount of damage being caused by an inefficient, incompetent regulator.

The public interest is not served when people are dying or killing themselves as a result of being part of this sector.

The public interest is also not best served when it is pursuing litigation in Tribunals and the Federal Court for small family businesses for seemingly irrelevant concerns and as we saw in some cases, administrivia, poorly understood 'complaints' that were never complaints.

It is in the public interest to know that Australia's vocational education and training sector is mostly regulated by a toxic, bullying culture, whereby ASQA's own employees at a senior management level walk into RTOs and say 'I'm here to close you down' and then as they walk out the door, hand the provider their business card and suggest that the provider should give them a call and they can help.

The public interest is also best served to know that when these issues are brought to ASQA's attention, that they chose to do nothing about it because the '*employee*' no longer works for ASQA.

The public interest is also not best served by a regulator that chases a provider causing millions of dollars of loss to small family businesses while costing the taxpayer potentially hundreds of thousands of dollars in fees and charges from the Australian Government Solicitor pursuing cases that should never have made it to the Tribunal in the first case.

The public interest is also not best served by a regulator who is aware that their current employees are leaving and setting up Consulting businesses and does not appear to manage the conflict of interest. The legislation requires that a conflict of interest must be managed whether it is perceived or real.

The public interest is not best served by rogue auditors walking into colleges and encouraging students to lodge complaints and seek refunds when they never had concerns to begin with.

The public interest is not best served when people die, are left paralysed or with amputated fingers as a result of training provided by public providers for which they were not penalised by but a private provider would be hung out to dry.

The public interest is not best served by a regulator who, since at least two years after it was established, was deemed to need intervention because its processes were so flawed. After multiple reviews and millions of dollars later, it is still incapable of performing its role in accordance with the legislation that established it.

The public interest is not served when more people who are victims of this predatory behaviour are so fearful of speaking out about the harm that has been caused that they'd rather keep quiet.

The public interest is not served when the Australian Parliament and the Minister are not interested in really addressing the issues but would rather provide tokenistic reviews and put bodies in place who do little but reinvent the wheel of reform, historically going back decades and reproducing the same response under a new name at a cost of millions of dollars to the taxpayer.

The public interest is not served by any of this behaviour that is swept under the carpet.

The public interest is not best served by Ministers making knee jerk changes to policy that cripple an industry with no, or insufficient transition requirements proposed.

People need to be accountable for this mess yet nobody is. It is a self-protection mechanism when an independent statutory authority is accountable to nobody and the most despicable outcomes, including, but not limited to, those previously mentioned arise. It is a disgrace that the Australian taxpayer is ultimately paying for this to occur and they don't even realise. It's an even bigger disgrace when that regulator charges exorbitant fees to providers for the privilege of experiencing such behaviour and outcomes and that same regulator is still pursuing full cost recovery.

Under the Australian Consumer Law, when providing a service, a service provider must provide Consumer Guarantees including for example that the service they provide is undertaken with due care and skill and is fit for purpose.

Interestingly, the Australian Consumer Law provides that:

> It is important to look at how the behaviour of the business affects the consumer's impression of a good or service. When deciding if conduct is misleading or deceptive, or likely to mislead or deceive, the most important question to ask is whether the overall impression created by the conduct is false

> or inaccurate. Even if a consumer discovers the true position before the conclusion of the transaction, the business will have contravened the ACL if the consumer has been enticed into 'the marketing web' by the misleading conduct[256].

Is the Australian taxpayer not being misled about the state of regulation in Australia's vocational education and training and international education sectors? Are the 4000 odd RTOs around the country being misled about the quality of regulation that they can expect? Is the Australian Parliament being misled about the quality of regulation that the vocational education and training sector in Australia is being exposed to? The recent review by the Australian National Audit Office ("ANAO") and the recent petition which may well have led to the review by the ANAO would certainly suggest that.

It is of grave concern that these types of incidents can continue to occur and individuals and families around the country are losing everything, including their lives and there is absolutely no avenue for recovering anything for the trauma and damage they've suffered.

Yes, it's in the public interest to know that despite what the people who were brave enough to tell their stories have lost, there is no avenue for them to pursue loss and damages, even when it is clear that the sanctions should never have been imposed in the first place.

In late 2019, a concerned group of VET stakeholders submitted a petition[257] to the Australian Parliament, its contents is reproduced below.

[256] Australian Competition and Consumer Commission, 'Avoiding unfair business practices: A guide for businesses and legal practitioners' <https://consumerlaw.gov.au/sites/consumer/files/2016/05/0553FT_ACL-guides_UnfairPractices_web.pdf>, page 6.

[257] Parliament of Australia, 'Petition EN1129 - Inquiry into the regulatory strategies, policies and activities of ASQA', <https://www.aph.gov.au/e-petitions/petition/EN1129>.

Petition Reason

The Australian vocational education and training (VET) sector has been in turmoil over recent years due to the actions of a small number of rogue operators. Such people have no place in our sector. We support any lawful initiative to improve the integrity and quality of vocational education and training. However, we have grave concerns about many of the regulatory strategies, policies and actions that the VET sector regulator, ASQA, has adopted and implemented over many years.

ASQA has:

- implemented an informal policy of trying to reduce the number of providers;
- unjustifiably cancelled registrations and rejected registration applications for a large number of legitimate and law-abiding operators;
- consistently failed to meet its Model Litigant obligations in regulatory disputes and has used the dispute process to force the closure of legitimate providers;
- skewed legislative interpretations to support its regulatory strategies, policies and actions;
- maintained an arbitrary and unofficial list of "persons of interest" whom, together with their associates, it has sought to exclude from the VET sector;
- implemented a secretive, inconsistent and unjust audit system resulting in unpredictable and unfair regulatory decisions;
- financially destroyed genuine and law-abiding providers, their owners and staff; and
- consistently failed to comply with its obligations.

Petition Request

We therefore ask the House to direct the Standing Committee on Employment, Education and Training to initiate a formal Inquiry into ASQA's regulatory strategies, policies and activities.

The expectation was that there would be a review into ASQA's practices. The response was a token one from the Minister saying that ASQA was in the process of implementing the recommendations from the Joyce and Braithwaite reviews. The concerns of the sector again it seemed were ignored. There is a school of thought that suggests the current review by the ANAO is in response to the petition. There are others that say that the terms of reference of the ANAO were so confined and restricted, that it will not achieve what is required by the sector and it is not aligned to the petition request.

What we do know is that the #enoughisenough campaign will continue to put pressure on ASQA to ensure the quality and integrity of the sector can be maintained or, at the very least, that it is documented for the purpose of historical matters that these concerns existed.

Another thing is also certain – the ICEA will be there, advocating for providers and doing what it can to uphold the integrity of the sector.

Resources

Free e-Course

The global COVID-19 Pandemic saw RTOs around the country strive to change their delivery models to an online learning environment in order to survive the pandemic.

Every staff member in an RTO needs to understand how the global COVID-19 pandemic affects their role in an RTO. Pandemics aside though, every staff member in an RTO needs to understand their role and responsibilities when delivering in an online learning environment.

Using the ASQA webinar related to 'Online Delivery' as the basis for this course, you can complete a range of activities and assessments related to the webinar designed to help you and your staff gather evidence for your next audit. Each person who successfully completes the course is issued with a certificate as evidence of current professional development in vocational teaching and learning (clause 1.13(c) of the Standards for Registered Training Organisations (RTOs) 2015).

What are you waiting for? To access the FREE e-Course on RTO Doctor Academy, follow this link:

> http://rto-doctor-academy.thinkific.com/courses/covid19-delivery
> and type the code **HUMANTOLL**.

Stay Up-To-Date

RTO Doctor occasionally sends out emails to its network advising of important changes or things you need to know to assist in keeping your registration safe. To receive these updates, sign up for the RTO Doctor Newsletter:

https://rtodoctor.activehosted.com/f/1

Free Facebook Group

Raelene has created a private space for people who have read this book and wish to discuss the topics raised, share their own experiences or ask questions. To join the group, visit the RTO Doctor Facebook Page where you will find a link that directs you to the group:

https://www.facebook.com/RTODoctor

RTO Doctor Academy

RTO Doctor has a range of online courses to help you stay compliant. Each person who successfully completes a course is issued with a certificate upon completion:

http://rto-doctor-academy.thinkific.com/

Get Help

- **Beyond Blue**
  Helpline: 1300 22 4636
  https://www.beyondblue.org.au/

- **Blue Knot Foundation**
  (02) 8920 3611
  Helpline: 1300 657 380
  https://www.blueknot.org.au/

- **Lifeline**
  Crisis Support: 13 11 14
  https://www.lifeline.org.au/

Commonwealth Ombudsman

The Ombudsman can investigate complaints about the actions and decisions of Australian Government agencies actions and decisions to see if they are wrong, unjust, unlawful, discriminatory or just plain unfair. The Ombudsman also seeks remedies for those affected by administrative deficiencies, and acts to improve public administration.

- **Complete the Online Form**
  https://www.ombudsman.gov.au/contact
  Helpline: 1300 362 072

Legal Assistance with ASQA Matters

- **Denison Toyer**

  Mr Peter Doukas - Solicitor

  E: Peter.doukas@denisontoyer.com

  T: +61 2 9267 7676

  (New South Wales)

- **GPZ Legal**

  Mr Nick Galatas - Solicitor

  E: gal@gpzlegal.com.au

  T: +61 3 9827 4291

  (Victoria)

- **The Centre for International Education Advocacy**

  Ms Raelene Bartlett
  E: raelene@rtodoctor.com.au
  T: 0408 144 002

Peak Bodies

- **ITECA** - https://www.iteca.edu.au/
  The Independent Tertiary Education Council Australia (ITECA) is a membership-based peak body bringing together independent providers in the higher education, vocational education and training sectors. Individually and collectively these providers share a commitment to providing students and their employers with the quality outcomes they are looking for. ITECA was also previously known as ACPET.

- **TAFE Directors Australia** - https://tda.edu.au/
  TAFE Directors Australia (TDA) is the peak national body which represents Australia's national network of publicly owned Technical and Further Education (TAFE) institutes and university TAFE divisions, and the Australia-Pacific Technical Coalition (APTC).

- **IEPA** - http://www.iepa.com.au/
  Independent Education Providers of Australia – was started in 2018 by a group of education professionals seeing a need for a truly representative association. We seek to provide industry leadership, lobbying on the behalf of members and promoting best practice in education.

- **IHEA** - https://ihea.edu.au/
  IHEA represents the majority of Australia's registered and accredited independent higher education providers.

Contact Raelene

Email: raelene@rtodoctor.com.au

Website: https://rtodoctor.com.au/

Facebook: https://www.facebook.com/RTODoctor

LinkedIn: https://www.linkedin.com/in/raelene-bartlett-7225808/

YouTube: https://www.youtube.com/channel/UCUnBuKgQWZnGz5zjbnxQLqQ

Other Books by Raelene

All the following titles are available to purchase on Amazon:

https://www/rtodoctor.com.au/books

- Legal Decision-Making Under the National Vocational Education and Training Regulator Act 2011 (Cth.): A Investigation Into Merits Review; and
- CRICOS CPR: Top 5 Tips to Rescue Your RTO.

Please Leave a Review!

I would love your feedback about this book. As an author, reviews are extremely important for our business. It would mean a great deal to me if you could please leave a review of this book on Amazon. Simply go to https://www/rtodoctor.com.au/books and you will be taken to the Amazon link. Thank you in advance.

Made in United States
Orlando, FL
05 November 2026

90231074R00282